FLORIDA STATE
UNIVERSITY LIBRARIES

JAN 2 4 2001

TALLAHASSEE, FLORIDA

TRANSITION, COHESION AND REGIONAL POLICY
IN CENTRAL AND EASTERN EUROPE

Transition, Cohesion and Regional Policy in Central and Eastern Europe

Edited by

JOHN BACHTLER and RUTH DOWNES
European Policies Research Centre, University of Strathclyde

GRZEGORZ GORZELAK
EUROREG, University of Warsaw

Ashgate

Aldershot • Burlington USA • Singapore • Sydney

© John Bachtler, Ruth Downes and Grzegorz Gorzelak 2000

All rights reserved. No part of this publication may be reproduced, stored in a retrieval system or transmitted in any form or by any means, electronic, mechanical, photocopying, recording or otherwise without the prior permission of the publisher.

Published by
Ashgate Publishing Limited
Gower House
Croft Road
Aldershot
Hampshire GU11 3HR
England

Ashgate Publishing Company
131 Main Street
Burlington, VT 05401-5600
USA

Ashgate website: http://www.ashgate.com

British Library Cataloguing in Publication Data
Transition, cohesion and regional policy in central and
    Eastern Europe. - (EPRC studies in European policy)
    1. European Union 2. Regional planning - European Union
    countries 3. European Union countries - Economic policy
    I. Bachtler, J.F. II. Downes, Ruth III. Gorzelak, Grzegorz
    338.9'4

Library of Congress Control Number: 00-132821

ISBN 1 84014 783 0

Printed and bound by Athenaeum Press, Ltd.,
Gateshead, Tyne & Wear.

Contents

List of Figures   *viii*
List of Tables   *ix*
List of Contributors   *xii*
Preface   *xv*
List of Abbreviations   *xvii*

PART I: DIMENSIONS OF TRANSITION

1. Introduction: Challenges of Transition for Regional Development   1
   John Bachtler, Ruth Downes and Grzegorz Gorzelak

2. The Progress of Transition in East Central Europe   11
   Michael Bradshaw and Alison Stenning

3. Transformation and the Interdependencies between Political and Economic Development   33
   Thiemo W. Eser

4. The Effects of Privatisation in Central and Eastern Europe: Evidence from Households in Three Central European Capitals   51
   Keith Grime, Zoltan Kovács and Vic Duke

PART II: NATIONAL REVIEWS

5. Bulgaria   71
   Julia Spiridonova and Nikolai Grigorov

6. Czech Republic   85
   Miloš Červený and Alois Andrle

7. Estonia   99
   Kaarel Kilvits

8. Hungary   115
   Gyula Horváth

9. Latvia   131
   Raita Karnite

10	Lithuania *Eduardas Vilkas*	143
11	Poland *Grzegorz Gorzelak*	153
12	Romania *Ioan Ianos*	167
13	Slovak Republic *Juraj Silvan*	177
14	Slovenia *Pavle Sicherl and Stanka Kukar*	195

PART III: THEMATIC PERSPECTIVES

15	Regional Disparity, Industrial Development and Technology Change in Hungary *Anne Lorentzen*	209
16	Inward Investment, Cohesion and the 'Wealth of Regions' in East-Central Europe *Adrian Smith and Petr Pavlínek*	227
17	The Spatial Dimension to Environmental Problems *Helmut Karl, Omar Ranné and John Macquarrie*	243
18	SMEs in the Visegrad Countries: On their Way to Europe? *Friederike Welter*	259
19	Cross-border Co-operation at Germany's Eastern Border: Institutional Limits to Multi-level Governance *Eiko R. Thielemann*	281

PART IV: POLICY RESPONSES

| 20 | Regional Policy in the Czech Republic and EU Accession
Jiří Blažek and Sjaak Boeckhout | 301 |
| 21 | Regional Development Policy in Poland in the 1990s
Marek Kozak | 319 |

22	Regional Policy Evolution in Hungary *Ruth Downes*	331
23	Regional Policy in Central and Eastern Europe: The EU Perspective *Jean-François Drevet*	345
24	Transition, Cohesion and Regional Policy in Central and Eastern Europe: Conclusions *John Bachtler, Ruth Downes and Grzegorz Gorzelak*	355

List of Figures

2.1	Growth in real GDP 1990-1998 (percent)	18
2.2	ECE-10 and EU-15: GDP per capita (PPP) – 1995	19
2.3	Transition economies: GNP per capita 1997	20
3.1	The interplay between political and economic development	44
5.1	Territorial administrative structure of Bulgaria	72
5.2	Regional unemployment in Bulgaria, August 1998	77
6.1	Territorial administrative structure of the Czech Republic	86
6.2	Regional unemployment in the Czech Republic	93
7.1	Administrative division of Estonia into counties	102
7.2	Regional unemployment disparities in Estonia	104
8.1	GDP per capita by counties, 1996 (thousand HUF)	122
8.2	Unemployment rate by small areas in Hungary, 1997	123
8.3	Eligible areas in Hungary, 1996	125
8.4	Planning and statistical regions in Hungary	129
9.1	Territorial administrative structure of Latvia	132
9.2	Regional registered unemployment in Latvia, August 1999	135
10.1	Territorial administrative division of Lithuania into counties (1995)	144
11.1	Administrative division of Poland from 1 January 1999	154
11.2	Companies with foreign capital in Poland, 1997	159
11.3	Regional GDP per inhabitant, 1996	162
12.1	Unemployment by county in Romania, July 1999	173
13.1	Territorial administrative structure of the Slovak Republic	179
13.2	Unemployment at district level in the Slovak Republic, June 1998	184
14.1	Territorial administrative structure of Slovenia	196
19.1	Interreg II procedure to approve projects (Brandenburg)	289

List of Tables

2.1	Socio-economic indicators for transition economies in 1996	16
2.2	Liberalisation, growth and inflation in selected transition economies, 1989-94	21
2.3	Growth in real GDP for selected transition economies	22
2.4	Inflation indicators for selected transition economies	23
3.1	The Washington consensus and East Asia	36
3.2	State of transformation in the CEEC 1994-98	39
3.3	Basic economic indicators for CEE countries	40
3.4	Trade off among privatisation routes for large firms	41
4.1	Changes in respondent work sectors, 1989-95	52
4.2	Respondent work sector by gender	53
4.3	Respondent work sector by age group	53
4.4	Respondent work sector by higher education	54
4.5	Respondent work sector by social class	54
4.6	Respondent work sector by respondent full/part time work	55
4.7	Housing stock by sectors (percent) 1990-1994	56
4.8	Ownership change 1989-96	57
4.9	Housing tenure by gender, age group, and education	60
4.10	Housing tenure by occupational class, employment sector, and unemployment	61
4.11	Household additional health insurance and household use of private health since 1989	62
4.12	Use of private health since 1989 by age group	62
4.13	Use of private health since 1989 by respondent social class	63
4.14	Levels of private school attendance and children's private tuition	63
4.15	Children's private tuition by respondent education level	63
4.16	Children's private tuition by respondent social class	64
4.17	Perceived impact of four types of privatisation on households	65
6.1	NUTS designation in the Czech Republic	87
6.2	Basic economic indicators for the Czech Republic 1989-1997	89
6.3	Regional disparities in the Czech Republic	96
7.1	Estonian counties and local administrative units	100
7.2	Basic socio-economic indicators in Estonia	103
9.1	Regional demographic profile of Latvia, 1998	133

9.2	Demographic statistics at beginning of 1998 (per 1,000 population)	134
9.3	Key labour market indicators 1997/98	135
9.4	Enterprises registered prior to 1 January 1998 (excluding peasant farms)	137
10.1	Structure of economy by GDP and employment in 1993 and 1997	147
10.2	Population and unemployment by counties	150
10.3	Employed population by economic activity (annual average, '000)	151
11.1	Economic development trends in Poland, 1989-1997	156
11.2	Strengths and weaknesses of the new Polish regions	165
13.1	Selected geographical and demographic characteristics in 1997	180
13.2	Components of creation of the gross domestic product - first half year 1998	182
13.3	Comparison of GDP levels for Slovakian regions and EU	183
14.1	Basic socio-economic indicators for statistical regions	202
18.1	Development of private enterprises and self-employment in the Visegrad countries	261
18.2	Registered and operational entrepreneurial activities in Hungary, 1996	263
18.3	Self-employment by status in Hungary	264
18.4	Main and second-job entrepreneurial activities in the Czech Republic	265
18.5	Self-employment in the Visegrad countries and the EU	266
18.6	Size structures in Central and Eastern Europe and the European Union, 1996	268
18.7	Size distribution of Hungarian and Slovakian enterprises in 1996	269
18.8	Sectoral size distribution in Hungary in 1995	269
18.9	Sectoral distribution in Central and Eastern Europe and the EU (percent)	271
18.10	SME in selected economic sectors of the Visegrad countries	272
18.11	Regional distribution of enterprises in 1996	273
18.12	Contribution to employment and GDP in Hungary	276
18.13	Contribution to employment in Poland in 1995	277
18.14	SME contribution to employment in Slovakia	277
19.1	Participating actors in the implementation of Phare and Interreg	287

20.1	Average unemployment rate (district maximum) in the Czech Republic	307
20.2	Principal difficulties in the preparation of the Czech programming documents	314
21.1	Basic data for 16 new Polish regions (*voivodships*), 1998	323
21.2	Budget of the new territorial self-government units, 1999	325
23.1	Comparison of German unification and enlargement to 26 Member States	346
23.2	Impact of the successive enlargements of the EU	346
23.3	Evolution of Phare allocations by country (1990-97)	349
24.1	Territorial administrative structures in CEE countries	364

List of Contributors

Dr. Alois Andrle, TERPLAN, Prague, Czech Republic.

Professor John Bachtler, European Policies Research Centre, University of Strathclyde, Glasgow, United Kingdom, j.f.bachtler@strath.ac.uk

Dr. Jiří Blažek, Department of Social Geography and Regional Development, Faculty of Science, Charles University, Prague, Czech Republic, blazek@prfdec.natur.cuni.cz

Sjaak Boeckhout, Netherlands Economic Institute, Rotterdam, The Netherlands, Boeckhout@NEI.NL

Dr. Michael Bradshaw, School of Geography and Environmental Sciences, University of Birmingham, United Kingdom, bradshmj@novell1.bham.ac.uk

Dr. Miloš Červený, TERPLAN, Prague, Czech Republic.

Ruth Downes, European Policies Research Centre, University of Strathclyde, Glasgow, United Kingdom, ruth.downes@strath.ac.uk

Jean-François Drevet, DG Regio, European Commission, Brussels, Belgium.

Vic Duke, School of History, University of Liverpool, United Kingdom, vicduke@liv.ac.uk

Dr. Thiemo W. Eser, Department of Urban and Regional Economics, University of Trier, Germany, eser@pcmail.uni-trier.de

Professor Grzegorz Gorzelak, EUROREG, University of Warsaw, Poland, euroreg@plearn.edu.pl

Dr. Nikolai Grigorov, National Centre for Regional Development and Housing Policy, Sofia, Bulgaria.

Keith Grime, European Studies Research Institute, University of Salford, United Kingdom, e.k.grime@salford.ac.uk

Dr. Gyula Horváth, Transdanubian Research Institute. Hungarian Academy of Sciences, Pécs, Hungary, horvath@dti.rkk.hu

Professor Ioan Ianos, Institute of Geography, Romanian Academy, Bucharest, Romania, geospat@fx.ro

Professor Helmut Karl, Friedrich-Schiller-Universität Jena, Germany, h.karl@wiwi.uni-jena.de

Dr. Raita Karnite, Institute of Economics, Latvian Academy of Sciences, Riga, Latvia, raimara@ac.lza.lv

Dr. Kaarel Kilvits, Institute of Economics, Estonian Academy of Sciences, Tallinn, Estonia, mail@sekr.tami.ee

Zoltan Kovács, Institute of Geography, Hungarian Academy of Sciences, Budapest, Hungary, zkovacs@helka.iif.hu

Marek Kozak, Polish Agency for Regional Development, Warsaw, Poland, m.kozak@sunik.pagi.pl

Stanka Kukar, Institute for Economic Research, Ljubljana, Slovenia.

Dr. Anne Lorentzen, Aalborg University, Aalborg, Denmark, al@i4.auc.dk

John Macquarrie, European Policies Research Centre, University of Strathclyde, Glasgow, United Kingdom.

Petr Pavlínek, Department of Geography and Geology, University of Nebraska, Omaha, USA.

Dr. Omar Ranné, Friedrich-Schiller-Universität Jena, Germany.

Professor Pavle Sicherl, SICENTER, Ljubljana, Slovenia, Pavle.Sicherl@link.si

Dr. Juraj Silvan, URBION, Bratislava, Slovakia, silvan@sazp.sk

Dr. Adrian Smith, Department of Geography, University of Sussex, United Kingdom, A.M.Smith@susx.ac.uk

Dr. Julia Spiridonova, National Centre for Regional Development and Housing Policy, Sofia, Bulgaria, Julia@Aster.Net

Alison Stenning, School of Geography and Environmental Sciences, University of Birmingham, United Kingdom, a.c.stenning@bham.ac.uk

Dr. Eiko R. Thielemann, Government Department, London School of Economics, London, United Kingdom, E.R.Thielemann@soton.ac.uk

Professor Eduardas Vilkas, Institute of Economics, Lithuanian Academy of Sciences, Vilnius, Lithuania, ejvilkas@ktl.mii.lt

Dr. Friederike Welter, Rhine-Westphalia Institute for Economic Research, Essen, Germany, welter@rwi-essen.de

Preface

The origins of this volume lie in the history of collaboration on regional development research between the editors and many of the authors over the past ten years. Through a series of international research projects, conferences and seminars debating the emerging regional development challenges and regional policy responses in Central and Eastern Europe, the idea of a book that would take a comprehensive, systematic look at the issues was born. After a decade of reform, the book was conceived as an opportunity to take stock of the regional problems and disparities associated with the transition process and the regional development policy challenges confronting regional, national and European policy-makers.

Regional development is, of course, a dynamic field in Central and Eastern Europe. Spatial differences are growing and changing quickly; the impact of reforms has recast the geography of advantage and disadvantage. Underlying abstract graphs plotting trends in GDP and unemployment is a reality of growing differentiation between regions, local communities and social groups, of a widening disparity between those that have benefited greatly from the shift to a market economy and those shattered by poverty, job loss and insecurity.

Until recently, regional policy was not generally seen as a priority area for government action. Urged on by the European Union this is now changing with the rapid emergence of regional development policy concepts, legislation, institutions and measures. It is still an open question, however, whether such policies are regarded merely as a presentational device to fulfil EU requirements or whether they will be able to make a difference to those regions and groups disadvantaged by economic liberalisation.

At the heart of this volume, therefore, is the relationship between transition and cohesion and the response of government. The book brings together contributors from Western, Central and Eastern Europe, presenting academic perspectives from geographers, regional economists and political scientists and the viewpoints of practitioners engaged in regional development. It encompasses region-wide overviews of developments across Central and Eastern Europe as well as accounts of the regional development situation in each of ten countries and a discussion of key thematic issues and regional policy responses.

Like any edited book, this is not a seamless volume, and there is no single view on the regional development challenges faced by the countries of Central and Eastern Europe. The editors have tried to create a framework within which to fit these different views and thereby produce a coherent, systematic and relevant overview of regional development and regional policy that will be of interest to academic researchers and practitioners alike.

We would like to thank all of the authors for their contributions, particularly the tolerance of those who submitted early. We are grateful to our colleagues in the European Policies Research Centre (University of Strathclyde) and the European Institute for Regional and Local Development (University of Warsaw) for their support and forbearance. In particular, we would like to thank Rosemarie Rey and Moira Lowe for their secretarial support and good humour.

John Bachtler, Ruth Downes
and Grzegorz Gorzelak

List of Abbreviations

AL	Average Liberalisation
BAZ	Borsod-Abaúj-Zemplen (Hungary)
BMWi	Bundesministerium für Wirtschaft
CBC	Cross-Border Cooperation
CDC	County Development Council (Hungary)
CEC	Commission of the European Communities
CEE	Central and Eastern Europe
CEEC	Central and Eastern European Countries
CEFTA	Central European Free Trade Agreement
CIS	Commonwealth of Independent States
CIT	Corporate Income Tax (Poland)
CLI	Cumulative Liberalisation Index
CMEA/COMECON	Council for Mutual Economic Assistance
CR	Czech Republic
CSF	Community Support Framework
CUP	Central Office of Planning (Poland)
DG	Directorate General (European Commission)
EBRD	European Bank for Reconstruction and Development
ECE	East-Central Europe
EEC	East European Countries
ERDF	European Regional Development Fund
ESA	European System of Integrated Economic Accounts
EU	European Union
FDI	Foreign Direct Investment
GDP	Gross Domestic Product
GNP	Gross National Product
HDI	Human Development Index
ISPA	Instrument for Structural Policies for Pre-Accession
ILO	International Labour Organisation
JIT	Just-In-Time
MoARD	Ministry of Agriculture and Regional Development (Hungary)
NDA	National Development Agency (Slovenia)
NEEC	North Eastern European Countries
NEM	New Economic Mechanism (Hungary)

NGO	Non Governmental Organisation
NIS	New Independent States
NPC-ESC	National Programming Committee for Economic and Social Cohesion (Czech Republic)
NUTS	Nomenclature of Territorial Statistical Units (EC)
OECD	Organisation for Economic Co-operation and Development
OTP	National Savings Bank (Hungary)
PARR	Polish Agency for Regional Development
PIT	Personal Income Tax (Poland)
PPP	Purchasing Power Parity
R&D	Research and Development
RDC	Regional Development Councils (Hungary)
RDF	Regional Development Fund (Hungary)
SAPARD	Special Accession Programme for Agriculture and Rural Development
SEEC	South Eastern European Countries
SEFA	Spatial Equalisation Financial Assistance (Hungary)
SME	Small and Medium Sized Enterprise
SOE	State-Owned Enterprise
SR	Slovak Republic
TBARD	Targeted Budgetary Allocation for Regional Development (Hungary)
UNDP	United National Development Programme
US	United States of America
USSR	Union of Soviet Socialist Republics
VW	Volkswagen
WTO	World Trade Organisation

PART I:
DIMENSIONS OF TRANSITION

1 Introduction: Challenges of Transition for Regional Development

JOHN BACHTLER, RUTH DOWNES AND
GRZEGORZ GORZELAK

Ten years ago, at the end of 1989, a series of historic events, symbolised most dramatically by the collapse of the Berlin Wall, opened the way for political and economic transformation across Central and Eastern Europe (CEE).[1] The political, social and economic reform of the 1990s has had a dramatic impact on the way the CEE countries are governed, their paths of economic development and the nature of their integration into the wider global framework. In what was often formerly perceived as a single 'eastern bloc', national differences have become increasingly apparent as individual countries have made their reform choices against unique historical, political and institutional backgrounds. Other levels of differentiation have emerged, through the spatial effects of economic reform within countries, producing regional disparities which have reinforced traditional patterns and created new ones. The application by ten CEE countries to join the EU has highlighted the implications of this spatial dimension of transition – both in terms of the requirement for a domestic regional policy response and the implications for the structural and cohesion policies of an enlarged Europe.

This volume is a timely contribution to the analysis and understanding of these issues. Its aim is to assess the impact of transition on economic and social cohesion in the CEE countries and the significance of regional policy. The book is structured in four parts. Part I examines the progress of overall transition, assessing not only economic aspects but also the political and social dimensions of the process. Part II provides a comprehensive overview of the regional aspects of reform in each of the ten CEE countries. The chapters analyse the pattern of emerging regional disparities, the reform of territorial structures and the form and nature of regional policy responses.

The third part of the volume examines the spatial dimension of transition from various thematic perspectives. It comprises case-studies illustrating technological change and industrial development, inward investment, the challenge of environmental problems, the growth and distribution of small and medium-sized enterprises and the issues of governance and cross-border cooperation. Part IV looks in detail at the differences in the emerging regional policy in three of the most advanced CEE countries, Hungary, Poland and the Czech Republic, as well as at the role of the EU in supporting regional policy and institutional frameworks. The concluding chapter of the volume draws together the principal aspects of macro- and regional-level transition before turning to the challenge of enlargement for structural and cohesion policies over the coming decades.

The complexity of transition

The post-socialist transformation initiated a decade ago in the CEE countries is singular in its speed and sudden change to a different economic system. Whether implemented gradually or through so-called 'shock therapy', transition has involved a series of economic reforms (notably macro-economic stabilisation, privatisation, structural reform, liberalisation and internationalisation) together with parallel political, social and cultural changes. While distinctive in major respects, similarities with experiences in more developed economies should not be overlooked. It is important to remember that it was only with the geo-political change following the Second World War that the CEE countries were forced into a socialist pattern of development, away from the economic paths followed earlier in the century. To some degree, the transition in the 1990s, therefore, resembles the start of structural change which took place in more developed economies a few decades ago, a process from which the former socialist countries were insulated by political ideology. Pursuing instead a path of industrial development, irreconcilable economic difficulties resulted which led ultimately to the collapse of the entire economic and political system - opening the way for a simultaneously delayed and accelerated process of restructuring.

Notwithstanding commonalities in the transformation process, the experience of transition has been highly differentiated among CEE countries. This differentiation is true, first of all, at a macro-economic level. There is a key relationship between the point at which countries decided to initiate real restructuring, the depth of the reform process and the pace of growth after the initial recession phase. Early, deep reforms were more quickly able to create the conditions for future growth, while the later the reform, the slower the growth. The economic and social costs, however, have been considerable and universal.

Differences in the speed of reform can be identified in the broad development patterns of countries such as Poland, Hungary and the Czech Republic on the one hand - but also Slovenia and Estonia and recently Slovakia too - and Romania, Bulgaria and many of the former (non-Baltic Soviet states on the other. In the latter case, reform has been consistently delayed for a range of reasons, while exposure to the new competitive environment has meant that negative socio-economic costs have been paid anyway. Within these broad groupings, further differentiation can be made. Poland initiated deep structural reform at an early stage, through its so-called 'shock therapy', and laid the foundations for future development - although the recent slowdown of structural reform and the continuing challenge of industrial restructuring have taken their toll on recent economic growth, which slowed down from seven to four percent. In the Czech Republic, initially heralded the transformation 'success story', early economic growth was achieved on the back of policies such as mass voucher privatisation which often hindered restructuring by placing a high degree of industry ownership into the hands of investment funds, run in many cases by State-owned banks. The 1997 currency crisis and stagnation, the subsequent austerity packages and now rising unemployment are all signs of the delayed tackling of painful reform.

These observations are reinforced in the theoretical hypothesis of post-socialist transformation following a J-curve pattern, reviewed in the chapter by *Michael Bradshaw* and *Alison Stenning*. According to this hypothesis, the costs of restructuring pave the way to future accelerated growth and, to a certain extent, are the conditions for this growth. An attempt to sidestep the costs of restructuring is a dangerous strategy which neither avoids the negative impact of socio-economic change nor moves the country from a situation of semi-permanent stagnation.

The complexity of the transformation process being undertaken in the CEE countries is evident in the multiple influences on reforms. As *Thiemo Eser* points out, these are not solely economic, but also include the political composition and stability of the ruling government, the nature and timing of the social costs of reform and the safety nets available to the population, as well as the popular will behind the reform effort. Analysis of reform needs to consider issues such as political pre-conditions and the institutional inheritance as part of wider, non-economic frames of reference.

The social ramifications of processes more often discussed from an economic viewpoint are also pertinent, given the potential for social discontent to derail the political will for reform. *Keith Grime*, *Vic Duke* and *Zoltan Kovács* pick up this theme in analysing the impact of privatisation on different household types in three CEE capital cities. They illustrate the rapid development of social inequalities, with spatial polarisation of social groups (along western lines) and a rapid process of social stratification in terms of housing and the use of private services such as health and education.

Macro-level differentiation in the experience of transition is now being reflected in the approach of the European Commission to enlargement. The former approach of starting negotiations with five CEE 'front-runner' or 'first-wave' countries (Poland, Hungary, Czech Republic, Slovenia and Estonia) was replaced during the Finnish Presidency of the EU (in the second half of 1999) with the decision to open negotiations equally with all 'applicant' countries and to link the rate at which talks are concluded to national progress in bringing economies and legislation into line with EU standards. The speed at which each 'candidate country' moves down the road to EU membership will now be linked directly to its national performance. While this approach has been welcomed mainly by countries not previously included in the 'first-wave' group, it could present difficulties or delays for other countries which have been negotiating entry terms but are currently experiencing difficulty in the preparations for membership.

The spatial dimension: national perspectives

The differentiated nature of transition is particularly apparent at regional and local levels in the CEE countries. Transformation has created new spatial patterns of economic and social inequality. The capital cities, for example, are usually flourishing, with relatively low unemployment rates, high levels of new firm formation and concentrations of foreign investment. These positive economic characteristics, as well as the reorientation of trade and investment patterns have also generally favoured western regions and disadvantaged those in the east. Old-industrial areas have particularly suffered from the closure or rationalisation of outdated and inefficient enterprises, often with a critical social cost. While emerging regional disparities have certain common elements, deep-seated historical and cultural factors, ethnicity, the specific influence of central planning and national characteristics all influence the ability of individual regions to adapt to the changing economic environment.

The individual national experiences of transition and regional development are discussed in detail in the second part of this volume. These chapters draw out some of the interesting differences between countries in terms of the speed of economic and political transition, the emergence of regional disparities and policy responses through the reform of territorial structures and the introduction of regional development policies. For example, Poland, Hungary, the Czech Republic, Slovenia and Estonia are the 'leaders' in CEE in terms of economic growth. However, Hungary (see chapter by *Gyula Horváth*) is the only country to have a well-developed regional policy while in the Czech Republic (*Miloš Červený* and *Alois Andrle*) and Slovenia (*Pavle Sicherl* and *Stanka Kukar*), regional policy has a relatively low priority and lacks a legislative base. In Poland (*Grzegorz Gorzelak*), a reform of territorial structures has been undertaken but regional policy has neither institutional leadership nor legislation.

Slovakia (*Juraj Silvan*) experienced political difficulties which negatively affected the path of economic development, and Bulgaria and Romania have been latecomers to the economic reform process; all three countries, however, have recently taken positive action in the field of regional development and policy. The creation of an effective regional policy was an election pledge of the new Slovak government, elected in autumn 1998, and moves are now being undertaken to create an appropriate institutional and legislative base and a more integrated policy approach. Regional policy legislation, although at a very early stage, also exists in both Romania (*Ioan Ianos*) and Bulgaria (*Julia Spiridonova* and *Nikolai Grigorov*) and a move away from the previously dominant sectoral approach is emerging. The issue of whether equality or efficiency goals should be followed is particularly pertinent in these countries where overall economic development levels are still very low.

For the smallest CEE countries, the validity and feasibility of regional policy may be questionable though all three have growing regional disparities. For Estonia (*Kaarel Kilvits*) and for Latvia (*Raita Karniie*), the primary concern is the difference between the capital cities and the rest of the country and workable institutional structures for regional policy have been established in both countries. By contrast, regional disparities in Lithuania (*Eduardas Vilkas*) are less marked, reflected in the lower priority accorded to regional development policy.

The EU accession negotiations, now being undertaken with all ten CEE countries, have universally raised the profile of regional policy. The process highlights the weakness of the existing legislative base in the CEE countries as well as the lack of appropriate institutional structures, both for co-ordinated policy-making at national level and for implementation through sufficiently strong regional-level organisations. The influence of the Structural Fund framework on the recent design of domestic regional policies is very apparent.

The spatial dimension: thematic issues

The progress of transition and reform is influenced by many interrelated J-curves of sectoral, organisational and institutional change, all of which play a role in overcoming internal systematic barriers and tensions. Each of these processes has a spatial expression, and their analysis can provide a different dimension to the understanding of transition and its impact at both national and sub-national levels.

Industrial restructuring and development has been (and remains) a central component of economic reform, and the spatial distribution of industry clearly determines the extent to which reform impacts on individual regions. The pattern of industrial concentration common to socialist development has exacerbated the social and economic costs for particular areas and, in some cases, has prevented restructuring because of the political fall-out which would result from widespread closure and resultant unemployment. Regional characteristics and preconditions also affect the ability of regions to encourage the growth of new enterprise or adaptation of working practices to more open competitive conditions. *Anne Lorenzen* picks up this theme and, using three Hungarian case-study regions, examines their different economic starting points and subsequent reactions to new industrial working methods. Regional differences to issues such as product innovation, organisational change, qualification profile and trade structure are drawn out and possible future divergent development paths highlighted.

Inward investment, another key contributor to the economic fortunes of the CEE countries, has flowed at very different rates into individual states and has often been highly spatially concentrated. The impact of the investment on local industrial restructuring, labour relations and supplier networks is not universally the same. *Adrian Smith* and *Petr Pavlínek* examine this issue using case-study material from the Czech Republic and Slovakia. Reliance on globalised corporate networks is questioned from the experience of certain regions, and the role of inward investment in enterprise restructuring is shown to differ considerably between regions. The policy implications of these findings raise issues for both national and regional-level policy-makers.

Small and medium-sized enterprises (SMEs) are promoted in Western Europe as an important source of economic growth, employment and innovation. The pertinence of SME development for the CEE countries is examined by *Friederike Welter*, focusing on the situation in Hungary, Poland, the Czech Republic and Slovakia. SME growth has been rapid, although much entrepreneurial activity is part-time, and enterprise size is skewed towards micro-companies. Historical patterns of private sector activity have favoured the growth of this sector in Hungary and Poland, where the legal and financial institutional framework is also furthest advanced. As in the EU, SMEs have a strong tendency to cluster in the most dynamic regions of CEE, but universally face pressures of competitiveness in a more open market environment.

Industrial restructuring, enterprise development and inward investment are obvious components of the process of economic transition. Other issues affecting the nature and progress of transition at national and sub-national levels include the environmental inheritance which poses particular challenges, not only domestically but also in light of the stringent environmental legislation of the EU. *Helmut Karl, Omar Ranné* and *John Macquarrie* review the principal environmental problems and the progress being made to overcome them. The expected difference in pollution levels between urbanised areas and rural regions is exacerbated in CEE countries as a result of the concentration of environmentally damaging production. The Upper Silesia region of Poland, for example, produces 60 percent of all industrial solid waste, 30 percent of all gases and 25 percent of all non-cleaned sewage. As highlighted in the case of inward investment, these regional differences pose real challenges for environmental and regional policy-makers alike. The integration of environmental sustainability into regional development measures is an issue not unique to CEE.

The question of the reform of institutional structures is examined by *Eiko Thielemann*. The perspective of multi-level governance is taken –

particularly important given the partnership principle of EU regional policy to which the candidate countries, following accession, will have to adhere. The case of cross-border co-operation between eastern Germany and Poland is analysed, looking at specific initiatives and the efficacy of their decision-making and implementation structures. The important potential role of regional and sub-regional actors, and the influence of different institutional structures and policy frameworks, point to the challenge facing CEE countries in the creation and operation of new territorial administrative systems.

The regional policy debate

As highlighted in the ten national chapters, a policy response to the spatially differentiated impact of economic reform is evident to differing degrees across CEE. Virtually every country has prepared some kind of regional development concept, although the necessary legislative base and institutional infrastructure (at national and regional levels) for the design and implementation of regional policy are at very different stages. More in-depth comparisons of the policy responses in three of the more advanced CEE countries are illuminating. *Ruth Downes* presents the Hungarian case where strong regional policy is most evident, rooted in 1996 legislation which created a robust legal basis and institutional structure and clarified the principles and objectives of policy. A wide-ranging National Regional Development Concept was developed in 1998 which laid down the framework for future development. At least as important is the emergence of regional development agencies and the allocation of increased budgetary resources for their support in 1999.

The regional policy responses in Poland and the Czech Republic are more *ad hoc* in nature, although recent developments have raised the profile and coherence of the policy area in both cases. *Marek Kozak* details the key reform of the territorial administrative structure in Poland, which introduced 16 highly decentralised regions at the start of 1999 to replace the former 49 provinces. These new regions comprise a good regional and local base for the implementation of future regional policy, despite the financial, organisational and regulatory challenges which still face their operation. Progress is being made towards this goal, but the final step to the development and introduction of a comprehensive regional policy is still to come. In the Czech Republic, *Jiří Blažek* and *Sjaak Boeckhout* point to the low profile of regional policy until the mid-1990s when several developments, including the creation of the Ministry for Regional Development and 14 regional development agencies, brought action in this policy area. Continuing problems facing Czech regional policy include a lack of co-ordination or clear strategy and a weak institutional structure displayed, in particular, in the lack of strong regional-level administration – issues that are recognised as common to many CEE countries.

The post-liberalisation process of regional policy formulation has been strongly driven by the EU. *Jean-François Drevet* reviews the financial and institution-building support provided by the European Commission, which has generally been focused on areas of greatest need but also providing capacity building and planning support. The influence of the EU has grown during the second half of the 1990s as the accession negotiations have increased in pace and the future availability of the Structural Funds has moved into central focus. The Structural Fund philosophy now underlies preparations in the majority of countries, both in terms of policy principles and institutional arrangements for implementation.

Finally, the concluding chapter by the editors summarises many of the issues explored throughout the volume and discusses the implications of enlargement for economic and social cohesion. It highlights the challenges confronting regional policymakers and considers the appropriateness of the EU's structural policy for the domestic regional policies of Central and Eastern European countries.

Note

1 The terminology used for discussing the former CMEA countries is ambiguous and loaded with potentially perjorative political, social and cultural overtones. In most of this volume, Central and Eastern Europe refers to the ten countries of Bulgaria, Czech Republic, Estonia, Hungary, Latvia, Lithuania, Poland, Romania, Slovakia and Slovenia. The principal exception is the wider definition used in Michael Bradshaw and Alison Stenning's chapter.

2 The Progress of Transition in East Central Europe

MICHAEL BRADSHAW AND ALISON STENNING

Introduction

The aim of this chapter is to assess the progress of selected transition economies in east central Europe (ECE) and the Baltic States. Those same states are the subject of the country scenarios presented in Part II of this volume. The chapter is divided into two main sections. The first section presents an assessment of transition progress within the parameters identified by the major international financial institution, namely the World Bank and the European Bank for Reconstruction and Development (EBRD). Because of the substantial data problems that exist, rather than use national statistics, this assessment makes use of data published by these agencies in their various reports. This first section poses three simple questions: what is transition, how does one measure progress and what is the pattern of progress across the selected transition economies? Each of these questions is worthy of a chapter in its own right. The purpose of this discussion is to provide a context for subsequent country case studies and thematic chapters. The second section of the chapter reviews policies for transformation. What are the major policies that have been implemented and how has the policy process varied across the selected transition economies? The chapter concludes by considering the relationships between policy and progress.

What is transition?

The dictionary definition of transition is a change from one state to another. In the context of recent development in ECE and the Baltic States, the change in state is from a Soviet-type socialist economic system towards some form of market-based economic system. The very term transition is problematic because it suggests a change from one known stable state to another stable state, in this case from plan to market. In fact, each version of the Soviet-type system was different and, as we shall see, the reform trajectories of each 'economy in transition' is proving to be different. As a consequence, each economy is likely to evolve into its own version of a market system and will occupy a unique position in the international economic system, just as the current Member States of the European Union (EU) have their own distinctions. However, this does not mean that there are not commonalities between transition economies and the progress made in transition - there are, and these are identified later in this chapter. The term transition also refers to changes beyond the economy. In reality, economic transition is not possible without simultaneous transitions in the political, social and cultural spheres. Consequently, it is commonplace to refer to the wider set of societal transition taking place in the post-socialist world as 'systemic transformation'. Those states that have made progress in economic transition have done so because they have been successful in reforming their political and social systems to create the institutions which support economic reform. Many of the states that have failed to make progress have failed because they have become involved in inter-state conflict and/or civil war or because their political and social systems have served to perpetuate the inefficiencies of the old system, rather than generate new growth. Thus, to understand more fully the progress of transition across the twenty-six transition economies identified by the EBRD it is necessary to consider all aspects of 'systemic transformation'. Nevertheless, this chapter focuses upon the process of economic transition, leaving later chapters to discuss social and political transformations.

Economic transition

According to the orthodox textbooks (see, for example, Gros and Steinherr, 1995) and the recommendations of the international institutions (World Bank, 1996), the transition from plan to market is brought about by a set of measures that together have been labelled the 'four pillars of transition'. Although individual authors tend to differ in the terms used to describe the key components of the transition, the four pillars can be described as: macro-economic stabilisation, privatisation and structural reform (including the financial system), liberalisation (in particular price liberalisation) and internationalisation (opening the economy to foreign trade and inward investment). According to de Melo et al. (1996), these measures should bring about the following changes in a formerly planned economy. The initial collapse of the planned system creates a period of macro-economic instability. For example, the liberalisation of prices may cause a period of high inflation. However, if stabilisation policies are implemented, inflation is brought under control and exchange rates stabilised. The disruption of the planned economy, loss of traditional markets and changes in domestic demand lead to decline in industrial production, referred to as: 'transitional recession'. In theory, the reallocation of resources, say from an inefficient industrial sector to an emergent service sector, eventually creates positive growth; transitional recession gives way to economic recovery (the so-called 'J-curve'). At the same time, policies to encourage private sector growth and foreign investment also generate growth. Thus, there is seen to be a process of creative destruction whereby the inefficient and distorted Soviet-type economy is replaced by a more balanced and effective market economy. Of course, this reallocation of resources across sectors and regions produces relative winners and losers, and it is recognised that transition has increased levels of inequality between regions and individuals.

Assessing transition progress

To assess the relative progress of the transition economies one must have a benchmark against which to judge the performance of individual states. Each year, the EBRD produces the *Transition Report*, which assesses the relative progress being made by the transition economies. According the EBRD's 1997 *Transition Report*, 'progress is measured against the standards of advanced industrial economies, recognising that there is no perfectly functioning market economy and that the institutional diversity among market economies does not present a unique end-point for the transition' (EBRD, 1997). For those transition economies seeking to join the EU there is an even more stringent set of criteria. The Agenda 2000 process has identified a set of political and economic criteria that must be achieved before a state can join the EU. Key among these 'Accession Criteria', also known as the 'Copenhagen Criteria', is the requirement that applicants demonstrate 'the existence of a functioning market economy as well as the capacity to cope with competitive pressure and market forces within the Union' (European Commission, 1997). The Agenda 2000 report identifies a set of conditions that define a 'functioning market economy':

- equilibrium between demand and supply is established by the free interplay of market forces; prices, as well as trade, are liberalised;
- significant barriers to market entry (establishment of new firms) and exit (bankruptcies) are absent;
- the legal system, including the regulation of property rights, is in place; laws and contracts can be enforced;
- macro-economic stability has been achieved including adequate price stability and sustainable public finances and external accounts;
- broad consensus about the essentials of economic policy;
- the financial sector is sufficiently well-developed to channel savings towards productive investment.

These criteria have much in common with the assessments used in the EBRD's *Transition Report*. In short, the transition is complete once the state has become a functioning advanced industrialised economy. The Agenda 2000 process also makes it clear that entry into the EU cannot be a means to achieve transition. The transition process must be completed and a functioning market economy in place *before* an applicant can be given serious consideration.

Patterns of progress

This section surveys the current level of development in all the transition economies and then focuses upon the ECE and Baltic states which are the most likely countries to meet the so-called 'Copenhagen criteria'. Table 2.1 provides basic socio-economic information on the transitional economies of ECE and the former Soviet Union. The table also includes the UNDP's Human Development Index (HDI) scores for each country. It is noteworthy that despite the variations in the economic indicators, there appears to be less variation in terms of quality of life. Figure 2.1 illustrates the degree of variation among the transition economies in terms of GDP per capita in 1997, while Figure 2.2 places the level of economic development in the ECE and Baltic States within the context of the current membership of the European Union. From this information, it is clear that there is considerable variation among the transition economies in terms of their relative levels of economic development. Much of this variation pre-dates the onset of transition. That many of the poorer transition economies seem to have more in common with the so-called 'developing world' than the advanced industrial economies leads one to question whether such an end point is a realistic target. Figure 2.3 shows that the transition record of the ECE and Baltic States has been quite different from the members of the Commonwealth of Independent States (and this is before the Russian economic crisis of 1998). The EBRD (1997) has identified three groups of countries: the countries at 'advanced stages' of transition (all the central European countries and the Baltic States); countries at 'intermediate stages' of transition (southern Europe and the Slavic republics of the former Soviet Union); and countries at 'early stages' of transition (the post-Soviet republics of the Transcaucasus and Central Asia). The fact that these groupings show a clear set of geographical divides suggests that the preconditions for transition are an important factor in determining the progress of transition.

In the context of the enlargement of the EU, the European Commission has concluded that five transition economies can now be considered to have functioning market economies: the Czech Republic, Estonia, Hungary, Poland and Slovenia. Even in these five there are areas, such as capital markets, that require further development. A sixth applicant, the Slovak Republic, was considered to be 'very close in terms of legislation and systemic features, but lacks transparency in implementation' (European Commission, 1997). A clear group of 'fast reforming economies' seemed to have emerged in ECE and the Baltic States. A group of economists at the World Bank has attempted to explain the patterns of transition (de Melo et al., 1996; World Bank, 1996). In their analysis they create a 'liberalisation index' which assesses the following areas:

- Internal markets - liberalisation of domestic prices and the abolition of state trading monopolies (weight: 0.3).
- External markets - liberalisation of the foreign trade regime, including elimination of export controls and taxes, and substitution of low-to-moderate import duties for import quotas and high import tariffs; current account convertibility (weight: 0.3).
- Private sector entry - privatisation of small-scale and large-scale enterprises and banking reform (weight: 0.4).

Table 2.1 Socio-economic indicators for transition economies in 1996

Country	Pop '96 Mill	Land area ('000 km^2)	GNP $ bill	GNP per cap $	GDP inc. % 90-96	Urb. pop. %	Trade as % GDP	HDI*	Rank out of 174	Emp. in agri. %
Albania	3	27	2.7	820	1.5	38	52	0.633	93	55
Bulgaria	8	111	2.4	1,190	-3.5	69	127	0.773	62	13
Croatia	5	56	18.1	3,800	-1	56	95	na	na	16
Czech Rep.	10	77	48.9	4,740	-1	66	117	0.872	37	11
Hungary	10	92	44.3	4,340	-0.4	65	79	0.855	46	15
Macedonia, FYR	2	25	2	990	-9.1	60	86	na	na	22
Poland	39	304	100.9	3,230	3.2	64	49	0.819	56	27
Romania	23	230	36.2	1,600	0	56	60	0.738	74	24
Slovak Republic	5	48	18.2	3,410	-1	59	126	0.864	41	12
Slovenia	2	20	18.4	9,240	4.3	52	111	na	na	6
CEE	**107**	**990**	**292.1**	**3,336**	**-0.7**	**59**	**90**	**na**	**na**	**20**
Armenia	4	28	2.4	630	-21.2	69	86	0.680	93	18
Azerbaijan	8	87	3.6	480	-17.7	56	62	0.665	96	31
Belarus	10	207	22.5	2,070	-8.3	72	96	0.787	61	20
Estonia	1	42	4.5	3,080	-6.5	73	159	0.749	68	14
Georgia	5	70	4.6	850	-26.1	59	44	0.645	101	26
Kazakhstan	16	2,671	22.2	1,350	-10.5	60	65	0.740	72	22
Kyrgyz Republic	5	192	2.5	550	-12.3	39	86	0.663	99	32
Latvia	2	62	5.7	2,300	-10.7	73	102	0.820	55	16
Lithuania	4	65	8.5	2,280	-6	73	115	0.719	81	18
Moldova	4	33	2.5	590	-16.7	52	118	0.633	104	33

Country	Pop '96 Mill	Land area ('000 km^2)	GNP $ bill	GNP per cap $	GDP inc. % 90-96	Urb. pop. %	Trade as % GDP	HDI*	Rank out of 174	Emp. in agri. %
Russia	148	16,889	356	2410	-9	76	42	0.084	57	14
Tajikistan	6	141	2	340	-16.4	32	228	0.616	105	41
Turkmen-istan	5	470	4.3	940	-9.6	45	na	0.695	90	37
Ukraine	51	579	60.9	1,200	-13.6	71	93	0.719	80	20
Uzbekistan	23	414	23.5	1,010	-3.5	41	69	0.679	94	35
Former Soviet Union	**292**	**21,950**	**525.7**	**1,339**	**-13**	**59**	**98**	**na**	**na**	**27**

Sources: The World Bank (1998); The World Bank and UNDP (1997).
Notes: * HDI: Human Development Index.

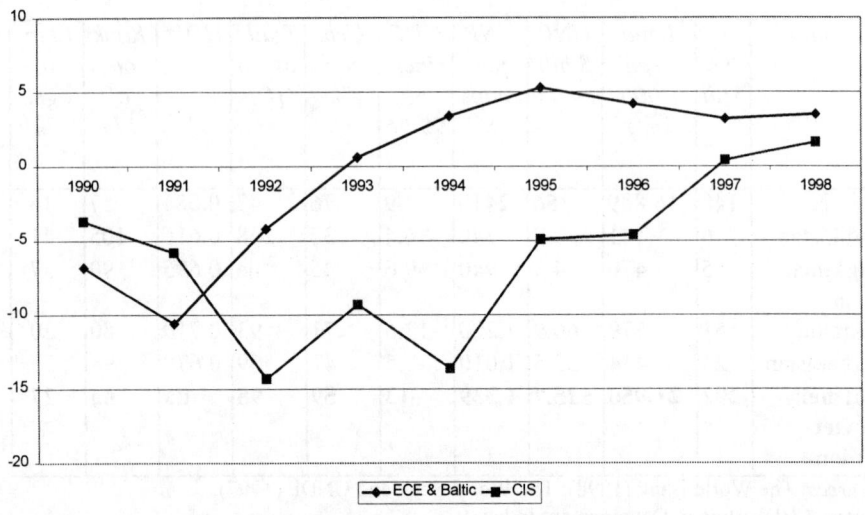

Figure 2.1 Growth in real GDP 1990-1998 (percent)

Source: See Table 2.3.

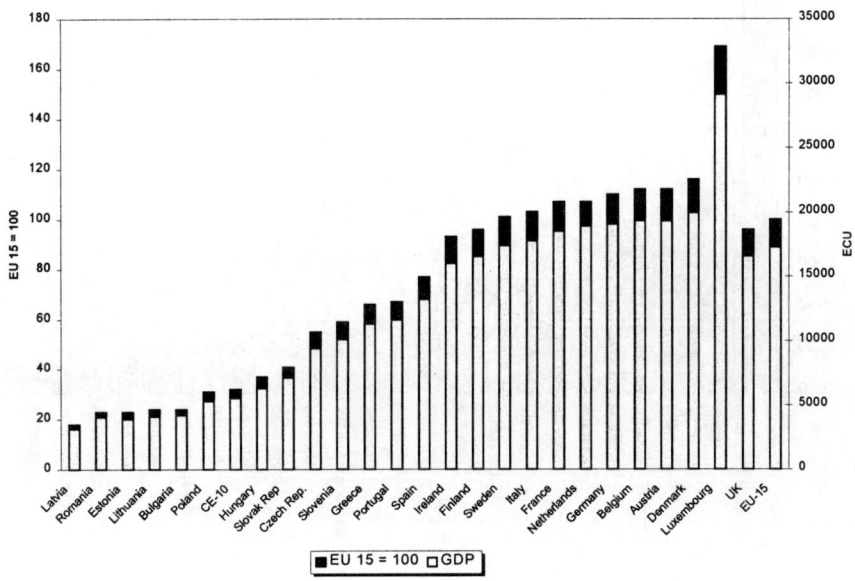

Figure 2.2 ECE-10 and EU-15: GDP per capita (PPP) – 1995

Source: http://europa.eu.int/comm/dg1a/agenda2000/

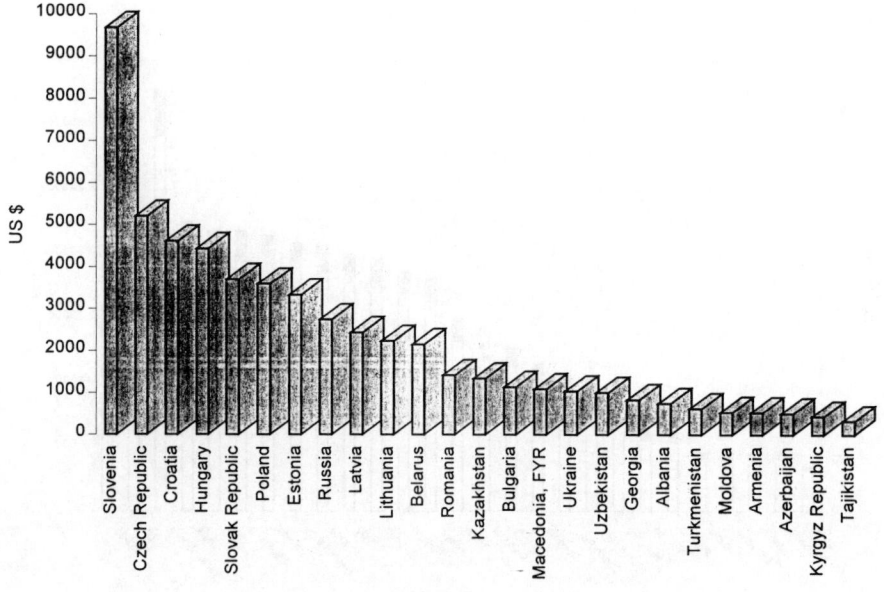

Figure 2.3 Transition economies: GNP per capita 1997

Source: World Bank (1998), World Development Indicators on CD-Rom.

The results of their analysis, as they relate to ECE and the Baltic States, are presented in Table 2.2. They conclude that 'country experience during the transition is strongly associated with liberalisation and that the return to positive growth is associated with declines in inflation to double digit or less' (de Melo et al., 1996).

Table 2.2 Liberalisation, growth and inflation in selected transition economies, 1989-94

	CLI^a 1994	AL^b 1993-94	Average annual inflation 1993-94 (%)	Average annual growth in GDP 1993-94 (%)	Average annual GDP in '93-94 as % of '89 GDP	Lowest GDP level as percentage of 1989 GDP
Advanced reformers						
Slovenia	4.16	0.82	26	3.0	84	81
Poland	4.14	0.84	34	4.2	88	82
Hungary	4.11	0.84	21	0.0	81	80
Czech Rep.	3.61	0.90	16	0.8	81	80
Slovak Rep.	3.47	0.86	19	0.4	79	77
Average	3.90	0.85	23	1.7	83	80
High-intermediate reformers						
Estonia	2.93	0.85	69	0.9	69	67
Bulgaria	2.90	0.68	81	-1.4	73	73
Lithuania	2.72	0.79	231	-7.3	44	44
Latvia	2.45	0.71	73	-4.4	60	59
Romania	2.29	0.66	194	2.2	69	67
Average^c	2.55	0.72	124	0.03	67	65

Source: de Melo et al (1996).
Notes: [a]CLI: Cumulative Liberalisation Index. [b] AL: Average Liberalisation. [c]This group also includes Albania and Mongolia.

More recent information on inflation and economic growth is presented in Tables 2.3 and 2.4. This information highlights the 'progress' made by ECE and Baltic States relative to the members of the Commonwealth of Independent States. The most successful states, in terms of economic growth, are those identified by the European Commission as potential candidates for EU membership. In assessing the pattern of progress, de Melo et al. (1996) conclude 'that there are strong common patterns among countries at similar stages of reform. The common legacy and the associated changes resulting from the initial disruptions in the socialist economic co-ordinating mechanisms and subsequent liberalisation measures go a long way toward explaining the transition experience'. On the question of the importance of pre-conditions versus policy, the World Bank (1996) report concludes that, while '[d]ifferences in initial conditions and structural characteristics...explain a good deal of the divergence of transition economies and policies across countries. They do not explain all- the sustained application of market-oriented reform policies, within a broadly "right" macro-economic environment, has been a critical ingredient in success'. The next section of this chapter reviews the implementation of those market-oriented reform policies.

Table 2.3 Growth in real GDP for selected transition economies

Country	1990	1991	1992	1993	1994	1995	1996	1997 Est.	1998 Proj.	1996 GDP as % 1989*
Bulgaria	-9.1	-11.7	-7.3	-1.5	1.8	2.1	-10.9	-7.4	4.5	68
Czech Republic	-1.2	-11.5	-3.3	0.6	2.7	5.9	4.1	1.2	2.0	96
Hungary	-3.5	-11.9	-3.1	-0.6	2.9	1.5	1.3	4.3	4.3	87
Poland	-11.6	-7.0	2.6	3.8	5.2	7.0	6.1	6.9	5.0	105
Romania	-5.6	-12.9	-8.7	1.5	3.9	7.1	4.1	-6.6	-3.0	88
Slovak R.	-2.5	-14.6	-6.5	-3.7	4.9	6.8	6.9	5.5	3.0	90
Slovenia	-4.7	-8.9	-5.5	2.8	5.3	4.1	3.1	3.3	4.0	95
Estonia	-8.1	-7.9	-14.2	-8.5	-1.8	4.3	4.0	11.0	5.0	71
Latvia	2.9	-10.4	-34.9	-14.9	0.6	-0.8	2.8	6.0	5.0	52
Lithuania	-5.0	-13.4	-37.7	-17.1	-11.3	2.3	5.1	5.0	5.5	41
CEE & Baltic States	-6.8	-10.6	-4.2	0.6	3.4	5.3	4.2	3.2	3.5	92
CIS	-3.7	-5.8	-14.3	-9.3	-13.6	-4.9	-4.6	0.4	1.6	56

Source: EBRD (1998).
Notes: * Estimated level of real GDP in 1996 as percentage of 1989.

Table 2.4 Inflation indicators for selected transition economies

Country	1991	1992	1993	1994	1995	1996	1997 Est.	1998 Proj.
Bulgaria	338.9	79.4	63.8	121.9	32.9	310.8	578.6	12.0
Czech Republic	52.0	12.7	18.2	9.7	7.9	8.6	10.0	9.0
Hungary	32.2	21.6	21.1	21.2	28.3	19.8	18.4	14.0
Poland	60.4	44.3	37.6	29.4	21.6	18.5	13.2	11.0
Romania	222.8	199.2	295.5	61.7	27.8	56.9	151.6	35.0
Slovak R.	58.3	9.1	25.1	11.7	7.2	5.4	6.4	na
Slovenia	247.1	92.9	22.9	18.3	8.6	8.8	9.4	8.6
Estonia	303.8	953.5	35.6	42.0	29.0	15.0	12.0	8.0
Latvia	262.4	959.0	35.0	26.1	22.7	13.2	6.0	5.0
Lithuania	345.0	1,161.1	188.8	45.0	35.5	13.1	8.5	9.0
CEE & Baltic States	229.7	199.2	35.6	26.1	21.6	13.2	10.0	9.0
CIS	147.0	1,352	2,082	1,220	101	32	13	11

Source: EBRD, 1998.

Policies for transformation

There has been considerable debate, both within east central Europe and beyond, over the tasks confronting those countries as they dismantle communism and attempt to construct new systems. Identifying the tasks is just the first step on the path to creating and implementing policies for reform and change. Very few of these debates and policy formulations have historical precedents or theoretical models to which to turn. For this reason, coupled with the enormity of the tasks and the stakes, a number of apparently diverse policies and approaches have been promoted. However, as Bideleux and Jeffries note, 'the virulence of the debate often hides substantial areas of agreement' (Bideleux and Jeffries, 1998), and discussions have in fact often been limited to ones of speed and sequencing, mostly notably on the relative merits of shock therapy/big-bang approaches as compared with gradualist policies. Ten years on from the tumultuous events of 1989, most commentators suggest that there was, and remains, a place for both rapid, overnight change and for more gradual approaches. Nuti and Portes, for example, argue that whilst some steps (such as price liberalisation, the decentralisation of foreign trade and the legalisation of foreign property) should be implemented immediately and simultaneously, processes of institution building and behavioural change (both individual and corporate) can only take place gradually (Nuti and Portes, 1993; see also Bideleux and Jeffries, 1998; Portes, 1992). Nevertheless, there remain die-hard reformers who argue that you cannot cross a chasm in two leaps, that gradualism carries dangers of reform failure (political and economic) and of getting stuck halfway, with a partially reformed economy.

Issues of speed and sequencing are most clearly played out in practice, as illustrated by the following review of the policies adopted by different east central European countries in different sectors of the economy. The focus lies with generally identifying commonalities and highlighting differences, serving as an introduction to later chapters with more specific regional and functional foci.

Price liberalisation

In many ways, the Polish Balcerowicz plan set the standard for price liberalisation by freeing ninety percent of all transactions overnight on 1st January 1990. Czechoslovakia (later the Czech and Slovak Republics) followed a similar policy, liberalising 85 percent of prices in 1991. However, countries such as Bulgaria, Romania, Slovenia and Hungary followed phased programmes of price liberalisation, freeing sets of prices gradually over the past ten years. Romania, for example, freed prices (to a limited extent) in three stages throughout 1990 and 1991, giving three months' notice of increases (Gros and Steinherr, 1995) whilst Bulgaria actually increased price controls through 1995 and 1996, liberalising most prices only in 1997. The freeing of the majority of prices, however, conceals the continued control and subsidy of many key goods and services. In nearly all the transition economies, price controls and state subsidies have been retained in the supply of domestic energy (gas and electricity), in housing rents, in passenger transport, in some medicines and in telecommunications. In Poland, for example, despite early and decisive action, 11 percent of prices remain controlled. In addition, many east central European states, such as Croatia, Macedonia and the Czech Republic have continued to offer minimum purchase prices for certain agricultural and food products. However, many of these states have also pushed through further liberalisation measures in 1997 and 1998, moving utility and housing prices closer to cost.

Privatisation and corporate governance

Privatisation has been a central plank of every programme of transition in east central Europe, where policies adopted provide a very good example of regional commonalities. Each country has, broadly speaking, divided the state-owned enterprise (SOE) sector into different categories and employed a variety of privatisation policies. Across the region, direct sales, auctions and leases to domestic capitalists, management (or management and employee) buy-outs, tenders, liquidations, restitution to former owners, direct sales to foreign companies and mass, voucher-based privatisation have all been used to varying degrees (Schwartz et al., 1994). Again, the major differential between countries has been the timing of ownership reforms, with late reformers such as Albania, Bulgaria and Macedonia only now beginning intensive programmes of privatisation. Nevertheless, key stages can be highlighted in the privatisation process. Small-scale privatisation - the selling of trade and service entities to employees and managers - has tended to be the first programme to be completed. This has often been swiftly followed by voucher-based mass privatisation programmes in which tradable vouchers are distributed to all or part of the population, to then be exchanged for i) shares in enterprises or ii) shares in investment funds, which, in their turn, purchase shares in a variety of enterprises. Later (current) phases of privatisation have tended to focus on finding strategic investors (domestic or foreign) for strategic, large enterprises. This sort of approach is currently being taken in Hungary, Poland, Lithuania and Romania.

Many of the states of the region have used some form of 'halfway house', such as a state-owned joint stock company, to manage the process of privatisation, such that even those companies awaiting full privatisation are commercialised, forced to balance their books and to appoint an accountable management board. Such management policies tend to be implemented through national property or privatisation agencies, or transferred to sectoral ministries or municipalities, and are aimed at improving corporate governance structures. There has been considerable debate over insider domination of firms privatised through sales to existing managers and employees (see, for example, Ellerman et al., 1991; Frydman and Rapaczynski, 1993) and over state-led programmes for the restructuring and privatisation of major enterprises such as gas and electricity companies, state railways and telecommunications firms, as well as large manufacturing plants, which implemented privatisation without restructuring.

The privatisation of state-owned enterprises has been mirrored by the on-going privatisation of land and housing markets. Patterns of change and policy choices in these fields have been more varied than in corporate ownership, and in many countries the state retains considerable control over housing and land markets, either through regulation, ownership or controlled pricing. In countries such as Croatia and Lithuania, housing privatisation is seen to be largely complete, whilst in Estonia, for example, issues of land registration cause continuing uncertainty. The development of land and housing markets across the region is complicated by demands for restitution of property to pre-war owners. These issues are complicated still further in states which have been characterised by major population movements, such as Poland and the states of former Yugoslavia.

Trade and foreign investment

The liberalisation of domestic prices was accompanied by the liberalisation of foreign trade, both into and out of the region, and by the legalisation of foreign investment and foreign ownership of economic assets. Most of the countries of the region have acceded to the World Trade Organisation (WTO) and have established multilateral and bilateral trading agreements within and beyond the region. The Baltic free trade agreement and CEFTA (the Central European Free Trade Agreement) are two of the main vehicles for trade liberalisation within the region, whilst attempts to join the EU are clearly an important motivator for opening national economies to international trade and investment. The general policy throughout the region has been for the conversion of quantitative trade restrictions to tariffs and the gradual reduction of tariffs across the board. Many countries are seen to have very liberal trade regimes, but many still retain both import and export controls on sensitive products, most particularly some agricultural and food products. At the present time, two contradictory tendencies can be identified in the region - i) the further opening of economies to international capital and goods (eg. the Czech Republic, Hungary and Slovenia) and ii) calls for increasing protectionism in certain sectors (eg. Estonia, the Slovak Republic and Croatia).

Each of the countries of the region has had a different approach to the role of foreign investors in the privatisation of enterprises and the development of new businesses. Hungary is frequently quoted as the country being most open to foreign involvement, whilst Poland is often represented as being more hostile to investment from foreign capitalists, as a result not only of excessive bureaucracy and red tape, but also of some politicians' nationalist rhetoric. The level of foreign ownership has increased through recent, large-scale sales to foreign companies - the sale of Latvija Gaze to Russian and German investors, and the possible sale of the two major Polish steelworks (Huta Katowice and Huta Sendzimira) to Western European consortia being examples of this tendency. In countries such as Lithuania and Slovenia, constitutional bans on the foreign ownership of land have recently been lifted along with the removal of restrictions on the repatriation of profits, reducing further possible deterrence to foreign investment in the region.

The region's currencies are increasingly externally convertible and, perhaps more importantly, relatively stable. Different approaches to stabilising exchange rates have been adopted, ranging from fixing or pegging rates to some combination of the German Deutsche Mark (DM) and US dollar, to establishing a floating band with central bank intervention. Though there have been some deliberate devaluations recently, national currencies tend now to be market-set.

Incomes and labour market policies

Profound economic restructuring, price liberalisation and increased international competition have all had a significant impact on wages and employment in the region. It has been widely noted (Winiecki, 1991) that reforms have been accompanied by declines in production and rising unemployment at the same time as previously universal welfare systems have been eroded and restructured. Thus, the management of employment and wages has been a critical issue across the region. Fears of inflationary spirals in the wake of dramatic price increases encouraged the introduction, in the early 1990s, in many countries of taxes on excessive wage increases. Governmental wage controls remain in some sectors in some countries, but the late 1990s has seen the strengthening of the role of trilateral commissions (the state, employers, employees) in setting wages, at least in the remaining state sector. In Slovenia, for example, collective agreements set minimum pay rates for nine education and skill categories, whilst in Poland wage negotiation is guided by indicative norms set by a trilateral commission. In addition to collective wage-setting agreements, every country in the region except Croatia has minimum-wage legislation which links a basic income to either a share of average earnings (around 40 to 65 percent) or to the retail price index (EBRD, 1997).

Structural change within the economy has intensified the need for active labour market policies to ease mismatches between labour supply and demand, in terms of skill, status and location (Gros and Steinherr, 1995). There is considerable emphasis, through privatisation, restructuring and business development, on job creation, but less on recognition that job creation requires mobility and often considerable adjustment on the part of the workforce. Retraining, the provision of small loans, counselling and even public works programmes have all been implemented to ease the restructuring of employment and work, but other structural issues such as a weakly developed housing market have, on occasion, rendered labour market policies ineffective.

Financial restructuring (government and corporate)

The central task in the financial sector has been the break-up of Soviet-era, one-tier banking systems and the creation of non-bank financial institutions. In each country, mono-banks have been transformed into smaller, but still large, regional (in Poland and the Czech and Slovak Republics) or sectoral (in Hungary) banks. With the break-up of state-run banks, new banking legislation has also been enacted to improve systems of regulation and supervision. As with state enterprises, some banks have been commercialised under ministerial ownership in preparation for privatisation, whilst others have engaged in joint ventures with foreign banks in an attempt to encourage sound banking practice. Across the region, bank debt and lending have been rescheduled, with recapitalisation taking place where necessary. A process of consolidation and merger has, in recent years, followed an early phase of excessive private bank creation.

Non-bank finance has been developed through the creation of money, stock and government bond markets. Some stock and inter-bank exchanges have been reopened (for example, Budapest in 1990), whilst others have been newly created (in Warsaw, Prague and Bratislava). In parallel to the development of exchanges, east central Europe has witnessed the expansion of the financial intermediary sector, often through the involvement of foreign accountancy, auditing and consultancy firms.

Government finances have undergone major transformations in recent years in terms of both incomes and expenditures. In the short term, incomes have fallen dramatically whilst expenditures, remaining at approximately the same level, have been significantly restructured. As a result, much of the region now possesses considerable budgetary deficits. As with privatisation, differences in the reform of taxes have largely been ones of timing. Hungary implemented a thorough overhaul of the taxation system early in 1988, whilst Poland carried out a phased restructuring throughout 1989 to 1993, and the Czech and Slovak Republics began with small-scale change before carrying out wholesale reform overnight in January 1993. Timing notwithstanding, the aims of reform have been remarkably similar - to shift the burden of taxation onto private enterprise, but at the same time to ease both the administrative and monetary burdens by increasing transparency and reducing overall levels of taxation, to level the playing field and remove preferential treatment of favoured enterprises and sectors, and to introduce new systems of personal taxation to reflect increasing income differentials amongst the population. One of the most pressing taxation problems is that of arrears and non-payment. In the Slovak Republic, for example, it is estimated that up to US$1.5 billion of state revenues have been lost in tax evasion, whilst in Croatia up to 25 percent of revenues have been lost to evasion (EBRD, 1997). Gros and Steinherr (1995) suggest that politically and socially powerful enterprises may be very successful at exerting leverage over the government to achieve the reduction or elimination of tax burdens. Of course, there are many individuals and enterprises who simply chose not to register, and it is in response to this that states have strengthened enforcement of tax policies, often through the creation of a tax police.

The enforcement of bankruptcy law has also recently been stepped up. Although such laws were introduced early in reform packages (1992 in Hungary, 1991 in Czechoslovakia), implementation was weak and few enterprises entered bankruptcy proceedings. This tended to mean that financial restructuring of firms and banks lagged also. Activity in more recent years has placed a stronger emphasis on increasing payments discipline and reducing inter-enterprise arrears, both through the enforcement of existing legislation (Lithuania and Poland) and through new laws, amendments and additions (in Croatia, Hungary, the Czech Republic and Romania) (EBRD, 1997).

Conclusion

Taking together the reviews of policies and progress, it is clear that the choice and implementation of policies cannot, alone, explain the 'success' or 'failure' of post-socialist transformation in the states of east central Europe. A wide variety of factors has been identified in the literature which may, in part, account for differences in the implementation and progress of reform policies. These include historical economic and political structures and orientation (from both socialist and earlier imperial eras), geographical and cultural proximity to western Europe (particularly in the light of EU accession), political stability, the social and regional context of reform (with particular reference to sub-national inequalities, the presence of ethnic minorities and the strength of certain 'interest groups' such as the Catholic church and Solidarity in Poland), the level of western involvement in transition, and, of course, the timing and technical implementation of reform policies (including the issue of whether countries began reforms prior to 1989). It is clear that each of these factors is played out very differently in each of the transitional economies and, for this reason, it is understandable that patterns of reform and progress differ across the region.

National and local contexts inevitably play a role in the mediation of reform policies, and, as a result, it is difficult to sustain any notion that capitalism can be installed in the east central European countries 'by design' (Stark, 1992). Reform policies, capitalist institutions and new economic practices cannot simply be created in a vacuum, but must navigate the rubble and foundations of older systems. The creation of new political and economic regimes rests not only on the accommodation or elimination of Soviet-era institutions, but also on the path of extrication from communism, and on wider questions of historical and geographical location.

This chapter has drawn attention to some of the commonalities of reform policies and progress, identifying general patterns and setting the transition from socialism in a wide regional context. In doing this, it lays the basis for more detailed explorations in later chapters of individual countries' experience and of sectoral and functional issues. Notwithstanding their common histories, the countries of east central Europe have fared very differently in the context of systemic transformation. To understand, and learn from, the processes of post-socialist transformation more completely it is critical to consider that variety of experience.

References

Bideleux, R. and Jeffries, I. (1998), *A History of Eastern Europe: Crisis and Change*, Routledge, London.

de Melo, Denizer, C. and Gelb, A. (1996), 'Patterns of Transition from Plan to Market', *The World Bank Economic Review*, vol. 10, pp.397-424.

Ellerman, D., Vahcic, A., Petrin, T. (1991), 'Privatisation Controversies East and West', *Communist Economies and Economic Transformation*, vol. 3, no. 3, pp.283-98.

European Bank for Reconstruction and Development (1998), *Economics of Transition*, vol. 6, London.

European Bank for Reconstruction and Development (1997), *Transition Report*, EBRD, London.

European Commission (1997), *Agenda 2000, Part Two: The Challenge of Enlargement*. http://europa.eu.int/comm/dg1a/agenda2000/.

Frydman, R. and Rapaczynski, A. (1993), 'Insiders and the State: Overview of Responses to Agency Problems in East European Privatisations', *Economics of Transition*, vol. 1, no. 1, pp.39-59.

Gros, D. and Steinherr, A. (1995), *Winds of Change: Economic Transition in Central and Eastern Europe*, Longman, London.

Nuti, D.M. and Portes, R. (1993), 'Central Europe: The Way Forward', in Portes R. (ed) (1993), *Economic Transformation in Central Europe: A Progress Report*, Centre for Economic Policy Research, CEPR, London.

Portes, R. (1992), 'Structural reform in central and eastern Europe', *European Economic Review*, vol. 36, pp.661-69.

Portes, R. (ed) (1993), *Economic Transformation in Central Europe: A Progress Report*, Centre for Economic Policy Research, CEPR, London.

Schwartz, G., Stone, M. and van der Willigen, T. (1994), 'Beyond stabilisation: the economic transformation of Czechoslovakia, Hungary and Poland', *Communist Economies and Economic Transformation*, vol. 6, no. 3, pp.291-313.

Stark, D. (1992), 'The Great Transformation? Social Change in Eastern Europe', *Contemporary Sociology*, vol. 12, no. 3, pp.299-304.

Winiecki, J (1991), 'The inevitability of a fall in output in the early stages of transition to the market: theoretical underpinnings', *Soviet Studies*, vol. 43, pp.669-76.

World Bank (1998), *World Development Indicators*, Washington D.C.

World Bank (1996), *From Plan to Market: World Development Report 1996*, OUP, Oxford.

World Bank and UNDP (1997), Human Development under Transition: Europe and the CIS, UNDP, New York.

3 Transformation and the Interdependencies between Political and Economic Development

THIEMO W. ESER

Introduction

Many recommendations have been made by economists regarding the transformation of the former socialist economies and the Central and Eastern European (CEE) countries. The majority of these are based on normative insights from economic theory and focus on the liberalisation, privatisation and stabilisation issue, strongly emphasising the liberalisation of markets and a slimmed-down public sector against the background of neo-classical economics. This approach has been questioned more recently in both the theoretical and also more applied literature.[1] Two main issues are apparent: first, the understanding of the role of state; and second, closely connected, the logic of interdependencies between political and economic development, as noted in the previous chapter. This chapter has three aims: to describe briefly the traditional view with reference to countries in transition; to show the shortcomings of this view with reference to developing countries; and to sketch a framework which may provide a basis for an improved consideration of these new insights through the incorporation of new theoretical approaches. Finally, conclusions concerning a new agenda for assessing transformation will be drawn.

Normative economic aspects of the transformation

After the iron curtain was lifted, it was clear that the socialist countries would try to achieve democratic structures and advance towards a market economy. A 'third way' for the development of economic structures has never been seriously taken into consideration. The main tasks of the transformation were, and still are, related to the reform itself (what has to be done), and how to deal with the transition process.[2]

As discussed in Chapter 2, key tasks in the commodity and factor markets sector are the liberalisation of prices, the reform of the business sector and the liberalisation of foreign trade. These reforms have hidden redistributional effects and have given rise to conflicts between diverse interests (as with reactions of management and workforce to privatisation) (Basten, 1996; Husain and Sahay, 1992; Aghion et al, 1993). Further, developments such as the reform and privatisation of firms, the adaptation of production structures (El Shagi, 1983), and the building up of an appropriate infrastructure take time. Similar redistribution issues and the reorganisation of relations between interest groups (state, enterprises, citizens) are inherent in reforms in the monetary sector such as monetary stabilisation, the introduction of new tax regimes and the creation of convertibility of national currencies. Of course, countries differ in preconditions such as the level of foreign debt, competitiveness of the national economy etc. (Edwards, 1989), and solutions have to be found for each individual transforming economy.

The dynamics of the transformation process were also discussed in the previous chapter: an initial collapse followed by a sustainable upswing of economic performance, with gross domestic product (GDP) following a J-shaped trend (Siebert, 1991) due to the costs and returns of the transformation (see Table 2.3 in Bradshaw and Stenning chapter). The trade-off seems to underestimate the returns compared to the real welfare gain. Due to inefficiencies in socialist times, GDP appeared much higher than actual performance during that time (Winiecki, 1991), while current GDP does not include the high level of black market activities (Dobozi and Pohl, 1995).

Furthermore, the break-down of the former institutional framework of economic activities did not coincide with the creation of new structures (Kornai, 1994). Initially, change to the governmental system caused unstable expectations and led to short-term planning horizons among actors, while the reallocation of property rights caused co-ordination problems between market participants (Niskanen, 1991).

Influencing the transformation process depends on the time factor (Kloten, 1993) ie. a time lag exists between the introduction of new institutions and the adaptation of the public and private actors to the new institutional structure. Of the two well-known approaches - shock-therapy and gradualism - an important pre-condition of the first is a fast adaptation to new institutional structures. Although this might lead to severe social and political tensions, in addition to economic problems, they might be overcome by the speed of the development itself (Rosati, 1991).

The gradualist approach suggests limiting the breakdown by introducing economic policy reforms more slowly, but necessarily requiring transformation to take longer. Thus, the timing and sequencing of reforms are key influences on the transformation process as both approaches have advantages and disadvantages. Once again, an important factor is the political rationale behind the choice of approach. Any kind of reform has to be approved somehow in the political process, particularly if burdens are unequally distributed (Roland, 1994).

The key point is that the transformation of the former socialist economies comprises a wide range of tasks, but the normative economic approach has neglected the political dimension ie. it has not considered the reaction of the citizens of the reforming countries. While the objectives of the transformation are relatively clearly defined, apart from having identified the problem of sequencing at the macro level, little research has been done on the causality and interdependencies between the introduction of measures and the possible reaction of the citizens. This is crucial for a number of reasons: political decisions about reforms have to be taken by politicians according to the specific situation in each country; there are different ways to create and build particular institutions; and there are many obstacles to the introduction of certain measures which place a high burden on the population.

Experience from the transformation of developing countries

Taking the debate a stage further, the question is whether the reforms will lead to a successful development of these countries? Experience with successful development following policy reforms can be drawn from developing countries. An investigation of these experiences highlights certain gaps in the explanation of some developments.[3]

Learning from successful reforms

In the case of developing countries, there is a comparable and widely agreed list of measures, the so-called "Washington consensus", which indicates the measures necessary to create conditions for successful development (see Table 3.1).

Table 3.1 The Washington consensus and East Asia

Elements of the Washington Consensus	South Korea	Taiwan
1. Fiscal discipline	Yes generally	Yes
2. Redirection of public expenditure priorities towards health, education and infrastructure	Yes	Yes
3. Tax reform, including the broadening of the tax base and cutting marginal tax rates	Yes generally	Yes
4. Unified and competitive exchange rates	Yes (except for limited time periods)	Yes
5. Secure property rights	In 1960s imprisonment of businessmen and threats of confiscation of assets	Yes
6. Deregulation	Limited	Limited
7. Trade liberalisation	Limited until 1980s	Limited until 1980s
8. Privatisation	No - government created many public enterprises during 1950-60s	No - government created many public enterprises during 1950-60s
9. Elimination of barriers to direct foreign investment	Heavily restricted	Subject to government control
10. Financial liberalisation	Limited until 1980s	Limited until 1980s

Source: Williamson, 1994; Rodrik, 1996.

This kind of check-list gives some initial guidance through the puzzle of factors which form the basis of successful policy reform. A brief overview of the scoring surprisingly reveals that even successful countries like South Korea or Taiwan scored only about 5-6 out of 10 on this list, mainly by meeting the first items (Rodrik, 1996). Although in the 1980s Latin American states introduced more of the measures outlined in the second part of the Washington Consensus, these countries have been obviously less successful than the Asian states.

So further explanations for the strength of the Asian countries have been investigated. One increasingly accepted hypothesis says that the Asian countries have much more effective government than others in Africa and South America (Krüger, 1993). Other important factors which have been identified are a better educated labour force, a more equal distribution and less powerful industrial and landed interest groups. This has meant less pressure on the government from rent-seeking lobbyists, and, therefore, the greater ability of the political leadership to supervise and guide the bureaucracy (Rodrik, 1996).

While the distributional argument is supported by empirical studies (Persson and Tabellini, 1994; Birdsall et al 1995), there is still a lack of research evidence about the underlying politico-economic arguments (Rodrik, 1996). Experience shows that, in developing countries, these reform recommendations have never been completely implemented, and there are no causal links between following these recommendations and the economic success of these countries. Each country has its own approach due to specific economic and political circumstances.

A further deficiency of many studies is the missing micro-institutional dimension which seems to have a strong influence on the success of the developing countries (Mummert, 1996). The hypothesis of Krueger (1993) supports this view that the governments in Asian countries are more successful than in South America. Institutions, in the sense of the new institutional economics, could be a key to further investigations about the success of developing economies. For example, one of the main lessons emerging from the debt crisis of some developing countries in the 1980s, has been that just proposing an 'optimal policy' is insufficient to adjust their economies. Support programmes and measures by international institutions, such as the World Bank and the International Monetary Fund, but also bilateral support programmes, are failing if these measures are not embedded in the political and social conditions of each country. Furthermore, the political rationale of the government and administrations of each country must be understood (Lafay and Lecaillon, 1993). This can be shown by the investigation of 'rent seeking' behaviour (Buchanan et al, 1980) on the basis of the New Institutional Economics. Institutions incorporate a stabilising element in the way that individuals are enabled to anticipate the others' behaviour. Rent-seeking activities of individuals mean that they try to gain additional income by abusing instead of supporting a Western-style rule of law (Pritzl, 1996). Individuals can achieve additional rents by influencing politicians towards interventions in favour of their interests. These activities distort the newly created incentive structure of liberalised markets and hamper the development of an incentive structure comparable to an advanced economy.

Although the transformation of the former socialist economies has key unique features, a number of similarities can nevertheless be drawn between developing and transforming countries (Nelson, 1993). These include, for example, the introduction of democracy, the privatisation of business, the liberalisation of markets and trade, and the reform of the government and its finances. The European Bank for Reconstruction and Development set up a system of indicators (see Table 3.2) for the classification of transforming economies which can be used to amend the criteria of the Washington Consensus of Table 3.1.

Comparing the institutional reforms indicated in Table 3.2 with key macro-economic data (Table 3.3 and see also Table 2.1), it is clear that a certain relationship does exist between inflation and growth rates on the one hand and the progress of reforms on the other. Even the categorisation appears to be suitable with the exception of Estonia which performs in both respects more like the CEEC than an NEEC. The absolute level of GNP does not appear to play a major role.

The key question is which factors are truly influential? The World Bank (1996), on the basis of practical experience, points to the following important conditions for successful policy reform:
- Consistent policies, combining liberalisation and price stability, even in the absence of clearly defined property rights and market institutions. A high rate of savings secures the internal finance of investments.
- Countries differ in the choice of rapid and deep reforms and more cushioned approaches. Dual-track approaches are not necessarily the worse way as long as the macro-economic balance is not undermined. A greater weight of economic performance is an important legitimating factor for an on-going government.

Table 3.2 State of transformation in the CEEC 1994-98[a]

Countries	Enterprises			Markets and Trade			Financial Institutions		Legal Reform
	Large-scale privatisation	Small-scale privatisation	Enterprise restructuring	Price liberalisation[b]	Trade, foreign exchange system	Competition policy[b]	Bank ref. interest liberal.	Security markets & non-bank fin. inst.[c]	Extens. & effec. of legal rules on invest.[d]
CEEC									
Czech R.	4/4	4/4+	3/3	3/3	4	3/3	3/3	3	4
Hungary	3/4	4/4+	3/3+	3/3+	4+	3/3	3/4	3+	4
Poland	3/3+	4/4+	3/3	3/3+	4+	3/3	3/3+	3+	4
Slovakia	3/4	4/4+	4/3-	3/3	4+	3/3	3/3-	2+	3
Slovenia	2/3+	4/4+	3/3-	3/3	4+	3/2	3/3	3	3
SEEC									
Bulgaria	2/3	2/3	2/2+	3/3	4	3/2	2/3-	2	3
Romania	2/3-	3/3+	2/2	3/3	4	3/2	2/2+	2	3
NEEC									
Estonia	3/4	4/4+	3/3	3/3	4	3/3-	3/3+	3	4
Lithuania	3/3	4/4	2/3-	3/3	4	3/2+	3/3	2+	3
Latvia	2/3	3/4	2/3-	3/3	4	3/3-	3/3-	2+	3
EEC									
Belarus	2/1	2/2	2/1	2/2	1	2/2	1/1	2	2
Moldova	2/3	3/3+	2/2	3/3	4	3/2	2/2	2+	2
Russia	3/3+	3/4	2/2	3/3-	2+	3/2+	2/2	2	3
Ukraine	1/2+	2/3+	1/2	2/3	3-	2/2	1/2	2	2

Source: EBRD 1994, 1997, 1998.
Notes: [a] Most advanced industrial economies would qualify for the "4+" rating for almost all transition indicators, a rating not included in the 1994 classification; [b] Both indicators were merged in 1994; [c] 1994 not classified; [d] Classified in 1997.

- Clearly defined property rights for firms, farms and real estate avoid an ownership vacuum, but diverse effects can occur which have to be considered in the restructuring process. Depoliticising the economic restructuring and opening the control to outsiders allows government to concentrate on key areas of the economy.
- Opening the markets causes greater uncertainties for individuals and a process of increasing inequality may be started with the creation of poverty. This also applies to adverse inter-generation effects of reform, which require the securing of pensions for elderly people.

Transformation in the transition countries in particular, suffers from a number of dilemmas. First, the liberalisation of prices, necessary to create the right relative prices, has led to falling production and employment. Second, the free convertibility of the currency, necessary to attract foreign capital, has led to a strong devaluation of the currency and to problems of stabilisation and payments due to foreign debt. Third, governments expected to stimulate entrepreneurship and revenue by privatisation but, in fact, the latter has not been achieved and the transition process has slowed (Bankim and Coricelli, 1994; see also Table 3.4).

Table 3.3 Basic economic indicators for CEE countries

Country	GDP per capita (PPP $) 1997	Level of real GDP 1997^a 1989=100	Inflation 1997 consumer/industrial	Public expenditure in % of GDP 1990/1997^b
CEEC				
Czech R.	10,97^a	90	8/5	41^c/42^d
Hungary	7,249^b	89	18/20	53/50^g
Poland	6,300^b	110	14/12	39/49^e
Slovakia	8,415	94	6/4	51^c/46^g
Slovenia	12,629^b	99	8/4	49/46^a
SEEC				
Bulgaria	3,780^b	63	1084/893	65/47$^{b, g}$
Romania	4,352^e	87	154/155	38/33$^{b, g}$
NEEC				
Estonia	4,431^g	76	11/7	34^i/40^h
Latvia	3,484^g	54	8/4	28^i/40^h
Lithuania	4,766^g	44	8/6	49^j/29$^{a, g, j}$
EEC				
Belarus	1,350^f	66	63/89	56^c/43$^{b, g}$
Moldavia	454^f	34	13/15	24^h/31$^{b, g}$
Russia	4,480^e	57	11/7	65^i/38$^{b, g}$
Ukraine	2,128^b	37	10/5	58^i/40^g

Sources: EBRD, 1996, 1997; BMWi, 1995, 1997, 1998; World Bank, 1997.
Notes: ^{a} Projection; ^{b}Estimate; ^{c}1993; ^{d}1994; ^{e}1995; ^{f}GDP in US $, current exchange rates; ^{g}1996; ^{h}1991, ^{i} 1992, ^{j} General Government Expenditure and Net Lending.

The following two conclusions can be drawn. First, successful development depends on factors often insufficiently taken into consideration. An important factor, in theoretical terms, is the institutional issue in the way it is described by the new institutional economics. Second, the political circumstances lead to different outcomes, eg. reforms may be more supported by the population of a particular country, or reforms may have been introduced but not properly enforced. In this case, it is obvious that there are many transition-related similarities between the former socialist and developing countries.

Table 3.4 Trade off among privatisation routes for large firms

Method	Objective				
	Better corporate governance	Speed and feasibility	Better access to capital	More government revenue	Greater fairness
Sales to outside owners	+	-	+	+	-
Management-employee buy-out	-	+	-	-	-
Equal access voucher privatisation	?	+	?	-	+
Spontaneous privatisation	?	?	-	-	-

Source: World Bank, 1996.

Understanding transformation: drawing on a wider analytical framework

An analytical framework ought to serve two functions: it should be based on theory in order to allow theory-led explanations and predictions; and it should cover a range of phenomena in practice in order to find the most important determinants for certain developments.

The theory of new institutional economics is not a homogenous body (Feldmann, 1995), but it seems to allow an application to transformation processes.[4] The above transformation measures, and those of the Washington Consensus, include institutional issues which ought to be investigated by a refined *property rights approach* which allows a more detailed analysis of certain sectors. Changing economic policies and, in particular, changing property rights lead to new incentive structures, and these changes have a strong influence on the performance of an economy as a whole. Furthermore, tools of *transaction costs theory* are important (Williamson, 1985). Indeed, transforming economies incorporate a number of 'sunk investments' by the former economic regime due to changes which have taken place. An application of this theoretical approach to transforming economies may uncover the rationale of the restructuring process (Bohnet and Reichardt, 1993). Another argument is introduced by Williamson (1994) who emphasises that "constitutions are relevant for the background support, but governance is where the main action resides" (Williamson, 1994). For instance, a distinction between internal institutions such as conventions, personal ethics, social norms and organisational rules and external institutions like state laws can be a useful analytical tool (Kiwit, 1995). These results may be supported by an analysis which is based on the positive elements of the *economic theory of constitutions* (Buchanan, 1990).

Transformation itself can also be regarded as a *principal agents'* problem, not only between individual voters and the government (Kalt and Zupan, 1990), but also between the government and its administration (Spiller, 1990). The relationship between politicians and their administration is an important element of policy reforms which gives rise to the question of whether there are any characteristics which may indicate why administrations follow more-or-less the political guidelines given by the political process. An analysis based on this approach may detect different conditions in transforming countries. What is also very important about transforming economies is the *path dependency* of the institutional change (Binmore and Samuelson, 1994; Herrman-Pillath, 1994).

This kind of analysis only partly addresses the fact that changes have to be supported by the population through government interference. Hence, another view is the political economy or *public choice* approach (Frey, 1985; Downs, 1967; Niskanen, 1987; Olson, 1991). This theory, in its more empirically sustained part, gives a research framework for the investigation of voting behaviour, the behaviour of politicians, parties and lobbyists groups under a range of conditions and institutional conditions. Moreover, it is interesting to look at the way in which variables such as the distribution of wealth, education and institutional arrangements affect the behaviour of these groups and therefore the outcomes of policy. Furthermore, the *institutional arrangements in politics* vary between transforming countries which influence the outcome of elections and accordingly the chosen path of the transformation process (Furtak, 1996). It has been already pointed out that the choice of individuals has a strong influence on successful transformation processes through the political process (Rodrik, 1996). Economic reforms and the public choice of a certain kind of measure cannot be kept apart when investigating the success of reforms. Reforms - wishful or not - can only work when a government has the power to enforce these kinds of policies.

By applying these theories to transformation processes it should be possible to gain a better understanding of processes in transforming economies. But a major problem with the application of these theories lies in their partial character. Therefore the investigation of single phenomena by different theoretical approaches needs to be incorporated in a more comprehensive framework.

A successful transformation process is influenced by cornerstones which are strongly interactive. First, there are *macro-economic policies* aimed at economic stability, like fiscal, monetary and exchange rate policies, which represent the frame of economic conditions for a market economy. Less important are *micro policies*, although they definitely have an impact on the success of reforms. Second, one has to take into account a further set of conditions: *political conditions,* and the question under which circumstances a government is willing and able to introduce policy reforms against deeply rooted practice. The interaction of the economic and political development is therefore an important constitutional element for the success of reforms. The idea of a framework combining these issues was proposed by Balcerowicz (1997). Extending these ideas, Figure 3.1 shows the main elements of the political and economic sectors and their interdependencies.

Within this framework, *actors* are influenced by their preferences. Their behaviour is usually based on the assumption of maximising their utility. How they actually act depends also on the *institutional framework* which determines a certain incentive structure. Assuming incomplete information and unsecured expectations, a voter or an entrepreneur may behave in a way which does not initially seem rational. However, insecurity may create situations like the 'prisoners' dilemma' which explain the rationality of preferences in a given institutional set. Further, *conditions in the political and economic sector* can be included. In the political sphere, for example, there are certain national 'traditions' such as the desire for independence in the Baltic countries or the defence of a position on the world stage by Russia.

POLITICAL SPHERE   **ECONOMIC SPHERE**

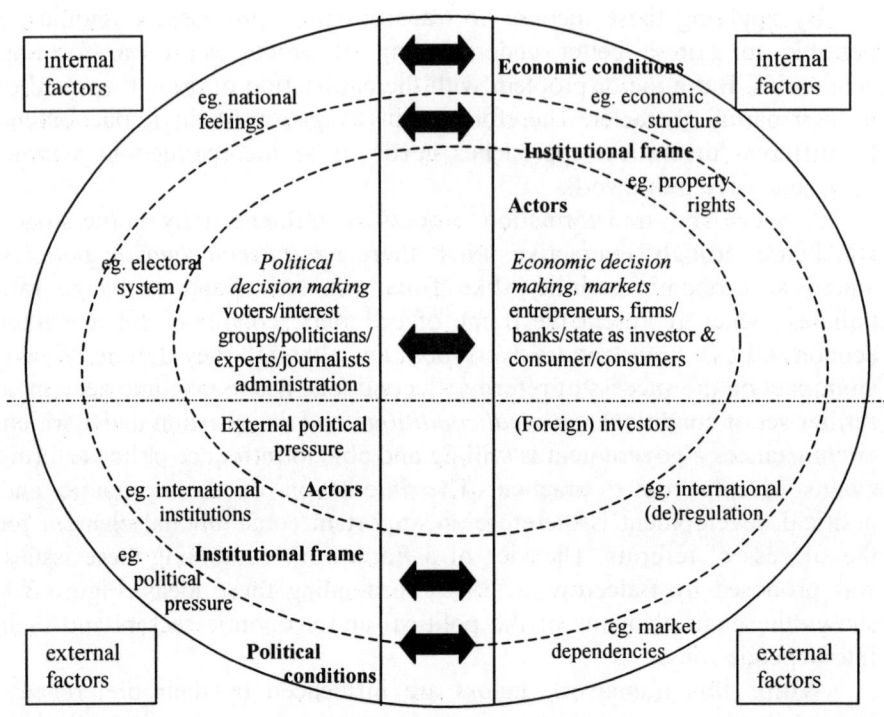

Figure 3.1: The interplay between political and economic development

Source: own compilation.

Clearly, some studies have already taken elements of this approach into consideration: eg. the *political economic situation* of developing countries due to indebtedness (Lafay and Lecaillion, 1993), agricultural policies (Krueger, 1996) or inward-looking development strategies (Kurer, 1996), single aspects of the transition like the privatisation issue (Estrin, 1994) or the privatisation itself without a connection to the transformation issue (Chen, 1996). Other studies try to include some politico-economic aspects by describing the transition process (Rodrik, 1995; Claque and Rausser, 1995; Gros and Steinherr, 1996) and the budgeting process (Guess, 1997).[5] All these studies give a broad idea of the institutional and political dimension but are far from an adequate use of the theoretical approaches which have been recently emerging in this field.

Balcerowicz (1997) proposed certain explanations for the interplay of political and economic development, apart from the usual assumption about the economic behaviour, for the specific case of transition countries. The new situation opened the political floor for non-typical politicians, or 'technocrats', more interested in the success of reforms than in long term political power. Successful countries placed a greater reliance on such technocrats.

There are also *positive and negative linkages* between the transition task and other political aims. The CEE countries had envisaged accession to the EU occurring simultaneously with reform progress. The possibility of EU accession contributed to the acceptance by CEE voters of harsher burdens during the transformation process. Recent negative developments in the Ukraine, and even more so in Belarus, may support the notion that the accession hopes have a wider domestic importance. It is true in many countries that former political ruling parties have returned to power in the second phase of reform as the burden of reform on voters has increased. Further, the culture of political co-operation may differ significantly between the European and Asian zones (Weitzman, 1993). Finally, the institutional framework in the political sphere depends to some extent on the starting conditions and, while convergence is expected in the longer term, the differences in speed and sequencing are currently a topic of research interest.

Conclusions

The aim of this chapter has been to open up a more comprehensive perspective on the transition process in the post-socialist countries. The starting point has been the argument that normative economics leads to a rather rigid recommendation for the transformation process. Experiences from Asian and Latin American countries show that the liberalisation of markets, definition of property rights and stabilisation of macro-economic conditions are not sufficient explanations of the success of transformation processes. These countries differ considerably in their approaches and they only partly follow recommendations from normative economic theory. Two main insights emerge when looking at these countries: (a) the role of the government in the transformation process; and (b) the interdependencies between economic and political development. In order to understand these interdependencies, a comprehensive approach to the evaluation and recommended transition measures is suggested through the use of more recent economic theories such as new institutional economics and the public choice approach. The approach outlined (inspired by a paper of Balcerowicz, 1997) distinguishes, at one level, between the economic and political sector and, at a second level, between actors, the institutional frame and political conditions. The approach also takes into consideration that the countries in transition have inherited institutions and preconditions in both the economic and the political sectors. Another important distinction refers to impulses from inside and outside the country. This analytical framework helps to structure and extract important factors for successful transformation processes and, thus, may be of help in refining policy recommendations.

Notes

1. Just to name two examples (theoretical literature see following sections): *The Economist* states in its headline: "The puzzling failure of economics" and criticises the attitudes of economists "to blame others for being too lazy or too stupid to understand their textbooks" (*The Economist* 1997, 13). The *OECD Observer* raises the question "Why do countries perform differently?" (Motohashi and Nezu, 1997) and comes to the conclusion that regular reforms and corporate governance play a decisive role.
2. I would like to thank Hans-Hubertus Bleuel for valuable discussion and his support for this chapter, (see also Bleuel, 1996).
3. The economic crisis which started in Asia is excluded, because causes and effects were unclear at time of writing.
4. The elements of this theory, namely the property rights theory, the principal agent theory, the transaction cost theory and the economic theory of constitutions are based on the common assumptions of methodological individualism, self-interest orientated behaviour with an extended utility function, bounded rationality (especially limited information) and costs comprise, beside the production costs, all costs related to the exchange of commodities. Thus, the new institutional economics fit in the general frame of assumption in economic theory and offer valuable extension of the economic theory (Feldmann, 1995).
5. Furthermore, the evaluation of the country reports prepared by the European Commission in connection with the Agenda 2000 offers a valuable source.

References

Balcerowicz, L. (1997), 'The interplay between economic and political transition', in Zecchini, S. (ed), *Lessons from Economic Transition*, Norwell MA, Kluver, pp. 153-68.

Basten, J. (1996), *Gewerkschaften in unterschiedlichen rechtlichen Umwelten - Ein Beitrag zur Logik gewerkschaftlichen Kooperationsverhaltens in Transformationsökonomien*, ORT.

Binmore, K. and Samuelson, L. (1994), 'An Economist's Perspective on the Evolution of Norms', *Journal of Institutional and Theoretical Economics*, vol. 150, pp. 45-63.

Birdsall, N., Ross, D. and Sabot, R. (1995), 'Inequality and Growth Reconsidered lessons from East Asia', *The World Bank Economic Review*, vol. 9.

Bleuel, H.-H. (1996), *Wirtschaftspolitik und Systemtransformation*, Universitäts Verlag, Wiesbaden.

Bohnet, A. and Reichardt, M. (1993), 'Der Beitrag der Transaktionskostenökonomik zu einer Theorie der Transformation von Wirtschaftsordnungen', *Jahrbücher für Nationalökonomie und Statistik*, vol. 212, pp. 204-26.

Buchanan, J. M. (1990), 'The domain of constitutional economics', *Constitutional Political Economy*, vol. 1, pp. 1-18.

Buchanan, J.M., Tollison, R.D. and Tullock, G. (1980), *Towards a Theory of the Rentseeking Society*, College Station, Texas.

BMWi (Bundesministerium für Wirtschaft) (1995) (1996) (1997) (1998), *Wirtschaftslage und Reformprozesse in Mittel- und Osteuropa*, Bonn.

Chen, Y. (1996), 'The optimal choice of privatising state-owned enterprise, a political economic model', *Public Choice*, vol. 87, pp. 223-45.

Claque, C. and Rausser, G. C. (eds) (1995), *The emergence of market economies in Eastern Europe*, Cambridge MA, Oxford.

Dobozi, I. and Pohl, G. (1995), Real Output Decline in Transition Economies - Forget GDP, try Power Consumption Data!, *Transition - World Bank Policy Research Department Newsletter*, no. 6, pp. 17-18.

Downs, A. (1967), *Inside bureaucracy*, Boston.

(The) Economist (1997), 'The puzzling failure of economics', *The Economist*, vol. 344, no. 8031, 23 August 1997, p. 13.

European Bank for Reconstruction and Development (1994), (1997), (1998) *Transition Report*, London.

Edwards, S. (1989), Real Exchange Rates, Devaluation and Adjustment, Cambridge, Ma.

El-Shagi, E.-S. (1983), Entwicklungstheorie und die List-Theorie über die Beeinträchtigung der Produktivkräfteentwicklung durch den Freihandel, *WiSt*, vol. 12, pp. 337-340.

Estrin S. (ed) (1994), *Privatisation in Central and Eastern Europe*, London.

Feldmann, H. (1995), 'Eine institutionalistische Revolution?', *Volkswirtschaftliche Schriften*, vol. 448, Berlin.
Frey, B.S. (1985), *Democratic economic policy*, Oxford.
Furtak, R.K. (1996), 'Zum Verhältnis von Staatspräsident und Regierung in postkommunistischen Staaten', in Luchterhand, O. (ed) *Neue Regierungssysteme in Osteuropa und der GUS*, Berlin, pp. 115-150.
Gros, D. and Steinherr, A. (1996), *Winds of change - economic transition in Central and Eastern Europe*, London, New York.
Guess, G.M. (1997), 'Transformation of bureaucratic states in Eastern Europe, public expenditure lessons from Latin America', *International Journal of Public Administration*, vol. 20, pp. 621-41.
Herrmann-Pillrath, C. (1994), 'Evolutionary Rationality, "Homo Economicus" and the Foundation of Social Order', *Journal of Social and Evolutionary Systems*, vol. 17, pp. 41-69.
Kalt, J. P. and Zupan, M. A. (1990), The apparent ideological behaviour of legislators - testing for principal-agent slacks in political institutions, *Journal of Law and Economics*, vol. 33, pp. 103-131.
Kiwit, D. (1995), *Path Dependencies in Technological and Institutional Change - Some Criticisms and Suggestions*, Diskussionsbeitrag 1095 des Max-Plank Institute for Research into Economic Systems, Jena.
Kloten, N. (1993), 'The Time Dimension of the Transition of Economic Systems', in Wagener, H.-J., *On the Theory and Policy of Systemic Change*, Heidelberg, pp. 121-34.
Kornai, J. (1994), 'Transformational Recession - the Main Causes', *Journal of Comparative Economics*, vol. 19, pp. 39-63.
Krueger, A.O. (1996), 'Political economy of agricultural policy', *Public Choice*, vol. 87, pp. 163-175.
Krüger, A.O. (1993), *Political Economy of Policy Reform in Developing Countries*, Cambridge, MA and Lexington.
Kurer, O. (1996), 'The political foundations of economic development policies', *Journal of Development Studies*, vol. 32, pp. 645-668.
Lafay, J.-D. and Lecaillon, J. (1993), *Political feasibility or adjustment - the political dimension of economic adjustment*, OECD, Paris.
Motohashi, K. and Nezu, R. (1997), 'Why do counties perform differently?', *The OECD Observer*, no. 206, pp. 23-27.
Mummert, U. (1996), *Institutionen und Wirtschaftspolitik in Entwicklungsländern*, in Max-Plank-Institut zur Erforschung von Wirtschaftssystemen, Dokumentation, Jena, pp. 7-8.
Nelson, J.M. (1993), 'The Politics of Economic Transformation - Is the Third World Experience Relevant?', *World Politics*, vol. 45, pp. 433-63.
Niskanen, W. A. (1987), 'Bureaucracy', in Rowley, C. K. (ed), *Democracy and public choice*, Oxford, pp. 135-40.

Niskanen, W.A. (1991), 'The Soft Infrastructure of a Market Economy', *Cato Journal*, vol. 11, pp. 233-38.
Olson, M. (1991), *Aufstieg und Niedergang von Nationen*, Tübingen.
Persson, T. and Tabellini, G. (1994), 'Is inequality harmful for growth?', *American Economic Review*, vol. 84, pp. 600-21.
Priztl, R.F.J. (1996), 'Verteilungskonflikte und Interessengruppen in Lateinamerika', *Aus Politik und Zeitgeschichte*, no. 48-49, pp. 38-46.
Rodrik, D. (1996), 'Understanding Economic Policy Reform', *Journal of Economic Literature*, vol. 34, pp. 9-41.
Rodrik, D. (1995), 'The Dynamics of Political Support for Reform in Economies in Transition', *Journal of the Japanese and International Economics*, vol. 9, pp.403-25.
Roland, G. (1994), 'The Role of Political Constraints in Transition Strategies', *Economics of Transition*, vol. 2, pp. 27-41.
Rosati, D.K. (1991), 'Sequencing the Reforms in Poland', in Marer, P. and Zecchini, S. (eds) *The Transition to a Market Economy, Part 1*, Paris, pp. 208-24.
Rowley, C. K. (ed) (1987), *Democracy and public choice*, Oxford.
Siebert, H. (1991), *The transformation of Eastern Europe*, Kieler Diskussionsbeiträge No. 163, Kiel.
Spiller, P. T. (1990), 'Politicians, interest groups, and regulators, a multi-principles agency theory of regulation, or "let them be bribed"', *Journal of Law and Economics*, vol. 33, pp. 65-101.
Weitzman, M.L. (1993), 'Economic Transition – Can Theory Help', *European Economic Review*, vol. 37, pp. 549-555.
Williamson, O. E. (1985), *The Economic Institutions of Capitalism*, New York.
Williamson, O.E. (1994), 'Institutions and Economic Organisation, The Governance Perspective', in The World Bank; *Annual Bank Conference on Development Economics*, Washington D.C.
Winiecki, J. (1993), 'Costs of Transition that are no Costs, On Non-Welfare-Reducing Output Fall', in Baldassarri, M. and Mundell, R. (eds), *Building a New Europ,*, vol. 2, New York, pp. 85-94.
Winiecki, J. (1991), 'The Political Economy of "Big Bang", Free market vs. New Keynesian Perspective', *BNL Quarterly Review*, vol. 46, pp. 407-28.
World Bank (1996, 1997), *World Development Report*, New York.

# 4 The Effects of Privatisation in Central and Eastern Europe: Evidence from Households in Three Central European Capitals

KEITH GRIME, ZOLTAN KOVÁCS AND VIC DUKE

Introduction

The process of privatisation and its effect on households in Central and Eastern Europe (CEE) is complex and varied. In Budapest, Prague and Warsaw, some forms of privatisation have proceeded along similar lines and at equivalent rates, while others, by contrast, have accelerated in one city and lagged behind in another (Duke and Grime, 1997). The state sector is being dismantled and, particularly in Poland and Hungary, many jobs have disappeared. Sometimes, sections of state industry have been privatised, and employees find themselves working for the former managers; sometimes they wake up to find that their workplace has been taken over by a foreign company, as in the case of the Staropramen Brewery in Prague or the Škoda car plant in Mlada Boleslav. This chapter concentrates on the impact of some of these changes on households and attempts to shed some light on which groups of people appear to be benefiting. It assesses which groups are most likely to be working in the private sector, outlines the changes that have occurred in the consumption of items such as housing, health and education, and indicates how satisfied people claim to be with the restructuring that has taken place since 1990.

The data presented here, except for Table 4.7, are from surveys conducted in Budapest, Prague and Warsaw during 1995. A common questionnaire was devised regarding general socio-economic aspects of the transformation process, and 1,000 households were interviewed in Budapest, 783 in Prague and 1,001 in Warsaw. Using data from the latest census in each country, eight neighbourhoods in each city were deliberately chosen to represent as wide a cross-section of the population as possible. Areas of high and low social status were included together with inner areas and high-density socialist housing areas constructed in the 1960s and 1970s. Within the neighbourhoods, households were selected randomly.

Privatisation and employment

Probably the most important shift which has taken place since 1989 in CEE is the privatisation of production ie. the change from state employment to working either in the private sector or being self-employed. Table 4.1 displays broadly similar trends in each city: both state and co-operative employment have decreased, whilst those employed in the private sector, the mixed sector and those who are self-employed have substantially increased.

Table 4.1 Changes in respondent work sectors, 1989-95

	Budapest			Prague			Warsaw		
	'89	'95	% change	'89	'95	% change	'89	'95	% change
% state	77	47	-30	93	40	-53	77	58	-19
% private	11	28	+17	2	36	+34	13	28	+15
% self-employ.	6	18	+12	1	16	+15	8	11	+3
% co-op	4	0.5	-3.5	3	0.5	-2.5	2	1	-1
% mixed	2	7	+5	0.5	8	+7.5	0.5	3	+2.5

Prague has experienced the most dramatic transformation in its employment patterns. It has moved from having the highest level of state employment in 1989 (93 percent) to the lowest in 1995 (40 percent). It has also undergone the biggest increase in private sector employment over the same period. Budapest has the second highest rate of decline in state employment, at 30 percent, while Warsaw exhibits a slower pace of change, but even here the decrease in state employment is approaching 20 percent. Prague has also had the largest increases in self employment, but it is closely followed by Budapest.

Several common patterns underlie the changes in employment. In all three cities, males are more likely to work in the private sector or be self-employed, whereas females are more likely to be still in the state sector (see Table 4.2). The gender imbalance in the residual state sector may herald an uncertain future for female workers. Moreover, the young are more likely to work in the private sector, whilst the old are substantially over-represented in the state sector (see Table 4.3).

Table 4.2 Respondent work sector by gender

	Budapest	Prague	Warsaw
Male % self-employed	23	20	12
Female % self-employed	13	10	8
Male % private	31	37	31
Female % private	23	35	27
Male % state	39	30	54
Female % state	56	50	61

Table 4.3 Respondent work sector by age group

	Budapest	Prague	Warsaw
18-39 % self-employed	16	17	13
40-59 % self-employed	19	14	8
60+ % self-employed	28	10	6
18-39 % private	37	42	39
40-59% private	21	34	24
60+ % private	12	13	12
18-39% state	43	32	46
40-59 % state	50	45	63
60+ % state	56	63	82

In Budapest and Prague, the private sector is associated with respondents without higher education (see Table 4.4), and by way of contrast, in all three cities, the more highly educated are more likely to work in the state sector, reflecting in part the concentration of administrative and professional jobs in the three capitals. Patterns in relation to self-employment are less clear cut, although in Budapest and Prague the higher educated are more inclined to be self-employed. A social class differential is apparent in the new sectoral patterns (see Table 4.5). Upper white collar workers are more likely to be employed in the state sector, which again confirms the administrative and professional status of the three cities. On the other hand the manual working class are now more likely to be employed in the state sector.

Table 4.4 Respondent work sector by higher education

	Budapest	*Prague*	*Warsaw*
Higher educated % self-employed	21	20	9
Not higher educated % self-employed	16	14	10
Higher educated % private	20	23	29
Not higher educated % private	34	40	29
Higher educated % state	52	49	61
Not higher educated % state	42	37	57

Table 4.5 Respondent work sector by social class

	Budapest	*Prague*	*Warsaw*
Upper white collar % state	61	57	73
Manual working class % state	42	35	64
Upper white collar % private	23	26	24
Manual working class % private	47	53	29

A final analytical point in relation to privatisation of production concerns the tendency for full time workers to be located more in the state sector, whilst part time workers are over-represented in the private sector (see Table 4.6). This is the case in two of the cities, with Prague the exception, where the opposite pattern occurs. The association in Prague between full time work and the private sector on the one hand, and part time work and the residual state sector on the other, perhaps reflects the greater progress made by the Czech Republic in reducing the importance of the state sector.

Table 4.6 Respondent work sector by respondent full/part time work

	Budapest	*Prague*	*Warsaw*
Full-time % state	48	39	59
Part time % state	42	68	44
Full time % private	27	37	28
Part time % private	38	23	39

Privatisation and housing

Another major aspect of privatisation to impinge on the everyday life of households and families is the rolling back of the state's role in providing essential services. Under the communist system the state was the overwhelming provider of such services as housing and, in a recent paper, Bodnár (1996) has suggested that tenure change in Budapest has resulted in increased social polarisation. She argues that this polarisation has arisen because housing privatisation in the 1990s has been strongly influenced by the pre-existing state socialist urban arrangements, which, certainly in the case of Budapest, Szelenyi (1983), Hegedüs (1987), Kovács (1990), and Hegedüs and Tosics (1994) have all suggested led to irregularities in housing allocation.

The housing tenure profile for 1990 and 1994 is presented in Table 4.7. *Public rental* includes housing units owned and controlled by central or local government, *private rental* consists of dwellings normally owned by private individuals but occasionally by organisations, while under the heading *semi-public rental* are included dwellings that are owned by associations, co-operatives or public enterprises. This latter form of ownership has been traditionally strong in Poland, approximately since the mid-1960s, public housing expenditure was spent mostly on the mass production of co-operative housing. *Owner occupied* means that the family living in the house or flat is also the owner. The complexity of the ownership structure of the state socialist housing system is well demonstrated by the fact that, for instance, in Budapest four different forms of owner-occupied housing could be distinguished before 1990 (Kovács and Wießner, 1994; Pichler-Milanovich, 1994). In addition to single-family housing there were co-operative dwellings, housing condominiums and National Savings Bank (OTP) dwellings. On the other hand, in Prague and Warsaw only single family houses were defined legally as *owner occupied*. *Other housing* are considered to be those special ownership forms which do not fit into the major sectors mentioned above (eg. common ownership co-operatives). A very specific type of tenure in Warsaw still is privately rented housing which was not nationalised after World War II but over which the owners lost control and the allocation, rents, and maintenance became the responsibility of local government.

Table 4.7   Housing stock by sectors (percent) 1990-1994

	Budapest		Prague		Warsaw	
	1990	1994	1990	1994	1990	1994
Public rental	54.0	33.0	59.5	38.0	44.8	29.5
Private rental	1.0	2.0	1.2	25.0	0.0	0.0
Semi-public rental	0.0	0.0	7.3	3.1	47.0	24.6
Owner occupied	45.0	65.0	12.5	13.0	6.2	15.7
Other	0.0	0.0	19.0	20.9	2.0	30.2
Total	100.0	100.0	100.0	100.0	100.0	100.0

Source: Hegedüs, Mayo and Tosics, 1996.

In 1990, as Table 4.7 shows, the public sector was dominant everywhere (above 50 percent) but in Warsaw the public and semi-public sphere reached an extraordinary 92 percent. In all socialist cities the privately rented sector was practically non-existent before 1990, which represented the main difference compared with Western European cities. The percentage of owner-occupied housing was the highest in Budapest, which can be related to the relatively liberal housing policy of the country prior to 1990. Comparing housing tenure in 1990 and 1994, it is clear that the proportion of publicly rented housing decreased in all three cities. The decline of the semi-public sphere in Prague and Warsaw was also very substantial. Ownership change in Budapest and Warsaw meant a clear shift from the public to the owner-occupied sector, whereas in Prague the growth of the private rental sector was the most spectacular. This is closely related to the Czech way of restitution, where the return of property nationalised by the communist regime became possible. In Prague, a large part of the older housing stock has been returned to the former owners, which led to a quick emergence of the private rental sector. In Budapest and Warsaw, direct restitution has not been on the agenda. However, former landlords or their heirs have received limited compensation in the form of vouchers which can be used for the privatisation of public dwellings.

There has been little debate over the need for privatisation since there is a general belief in Eastern Europe that market mechanisms are a more efficient way of organising the production and exchange of goods than the previous systems of central planning (Clapham, 1995). In all three cities the selling of state housing has meant a 'give-away privatisation', with sales, in many cases, at less than 15 percent of estimated market value.

Table 4.8   Ownership change 1989-96

	Budapest		*Prague*		*Warsaw*	
	Count	*%*	*Count*	*%*	*Count*	*%*
Ownership changed 1989-1995	406	40.6	136	18.1	115	11.5
Ownership change estimated for 1996	77	7.7	97	12.9	95	9.5
Total	483	48.3	233	31.0	210	21.0

In order to get a more comprehensive picture about the dynamics of the restructuring of the housing market, respondents were asked about ownership change which had taken place since 1989, and ownership change which was expected until the end of 1996 (Table 4.8). In Budapest, nearly half the dwelling stock in the sample has gone through or intended to go through ownership change in the first six years of transition, but in Prague and Warsaw the figure was considerably lower at 31 percent and 21 percent respectively. This is clear evidence that changes in the tenure structure have been most intensive in Budapest, less in Prague and least in Warsaw.

The way in which ownership change has taken place has great relevance, and there is a substantial difference between the three cities. In 88 percent of the cases in Budapest the household was directly involved in the ownership change, in Warsaw it was 70 percent, but in Prague only 25 percent. This highlights the different nature of the privatisation strategies applied in the different cities. In Budapest, the direct selling of flats to sitting tenants was dominant, while in Prague a large part of the housing market was transferred to a third party via restitution. This brings three questions to the fore: how is housing privatisation perceived by the public, how do people judge the different models of restructuring, and which model of restructuring provides the best chance for improvement in housing conditions and housing provision?

The survey showed that the people of Budapest were generally more satisfied with housing privatisation than the citizens of Prague or Warsaw, but even in Budapest only one-third declared themselves to be satisfied. Some 36 percent of Budapest respondents were dissatisfied but in Prague (48 percent) and in Warsaw (51 percent) dissatisfaction was much higher. The level of satisfaction correlates highly with the speed and method of privatisation. In Budapest where privatisation was quick, and normally meant a direct sale of social housing to the former tenants, a higher proportion of people are satisfied. The least satisfied are people in Warsaw where privatisation proved to be the lowest and slowest. In Prague, the respondents were less satisfied than in Budapest, but the level of dissatisfaction did not reach the Warsaw scale. In Prague, 40 percent of the households had a mixed (both positive and negative) opinion about privatisation which can be associated with the practice of restitution, where a substantial proportion of the tenants are excluded from the privatisation process.

Influences on housing privatisation

The following section examines (Tables 4.9 and 4.10) the influence of gender, age, educational attainment, occupational class, employment sector and unemployment in relation to housing privatisation and suggests that housing is of symbolic importance in the transition because it is a highly visible example of the retreat of the state and is of economic importance because of the potential economic gain derived from property ownership. There appear to be no significant gender differences in any of the cities, and age appears to have no influence in Warsaw. In Budapest, however, the old have been more involved in privatisation, whereas in Prague the old already exhibited a higher level of owner occupation in 1989. In Prague and Warsaw, the more highly educated experienced a higher rate of privatisation in addition to already displaying a higher percentage of ownership. In Budapest, there is no significant difference in the rate of privatisation but the higher educated were already more into owner occupation in 1989.

There is a clear class pattern in two of the three cities, with Prague the odd one out. In Budapest and Warsaw, entrepreneurs and upper white collar workers are most likely to own their house or flat, while lower white collar and manual workers are most likely to still be in the state sector. Warsaw best exemplifies class inequalities in owner occupation with the percentage owned in descending order entrepreneurs (79), upper white collar (70), lower white collar (60), and manual (35). The Prague anomaly is that the manual working class display the highest rate of owner occupation. This might be due to the equalising impact of restitution and also the tendency to a more egalitarian society under state socialism mentioned earlier. There is no clear indication as to which social class privatised most between 1989 and 1995; in Prague and Warsaw it was the upper white collar workers while in Budapest it was the lower white collar employees. There are no consistent differences between private and state sector employees, although state employees are more likely to own their own house/flat in Budapest than in Prague or Warsaw. In Prague, only nine unemployed people were identified in the three tenure groups which was too few to analyse. In the other two cities, however, a relatively high percentage of unemployed respondents live in state housing.

In Tables 4.9 and 4.10 respondents renting from co-operatives and private landlords have been excluded. An *owner* is defined as someone who owned in 1989 and was still living in, and owning the same house/flat in 1995, a *privatiser* as someone living in the same house/flat as in 1989 but in the ensuing period had bought it from the state, and *state* as someone in state housing in 1989 and still in the same house/flat in 1995. *Tenure* was recorded by asking the respondent and *privatisation* was defined as exit from the state sector. On both counts the practice of Bodnár (1996) was followed.

Table 4.9 Housing tenure by gender, age group, and education

Variable	Category	Housing Tenure	Budapest	Prague	Warsaw
Gender	Male	% owned	46(393)*	36(204)	61(269)
	Fem.	% owned	45(447)	36(256)	58(388)
	Male	% privatised	44	6	12
	Fem.	% privatised	41	5	13
	Male	% state	10	57	27
	Fem.	% state	14	59	29
Age group	18-39	% owned	40(222)	30(160)	61(159)
	40-59	% owned	49(323)	31(147)	57(253)
	60+	% owned	45(291)	50(133)	61(244)
	18-39	% privatised	42	6	11
	40-59	% privatised	37	5	14
	60+	% privatised	49	6	11
	18-39	% state	18	64	28
	40-59	% state	14	64	29
	60+	% state	7	44	28
Education	Not H.E.	% owned	42(551)	35(371)	55(459)
	H.E.	% owned	50(284)	39(89)	69(182)
	Not H.E.	% privatised	42	4	10
	H.E.	% privatised	43	12	18
	Not H.E.	% state	16	61	35
	H.E.	% state	6	48	13

Note: * The figures in brackets are the number of respondents in that particular category.

Table 4.10 Housing tenure by occupational class, employment sector, and unemployment

Variable	Category	Housing Tenure	Budapest	Prague	Warsaw
Occupational Class	Entrepreneur	% owned	57(58)[b]	31(32)	79(38)
	Upper white collar	% owned	54(153)	30(56)	70(98)
	Lower white collar	% owned	37(97)	22(86)	60(103)
	Manual	% owned	40(82)	45(65)	35(72)
	Entrepreneur	% privatised	28	6	5
	Upper white collar	% privatised	39	13	19
	Lower white collar	% privatised	51	2	10
	Manual	% privatised	37	3	10
	Entrepreneur	% state	16	63	16
	Upper white collar	% state	7	57	10
	Lower white collar	% state	12	76	30
	Manual	% state	23	52	56
Employment Sector	State	% owned	50(190)	29(102)	55(180)
	Private	% owned	40(103)	32(81)	62(85)
	State	% privatised	40	6	15
	Private	% privatised	43	3	9
	State	% state	11	65	30
	Private	% state	18	65	28
Unemployment	Unemployed	% owned	41(27)	[a]	56(27)
	Unemployed	% privatised	19	[a]	11
	Unemployed	% state	41	[a]	33

Notes: [a] The total number of unemployed people in Prague in the tenure groups used in this table was only 9; [b] The figures in brackets are the number of respondents in that particular category.

Privatisation of health care and education

Health care remains overwhelmingly the preserve of the state in each city. There has been a steady growth in households taking out additional private health insurance (see Table 4.11). On the other hand, the use of private health care as a one-off treatment such as a private dentist has been extensive since 1989. In Budapest and Warsaw, over half of the households have used some form of private health care.

Table 4.11 Household additional health insurance and household use of private health since 1989

	Budapest	Prague	Warsaw
% additional health insurance	7	7	14
% used private health since 1989	55	39	62

Table 4.12 Use of private health since 1989 by age group

	Budapest	Prague	Warsaw
18-39 % used private health	70	44	80
40-59 % used private health	54	44	61
60+ % used private health	36	25	47

In each city the younger respondents are more likely to have used private health care (see Table 4.12). Such evidence suggests a potential for further growth in private health care. Table 4.13 shows a clear relationship between social class and private health usage in both Budapest and Warsaw where the manual working class are much less involved. Warsaw displays a particularly strong class pattern. Prague is again the odd one out with all employment groups using private health care in approximately similar proportion but with entrepreneurs the lowest of all!

Like health care, education continues to be provided predominantly by the state sector. Of those respondents with children of school age, only a very small fraction attend private schools (see Table 4.14). Mirroring the health situation above, paying for a small amount of private education is a different matter. Around half of the households with children in each city have paid for some private tuition, usually for learning English.

Table 4.13 Use of private health since 1989 by respondent social class

	Budapest	Prague	Warsaw
Entrepreneur % used private health	78	31	90
Upper white collar % used private health	75	43	81
Lower white collar % used private health	66	47	71
Manual working class % used private health	47	42	52

Table 4.14 Levels of private school attendance and children's private tuition

	Budapest	Prague	Warsaw
% attend private school	5	5	6
% pay for private tuition	49	48	54

Higher educated respondents are markedly more likely to utilise private tuition for their children in all the cities except Prague (see Table 4.15). Table 4.16 also highlights a less clear cut social class pattern for Prague in relation to the take-up of private tuition. However, for all three cities the lowest amount of private tuition occurs in the manual working class.

Table 4.15 Children's private tuition by respondent education level

	Budapest	Prague	Warsaw
Higher educated % private tuition	67	48	75
Not higher educated % private tuition	37	50	49

Table 4.16 Children's private tuition by respondent social class

	Budapest	Prague	Warsaw
Entrepreneur % private tuition	68	46	68
Upper white collar % private tuition	69	57	77
Lower white collar % private tuition	42	53	62
Manual working class % private tuition	29	41	39

Participation in privatisation

In addition to measuring the extent to which respondents and households have reduced their involvement with the state, both at the workplace and in the consumption of essential services, respondents were asked whether the household had been affected by, or taken part in, the four main types of privatisation legislation in their respective countries, namely the small privatisation (of small businesses and shops), the large privatisation (of large industrial enterprises), restitution (of property to previous owners), and housing privatisation (sale of state houses or flats). Although not completely identical in each of the three countries, there is a broad overlap in what was involved in each and the terms were understandable to the respondents.

The perceived impact of the four types of privatisation is summarised in Table 4.17. Levels of impact are relatively low in Budapest with the notable exception of housing, and to some extent restitution. Prague is fairly high on small privatisation but particularly high on large privatisation; fully 66 percent have taken part in the mass scheme of voucher privatisation. The Warsaw respondents display a high level of involvement in the small privatisation.

The pattern of respondent perceptions of privatisation impact displayed in Table 4.17 mirror real policy differences and successes between the three countries. Budapest's success in privatising housing (described above) is matched by the relative perceptions of our respondents. Similarly, Prague's successful voucher privatisation scheme for large industries, and rapid execution of small privatisation are shown to have impacted on the households. In Warsaw, it is small privatisation which has had most impact, reflecting Poland's early legislation and rapid execution of small privatisation. (For these policy differences in detail see Duke and Grime, 1994.)

Table 4.17 Perceived impact of four types of privatisation on households

	Budapest	*Prague*	*Warsaw*
% impact of small privatisation	12	34	49
% impact of large privatisation	8	38	17
% impact of restitution	19	19	6
% impact of housing privatisation	44	16	16
% taken part in voucher privatisation	not applicable	66	not applicable*

Note: * Data refers to 1989-95 - a voucher type privatisation was subsequently introduced in Poland in 1997 and involving 90 percent of those entitled to participate.

Conclusion

The first section of this chapter showed that, overall, males are more likely to be employed in the private sector than females. When age is taken into account, young people of both sexes are likely to be found in the private sector, probably because they are more flexible in their behaviour than people in an established career pattern and continue to function in much the same way as they did before the changes. So, in Warsaw, no less than 82 percent of the over-sixties are employed in the state sector and only 6 percent are self employed. However, generalisation is difficult because in Budapest only 56 percent of the over-sixties are state employees and 28 percent are self employed. In both Prague and Budapest, manual workers are more likely to be employed in the private sector, but in Warsaw they are most emphatically still employed in the state sector. In all three cities, upper white collar workers are most definitely employed in the state sector and, probably because there is a high degree of correlation between upper white collar employees and those who have had a higher education, the more highly educated a person, the more likely he or she is to be working in the state sector (although in Warsaw the percentages differ very little).

In the second section, three quite different restructuring models used in the restructuring of housing tenure were identified. In Budapest, there was a relatively quick, purely "give away", type of privatisation to existing tenants, at a very low price. In Prague, a somewhat slower, mixed type of privatisation took place, involving tenants and private individuals in restitution and less emphasis on selling state property, while in Warsaw a less liberal, relatively slow but more market-based privatisation was undertaken.

The quick and cheap privatisation strategy (Budapest) received most support but not overwhelmingly so. This does not mean that this is the ideal solution, because in Budapest the shrinking state sector is becoming more and more the shelter for marginalised households. Thus, the Budapest form of privatisation increases the unfavourable tendencies of polarisation and segregation of social groups and leads to increasing differentiation of housing classes.

The evidence on housing privatisation suggests that social inequalities are developing very quickly. Significant differences in housing tenure are evident for several social characteristics. Particularly distinctive are higher educated respondents who are clearly advantaged in each of the cities; conversely, unemployed respondents are disadvantaged in every case. In many respects distribution patterns in post-communist cities are converging on western models of social polarisation.

The final section examined the relationship between the use of various private services and age and social class. In general, it is the younger people who are using private health and, not surprisingly, the more highly educated and those in the entrepreneurial and upper white collar class who are paying for private tuition. One final point is that Prague, on many of the items examined, is quite often diametrically opposed to Warsaw and Budapest. This could, of course, be caused by sampling error, but this is probably not the case. Instead, it can be concluded that the effects of privatisation have had a differential impact in Prague, Warsaw and Budapest.

Acknowledgement

The data presented here is taken from a much wider study funded by the European Union programme *Co-operation in Science and Technology with Central and Eastern Europe CIPA CT93 0082*. In particular we must mention the project's team leaders. They were Anna Karwinská, Department of Sociology, Academy of Economics, Kraków; Ludk Sýkora, Department of Geography, Charles University, Prague; and Grzegorz Wcawowicz, Institute of Geography, Polish Academy of Sciences (one of the co-authors, Zoltan Kovács, was the Budapest team leader). Thanks are also warmly extended to Professor Jan Kowalski, Institute for Economic Policy Research, University of Karlsruhe, who was also a member of our research team, for his constant help and encouragement and also to Mike Ingham, European Studies Research Institute, the third member of the Salford team. Having said all of this, the views expressed here are ours and do not necessarily reflect those of our colleagues working on the project.

References

Bodnár, J. (1996), 'He that hath to him shall be given: housing privatisation in Budapest after state socialism', *International Journal of Urban and Regional Research*, vol. 20, no. 4., pp. 616-36.

Clapham, D. (1995), 'Privatisation and the East European housing model', *Urban Studies*, vol. 32, nos. 4-5, pp. 679-94.

Duke, V. and Grime, K. (1994), 'Privatisation in East Central Europe: similarities and contrasts in its application', in Bryant, C. and Mokrzycki, E. (eds) *The New Great Transformation*, Routledge, London, pp. 144-270.

Duke, V. and Grime, K. (1997), 'Inequality in post-communism', *Regional Studies* vol. 31, no. 9, pp. 883-90.

Hegedüs, J. (1987), 'Reconsidering the roles of the state and the market in socialist housing systems', *International Journal of Urban and Regional Research*, vol. 11, pp. 79-87.

Hegedüs, J. and Tosics, I. (1994), 'Privatisation and rehabilitation in the Budapest inner districts', *Housing Studies*, vol. 9, pp. 39-54.

Hegedüs, J., Mayo, S.K. and Tosics, I. (1996), 'Transition of the housing sector in the East-Central European countries', Budapest.

Kovács, Z. (1990), 'Rich and poor in the Budapest housing market' in Hann, C.M. (ed), *Market Economy and Civil Society in Hungary*, Frank Cass, London, pp. 110-24.

Kovács, Z. and Wießner, R. (1994), 'Housing market in transition: the case of Budapest', Paper presented at the IGU Regional Conference "Environment and quality of life in Central Europe: problems of transition." Prague, 22-26 August (CD-ROM).

Pichler-Milanovich, N. (1994), 'The role of housing policy in the transformation process in Central East European cities', *Urban Studies*, vol. 31, no. 7, pp. 1097-1115.

Szelenyi, I. (1983), *Urban inequalities under state socialism*, Oxford University Press, Oxford.

PART II:
NATIONAL REVIEWS

In the context of the broad economic, political, institutional and social processes of transformation discussed in the previous three chapters, the following section considers individual national experiences. In ten short chapters, these 'national reviews' provide a brief outline of the progress of transition and the implications for regional development in Bulgaria, the Czech Republic, Estonia, Hungary, Latvia, Lithuania, Poland, Romania, the Slovak Republic and Slovenia. Each chapter describes the main patterns of regional disparity and problems, the territorial and institutional structures and the current status of regional development policies.

PART II:
NATIONAL REVIEWS

5   Bulgaria

JULIA SPIRIDONOVA AND NIKOLAI GRIGOROV

Introduction

Despite the relatively small size of the country, notable regional disparities are evident in Bulgaria. These can be seen in a range of areas including the distribution of resources and production facilities, living conditions and the share of individual regions in the generation of national economic growth.

The first serious regional disparities in demographic, social and economic development patterns were officially noted in the early 1980s. The roots of these regional imbalances can be traced back to a number of factors including the industrialisation process, intervention in ownership rights through nationalisation and the establishment of co-operatives, and the relatively 'closed' nature of the national space. These processes had a negative impact on the development of urbanised territories and rural areas and caused grave problems in the western and southern border regions.

The economic crisis of the 1990s aggravated the problems and disparities in regional development, with underdeveloped regions being the worst affected. In the early stages of the transition to a market economy, an overall deterioration in regional indicators, including in the better developed regions, gave the appearance of lessening levels of disparity. Later, however, different trends and rates of development at regional and municipality level emerged and regional inequalities grew considerably, taking on critical proportions in certain regions.

Territorial administrative reform

The introduction of the territorial administrative reform and the consolidation of local self-government is a new element in the implementation of the process of transition. The roots of the reform were in 1991 with the approval of the new Constitution that defined Bulgaria as a 'unified state with local self-government'. The Law on Local Self-

Government was passed the same year and underwent comprehensive changes in 1995, accompanied by the approval of three new laws in this field.

The regions (*oblasti*) comprise the administrative territorial unit for the implementation of regional policy and State administrative tasks. At the end of 1998, Bulgaria had nine regions (see Figure 5.1). These units were structures of the State (national) administration and not elected bodies. The initiation of a government programme on the creation and activities of territorial administrative authorities resulted in an increase to 28 in the number of regions from 1 January 1999. The objective of this change is to make use of the decentralised State structures which continue to operate at the former county (*okrug*) level.

Figure 5.1 Territorial administrative structure of Bulgaria

The 262 municipalities comprise the local-level units in Bulgaria. The municipality is the basic territorial administrative unit at which local self-government is exercised. The population elects a Municipal Council to act as the local self-government body and a mayor as the executive government body.

The current state of transition

The experience of economic and political transition to date in Bulgaria has not been wholly positive. Bulgaria is one of the countries which has found difficulty in adapting to new conditions and changes resulting from a combination of domestic and foreign factors. The following points summarise the main characteristics of Bulgaria's transition to a market economy.

- *Lack of consistent approach to the implementation of transition-related measures.* This is due principally to the numerous changes of government and the absence of a strategic approach to link macro-economic changes to supporting policies. On-going developments, however, have still resulted in a relatively rapid transformation of the economy from a centrally-planned to a private-sector dominated structure. In 1998, for example, the private sector produced more than 60 percent of the country's GDP.
- *Delay of structural reform.* This process was pushed forward more actively during 1998, and 1999 has been a very important year for the successful implementation of the reform.
- *Dramatic decline in GDP levels.* The economic crisis caused a fall of more than one third in GDP compared to the situation at the start of the transition period. Although the level of GDP has fluctuated during the period, the overall direction of the trend has been downwards, reflected in negative rates of economic growth. The evaluations for 1998, however, show a more positive development of GDP levels, following the negative trends of 1996 and 1997.
- *High social price of transition.* This has been the case throughout the 1990s as the economic crisis, characterised by high inflation (until the start of 1997), rapidly rising unemployment and insufficient social protection, has caused widespread impoverishment of the population. The average real monthly income per head has been falling consistently and, in 1996, was only 34 percent of the 1990 level.
- *Diminishing inflation rate since mid-1997.* This is related to the introduction of a Currency Board in mid-1997 and measures to limit

the budget deficit. The results of structural reform efforts and changes to the income taxation system are also contributing to the rehabilitation of the State budget.
- *Worsening of regional problems.* An underestimation of regional development issues during the period of transition, coupled with the absence of clear-cut priorities within the national structural policy and a general shortage of financial resources, has exacerbated of regional disparities and difficulties. The requirement for an active regional policy, oriented towards the better utilisation of regional factors of economic growth, the resolution of critical regional problems and the creation of conditions for reducing regional disparities, comprise the basis of the Law on Regional Development which was approved by the Government in 1998.

Demography

The population of Bulgaria was 8.28 million at the end of 1997. The persistently unfavourable trends in national demographic development point to a demographic crisis in the country. According to census data, the last positive natural population growth occurred between 1976-1985 with a mean annual growth of 0.2 percent. In the period 1985-92, however, the population level fell by an annual average of 0.8 percent and a continued annual average fall of 0.5 percent was registered between 1993 and 1997.

An analysis of the regional population distribution shows that the disparity between northern and southern Bulgaria, recorded at the end of the 1980s, is still in evidence. In 1990 and 1991, when there was a nationwide negative natural growth rate, this index was –3.4 percent in northern Bulgaria but only –0.25 percent in southern Bulgaria. In 1997, this index for southern Bulgaria was –5.9 percent but exceeded 12-13 percent in north-western and northern Bulgaria, indicating the emergence of a serious depopulation trend.

The considerable regional variation in demographic potential is also mirrored in terms of population distribution, with an overall trend towards the emergence of regions with a regressive demographic re-population capacity. Within this overall situation, differing grades of severity can be recognised. Twelve regions (Veliko, Tirnovo, Vidin, Vratsa, Gabrovo, Kyustendil, Lovetch, Montana, Pernik, Pleven, Rousse and Yambol) appear to face the worst situation. Only a very small number of their constituent

municipalities display a relatively normal age structure which has the capacity to sustain at least a minimum level of natural population growth.
- Fifteen regions (Blagoevgrad, Bourgas, Varna, Dobrich, Kardjali, Pazardjik, Plovdiv, Razgrad, Silistra, Sliven, Smolyan, Stara Zagora, Targovishte, Haskovo, Shumen) feature a relatively favourable population age structure and the continued potential for demographic and labour market renewal. At sub-regional level, there are broad differences between the municipalities, and it is worth noting that negative demographic trends are also evident even at this level.
- The population in the Kardjali, Razgrad, Silistra, Targovishte and Haskovo regions began to decline after 1989 purely as a result of a negative external migration balance, further exacerbated by negative natural population growth in some of the municipalities.
- In terms of child-bearing population potential, birth rate, death rate and age structure, Sofia-City and Sofia Region cannot maintain a natural reproduction rate of the population.

The demographic development of the municipalities is characterised by very broad differences. About one third of the municipalities demonstrate the capacity for positive natural reproduction, and a further fifth are able to maintain the level of natural reproduction. About half of the Bulgarian municipalities show a trend towards a negative reproduction rate, and the population structure, proportion of the child-bearing population, fertility levels and death rates all point towards negative natural growth rates. The majority of these municipalities are located in the western border regions of the country.

The basic demographic processes are the result of interrelated and interdependent processes of overall social and demographic development. The roots of the observed negative demographic trends date back to earlier decades, although the changing socio-economic environment has further contributed to the deterioration of demographic indices.

Employment and unemployment

The unfavourable processes in the national economy have had a corresponding impact on employment rates. The number of employed persons fell over the period 1990-1997 from 4.1 to 3.2 million, a drop of around 898,000 people. The sectoral re-distribution of the labour force has been occurring in parallel with the absolute fall in the employed population. Ownership changes have led to an increasing share of employment within the private sector and, by the end of 1997, 51.2 percent of the total employees were active in this sector.

A degree of stabilisation was evident in the labour market in 1994 and 1995 following a dramatic decline of almost 21 percent in the number of employed people in the first three years of transition. In absolute terms, by the end of 1997, ca. 521,000 people had lost their jobs but the mean annual growth in unemployment was −0.3 percent in 1996 and 1997. Unemployment remained consistently high at around 20 percent until March 1996 when a downward trend became evident, and the rate fell to 13.6 percent in 1997.

In regional terms, the highest fall in employment rates has been noted for the regions of Vidin, Vratsa, Montana, Smolyan, Shumen, Targovishte and Haskovo. The overall picture contains considerable municipality-level disparity, with the mean annual unemployment rate for 1998 varying from 3-4 percent (Sofia, Bourgas, Varna etc.) up to more than 30-40 percent (Kaolinovo, N. Kozlevo, Kaynardja, Rouzhintsi, Damyanovo, Antonovo).

Despite the variation in specific indicators, the picture of regional disparities remains constant within certain overall boundaries. This implies the existence of long-term structural unemployment and the formation of 'black spots' of permanent unemployment. The populations in affected municipalities require considerable State support in terms of specific measures to combat these developments.

Rising unemployment is a result of the current economic crisis. Initially, the root cause was a fall in production activities and the closure of entire production lines, companies etc. rather than structural changes in the manufacturing sector or technological innovation. In the period after 1996, however, unemployment was also fuelled by structural changes in the economic sector. Bulgarian unemployment is characterised by a high level of youth unemployment as well as a notable proportion of the unemployed having low skill and educational levels.

In terms of regional disparities in unemployment (see Figure 5.2), the following factors have an important impact:
- *natural conditions and geographic location*, given that the majority of the municipalities worst hit by unemployment are situated in mountain areas;
- *the state of the economy*, its sectoral structure and level of production decline; and

- *qualitative characteristics* of the labour force.

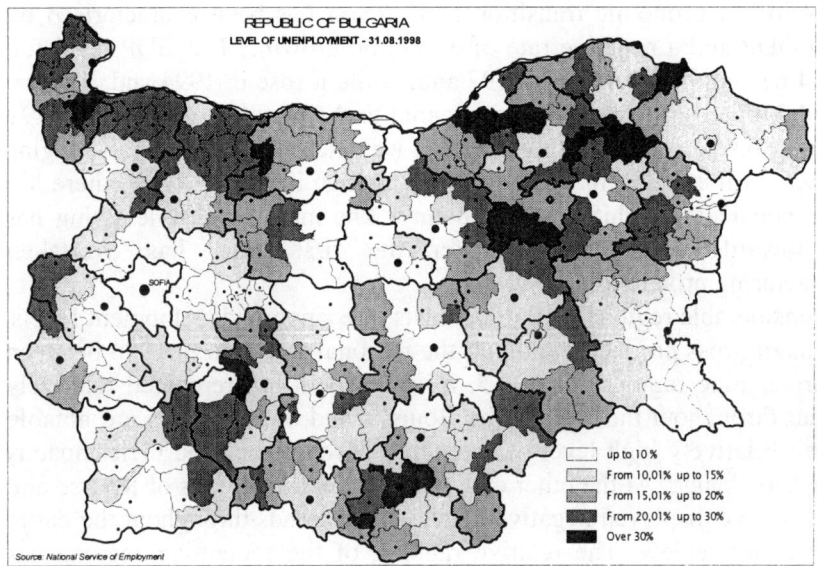

Figure 5.2 Regional unemployment in Bulgaria, August 1998

In parallel with changes in employment and unemployment rates, significant structural changes in the patterns of employment can also be noted. There has been an increase in the relative share of those employed in the tertiary sector which currently accounts for between 40-45 percent of the total number of employees. This process is particularly evident in regions where the regional centres offer important service functions (Sofia, Varna, Plovdiv. etc.).

Employment in the private sector already exceeds 50 percent according to official statistics and was 52.6 percent in 1997. Regional disparities are related to the differing rates of development in the privatisation process, the agrarian reform, and the entrepreneurial activity of private businesses, whether domestic or foreign-owned. The share of those employed in the private sector is highest in the regions of Sofia, Varna, Ganrovo, Veliko Tirnovo and Lovetch and the lowest in Montana, Vidin and Haskovo.

Economy

The period of economic transition in Bulgaria has been characterised by falling GDP and a negative rate of economic growth. The GDP level fell by 33.4 percent between 1990-1997 and, while it rose in 1994 and 1995 by 1.8 and 2.6 percent respectively compared to the previous year, if the 1991 level was taken as the starting point, it was clear that the overall lagging trend was still evident. In addition to the change in overall GDP, there has been a considerable shift in its structure. The most noticeable swing has been towards services which, for the first time, has overtaken manufacturing production.

Considerable regional variation exists in economic development levels. In terms of gross production output, the regional variation in 1996 between the former nine regions was 1:3.5, a level which has remained relatively constant throughout the 1990s. The Bourgas and Sofia regions are notable for their relatively high level of economic development and their capacity to adapt to change. At the other end of the scale, the regions of Rousse and Montana have displayed negative development trends throughout the entire period under review. The relative ranking of the remaining regions has fluctuated during the 1990s. It is anticipated that regional disparities will increase with the introduction of the 28 new regions.

At municipality level, comparisons of economic development reveal greater levels of disparity. Studies carried out during the period under review report differences of over 100 times in the values for production output, assuming that Sofia-City is not taken into account. The picture remains broadly similar if production output per head of population is used as the indicator.

Analysis shows that 16 municipalities display the best capacity to adapt (see Figure 5.3) and have led the way during the transition period. The indicators used to identify these leading regions are: gross production output per inhabitant; the rate of change of gross production output during the relevant period; relative share of employment in the private sector; and the volume of foreign investment. These areas are located principally in central regions within the sphere of influence of large cities - Sofia, Bourgas, Plovdiv, Varna, Rousse, Sliven, Shumen, Veliko Tirnovo, Gabrovo, Pleven, Blagoevgrad, Stara Zagora, Haskovo, Troyan, Pazardjik. The capital accumulation in these areas is based on the build-up of considerable assets within a range of industrial and infrastructure-related sectors. Within the current economic climate, these areas display an ever-increasing ability to attract capital investment, business activities and innovative enterprise. This is related to the increasing importance of place and the possibility for diverse business opportunities as attractive location factors for economic activity.

The underdeveloped areas of the country comprise about 20 percent of the national surface area (see Figure 5.3), the principal criteria used for their classification comprising: production output per inhabitant; the rate of change of gross production output during the relevant period; the rate of long-term unemployment; the average salary per inhabitant; and the level of development of the social and technical infrastructure.

This group comprises some 66 municipalities which lag considerably behind in terms of their social and economic development. These municipalities have encountered grave difficulties with respect to employment, income levels, manufacturing, technical and social infrastructure. The majority are border areas or are peripheral to large development centres. The increasing level of disparity between these and other municipalities is becoming serious and, in some cases, critical.

The identification of regions characterised by industrial decline is seriously hampered by the fact that the majority feature a combination of both structural problems and production decline. The industrial output of the entire country has been extremely seriously affected by the economic crisis, with the 1997 output levels only 55.3 percent of the 1989 equivalent.

The following indicators have been used to identify regions of industrial decline: level of industrial employment; dominant mono-structure of industrial production focused on the primary sector (energy, mining, metallurgy, etc.); fall in industrial production output; level of permanent unemployment; and level of employment decline in industry during the period under review. Seven regions of decline can be identified using these indicators.

A number of key factors affect the emergence of regional disparities in Bulgaria. First, the *structure of the economy and degree of manufacturing specialisation*. The structure of the economy and the pace and nature of structural change are key determinants of regional disparities. Both 'passive' and 'active' structural change can be identified. 'Passive' structural change is caused by a range of factors such as the impact of the economic crisis, the differing degrees of production decline, the launch of new production lines and increased sectoral output in areas with competitive advantage. 'Active' structural change is initiated by State actions to promote economic reform, focusing particularly on the process of privatisation or the liquidation of ailing companies, as well as the organisational and technical restructuring of companies. An evaluation of the regional consequences of structural reform provides no reason to identify serious 'black spots' within the national territory.

Second, the *level of development and efficiency of infrastructure provision*. The starting potential for development plays an important role in the regional transformation process. One of the key underlying reasons for less advantageous starting positions and poorer adaptability among municipalities is the underdevelopment of their manufacturing infrastructure. This impedes their ability to react rapidly to new innovative manufacturing opportunities or to expand efficiently existing facilities. Equally, those municipalities with a better infrastructure base display greater flexibility as their development efforts are not oriented towards keeping an obsolete structure intact but rather to developing new opportunities and horizons.

The regional distribution of technical infrastructure also shows considerable regional disparities. These manifest themselves to a lesser extent at the regional (*oblasti*) level, although their importance increases considerably at municipality level, and a strong core-periphery difference is also evident.

Third, the *level of investment activity*. The lagging position of Bulgaria in attracting foreign investment capital has a corresponding impact on the dynamics and quality of overall economic development. Over the period 1991-96, investment worth US$ 830.9 million entered the country, of which US$ 766.6 million comprised direct investment. In 1997 alone, FDI flows of US$ 636.2 million came into Bulgaria and the volume of foreign capital invested now exceeds US$ 1.2 billion. Direct FDI through the privatisation process accounts for 41 percent of the total volume, a further 4.6 percent has come through the capital market and the remaining 54 percent comprises 'green' investment and additional investment outside existing companies. The distribution of direct foreign investment by sector for the period 1991-1997 shows that interest is strongest in industry (55 percent), followed by trade (17 percent), finance (9.5 percent), and transport and tourism (6 percent each). More than half of the investments in industry go into the food and beverage industry, non-ferrous metallurgy, the clothing industry, electrical engineering and electronics.

The regional distribution of foreign investment at the end of December 1997 showed a strong concentration in the capital city (41.5 percent), followed by Varna Region (17.5 percent), Sofia Region (12.8 percent) and

Lovetch Region (9.4 percent). Projected on the 28 newly established regions, the share of foreign investment is highest in the regions of Varna, Sofia and Sofia-City, which account for 57 percent of the total volume of investment in industry nationwide. In the transport sector, the volume of investment is highest in Sofia-City (93 percent) and Bourgas Region (5.8 percent). In terms of tourism, Sofia-City again accounted for 92 percent of the foreign investment in Bulgaria at the end of 1997, followed by the Region of Dobrich (5.5 percent).

Finally, the *nature of the human resource base*. This includes factors such as educational background, skills level, traditions, entrepreneurship, and local business activity.

There are a number of factors which appear able to promote development. These include expanding the processes of local self-government and capacity building for mayors and local authorities to improve their skills in promoting development and creating structures that support local business activity eg. regional development agencies, business incubators etc. Such activity is evident, for example, in the regions of Bourgas, Smolyan, Plovdiv, Pazardjik, Rousse, Pernik, Blagoevgrad and Varna.

Regional policy and regional development institutions

Government policy has addressed the issues of regional development and the serious spatial consequences of the economic crisis and structural reform measures to differing degrees and with varying success. Regional development-related actions have been implemented within the framework of different ministries and sectoral policies, and funded by the State budget or special-purpose sectoral funds.

A number of initiatives are currently in different phases of drafting or implementation. These include regional programmes for the promotion of employment in unfavourable regions (Ministry of Labour and Social Policy), for alternative employment (Ministry of Industry), for overcoming environmental problems (Ministry of Regional Development and Public Works) as well as specific activities, programmes and schemes to combat regional disparities.

The problems of regional development have become increasingly topical and have been the subject of several legislative acts over the past 2-3 years. In terms of regional support measures, some taxation and credit conditions have been introduced, as well as a number of investment subsidies. In addition, other measures targeted at underdeveloped regions are envisaged in the Law on Foreign Investments, the Law on the Protection of Agricultural Producers, the Law on Protection of the Unemployed and on the Promotion of Employment and environmental laws.

The necessity of a legal framework for regional policy has resulted in the drafting of a specific Law on Regional Development and its submission to the Parliament of the Republic of Bulgaria for approval. The law lays down provisions concerning the co-ordination and administration of regional development and the procurement of dedicated resources for its implementation. The major objectives of the law include the creation of preconditions for the sustainable and balanced development of all regions, the reduction of inter-regional disparities in employment rates and income, and the implementation of regional and trans-border co-operation and European integration.

The tools for implementation of regional policy include:
- a National Plan for Regional Development which defines the objectives, principles and priorities of regional development in the country for the next six years;
- the designation of regions for specific targeted measures comprising growth regions, development regions, trans-border co-operation regions and regions facing specific difficulties;
- regional policy measures such as investment subsidies, interest subsidies, direction investment, preferential state and local charges, financial guarantees etc; and
- provision for certain administrative measures governing, for example, the allocation of municipal building plots for construction activities or the granting of building permits.

According to the Law on Regional Development, a Regional Development Board is to be established by the Council of Ministers which will co-ordinate the activities of all organisations and bodies involved in the implementation of the national plan. At the regional level, a Regional Board will be created in each region comprising representatives of the municipal authorities freely elected by the population. This Board will discuss decisions relating to the administration and planning of regional development in its area.

The principal function of the Law is to integrate the activities of relevant institutions to ensure that the stated objectives and tasks of regional development are met in the future.

References

Institute of Economics of BAS (1998), *Bulgaria's economy until 2000*, Sofia.
National Institute of Statistics (1997), *Socio-economic development of Bulgaria 1996*, Sofia.
National Institute of Statistics (1998), *Statistical Yearbook of the Republic of Bulgaria*, Sofia.
National Institute of Statistics (1998), *The main macro-economic indicators of the Republic of Bulgaria*, Sofia.

6 Czech Republic

MILOŠ ČERVENÝ AND ALOIS ANDRLE

Introduction

The Czech Republic was established on 1 January 1993 following a separation of the previous Czech and Slovak Federal Republic into two independent states. The Czech Republic has an area of 78,866 km^2 and borders Germany, Poland, Austria and Slovakia. The Czech population at the end of 1996 was 10.4 million with a population density of 131 inhabitants per km^2 and an urban population share of 70.5 percent.

The principal changes in the political, economic and social situation started within the former Czechoslovakia in November 1989. The initial position of the Czech Republic was very favourable having, for example, the highest level of per capita GDP of the CEE countries (except Slovenia) and low inflation, unemployment and foreign debt. Following a very deep decline in economic activity between 1989 to 1992, the process of economic recovery continued relatively favourably until 1995. In 1998, however, economic growth was actually negative (by more than two percent), although in most other countries the process of transition continued more successfully. The Czech Republic also applied for EU membership in January 1996 and negotiations are still in progress.

This chapter reviews the progress of national economic transition before turning in more detail to the regional territorial structures and emerging regional disparities within the Czech Republic. It concludes with a brief summary of the regional policy response - a subject dealt with in more detail in Chapter 20.

The territorial administrative structures

The Czech Republic currently comprises eight administrative regions (*kraj*), 77 districts (including Prague) and 6,242 communities (see Figure 6.1). Since 1990, sub-national elected bodies have existed only at the community level. Offices with a nominated head have been established at district level, and no political authorities (elected or nominated) operate in the regions. The only region-level administration comprises courts, financial offices, police and other sectoral bodies.

A new system of administrative regions with elected self-government bodies is to come into force from the start of January 2000 (see Figure 6.1). The legislative basis for the creation of these 14 higher self-government territorial units (Prague and 13 regions) is a Constitutional Act of 3 December 1997 and the new regions are to be named after their central cities. The preparation of the necessary legislation, the definition of their responsibilities, the election rules, logistics and other preconditions for their operation have been delayed. The election of the self-government bodies is now unlikely to take place before the end of 2000.

Figure 6.1   Territorial administrative structure of the Czech Republic

The creation of these new territorial units has not fulfilled many of the conditions requested by Eurostat. One of the key issues is that they are too small to comprise NUTS II units. For this reason, the government decided to establish eight territorial units which would be used for the purposes of structural analysis and the implementation of EU Structural Funds. Their function would be principally analytical and statistical, and they would be allocated neither administrative functions nor official management bodies. Of the 14 new regions, only Prague, Mid-Bohemia and Ostrava can be NUTS II regions. In the other cases, the NUTS II regions comprise a number of the new regions as shown in Table 6.2.

Table 6.1 NUTS designation in the Czech Republic

NUTS II	NUTS III (regions)
Prague	Prague
Mid-Bohemia	Mid-Bohemia
South-West	České Budějovice
	Plzeň
North-West	Karlovy Vary
	Ústí nad Labem
North-East	Liberec
	Hradec Králové
	Pardubice
South-East	Jihlava
	Brno
Mid-Moravia	Olomouc
	Zlín
Ostrava	Ostrava

The existing 77 districts are considered as NUTS IV regions and the 6,242 communities as NUTS V.

The average area of the NUTS II regions is 9,858 km^2. Apart from Prague (496 km^2), the smallest is Ostrava with 5,555 km^2, and the largest is the South-Western NUTS II region which covers 17,617 km^2. In population terms, the average size is 1.28 million inhabitants, the smallest being Mid-Bohemia with 1.1 million inhabitants and the largest, South-East, with 1.7 million. There is also considerable variety in the population density of the NUTS II regions. Prague clearly has the highest population density with 2,429 inhabitants per km^2, with the remaining NUTS II regions ranging from 67 inhabitants per km^2 in the South-West to 232 in Ostrava (the national average being 131 inhabitants per km^2). To some degree, these figures reflect differing economic structures – the South-West NUTS II region has a rural and forestry base, while Ostrava is characterised by industrial activity, mining and metallurgy.

In terms of NUTS I, the Czech authorities have proposed that the whole country be considered under this category although, by size and population, two NUTS I regions could be established corresponding to the historical lands of Bohemia and Moravia. This would, however, contradict the proposed NUTS II delineation, as the South-East NUTS II regions incorporate both southern Moravia and a large part of the historical area of Bohemia.

Current state of the transition

The course of economic transition in the CEE countries has involved a number of processes including a shift in property ownership, the liberalisation of prices, the free exchange of currency and capital transfers, the creation of a new tax system and the establishment of market institutions. Price liberalisation in the Czech Republic is now virtually universal and a currency devaluation was carried out in 1991. The consumer price index ranged between 9-10 percent p.a. in the period 1994-98, although this was linked to the increase in some still regulated prices. The index did start to fall by the end of 1998 and this trend has continued in 1999. The fixed exchange rate of foreign currencies has now been abolished and the currency is fully convertible. The main economic indicators for the period 1989-97 are provided in Table 6.2.

The process of privatisation has been completed in most sectors and, in 1996, the non-State sector generated 75 percent of total GDP. The division of large companies did have certain ramifications for their technological and R&D competencies and vocational training often ceased to exist within the newly created smaller units. The remaining State-owned entities comprise several banks and some public services (distribution of electricity and gas, railways, mail service etc.). Foreign investment has played an important role in the privatisation process, with more than a quarter of foreign investment in industry concentrated in transport equipment and a further fifth in food and tobacco. Germany is the principal source of this investment, accounting for 28 percent, followed by the Netherlands and the USA (14 percent each), Switzerland (11 percent) and France and Austria (eight and seven percent respectively).

Table 6.2 Basic economic indicators for the Czech Republic 1989 - 1997

Indicator/Years	1989	1991	1992	1993	1994	1995	1997
GDP (1989 = 100)	100.0	87.5	84.6	85.1	87.8	93.4	98.0
Employ. in civil sector[a] ('000)	5,403	5,059	4,927	4,848	4,885	5012	4,990
Average monthly wages (CSK[b])	3,170	3,792	4,644	5,817	6,894	8172	10,695
Unemployment (%)		4.13	2.57	3.52	3.19	2.93	5.23
Tangible fixed assets (1990=100)		67.5	78.7	85.0	99.4	127.1	136.3
Consumer price index (1989=100)	100.0	171.8	190.8	230.5	253.5	276.7	326.5
Balance of foreign trade (Mrd CSK)	-0.1	24.8	-45.3	10.1	-20.6	-95.7	-140.8

Source: Central Statistical Office, 1997, Ukazatele sociálního a hospodářského rozvoje ČR 4/97. Ekonom 41/98.
Note: [a] includes secondary jobs, average figures. Employ = employment; [b] £1=57.4 CSK, December 1999.

The social impact of transition has been significant and is seen particularly in unemployment trends. The unemployment rate was relatively low until the end of 1996 (3.5 percent) but subsequently increased considerably. It reached 5.2 percent by the end of 1997, 7.5 percent by the end of 1998 and was 8.3 percent in February 1999. The unemployment rate exceeded ten percent in 21 districts (of a total of 76 districts). The average wage in 1996 was marginally higher than the 1989 level, although this fails to reveal the disparities in living standards between different social groups. For example, 62 percent of total employees receive less than the average wage. Income disparities have also increased in spatial terms – in 1989, the average wage level in Prague was only 6.4 percent higher than the national average but, by 1997, this had increased to 31.5 percent.

Population

The overall balance of the Czech population has been decreasing slightly during the 1990s, with the natural decrease (67,761 people between 1991-97) insufficiently outweighed by in-migration (67,279). The birth rate has fallen from 19.1 per 1,000 inhabitants in 1975 to 12.6 in 1990 and only 8.8 in 1996. The death rate has also declined, falling from 12.6 in 1990 to 10.9 in 1996, and resulting, since 1994, in a natural population decrease. There is a more positive picture with other demographic indicators such as infant mortality, where the number of deaths per 1,000 live births has fallen from 12.5 p.a. in 1985 to 10.8 in 1990 and 5.9 in 1997. This is comparable with other developed countries. Similarly, life expectancy has been rising, particularly for males, increasing from 67.5 in 1990 to 70.5 in 1997. For females, the corresponding figures were 76.1 in 1990 and 77.5 in 1997.

The latest medium-term projection of the Central Office of Statistics shows a decline in overall population from 10.29 million in 1997 to 10.27 million in 2005 and 10.18 million in 2020. As a result, the age structure of the population is likely to become more imbalanced, the proportion of people aged 60 and over rising from 18 percent of the total population in 1997 to a projected 26 percent in 2000.

Regional differences in population development exist among the present administrative regions. Over the seven-year period 1991-1997, four of the fourteen future regions reported a decline in total population. The greatest decline (-14,847 persons) was reported in Prague and significant falls were also noted in the Mid-Bohemian and Plzeň regions, with a more negligible decrease in the region of Hradec Králové. Natural decrease was the principal cause of this trend – in fact, natural decrease was evident in ten regions in total with only four registering a natural population increase. The greatest natural decrease was actually found in Prague (more than 30,000 people) and its surrounding Mid-Bohemian region. The migration inflow exceeded the natural decrease in population in Prague until 1992, but total population has subsequently declined with a fall in both the number of births and the net inflow of migrants.

Migration flows have compensated in large part for the natural decrease, both nationally and in many regions. At national level, there was a positive net balance of 62,279 persons over the seven-year period, although a further ca. 200,000 illegal immigrants could probably be added to this total. Regional data covers international as well as domestic migration, and the highest levels of net migration are reported in Prague (almost 15,000 persons), followed by Mid-Bohemia, Brno, České Budějovice and other regions. The only region with a negative balance of migration is Ostrava, possibly caused by a large number of Slovak and Polish workers involved in the coal-mining and metallurgy industries which are now undergoing restructuring.

Regional population changes also affect the relative age compositions. While exact data is only available from the population census, which is not strictly comparable to EU statistics, it can be seen that the share of population in the youngest age group (0-14) is lowest in Prague followed by Mid-Bohemia and Plzeň. The Moravian regions have the highest proportion of this group as well as the northern regions of Bohemia (Karlovy Vary, Plzeň, Liberec).

Labour market

Employment levels have declined slightly during the transition period, from 52.6 percent in 1991 to 51.0 percent in 1997. The highest regional employment levels are in Prague (52.1 percent) and the West-Bohemian regions (52.1 percent) and the lowest levels in both Moravian regions (48.5 percent in South-Moravia and 48.8 percent in North-Moravia). These levels, however, remain considerably higher than in many EU countries. Employment in the public civil sector (principal job only) fell from 5.17 million in 1989 to 4.62 million in 1992 but subsequently rose again to 4.86 million in 1996. A considerable number of people released from this sector left the official workforce entirely for a range of reasons including retirement or involvement in the shadow economy.

In terms of sectoral structure, employment in the primary sector (agriculture, forestry) has declined from 13.2 percent in 1989 to 5.3 percent in 1997. Employment in the secondary sector (industry, construction) has also declined from 48.5 percent to 40.1 percent, although still higher than in EU countries. Conversely, employment in the tertiary sector has increased not only in terms of its relative share (from 38.4 percent to 54.6 percent), but also in absolute terms (by more than 400,000 persons). Commerce comprises the greatest proportion of the tertiary sector (16.2 percent of total employment), although the highest growth rate between 1989 to 1996 was recorded in banking and insurance (3.5-fold increase).

The economic structure at sub-national level differs between districts. The North-Bohemian and North-Moravian regions are the most industrialised areas and have correspondingly been the main targets for restructuring. Their shares of employment in the secondary sector (industry and construction) were 55 and 47.7 percent respectively in 1997. These two regions also have, with the exception of Prague, the smallest share of primary sector employment (3.9 percent and 4.7 percent). The highest share of employment in agriculture and forestry is found in the East-Bohemian region (11.9 percent), followed by South-Bohemia (9.5 percent).

In terms of the tertiary sector, the highest share of employment is unsurprisingly found in Prague (73.8 percent). West-Bohemia ranks second (53.5 percent), and these two regions also have the lowest levels of secondary sector employment (39.9 percent in West-Bohemia). The largest city in West-Bohemia, Plzeň, is the location of the biggest machine works in the Czech Republic (Škoda works), and the high tertiary sector employment in this region is related in part to proximity to the western border of the Czech Republic. South Moravia ranks third of the Czech regions in tertiary sector employment (51.5 percent), influenced by the location of Brno, the second largest city in the Czech Republic, where the service sector accounts for 64.7 percent of employment.

The differing economic structures also affect the average wage levels. In Prague, for example, the monthly average wage of the employed population in 1997 was 31.5 percent higher than the national average. This is principally a result of the high level of employment in banks and financial institutions, central government offices, and foreign company HQs. The lowest wage level was in the East-Bohemian region (90 percent of the average) due to the importance of agriculture and the high representation of textiles in the region's industrial base. At district level, the lowest wage rate was found in the districts of Bruntal and Jeseník in remote areas of northern Moravia.

The rate of unemployment recorded by the Labour Offices remained low for several years at the start of the transition process. However, from 1997 it began to increase, reaching 5.2 percent by the end of 1997, 7.5 percent at the end of 1998 and 8.3 percent at the end of February 1999. The regional disparities in unemployment are high (see Figure 6.2), lowest levels of unemployment are in Prague and its surrounding districts, and the highest rates in the coal-mining basins in North-Bohemian and North-Moravian regions as well as in southern Moravia in mainly rural districts with intensive agriculture. The unemployment rate exceeded ten percent in 23 districts, seven of which were in the Ústí n.L. region, five each in the

Ostrava and Olomouc regions, three in the Brno region and one each in the regions of Zlín, Mid-Bohemian and Jihlava.

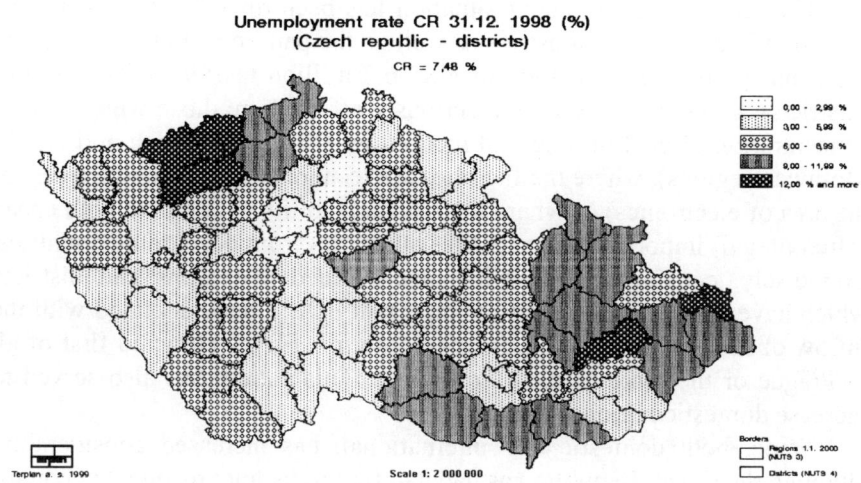

Figure 6.2 Regional unemployment in the Czech Republic

Economy

The level of GDP in the Czech Republic fell to its lowest point in 1992 before regaining an upwards trend. The highest annual growth rate was achieved in 1995 (6.4 percent) but has subsequently fallen, reaching only one percent in 1998 with a further potential decrease forecast. Per capita GDP nevertheless still stands at 58.7 percent of the EU average, the second highest of the CEE countries after Slovenia. Free-market policies previously prevented the formulation of longer-term development strategies for particular sectors, but the introduction of a new policy approach resulted in the drafting of such strategies, both for regions and sectors, and their consideration during 1999.

Industry (mining, manufacturing and utilities) has suffered a considerable fall in output, falling in 1993 to 66 percent of the 1989 level but subsequently rising again to 79 percent in 1996. The steepest decrease was in mining, and coal mining in particular, which has had serious regional ramifications. The level of industrial productivity in the Czech Republic is estimated to be less than half of the average EU productivity rate.

The regional development situation has been directly affected by the recession in a range of industries as well as the pattern of FDI flowing into the country (an estimated total of US$ 6.7 million in 1997[1]). The regions (districts) which have been most seriously affected are those which have a concentration of coal mining and metallurgy (North-Bohemian and North-Moravian regions), where the factories are technologically backward (eg. in the area of electronics) or where there is an inability to compete with cheap (often illegal) imports such as textiles and shoes from developing countries. Conversely, considerable benefits have accrued to regions and districts which have been the recipients of important FDI, often associated with the inflow of modern technology. In general terms, FDI is attracted first of all to Prague or the hinterland of large cities. This pattern has also served to increase domestic regional disparities.

Trade, both domestic and international, has increased considerably, although the Czech Republic has had a deficit in its total payment accounts. In 1998, the balance of foreign trade improved slightly, although FDI levels were low. The creation of a Czech export bank and the Export Guarantee and Insurance Company are likely to have a positive effect on the promotion of exports. The share of the EU in both Czech exports and imports has risen consistently and now accounts for 60 percent of all trade.

The process of transition has been associated with the creation of new enterprises. In 1996, approximately 35,000 economic subjects were recorded with their principal office abroad or under foreign ownership. In terms of non-financial enterprises, economic subjects under foreign control account for 6.2 percent of total employment in that area, illustrating the increasing influence of foreign investors within the Czech economy. In terms of spatial distribution, the large towns are the principal sites of company headquarters and Prague, which has 11.7 percent of the total population, accounts for the headquarters of 32 percent of all business companies and 36 percent of all joint-stock companies. The national average for the number of private entrepreneurs per 1,000 inhabitants is 121 but rises as high as 167 in Prague and 140 in Brno.

Regional disparities and policies

Regional disparities which have been emerging during the course of political and economic transition have partially been discussed above. This section draws out some of the principal areas and provides a brief overview of the regional situation and the policy response.

Prague is the only region where per capita GDP is considerably higher than the Czech average and, in 1995, it was actually higher than the EU average. The disparity between Prague and the other Czech regions has increased in recent years and all the remaining regions are below the national average. The very low level of the Mid-Bohemian region is misleading. The region has a very high level of commuting into Prague for employment, and GDP is calculated on the basis of place of work rather than residence. The bottom ranking of North-Moravia is a result of restructuring in the coal mining, metallurgy and heavy industries. However, in general, the disparities in per capita GDP in the regions outside Prague are relatively low.

The pattern of regional disparities in terms of average wages is similar to that for GDP figures, with the highest levels in Prague and the lowest in the East-Bohemian region (where there is the highest percent age of employment in agriculture and forestry). The wages in South-Bohemia and South-Moravia are also very low for similar reasons of high primary sector employment and low levels of urbanisation.

Unemployment is higher in coal-mining districts including North-Bohemia and North-Moravia and the future regions of Ústí and Ostrava. In addition, the Kladno district also has very high levels of unemployment due to the crisis in the metallurgy industry where there is a dispute over the ownership of the central steel-producing plant.

There has been no consistent regional policy response in the Czech Republic in recent years. The most effective measure since 1993 has been SME support which prioritises particularly underdeveloped areas. Two types of district are covered by this initiative and a list of eligible areas is drawn up and adjusted annually. The first group comprises economically weak districts, measured by indicators such as low income, employment levels, percentage of agricultural employment and population density. In 1999, the following districts were included within this category: Bruntál, Břeclav, Český Krumlov, Jeseník, Klatovy, Louny, Prachatice, Tachov, Třebíč a Znojmo. Three of them are located within the South-Moravian region, two each in North-Moravia, South-Bohemia and West-Bohemia and one in the North-Bohemian region.

The second group is made up of those districts undergoing structural difficulties, as measured by factors such as the level of mining activity, industrial employment and the unemployment rate. In 1999, this included the following districts: Děčín, Chomutov, Karviná, Kladno, Most, Ostrava, Přerov, Teplice. Four of these are in North-Bohemia, three in North Moravia and one in Mid-Bohemia.

Table 6.3 Regional disparities in the Czech Republic

Regions	GDP per capita 1993		GDP per capita 1995		Aver. wages 1996	Unemp	Urban pop.	Emp. 1996 in agric. & forestry
	CR =100	EU =100	CR =100	EU =100	CR = 100	Dec 97 (%)	1996 (%)	(%)
CR total	100.0	54.0	100.0	58.7	100.0	5.2	70	5.9
Praha	169.2	91.4	182.0	106.8	129.5	0.9	100	0.3
Mid-Bohemia	80.3	43.4	78.4	46.0	98.0	4.6	54	6.9
South-Bohemia	93.4	50.4	91.0	53.4	93.5	3.9	64	9.5
West-Bohemia	98.2	53.0	95.9	56.3	97.1	4.4	72	6.5
North-Bohemia	91.1	49.2	91.1	53.5	97.1	8.6	81	3.8
East-Bohemia	89.3	48.2	88.4	51.9	89.9	4.4	65	11.6
South-Moravia	94.9	51.2	91.0	53.4	93.2	5.3	61	6.6
North-Moravia	88.8	47.9	88.7	52.0	97.9	7.7	71	4.7

Source: Central Statistical Office statistics.

Finally, in terms of regional policy aims and objectives, the principal current activity relates to the preparation of documentation required for participation in the EU Structural Funds. A preliminary working document ('Regional and Sectoral Analysis of the Czech republic') was completed in

1998 and a Strategy for Regional Development of the Czech Republic is expected in 1999. Further details on the emerging regional policy of the country are provided in Chapter 20.

Note

1   Vienna Institute for International Economic Studies (1998), *Handbook of Statistics – countries in transition 1998*, Vienna.

7 Estonia

KAAREL KILVITS

Introduction

Notable regional disparities and problems are evident in Estonia despite the country's relatively small size. The current accession negotiations with the European Union have increased the topicality of regional disparities and problems. While problem regions of various kinds clearly exist in EU Member States, the recent political and economic changes in Estonia have resulted in acute regional difficulties which are not always of a classical nature.

The collapse of the Soviet Union and the socialist system as a whole meant that Estonia, as a former constituent republic of the Soviet Union, was placed in a very different starting position from other Central and Eastern European countries. The structure of the Estonian economy, the planning indicators and other key economic drivers were all dictated from Moscow and primarily served the interests of the Russian empire. The resulting structure of the Estonian economy is not suitable for the needs of a newly independent country undergoing the process of transition from a planned to a market economy.

Against this context, this chapter provides an overview of the regional disparities emerging in Estonia as well as an analysis of their origins and future development scenarios. An overview of the regional policy response is provided in conclusion.

Territorial administrative structure

Estonia is a unitary state divided into 15 legally established counties (Figure 7.1 and Table 7.1). At sub-regional level, the Constitution considers rural municipalities and towns as local administrative units. As of 1 January 1998, there were 47 towns and 207 rural municipalities in the country (Statistical Yearbook of Estonia 1998).

The current administrative system in Estonia is both expensive and complex. Extensive reform was proposed at the end of 1996 by the Minister of Finance, the Minister of Transport and Communications and the Minister of Economic Affairs and caused considerable debate. The goal of the suggested reform was to create an economic, people-oriented administrative system in which the limited national resources could be taken into account.

Table 7.1 Estonian counties and local administrative units

County	Area	Population		Administrative units	
	(km^2)	1.1.98	% total pop.	Cities and towns	Municipalities
Harjumaa (+ Tallinn)	4,331	538,149	37.0	7	19
Hiiumaa	1,023	11,862	0.8	1	4
Ida-Virumaa	3,364	197,530	13.6	7	16
Jõgevamaa	2,604	41,622	2.8	3	10
Järvamaa	2,623	43,368	3.0	2	14
Läänemaa	2,383	31,949	2.2	2	11
Lääne-Virumaa	3,465	76,144	5.2	4	15
Põlvamaa	2,165	35,956	2.5	2	13
Pärnumaa	4,806	100,457	6.9	3	20
Raplamaa	2,980	40,153	2.7	1	13
Saaremaa	2,922	40,202	2.8	1	16
Tartumaa	3,089	151,301	10.4	3	19
Valgamaa	2,047	38,985	2.8	3	11
Viljandimaa	3,589	62,782	4.3	6	14
Võrumaa	2,305	43,384	3.0	2	12
	1,529*				
Estonia	45,227	1,453,844	100.0	47	207

Source: Statistical Yearbook of Estonia, 1998.
Note: * The part of Lake Peipsi and the area of Lake Võrtsjärv which have not been divided into counties.

As mentioned above, Estonia currently has 254 units of local government. The municipalities are very small, the majority having between 1,000-2,500 inhabitants. In 80 municipalities, the centres have less than 500 inhabitants and, in a further 140, the centres have less than 1,000 people. In order to create a reasonable scale for social and economic activity and interaction, centres of at least 2,000 inhabitants are required. Given that many inhabitants registered as living in municipalities have actually moved into towns, the actual size of numerous municipalities is probably even smaller. It is clear that the present number of local government units is too large. Of the 254 local governments, only 17 do not need government subsidies.

Reducing the number of local government units would, however, meet with strong resistance. Such opposition would be expected from government officials employed at this level, as well as local inhabitants opposing the merger of local municipalities because of longer travel distances to the municipal centre and a distancing from the source of local democratic power and decision-making. County centres, which have developed mainly from the former *kolkhoz* and *sovkhoz* centres, have served as so-called centres of attraction for nearly 40 years and the removal of local government functions would threaten their existence. Where municipalities are merged, difficult decisions relating to the location of the local government would have to be faced, with the corresponding impact (understood by the population) on future local infrastructure investment and development. While such a move is economically justifiable, it is more questionable from a socio-political and regional political viewpoint – the artificial merging of municipalities could create a new periphery.

The costs of mergers should also be taken into account as an objective obstacle - the estimated cost of merging two small municipalities is around two million Estonian kroons[1]. Subjectively, there are also issues of identification with a certain administrative unit. The voluntary merging of local governments, while having greater popular support, does also have the danger that only the stronger municipalities, with appropriate revenue bases, will join together leaving the weaker municipalities isolated.

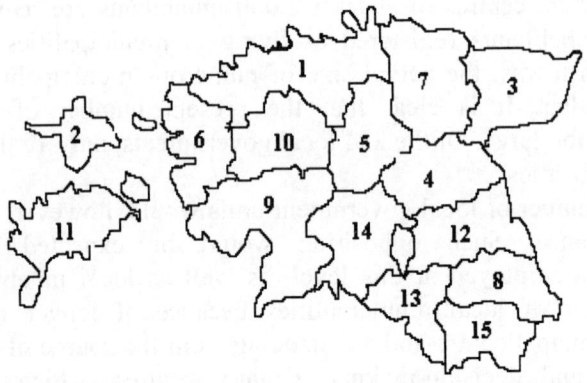

1.	Harjumaa	8.	Põlvamaa
2.	Hiiumaa	9.	Pärnumaa
3.	Ida-Virumaa	10.	Raplamaa
4.	Jõgevamaa	11.	Saaremaa
5.	Järvamaa	12.	Tartumaa
6.	Läänemaa	13.	Valgamaa
7.	Lääne-Virumaa	14.	Viljandimaa
		15.	Võrumaa

Figure 7.1 Administrative division of Estonia into counties

Regional disparities

Regional disparities are evident in Estonia in a number of key areas and are summarised in Table 7.2.

Table 7.2 Basic socio-economic indicators in Estonia

County	Working age population (16-60/55)		Registered unemployed jobseekers		Aver. gross wages	Local budget revenue per inhab.
	Jan. 98	% total pop	Aug. 98	% working pop.	1st quarter 1988	1997 EEK
Harjumaa (+ Tallinn)	329,180	61.2	8,120	2.5	4,545	3,999
Hiiumaa	6,512	54.9	270	4.1	3,111	3,365
Ida-Virumaa	115,829	58.6	7,117	6.1	3,161	2,770
Jõgevamaa	22,862	54.9	944	4.1	2,695	2,515
Järvamaa	24,301	56.0	818	3.4	3,073	2,966
Läänemaa	18,252	57.1	786	4.3	3,029	3,646
Lääne-Virumaa	42,224	55.5	892	2.1	3,423	2,587
Põlvamaa	19,418	54.0	904	4.7	3,077	3,091
Pärnumaa	54,879	54.6	1,036	1.9	2,958	3,959
Raplamaa	22,151	55.2	1,046	4.7	3,118	3,059
Saaremaa	22,413	55.8	784	3.5	3,208	3,059
Tartumaa	86,780	57.4	1,662	1.9	3,151	2,853
Valgamaa	21,234	54.5	1,366	6.4	2,736	2,348
Viljandimaa	34,470	54.9	1,226	3.6	2,945	2,991
Võrumaa	23,523	54.2	1,412	6.0	2,674	2,477
Estonia	844,028	58.1	28,383	3.4	3,743	3,342

Source: Statistical Yearbook of Estonia 1998; Estonian Statistics.

The Table highlights a number of key regional socio-economic trends including:
- *Unemployment* - the percentage of unemployed job seekers is highest in Valgamaa, Ida-Virumaa and Võrumaa and lowest in Pärnumaa, Tartumaa and Lääne-Virumaa (see Figure 7.2).

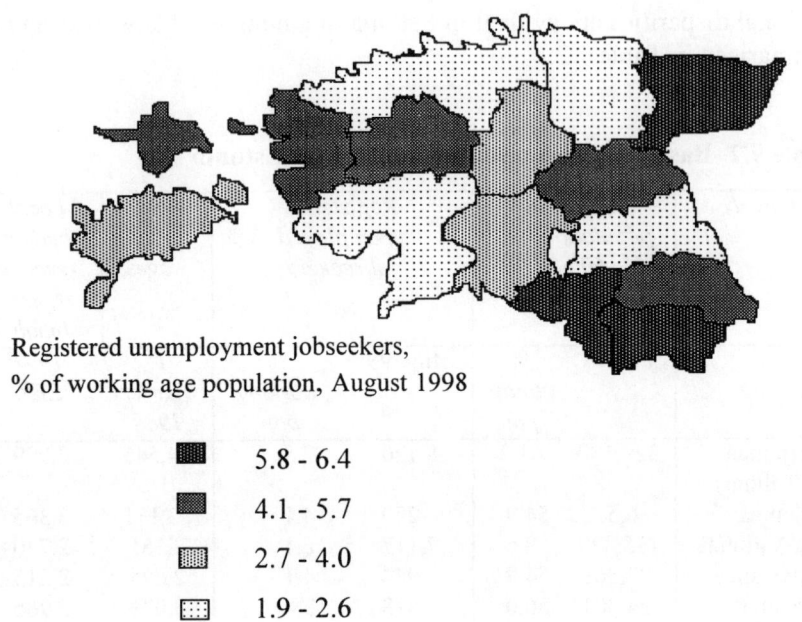

Registered unemployment jobseekers,
% of working age population, August 1998

■ 5.8 - 6.4
■ 4.1 - 5.7
▨ 2.7 - 4.0
▨ 1.9 - 2.6

Figure 7.2 Regional unemployment disparities in Estonia

- *Average gross wages* - lowest in Võrumaa, Jõgevamaa and Valgamaa (rural regions) and highest in Harjumaa (the main industrial region). The net income per family member is 40 percent lower in north-east and south Estonia and 30 percent lower in north, central and western Estonia than in Tallinn.
- *General socio-economic situation* - worst in Võrumaa, Jõgevamaa, Valgamaa and Põlvamaa in 1998 and most favourable in Harjumaa (which includes Tallinn), the most developed region of Estonia.
- *Standard of living* – on the basis of officially declared earnings, regional disparities are considerable. In 1997, there was a 1:2.4 ratio in the individual income tax revenue per inhabitant between the worst (Võrumaa - EEK 1,169) and best (Harjumaa - EEK 2,810) counties. The standard of living in Tallinn and its suburbs is in sharp contrast to south-east and south Estonia.

Significantly, there is a large Russian ethnic minority in Estonia, accounting for 28 percent of the population. Ethnic Estonians comprise 65 percent of the population and other minorities include Ukrainian (2.6 percent), Belarussian (1.5 percent) and Finnish (0.8 percent). The percentage of Russians living in the Tallinn is around 40 percent of the total population of the capital.

Entrepreneurship and business development

Within the framework of the former Soviet Union, the territorial pattern of Estonian industry became highly concentrated. In 1990, approximately two thirds of the local production capacity was located in only two counties - Harjumaa (containing the capital, Tallinn) and Ida-Virumaa (Narva and Kohtla-Järve). This pattern has been further exacerbated in recent years with over 80 percent of foreign direct investment between 1991-1998 flowing into Harjumaa. Indeed, the regional disparities in Estonia are worse in 1999 than in 1990.

Harjumaa contains a disproportionate share of enterprises, accounting for 47 percent of all registered businesses at the end of 1998 but only 37 percent of the total population. The regional variation ranged from 17 registered businesses per 1,000 inhabitants in Ida-Virumaa to 45 in Harjumaa, with a national average of 35 per 1,000 inhabitants. This clearly reflects marked inter-regional and urban-rural contrasts in the rate of new firm formation.

Overall, the majority of enterprises are concentrated in the major towns. According to research financed under the EU's Phare programme (Estonian Ministry of Economic Affairs and Netherlands Economic Institute), the three outstanding counties in terms of a company-based index of economic success were Harjumaa, Järvamaa, and Tartumaa. Raplamaa, Saaremaa, Viljandimaa and Jõgevamaa are classified as having an 'average performance', with the former two performing marginally better than the latter two. In terms of entrepreneurship, Ida-Virumaa, Hiiumaa, Võrumaa and Põlvamaa are clearly disadvantaged, with Ida-Virumaa emerging as having the least favourable situation in the country. Valgamaa also tends to fall into this disadvantaged category and, although its index of economic success is slightly better than the others, its investment environment is not sufficiently good to be classed within the 'average performance' group.

Estonia can essentially be viewed as a 'centre', comprising Tallinn and its suburbs of Harjumaa, and a 'large arc' of surrounding counties, from Lääne-Virumaa to Läänemaa. Tartu and Pärnu are so-called supporting centres within the 'periphery' which comprises the complex of South-East counties, Ida-Virumaa and the insular Hiiumaa. The only county not included in this classification is Saaremaa, which could be considered as part of the 'periphery' due to its location and insular position, but its more advanced economic development pushes it outside this category.

While the regional development disparities are clearly a concern for a relatively small country such as Estonia, there is some hope for the peripheral counties. Successful business ventures are evident everywhere and inter-county differences are wider than inter-regional ones. Further, technical and business-related infrastructure is available throughout the whole of Estonia.

Agriculture – a key source of regional problems

In post-war years, a collectivisation of agriculture based on owner-run farmsteads was carried out. Agriculture became specialised in the production of meat and milk for the markets of the Soviet Union. Major investments were made in the central settlements of *kolkhozes* and *sovkhozes* resulting in the decline, and sometimes abandonment, of small villages. Many small schools were closed and the rural population became concentrated in collective or state farm centres. To put it figuratively, Estonia was turned into a pig farm of the Soviet Union.

Under the new political and economic conditions of the 1990s, the structure of Estonian agriculture has changed drastically. Large-scale farms were abolished following legislation in April 1993 and, by 1998, Estonia had around 20,000 farmsteads and 1,000 co-operatives in place of the former 300 *sovkhozes* and *kolkhozes*.

Such rapid structural changes have been painful and their economic and social effectiveness is questionable. Although *kolkhozes* and *sovkhozes* cannot be regarded as an effective form of agricultural production, it is still true that large-scale production has indisputable advantages over small-scale farming. As a consequence of the structural crisis and other factors, such as a noticeable contraction of the Eastern market and contradictory agricultural and land reform initiatives, agricultural output has decreased notably in recent years.

From a national standpoint, the main problem is not, in fact, falling agricultural output. Indeed the current output of most agricultural products is higher than domestic demand, although the export of agricultural produce is not a cost-effective undertaking in the modern world. The most pressing problems in the agricultural regions are more in areas such as employment (especially in the former *kolkhoz* and *sovkoz* centres), social issues, village life and the overall rapid changes in the regional structure.

Future regional development scenarios

From the standpoint of classical regional policy, the economic structure in Estonia is undoubtedly overly dominated by Tallinn. This focus might, however, be more logical from an economic point of view given the need for a degree of capital and labour concentration to encourage economic growth. Moreover, in comparison to developed western countries, Estonia has a low average population density of 32 inhabitants per km^2, and even lower in certain southern areas of the country.

Tallinn is the capital of Estonia and is its most important port and therefore has a leading role in the promotion of a market economy and improved living standards. There is an opinion that the objective process of territorial differentiation is inevitable and that regional policy is unlikely to be able to counteract the evident urbanisation process. Decentralisation is not likely to be promoted to any great extent, regardless of the level of finance committed.

A range of development scenarios is possible in principle, including the following division of Estonia into two parts. One part would comprise very sparsely populated peripheral districts (border areas, areas with poor accessibility, islands) where there is out-migration of the population, and the qualified labour force in particular, in search of employment. In general, a 'brain drain' is evident with the most capable, entrepreneurial and creative sections of the population leaving first to maximise their potential elsewhere. The skilled sections of the population commute initially to the county centres until the opportunity to move closer to the workplace appears. The unskilled remain in the peripheral villages. The result is that the existing housing stock, as well as the infrastructure as a whole, remains underused in outlying areas. This process has serious consequences for the growth potential of the district concerned - as a rule, when the most active inhabitants leave the area, the growth potential declines and the community is less capable of adapting to innovation. In several regions in Estonia, the local growth potential (ie. readiness for innovation and social and business activity) has fallen to a level which makes development on the basis of local political and economic initiative impossible. Considering the small size of Estonia, the distances between outlying regions and the major economic centres pose no particular problems, but difficulties lie more in the ageing local population, their low educational level and passive attitudes. Research has shown that the major problem of the south Estonian labour force is a scarcity of middle managers. The revenue base of the local government is usually very low, and the age and educational structure of the inhabitants is unfavourable.

The second part of Estonia would include the rapidly growing Tallinn metropolitan area with its rising prices, increasing crime rate, strained road infrastructure and communication networks, and rising industrial and traffic pollution. The quality of life will gradually deteriorate and an influx of people from rural areas could lead to the emergence of ghettos, a forcing down of wage rates and increased demand and competition on the labour and housing markets. Currently a third of the Estonian population live in Tallinn, two thirds of the national money circulates in the city, and it is the location for over half of the country's crimes. The emergence of disadvantaged city districts is likely, with a corresponding fall in house prices and rise in crime and the requirement for significant government intervention. Equally, internal urban disparities will be increased with the emergence of privileged areas.

The above development scenario started to emerge a long time ago, although official statistics record that the rural population has been stable over the last five years. Statistics based on the registration of an individual's place of residence do not reflect the real situation given that there is neither a current law obliging people to define their place of residence nor an exact survey relating to change of residence. In addition, it is in the interests of the local government to show the number of inhabitants to be as high as possible as State budget subsidies are allocated on the basis of population. The expected decline in urban housing prices and availability of space with the return of many immigrants to Russia and other CIS countries has not occurred, principally due to the compensating influx of people from rural areas. One positive aspect of this development scenario is the increase in labour mobility which is important for rapid economic growth.

There are a number of options available for addressing this trend. The migration flows could be left entirely to market forces with the possibility of further social and spatial stratification. Another option is to pursue active and systematic regional, labour and social policies. This would certainly raise government expenditure but, in the long run, might help to avoid much higher expenditure related to the socio-economic issue of ghettos and urban problems. State intervention is certainly necessary to avoid the disparities between the rich and poor becoming so great that they threaten societal stability. Estonia should not become the city-state of Tallinn and the counties provide a regional basis which is wider than this view.

Other factors will also influence the pattern of the country's future regional development. These include, for example, the level of tax levied on fuel. High fuel taxes would be accompanied by a rising cost of living and increasing urban-rural disparities, while a low level of tax would be associated with increased traffic levels and pollution. In recent years, over half of the jobs available in rural areas have been lost. New jobs have been created in towns, but housing construction has not kept pace and rental and purchase prices have increased. As a result, daily commuting has increased considerably and thus any considerable rise in fuel tax would impact commuters and threaten a migration movement into urban areas.

Estonian regional policy

As introduced in 1995, the goals of Estonian regional policy are:
- creating stable living conditions for people in all regions, including the availability of employment, education, health care and other elementary services, and a healthy environment;
- supporting the economic development potential for all regions;
- creating and maintaining a regional balance in the development of population and settlement;
- sustainable development; and
- securing the territorial integrity of the country.

The main tasks of regional policy in Estonia are considered to include:
- creating conditions which enable prosperous entrepreneurship in all regions of the country;
- developing a communications infrastructure for the whole country;
- promoting a more effective regional restructuring of the rural economy;

- creating economic growth potential in developing regions;
- ensuring the availability of primary services (basic education, first aid, communication, etc.) across the territory; and
- creating a national database for monitoring and guiding regional development, and making this information publicly available.

Regional policy is implemented primarily through the provision of State support for local initiatives designed to influence economic, infrastructure and social development. The State supports regional policy measures in co-operation with the local population, entrepreneurs and their unions, institutions and local government.

In order to achieve a higher level of efficiency in the use of finance, the State is focusing on the promotion of regional policy through the co-ordination of various institutions. Regional economic grants and financial support are regarded as temporary measures for increasing and restoring local potential. Permanent measures are introduced only in exceptional cases. The status of developing regions is awarded by the government only to regions where the socio-economic situation is very unfavourable, a high rate of unemployment is anticipated, there is considerable out-migration or a much lower comparative standard of living is evident.

Given the objectives, tasks and principles of regional policy, as outlined in the Regional Policy Concept and other related regulations, all government institutions are involved to some degree in its implementation. The policy area is co-ordinated by the Ministry of the Interior, which provides relevant guidance. Many government institutions have established sub-groups to analyse and carry out regional development in their particular sphere of influence. A State Regional Policy Council is to be established, with representatives from state institutions and local government, to elaborate regional policy and strategies and co-ordinate their implementation.

At sub-national level, regional policy is carried out by county governments, which monitor development trends and implement State regional policy initiatives within their jurisdiction. All regional policy measures and decisions relating to their territory which originate outside the county government itself must have the agreement of the relevant county government prior to implementation. Regional development plans and programmes will be drafted and implemented by county-level State institutions in conjunction with local governments.

The following regional policy measures are implemented in the country:
- spatially differentiated credit conditions and local public transport subsidies;
- regional business start-up, development and training support;
- regional development and support of business networks and development centres;
- support of local development initiatives for concrete projects;
- subsidised transport between the islands and the mainland and electricity on the islands;
- other subsidies to local governments (from the fund to support municipal budgets); and
- preparation of regional development programmes.

The Regional Development Concept approved in October 1995 allows for the financing of six regional development programmes from the State budget. These programmes are targeted at combating a further polarisation of the national economy and preventing associated macro-economic problems. They comprise:
- *Programme for the periphery*: to create new jobs, reduce out-migration and increase the local development potential in peripheral rural districts;
- *Programme for the islands*: to ensure the provision of essential services (transport, communication, electricity, first aid, education) to people living in permanently populated islands, and to increase the competitiveness of the local economy;
- *Village support programme*: to arouse local self-initiative in villages;
- *Programme for mono-functional settlements:* to diversify the economic structure of mono-functional residential areas (towns with over 1,000 inhabitants where most inhabitants have been employed by a single enterprise or industrial sector) by creating alternative employment opportunities using the existing labour force, facilities and equipment, and improving the infrastructure of the towns and connections with regional-county centres;
- *Programme for border regions*: to promote the development of border areas in conformity with the obligations of state defence and border protection; and

- *Ida-Virumaa programme*: to integrate the Russian-speaking population in this area into Estonian society, preserve and strengthen the Estonian-speaking population, increase the economic and social stability, improve the entrepreneurial climate and ensure the effective and sustainable use of natural resources.

Despite the existence of many institutions dealing with regional policy and State support programmes, Estonian regional policy suffers from a lack of political agreement about the redistribution of national income to promote homogenous national development. The rapid economic growth expected in the short term will probably result in the emergence of a wider gap between Tallinn (Harjumaa) and peripheral regions, although it is anticipated that the standard of living in peripheral areas should also start to rise.

Regional policy was cited as a priority in the 1998 State budget although the financial allocation given to peripheral areas cannot yet be classified as regional policy. Further, other budget expenditure items are currently included under the regional policy banner but, in reality, have little to do with regional development. These include, for example, expenditure on land cadastre, land management, environmental monitoring, geological surveys, projects of applied microbiology and various other national undertakings. The country still faces a considerable challenge in developing an effective regional policy to combat the rising regional disparities and problems.

Note

1   £1 = 25.2 kroon (EEK) (December 1999).

References

Berg, B. (ed) (1997), *Estonian Economy and European Integration*, The Research Institute of Finnish Economy, Helsinki, p. 289.

Berg, B., Kilvits, K. and Tombak, M. (1996), *Technology Policy for Improving Competitiveness of Estonian Industries*, The Research Institute of Finnish Economy, Helsinki, p. 236.

Eesti Vabariigi Majandusministeerium (1998), *Eesti majandusülevaade 1997–1998*, Tallinn, p. 159.

Estonian Human Development Report 1998, Tallinn, p. 127.

Estonian Statistics No 1/1998 – 12/1998.

Mäeltsemees, S. (1995), 'Local Government Reform', in Lugus, O and Hachey, G.A. Jr. (eds), *Transforming the Estonian Economy*, Estonian Institute of Economics, Tallinn, pp. 126–39.
Ministry of Economic Affairs (1997), *Estonian Economy 1996–1997*, Tallinn, p. 183.
Statistical Office of Estonia (1998), *Statistical Yearbook of Estonia 1998,* Tallinn, p. 324.
Terk, E. (1999), 'Regionalist View of Estonian Entrepreneurship', *The Baltic Review,* vol. 16, pp. 18-19.

8 Hungary

GYULA HORVÁTH

Introduction

In a European context, Hungary can be regarded as a small- to medium-sized country with its population of ca. 10.3 million. However, the regional disparities in the country, reinforced by the period of socio-economic transformation, are considerable and their management has become an important political issue. The spatial structure of the country is still not suitable for the conditions required to promote a modern market economy. The increasing level of social and economic innovation, as well as the country's integration into the European regional division of labour, are hindered by a lack of cohesion and infrastructure links between the Hungarian regions and by the under-developed character of regional centres.

This chapter examines the regional territorial structure of Hungary and the patterns and causes of regional development and disparity trends. It concludes with an overview of regional policy outlining the types of disadvantaged region and the measures in place to encourage their growth – a topic developed in more detail in Chapter 22.

Regional structure

Hungary is a unitary state comprising 19 counties (see Figure 8.4), plus Budapest which has a similar legal status. Local government reform in 1990 created local authorities (or settlements) as unlimited legal subjects and increased their number to over 3,000. This system is highly fragmented with over 35 percent of the 3,000 local authorities having fewer than 500 inhabitants, and the average size being 3,400 inhabitants, lower than the European average. The 1990 reform also increased the powers of local government level vis-à-vis the counties. The counties can now assume only those functions which the local governments at the settlement level cannot, or do not wish to, perform. This considerably limits the counties in terms of their economic development functions. County development councils have been established and regional development councils are also currently being set up. More details on this institutional framework for regional development are given later in the chapter.

Hungary's current regional structure displays a number of key characteristics. First, the country is homogeneous from an ethnic, linguistic, and historical point of view. Over 90 percent of the population speak Hungarian as mother tongue, and the Hungarian language does not have regional dialects which differ markedly. Traditionally, the country has had a uniform, centralised public administration system. The autonomy of the territorial units is very limited, there is no tradition of federalism and regionalism is weak. Homogenisation was overt, especially in the socialist era, although now the trend is shifting to some degree.

Second, the spatial structure of Hungary is highly mono-centric. The capital, Budapest, has a very large population share (about 20 percent of total population) and plays a disproportionate role in intellectual and cultural life, as well as in politics. Budapest is the only large city in the country, and, in some ways, the entire country comprises its periphery. Different governments have attempted to reduce the size and role of Budapest (and its metropolitan area) a number of times, but most have failed. The only policy which had a clearly quantifiable effect was the industrialisation of peripheral regions between 1950–1980 when the share of industrial employees in Budapest fell from 50 percent in 1950 to a level proportional to its population share. In terms of innovative activities in other sectors, the capital plays a dominant role and, despite political statements to the contrary, there has been no significant decentralisation of higher education, business services or R&D. In 1996, for example, there was a three-fold difference in the per capita GDP between Budapest and Szabolcs-Szatmár-Bereg county.

Third, the most prominent feature of regional development disparities in Hungary is the east-west divide, with the Danube river acting as an important dividing line. In recent years, this contrast has become more pronounced. The Great Plain, covering around a half of the country's area, is a traditional agricultural region which the process of industrialisation, carried out during the 1960s and 1970s, failed to modernise. The Great Plain also requires special attention because of its particular ecological and human settlement conditions which are unique in this part of Central Europe.

Finally, smaller areas of economic crisis can be identified within the larger regions. In particular, these include agricultural areas with a poor resource base located in hilly regions and where little alternative economic activity is possible principally because of poor transport links. Out-migration from these areas has been a longer-term trend, and many of the de-populated villages now contain either an ageing population or marginalised populations such as gypsies.

Regional socio-economic development trends

Population

Population decrease is anticipated in Hungary on the basis of age structure and current demographic trends. In 1990, the Hungarian population was 10.3 million and this total is expected to fall to 9.7 million by 2010 – a fall of approximately seven percent over two decades. This decrease would only be counter-balanced by a very high rate of international migration, which is unlikely to occur. The size of different age groups is likely to fluctuate considerably because of the unequal spread of ages through the population as a whole.

Demographic processes vary widely in the different regions of the country and include:
- above-average population decrease along the southern borders of the country;
- lower rate of population decrease in the northern part of the country, although stagnation can be identified in smaller districts (principally in certain areas of Szabolcs-Szatmár-Bereg county, eastern regions of Borsod-Abaúj-Zemplén and some industrialised areas of Veszprém and Fejér, which previously attracted significant immigration);
- a better demographic situation in rural towns than in village areas as a result of previous immigration and age structures and, because the ageing of the population structure is less marked, the fall in population over the last two decades has only been 2–4 percent, as opposed to the 8–12 percent natural demographic decrease in village regions and the influence of migration trends.

The difference between urbanised areas with higher population density and rural areas of lower population density has been increasing in Hungary. In 1990, 53 percent of the Hungarian population lived in the 20 largest urbanised zones, a rate which is expected to reach 60 percent by 2010.

The nature of migration is also changing. First, the rate of migration between the large regions has decreased and is likely to remain at a low level. The main motivation for longer-distance migration has disappeared with the emergence of unemployment as a general phenomenon, the halting of large-scale housing construction programmes, and the overall availability of social services and unemployment benefit. The lack of housing, particularly in the rental market, also presents a serious obstacle to the mobility of labour.

Second, the age group of migrants is becoming younger. This is due principally to the increase in attendance at secondary and high schools and the growing role of educational institutions as an incentive for regional mobility. Third, since 1990, the permanent migration balance of settlements with county-rights has been negative and this trend is likely to continue over the next 10-15 years. In Budapest, as well as several large rural towns, there is likely to be a continuation of the trend towards decreasing population in inner districts which started more than 20 years ago. A population fall in large housing estates, evident since 1990, is also continuing. The inhabitants moving from these areas settle in the outlying areas of towns, although still within the urbanised belt.

Fourth, international migration remains relatively low, although higher than during the period to the mid-1980s. It is likely that a portion of Hungarian minorities currently in neighbouring countries will return to Hungary, settling in border regions to maintain ties with their former homes. This could further exacerbate the problems of the already disadvantaged eastern regions of the country. Lastly, an increase in the proportion of the Romany population is likely to continue in peripheral villages where population decrease is rapid, as well as from the depopulating town centres and housing estates in Budapest and other large towns.

Regional development policy could help to create conditions to promote more favourable demographic trends to help stem the out-migration of younger and more educated people in particular. This could partially be achieved through combating regional disparities and improving overall conditions in underdeveloped regions.

Living standards and social differentiation

The 1990s have witnessed a significant increase in social inequality in Hungary. Over the past five years, differentiation in income and property, started in the 1980s, has continued at an accelerated pace. Extreme income disparities can be identified between different professions, sectors and regions. In the 1980s, around a million people, or ten percent of the population, lived below the poverty line and, by the mid-1990s, this had increased to almost 25 percent. The direct causes of increasing poverty, which include housing provision, and rising unemployment are particularly prevalent among the poorly educated, dependent and unskilled populations living in villages. From a social viewpoint, the fall in the ratio of earners to dependants causes considerable tensions. This is a result of trends in the age structure and a fall in the proportion of the working-age population, as well as increasing unemployment. The ratio is particularly poor in regions with a high proportion of elderly and unemployed persons.

The emergence and rapid growth of open unemployment has been a very important contributor to the increase in income disparities. Unemployment affects about a fifth of families and households, and characteristically families with lower income levels. Between 1990 and 1994, more than 1.4 million jobs were lost or 25 percent of the total number of jobs in the country – exacerbated by a parallel trend in falling wage levels. Around 40 percent of those who lost their jobs were out of employment for more than 12 months. Regional differences are significant, with the northern industrial area and the north-eastern counties being the worst affected.

The earning possibilities within the shadow economy, available to a large proportion of the population under the former socialist system, have now decreased. The opportunities for so-called household or small-scale production have been reduced, there has been an overall fall in market demand and the links between large factors and small-scale agricultural production have largely been broken.

There is a spatial dimension to the newly emerging social problems. The enhanced differentiation between settlements highlights the underlying strength of the local economy. Development options open to local governments are considerably influenced by the different levels of income tax earnings. This means that the cities with county-rights and the more important employment centres have maintained or even increased their favourable positions despite the transformation of the local economy, while the burdens of industrial restructuring have been imposed on the rural areas. Social stratification is strongly influenced by location and the status of a particular settlement. A close link can be made between distribution of the social classes and settlement categories. The elite and upper middle class are represented most strongly in Budapest and larger developed towns, while social mobility and the proportion of upper classes is much smaller at lower levels of the settlement system.

Acute crisis regions have developed where structural, employment and social tensions generated by underdevelopment and industrial decline appear simultaneously. Small villages face some of the worst difficulties in terms of lack of working-age population, while the number of unskilled, unemployed people of low education is particularly high in the underdeveloped, hinterland border regions. In the face of such difficulties, the traditional pre-1990 approaches to social policy are unable to handle the current problems of poverty and inequality under market economic conditions and are particularly unsuited to tackling the spatial dimension of social problems.

Economic processes

Two factors are central in the creation of the economic spatial structure. First, historical trends established a centre-periphery relationship within the country. In the course of previous decades, the State-run economy strengthened the economic centres in a hierarchical fashion, creating a system of peripheral areas reliant on the centres. The introduction of economic reform pushed the peripheral areas into greater difficulties given their diminished ability to develop their own interests and their biased system of linkages to the economic centres.

The other determining factor influencing the spatial economic structure of Hungary is the regional location and distribution of the material and mining industry. Patterns of industrial location emerged, as in Western Europe, as part of the historical industrialisation process although, in Hungary's case, this was delayed into the first half of the 20th century. The spatial distribution of industry has been maintained into the 1990s and its obsolete character has created industrial crisis regions. This situation can only be resolved through far-reaching industrial restructuring which, as in the case of west European heavy industry, is likely to take a long time.

The current spatial structure which has emerged during the transition to a market economy is characterised by a number of features. The role of

Budapest remains central, particularly in the area of international economic relations and capital investment. The related economic opportunities, however, have spread not only to the immediate hinterland of the capital, but also to several large towns throughout the country. This has helped to develop the role of such towns and led to positive economic development in most cases. The majority of medium-sized towns, however, are still in an uncertain economic position.

Economic development in the peripheral areas is even more problematic. The economic transition resulted in a weakening of their dependent role and the underlying conditions are often insufficiently good to attract foreign direct investment. The border areas face particular issues, both positive and negative. In regional development terms they are often the most remote but cross-border co-operation can, in some cases, offer new economic growth opportunities. This is certainly evolving along the western border regions of the country. Tourism development has also been a source of new economic activity – particularly tourism which is not seasonally restricted.

The nature of economic transition and its continued uncertainties make projections of economic development processes and prospects only possible in the medium-term. It can be reasonably assumed that the economy will become more dynamic over the next few years, in comparison to the current growth rate of only 1-2 percent, although highly dynamic growth cannot yet be taken for granted. The most active growth areas include market services (trade, telecommunications, financial services, tourism and other business services) while only limited improvement can be expected in other areas such as agriculture.

A comparison of per capita GDP in 1994 and 1996 shows growth in overall terms but a relative stability in the spatial structure and distribution of economic development. Per capita GDP rose from 425,000 HUF[1] in 1994 to 672,000 HUF in 1996. Budapest retained its dominant position well above the national average, and the counties of Győr-Sopron-Moson and Vas exceeded it only very slightly. The relatively developed counties of Zala, Fejér, Tolna and Csongrád counties achieved only 90–100 percent of the national average. In terms of GDP growth rates, per capita GDP increased most in the counties of Komárom-Esztergom and Veszprém and in Transdanubia specifically, with only the county of Tolna showing a rate of growth lower than the national average.

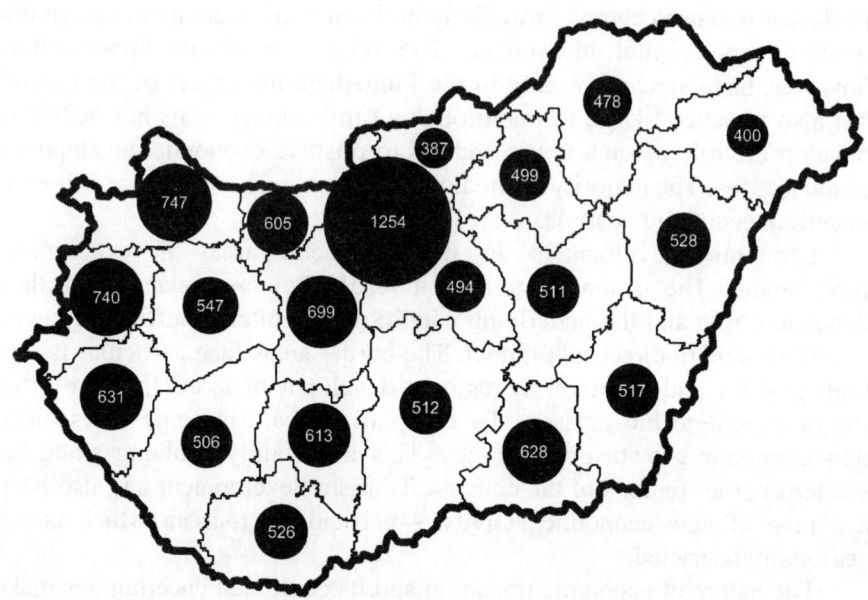

Source: Regional Statistical Yearbook, 1996

Figure 8.1 GDP per capita by counties, 1996 (thousand HUF)

The lowest per capita GDP rates during this period were recorded in Nógrád and Szabolcs-Szatmár-Bereg, with the pace of growth slower in the former than the latter county. The GDP level increased in Heves and Borsod-Abaúj-Zemplén although still did not exceed 75 percent of the national average, and the increases were insufficient to bring the northeastern region of the country into line with the other regions. Interestingly, however, the pace of growth in central regions did lessen during this period as evidenced by the below-average rates in Pest, Budapest, Nógrád and Szolnok. This modest development in the north-eastern part of the country can be attributed partly to regional development support while the growth of the two Transdanubian counties can be explained by private capital investments (see Figure 8.1).

The rise in unemployment also has a marked spatial dimension (see Figure 8.2). Areas most affected by unemployment are generally in regions characterised by the loss of heavy industry and mining, severe underdevelopment and employment decline. Employment decline affects not only the actual location of the jobs but also the labour market area as a whole. The situation in industrial crisis regions is particularly problematic as the population was often heavily reliant on single, large firms and the lack of skills or other factors increased the difficulty in moving to another area in search of work.

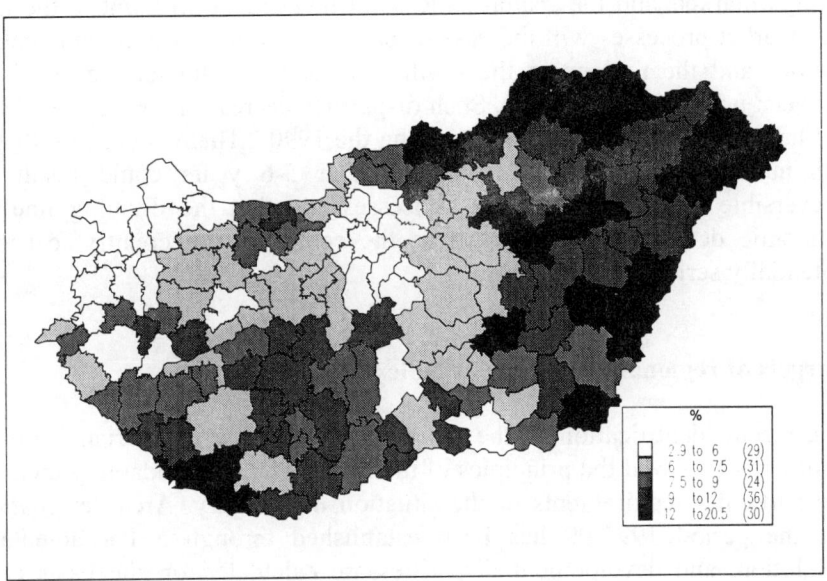

Source: Regional Statistical Yearbook, 1997.

Figure 8.2 Unemployment rate by small areas in Hungary, 1997

In terms of investment activity, over half the investment in the production sector has originated from foreign capital. This reflects, in part, the limited possibility for domestic capital accumulation and the lack of motivation to invest. The capacity for resource generation within the economy is insufficient for the modernisation of a range of sectors including industry, and this situation is unlikely to change in the short-term. This situation is likely to reinforce the advantageous position of larger towns (and Budapest in particular) and industrial districts with good infrastructure. In the absence of specific investment incentives, the weakened position of the less-developed regions is likely to be reinforced.

Foreign investment capital is a decisive factor in the spatial distribution of investment, production growth rates and the regional allocation of capital. Currently, 80 percent of such investment is concentrated in western Hungary and in Budapest and its hinterland.

The differing pace of development between sectors, the dynamics of the foreign markets and the spatial patterns of investment all point to the fact that market processes will increase disparities between western and central regions and the regions in the north and south of Hungary, as well as between urban and rural areas. Such disparities decreased during the 1980s but have been steadily increasing during the 1990s. There is concern that a continuation of these trends for a further 5-6 years could result in irreversible or barely reversible processes and that the dividing line of economic development will shift to the centre of the country, causing potentially serious social tension.

Targets of regional development policy

The recent identification of the main target areas for Hungarian regional policy has followed the principles of the European Union, adapting them to the particular requirements of the situation in Hungary. Area designation for the period 1997-99 has been established through a Parliamentary resolution, and development disparities are calculated on the basis of a complex indicator system using a range of different variables. The designated areas comprise those regions where the indicator values are considerably below the national average. Four main types of problem area have been identified: socially and economically underdeveloped regions; regions requiring industrial restructuring; underdeveloped rural regions; and regions facing long-term structural employment which fall outside the other designations (see Figure 8.3).

Socio-economically underdeveloped regions are those areas where the complex indicator (combining 28 individual indicators and including a weighting for regional centres) is lower than the national average. Under this classification, 76 districts are currently eligible, principally in the north-eastern counties. Over the last five years, nearly 80 percent of the resources of the Regional Development Fund have been concentrated on the four counties of Borsod-Abaúj-Zemplén, Szabolcs-Szatmár-Bereg, Hajdú-Bihar and Nógrád. This has resulted in significant improvements, particularly in infrastructure provision. There has been a lower rate of expenditure on enterprise promotion and job creation (26 percent) although this is to increase in future years as infrastructure provision alone is insufficient to generate economic growth and employment. The further improvement of economic and business infrastructure, and a broadening of enterprise services, will also be important areas of future support.

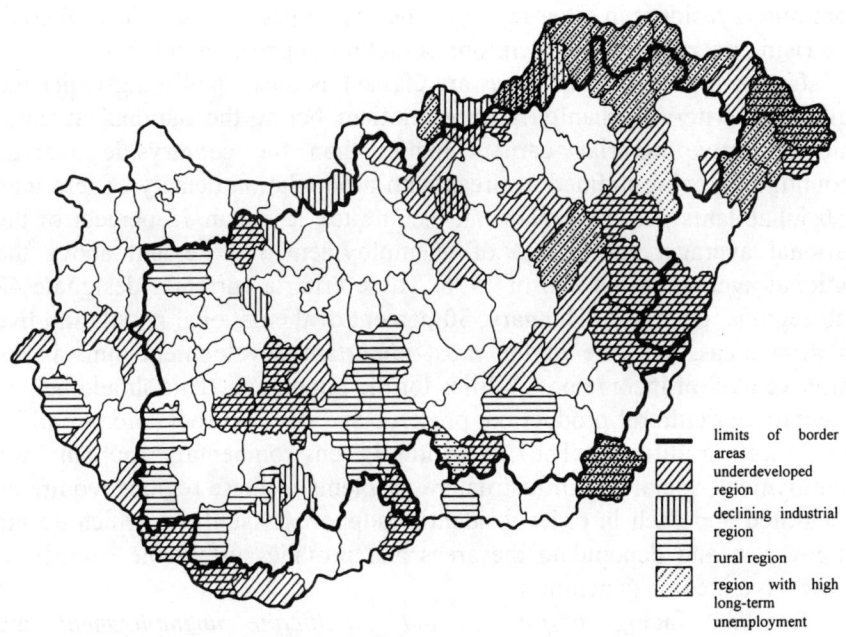

Source: Governmental Decree 219/1996. Designed by the author.

Figure 8.3 Eligible areas in Hungary, 1996

Areas of industrial restructuring are defined as those statistical areas where the number of industrial employees is double the 1990 national average and the fall in the proportion of industrial employees between 1990-95 and the rate of unemployment in 1996 is above the national average. These criteria designate regions in the Borsod-Abaúj-Zemplén and Veszprém counties. Regions where the number of industrial employees is 1.5 times the national average are also eligible for support. The radical decline of the number of industrial employees in general, and in certain industrial sectors (mining, metallurgy, defence, textile and clothing industry, machinery, some branches of construction industry) in particular, has contributed significantly to the number of regions in this category. There is considerable spatial concentration of industrial related development problems. This has been intensified both by the relocation of some industrial sectors into more dynamic and economically favourable regions and the fact that the crisis industries employed a large number of commuters resident in other regions. The real impact of the industrial crisis and rising unemployment, therefore, sometimes appears in other areas.

Underdeveloped rural areas are classed as those qualifying under the following criteria: urbanity/rurality quotient below the national average; rate of active agrarian earners higher than the countryside average (countryside being defined as areas with a population density of less than 150 inhabitants per km^2); personal income tax less than 75 percent of the national average; and a rate of unemployment 133 percent above the national average at the end of 1996. These criteria currently designate 42 sub-regions. Overall in Hungary, 30 percent of the national population live in rural areas, and one of the most important development aims is the improvement of income possibilities for the population. This should help to maintain agricultural production, preserve and develop social communities and rural traditions. The agricultural, environmental, tourism and employment, social and infrastructure problems of these regions require an integrated approach in order to identify support possibilities which do not impoverish and depopulate the areas and provide sustainable sources of alternative income generation.

Regions facing *long-term and significant unemployment* are categorised as those where long-term unemployment is more than 133 percent of the national average in 1994, 1995 and 1996. This indicator currently identifies 37 statistical areas. In some regions, this is caused not just by changes in the economic structure but also by the restriction and increasing cost of commuting, potentially resulting in job losses for those people who live in one region but work in another. The support measures for this type of problem have to be applied over larger spatial areas, although targeted intervention to promote transport improvements, job creation, training structures and labour mobility are justified in areas where the problems are particularly severe.

Several *border areas* can be designated under some of the above categories and face similar problems. Border regions face particular difficulties as well as special advantages in terms of their development prospects. The growth of the areas on both sides of the border is linked, and the promotion of cross-border development requires co-operation of the local economies, local governments and economic chambers, and a joint approach to common problems, particularly in the field of environmental protection. A positive example of cross-border co-operation is under the ten-year old Austro-Hungarian Regional Organising and Planning Committee involving the leaders of the relevant local governments. However, a large number of Hungarian border areas linked to neighbouring Ukraine, Slovakia, Romania, Serbia and Croatia are in already underdeveloped regions. The belt of border areas is exposed to some of the highest levels of social stress, exacerbated by the high number of immigrants from neighbouring countries who have moved into these areas to live.

Legal and financial frameworks of Hungarian regional policy

Hungary was among the first of the Central and Eastern European countries to develop a new institutional system for regional development. The milestone legislation in this process was the Act XXI on Regional Development and Physical Planning, adopted by the Hungarian Parliament in 1996. Since this Act came into effect, the institutional system for regional development has been gradually expanded at national, county, regional and sub-regional levels.

The first strategic task at government level was to establish the legal framework for regional policy. The Parliament discussed and adopted a resolution on the principles of regional development subsidies and decentralisation, as well as on area designation criteria, in 1997. Subsequently, the government has re-adjusted the regulations relating to the use of funds for regional development and equalisation purposes. The distribution of subsidies among the counties and the classification of eligible regions have also been revised.

The basic structure of the institutional system for regional development was established by the end of 1996. *County development councils* have been created by the 19 county general assemblies, despite the difficulties associated with the introduction of new and previously unknown institutional structures. The organisation of the county development councils reinforced the self-governing character of the municipalities, and municipality associations were created to ensure their involvement in the drafting of development policies for their areas. These two developments have improved institutional co-operation. At national level, the National Council for Regional Development has been established by the national authorities and the county development councils. It is responsible for making proposals, undertaking co-ordination tasks for the government and, more recently, drafting the National Regional Development Concept.

The next phase in the creation of institutional structures for regional development is the organisation of *regional development councils*. The Development Council of Budapest and the Balaton Development Council, in the Lake Balaton area, were established in 1997, while the wider organisation of regional co-operation has been a bottom-up process initiated by county councils. Regions to be governed by a regional development council must be stable, they must provide an appropriate base for the provision of information and together they should cover the entire Hungarian territory. For these reasons, planning and statistical regions were proposed as a suitable territorial division and, following a Parliamentary resolution in 1998 on the National Regional Development Concept, the country was divided into seven such regions (see Figure 8.4).

The development of a financing system for regional policy is also progressing and, although resources are scarce, the government has steadily increased the funds available for regional development purposes. In 1997, the regional development budget for economic development was approximately HUF 10.4 billion, of which HUF 7 billion came from privatisation income. This budget was increased by a further half billion HUF in 1998. The regional equalisation budget for local authorities was expected to increase from HUF 8-9 billion by 1998 and was designed solely for decentralised decision-making mechanisms. A new source of regional development funding introduced in 1998 was the HUF 4 billion fund for decentralisation subsidies which takes the place of the previously centrally managed budget. County development councils have important responsibilities for the targeting and utilisation of this fund.

The range of regional policy specific instruments is supplemented by corporate tax incentives. Tax incentives were already granted in 1997 for investments over HUF 1 billion in areas with a high rate of unemployment and in enterprise zones. Provisions for investments over HUF 3 billion were added in 1998 and new ten-year tax-on-return incentives are available for socially and economically underdeveloped regions and their centres. Lastly, Parliament has also passed decisions on the support of individual programmes for the development of counties in the most disadvantaged regions.

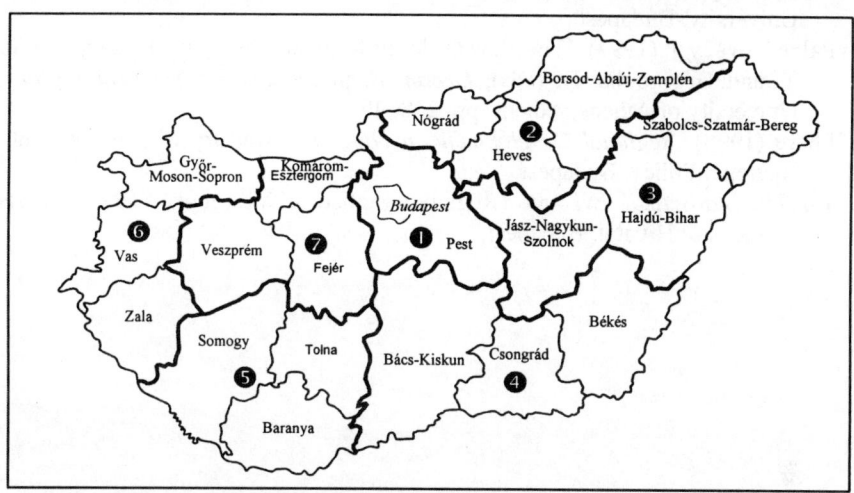

Key: ❶ Central Hungary ❷ North Hungary; ❸ North Great Plain; ❹ South Great Plain; ❺ South Transdanubia; ❻ West Transdanubia; ❼ Middle Transdanubia

Figure 8.4 Planning and statistical regions in Hungary

Note

1 £1 = 406 forints (HUF) (December 1999).

References

Enyedi, G. (1996), *Regionális folyamatok Magyarországon az átmenet időszakában* (Regional processes in Hungary in the transitional period), Hilscher Rezső Szociálpolitikai Egyesület, Budapest.
Government of the Republic of Hungary (1998), *National Regional Development Concept*, Budapest.
Hajdú, Z. (ed) (1998), *Regional Transformation and New Structures in Hungary*, Centre for Regional Studies, Hungarian Academy of Sciences, Pécs.
Horváth, G. (1998), *Regional and Cohesion Policy in Hungary*, Centre for Regional Studies, Hungarian Academy of Sciences, Pécs.
Ministry of Environment and Regional Policy (1997), *Country Profile: Hungary's Regional Development Policy*, Budapest.

Nemes Nagy, J. (1997), *Integration and Transition in Europe*, Eötvös Lóránd University, Budapest.
Pálné Kovács, I. (1997), 'The New Order of Regional Policy in Hungary', in Sellis, T. and Georgoulis, D. (eds), *Urban, Regional and Environmental Planning*, University of Athens, Athens. pp. 238–49.
Phare (1998), *Regional Development in Hungary*, Ministry of Environment and Regional Policy, Budapest.
Területi Statisztikai Évkönyv (Regional Statistical Yearbook) (1997), Központi Statisztikai Hivatal, Budapest.

9 Latvia

RAITA KARNITE

Introduction

The profile of regional development and regional policy issues has been increasing in Latvia in the context of national economic growth and European integration. While Latvia is a small country with relatively homogeneous natural and economic conditions across its territory, regional disparities are still evident. These are most marked at local government level where both well-developed and disadvantaged territories can be found within the same region. At the higher district level, the differences are less pronounced and location appears to play a much larger factor. In this chapter, which analyses the nature of regional disparities as well as the policy response, a broad regional division is used as the basis for analysis. This comprises a set of seven main cities and four groups of administrative districts - Kurzeme (Western Latvia), Zemgale (Southern Latvia), Vidzeme (Northern Latvia) and Latgale (Eastern Latvia) – which are linked to historical regional divisions.

Territorial administrative structure

The administrative division of Latvia (see Figure 9.1) at the start of 1998 comprised seven cities, treated as single-level local governments, 26 districts (upper level local governments), together incorporating 77 towns and 486 civil parishes called *pagasts* (lower level local governments).[1] A comprehensive process of administrative reform is currently on-going in Latvia which is likely to change this structure. The higher level administrative units are currently too small for the implementation of State management functions, although larger administrative units could hinder the ability to implement democratic self-government in rural areas. Administrative territorial reform will need to address these problems, possibly providing for the enlargement of higher level administrative units on a voluntary basis.

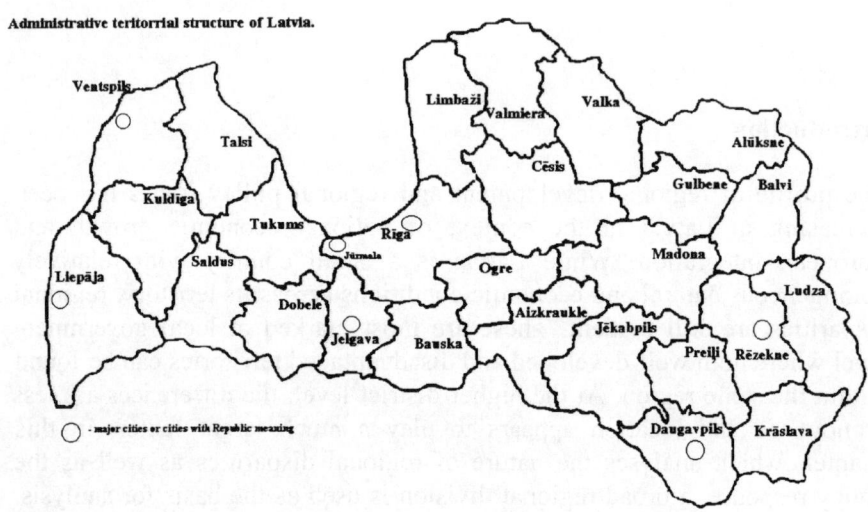

Figure 9.1 Territorial administrative structure of Latvia

The Latvian Regional Development Concept defines a region as a relatively homogeneous area of territory (a group of towns and rural local governments, an administrative district, a group of administrative districts) which have common features or problems. This definition allows the relatively free interpretation of terms such as regional division, regional development, analysis of regional development and so on. The historical division of Latvia into four regions (named above) is also used for planning purposes, although there is no formal institutional reflection of this division. There is currently no single pattern of regional division in Latvia, and different units are used for different purposes eg. administrative structure, internal security, labour service, judicial system, electoral structure etc. Each of these divisions respects the territorial administrative system of the country, although almost all exceed the borders of single administrative districts.

Regional disparities and regional problems

Demography

There are considerable differences in population at local government level, ranging from 89,000 inhabitants in Riga's district to 13,000 in the country's smallest district, Ventspils. The figures for rural districts include their towns in all cases, excepting the seven main cities. The principal cities vary in size from 806,000 inhabitants in Riga to 41,000 in the smallest city of Rezekne. The area of rural districts (but not the historical regions) is relatively even, and it is the differences in living and working environments which characterise regional disparities. The population density in urban areas ranges from 590 to 2,625 inhabitants per km^2 and falls as low 5.7 in rural districts.

The demographic structure of the population is considerably less favourable in rural areas, with marked local differences (see Table 9.1).

Table 9.1 Regional demographic profile of Latvia, 1998

Region	Resident pop'n by region	Structure				Demographic burden[b]
		Total	Below working age	Of working age[a]	Over working age	
Cities	50	100	17	60	23	664
Rural	50	100	22	55	23	794
Kurzeme	10	100	23	55	22	822
Zemgale	5	100	23	58	19	737
Vidzeme	23	100	22	56	22	773
Latgale	12	100	20	55	25	836
Total	100	100	19	58	23	726

Source: Central Statistical Bureau of Latvia, Latvian Statistical Institute, 1998.
Notes: [a]Males aged 15–59 years, females aged 15-55; [b]Population under and over working age per 1,000 population of working age.

This variation is linked to the urbanisation policy of the socialist State and current socio-economic trends. Given higher unemployment levels in rural areas, and in Latgale in eastern Latvia in particular, many job seekers migrate to urban areas in search of work. In the most critical cases, rural *pagasts* have very few or no births per year.

The natural increase in all territories is negative, although this is more pronounced in rural than urban areas. The most marked negative birth rates are in Latgale (see Table 9.2). Latgale comprises five administrative districts and, despite the input of financial and other kinds of support under successive political regimes, has traditionally been and still remains the poorest part of the country.

Table 9.2 Demographic statistics at beginning of 1998 (per 1,000 population)

	Births		*Deaths*		*Natural increase*	
	Min	Max	Min	Max	Min	Max
Cities	6.1	7.5	11.4	14.0	- 7.8	- 4.0
Rural	7.3	10.3	11.4	21.7	-14.4	-2.4
Kurzeme	9.0	10.3	12.8	15.3	- 6.0	- 2.8
Zemgale	9.0	10.3	11.8	15.6	- 5.3	- 2.4
Vidzeme	8.1	9.6	11.4	16.0	- 6.8	- 2.8
Latgale	7.3	9.2	15.0	21.7	- 14.4	- 6.3
Total	7.6		13.6		-6.0	

Source: Central Statistical Bureau of Latvia, 1998.

Unemployment and employment

Unemployment figures (as a percentage of the economically active population) varied at the start of 1998 between 3.1 and 11.8 percent in the cities and 4-29 percent in rural districts (see Table 9.3). Monthly (gross) wages and salaries average 120 LVL^2 nationally, rising to 215 LVL in certain cities and falling to 74 LVL in some rural areas. The lowest figures are generally for Latgale where the ratio of pensioners is highest and the proportion of socially disadvantaged groups is most significant. Table 9.3 shows that the ratio of public sector employees is higher in rural territories and Latgale, corresponding to lower individual economic activity in these areas.

Table 9.3 Key labour market indicators 1997/98

	Wages and salaries, LVL		Employed in public sector		Unemployment at beginning of 1998*	
	Min	Max	Min	Max	Min	Max
Cities	98.3	215.7	41	57	3.1	11.8
Rural:	74.3	121.0	43	68	4.0	29.0
Kurzeme	85.1	102.8	43	59	4.3	10.8
Zemgale	84.0	93.9	46	52	7.0	10.1
Vidzeme	83.3	121.0	43	61	4.0	13.1
Latgale	74.3	88.6	52	68	14.2	29.0
Total	120.0		48		7.0	

Source: Central Statistical Bureau of Latvia, 1998.
Notes: * as percent of economically active population.

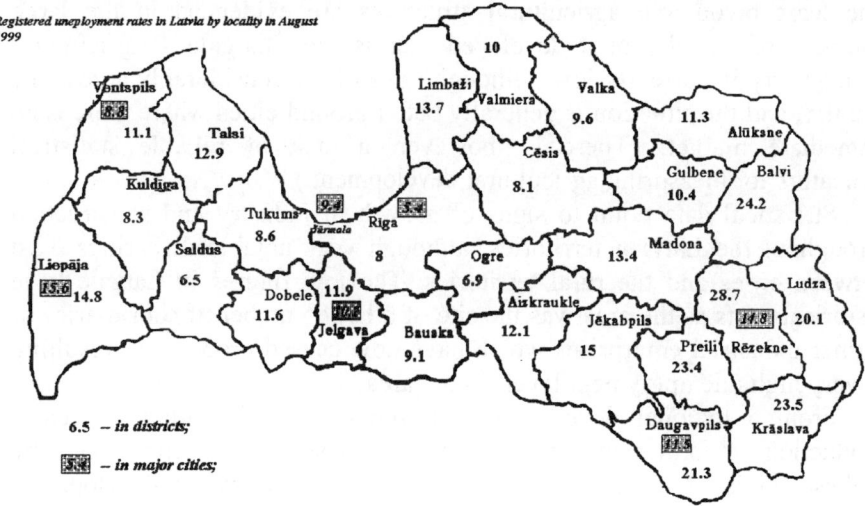

Figure 9.2 Regional registered unemployment in Latvia, August 1999

Economic and sectoral development

It is clear that economic development is an important precondition for the elimination of regional disparities. Regional development patterns in Latvia are greatly influenced by the consequences of the economic development policy implemented by the former socialist State. The most agricultural regions in the country are also the least developed. It is, however, recognised that Latvia is an agricultural country, and both farmers and policy-makers in the post-independence period accept that agriculture is not simply an economic activity but an important lifestyle which must be supported. This approach has hindered the restructuring and modernisation of agriculture and its adaptation to new economic conditions and markets. The liberalisation of prices, low domestic demand, the loss of eastern markets and inaccessibility to western ones and a dramatic fall in production have all negatively affected Latvian agriculture, in addition to its already relatively low starting point. Unfavourable structural patterns, legislative shortcomings and unfair trade further exacerbate this situation. The least favourable agricultural structures are evidenced in the large number of small underdeveloped farms in Latgale. Agricultural productivity is currently low, although rates differ considerably across the country, and the situation is generally better around cities where there is an immediate market. (There is, however, a lack of reliable statistical indicators for measuring agricultural development.)

Statistical data point to signs of growth in industry and construction throughout the Latvian territories, although very notable disparities exist between cities and the rural territories. The low figures in Latgale have historical roots as the area was the site of a large number of subsidiaries of former industrial enterprises which have now ceased production, resulting in very high unemployment levels in the area.

From a regional development viewpoint, it is important to renew production in former industrial centres as these regions often have the highest levels of unemployment. The only way to restore development levels is to restructure the old industrial enterprises into new ones, although this is far from an easy task. One obstacle to this process is the population structure of the regions in question which generally includes a concentration of workers and specialists in one specific form of production. A further difficulty is a lack of investment capital necessary to turn inefficient buildings into a modern industrial infrastructure.

Data relating to the distribution of investment shows that there is a reluctance to invest in the rural territories of the country (see Table 9.4) and the same trend applies to the incidence of foreign direct investment. The latest statistical data from the end of June 1998 show that 47 percent of the FDI stock was concentrated in Riga, with a further 13 percent in the second largest city of Daugavpils (located in Latgale). Taken together, the seven main cities accounted for 67 percent of total FDI with only 11 percent distributed through the rest of the country. Twenty-two percent of the FDI stock is not classified, and therefore may also be concentrated in urban areas. There is a correspondingly higher level of economic activity and performance in the areas with high investment levels (see Table 9.4). Some explanation for these trends may be found in the changing business behaviour resulting from increased competition and globalisation. Globalisation has introduced greater mobility of capital which still tends to be located in regions where the overall economic environment is better. Increasing competition and globalisation therefore can result in a concentration of business resources and activities in developed regions.

Table 9.4 Enterprises registered prior to 1 January 1998 (excluding peasant farms)

	Number of enterprises		Active enterprises	Active enterprises as percent of total	Active enterprises per 1,000 inhabitants
	Total	% of total			
Cities	65,625	70	38,951	59	32
Rural	28,238	30	14,705	52	12
Zemgale	2,613	3	1,210	46	9
Vidzeme	14,679	16	7,930	54	14
Latgale	4,940	5	2,440	49	8
Kurzeme	6,006	6	3,125	52	13
Total	93,863	100	53,656	57	22

Source: Central Statistical Bureau of Latvia, Latvian Statistical Institute, 1998.

Technological progress is another consideration which has to be taken into account in addressing the regional development challenge. New technologies, and information technology in particular, can expand business activities geographically but also sometimes require high levels of communication and skilled workforces. These are not always available in areas distant from business centres.

Infrastructure and welfare

The approach to regional development policy in Latvia is focused on measures which encourage the creation of a favourable economic environment rather than direct financial support in a particular territory. For this reason, one of the main directions of the government's support policy is the development of infrastructure. Latvia inherited a good infrastructure provision from former Soviet times although much of it is now expensive and obsolete. The road network and telecommunications are the most problematic infrastructural components. Latvia is currently implementing a comprehensive programme of telecommunications reform including the development of networks, the modernisation of the state-owned telecommunications company and increased competition in this sector through the promotion of private sector companies. The implementation of the Transport Development Programme in 1997-98 improved the situation of the roads and established a firmer financial basis through the Road Fund. It is important to note that the long-term policy of provision by the former socialist State has resulted in the less-developed regions having a similar, if not better, infrastructure provision than the remainder of the country. The Public Investment Programme is a further important government instrument used to promote regional development which, in addition to transport and communications, also supports the energy sector, environmental protection, education, research and development, welfare and health, common agriculture infrastructure, defence and internal affairs and art.

The education infrastructure is distributed relatively evenly across the country's territory which permits educational access without the necessity to leave the place of residence. However, there is a current trend for young people, following the completion of basic education, to move to business centres and away from the less-developed regions. This has important implications for the non-material aspects of regional policy such as the encouragement of local loyalty and confidence among the population.

In the case of certain welfare indicators such as health care provision and educational resources, Latgale does not differ significantly from the rest of country. Indeed, in terms of the provision of housing and the quality of apartments, Latgale even scores higher than the remainder of Latvia.

This is linked principally to the results of the Latgale development policy undertaken by the socialist State. Indicators which are more linked to individual prosperity, such as passenger car ownership, are again lower for Latgale in national comparison.

Regional policy development

Regional policy has experienced a rapid development over recent years. The Ministry of Environmental Protection and Regional Development is the principal institutional body with responsibilities in this area, and the basic principles of Latvian regional policy are set out in the 'Concept of Latvian Regional Development Policy', adopted by the Cabinet of Ministers in 1996. The Concept stipulated the need for a legislative cornerstone for the country's sustainable development and, accordingly, the law 'Planning for Territorial Development' was adopted at the end of 1998. The main objectives of Latvian regional policy include the elimination of regional disparities and both the provision of balanced development within the country and individual territorial units and the maintenance and promotion of their individual identities. A high proportion of Latvian regional policy measures is focused on territorial and socio-economic planning. The Regional Development Concept underlines the role of local governments as the main actors in development planning.

The Latvian 'Concept for National Planning' is another important document in the field of regional planning and was adopted by the Cabinet of Ministers in January 1998. This Concept is used to determine the optimal approach to exploiting the Latvian territory. Further regulations on territorial planning were passed in February 1998 to improve the legislative basis of the existing planning process and supersede former regulations from this area (dating from 1994). These regulations and laws envisage the State financing of planning measures with local governments having the right to apply to the Ministry for Environmental Protection and Regional Development for grant aid.

Within the framework of regional development policy, particular attention has been paid to the issue of rural development. The Programme for Rural Development, a wide-ranging and comprehensive policy document, was prepared and adopted by the Latvian Parliament in June 1998. Rural development under this Programme is considered a complex of activities including agricultural development and the parallel promotion of other sectors. Rural development requires the close co-operation of sectors and different government levels. The Programme deals principally with rural areas but also includes small towns within its remit.

The stimulus for local governments to initiate planning and improve co-operation with neighbouring units has resulted in the creation of so-called 'planning regions' in Latvia. These comprise an informal amalgamation of local governments working together on regional development projects. These groupings are currently viewed as the potential basis for the future implementation of EU regional policy measures. Latvian local governments are already developing the skills required to participate in EU regional development related cross-border and inter-regional co-operation programmes such as Credo and Ecos-Ouverture.

The creation of the Regional Development Fund in 1997 comprises the principal government measure in the field of regional development. The Fund provides financial grants for eligible regions which could comprise a particular area, local government or group of local governments. In order to determine eligibility, the administrative units are ranked according to a number of indicators: percentage coverage of industry and infrastructure as proportion of the total area; unemployment rate as a percentage of the total working age population; per capita personal income tax; demographic structure; population density; and number of people per 1,000 inhabitants with higher and secondary education at the age of 18 or over. In 1998, the sum of the six criteria varied amongst the 566 Latvian administrative units from 285 (the best) to 4,271 (the worse). The creation of local regional development agencies at a level higher than administrative district and their financial provision is the next step - although this process has only just been initiated.

It is worth noting that the availability and quality of territorial statistics has improved in recent years. Regional development was poorly monitored and reported in the early 1990s with regional statistics covering only administrative districts and cities and then only for certain topics. In 1996 and 1997, the Administration of Local Government Affairs of the Ministry of Environmental Protection and Regional Development issued collections of demographic and financial data for all local governments, and this information has subsequently been incorporated into official statistical issues. In 1998, the monitoring of regional development was renewed and a number of publications were produced including a statistical yearbook on 'Administrative Districts and Major Cities of Latvia'. In parallel with yearbooks, monthly and quarterly regional statistical information is now available. The most critical shortcoming of the existing regional statistics is their lack of detail with only a very few statistical indicators being presented at the level of local administrative unit. The existing coverage of regional statistics is too small for genuine use in the identification of regional problems.

Conclusions

Regional policy in Latvia has undergone a recent period of rapid development. This is having a positive knock-on effect in achieving more balanced regional development within the country. Important regional disparities do exist in Latvia despite the small size of the country and the relatively homogeneous natural and economic conditions. This is particularly noticeable at local level (*pagasts* and towns). The principal broad-brush disparities in Latvia include those between eastern Latvia and the remainder of the country, between urban and rural territories and between the capital city of Riga and the remainder of the country in terms of investment, economic development, education and personal welfare.

The identification of objective reasons for regional disparities in Latvia is a relatively difficult task, and thus the main objective of Latvian regional policy is to achieve balanced economic development throughout the country. Latvia pursues an active regional policy which is expected to provide an equalised economic environment throughout the territories, State support for infrastructure development and the promotion of initiative, self-confidence and responsibility amongst local populations.

A number of key challenges face the future development of regional policy in Latvia. First, the continued modernisation of the country's infrastructure provision, including higher and professional education, is of key importance given its role as a development factor. Progress in this area would contribute to an equalisation of the economic environment. Second, the role of regional local governments in the promotion of regional development needs to be increased. This would require the regions to have institutional decision-making powers, and administrative reform and the co-operation of local governments would be important steps towards achieving this aim. Third, it is necessary to improve the balance between urban and rural development. This is a difficult task for regional policy and requires a new understanding of development factors and a re-evaluation of the significance of individuals for regional development. Lastly, regional policy must incorporate a more international dimension in the light of similar or directly linked regional problems between countries. This forms the basis for cross-border co-operation and new opportunities for regional development.

Notes

1. All data if not otherwise indicated are from 'Administrative Districts and Major Cities of Latvia', Central Statistical Bureau of Latvia, Latvian Statistical Institute, Riga, 1998).
2. £1 = 0.9 lat (LVL) (December 1999).

References

Central Statistical Bureau of Latvia (1998), *Administrative districts and major cities of Latvia*, Latvian Statistical Institute, Riga, p.10.

Central Statistical Bureau of Latvia (1998), *Investment in Latvia*, Quarterly Bulletin, No. 2, Riga, pp 43-48.

Central Statistical Bureau of Latvia (1998), *Towns and Civil Parishes in the Administrative Districts of Latvia - A Collection of Statistical Data*, Latvian Statistical Institute, Riga, Part I, p. 479, Part II, p. 451.

Ministry of Environment Protection and Regional Development (1998), *Regional Development. Legislative Acts, Regulations and Concepts*, Riga, p.110.

The Administration of Local Government Affairs of the Ministry of Environmental Protection and Regional Development (1998), *Local Government Budgets 1997*, Riga.

The Administration of Local Government Affairs of the Ministry of Environmental Protection and Regional Development (1997), *Local Government Budgets 1996*, Riga.

10 Lithuania

EDUARDAS VILKAS

Introduction

Lithuania has entered a stage of fast and stable economic growth following a fundamental social and economic transformation undertaken in highly unfavourable systemic conditions. Despite the economic crisis in Russia, which negatively influenced sales of many Lithuanian products, relatively high GDP growth of ca. five percent was still expected in 1998. The processes of industrial restructuring and modernisation have been particularly intense over the last two years as a result of earlier privatisation and foreign investment. Considerable progress was also achieved in the upgrading of the physical and market infrastructure. Less positively, the current account deficit has approached ten percent of GDP over the last two years.

The transition process has created problems in regional economies as the decline in production has not been evenly spatially distributed and the potential of individual territories for restructuring and growth differs markedly in the medium term. Further, the reform of public administration, including regional administration and self-government has only passed the first stage. The process of territorial administrative reform, as yet incomplete, poses additional difficulties in solving the newly emerging problems of regional economic and social development. This chapter addresses these issues looking initially at overall economic reform and dealing with the impact of the former integration into the Soviet Union before turning in more detail to the regional dimension of economic growth and charge.

Territorial administrative reforms

Lithuania inherited the following administrative territorial units from the Soviet period: 11 towns and 44 regions (*rajonas*), directly responsible to central government, and a further 530 towns and villages (*apylinke*) within these units. All the units had some form of representative council. This territorial structure differed both from current European practice and from the pre-war division in Lithuania, and a new structure was introduced in 1993. This attempted to combine efficient self-government with a system that could be used to implement the socio-economic policies of the government and is modelled on the French example.

The proposal was to create ten new counties, *apskritis,* the governors of which would be appointed by central government, and 93 municipalities with directly elected councils. The relevant law was passed in 1994, together with the required legislation to implement the reform in two main stages.

Figure 10.1 Territorial administrative division of Lithuania into counties (1995)

The first stage, completed in 1995, established the ten counties (named after their principal cities), dissolved the 530 lower level administrative units and transformed the 11 towns and 44 regions into municipalities (see Figure 10.1). Visaginas town was later added as a further municipality.

The ten counties correspond to European standards in size and other parameters, and no plans exist to reorganise them further apart from minor boundary changes. The creation of the municipalities, however, is far from complete and is expected to take at least five years. The next stage will be undertaken in 2000 in conjunction with the municipal elections and will comprise the creation of an additional 11 new municipalities. The number of municipalities will then be further increased, initially to 93 and then to almost double that number, bringing it in line with European standards. The following criteria will be followed in the creation of new administrative units: the population must be 10-12,000; the municipality centre must contain at least 5,000 inhabitants, or 1,800 where the centre is within the suburban area of a city; the distance of the new centre from the current centre should be 20 km.; and the economic potential of the new municipality should not deviate significantly from the national average.

Structural change in the Lithuanian economy

In addition to the classic factors which affect economic structure and growth (natural resources, geographic location, labour force), the impact of centralised planning within the former Soviet economy was very significant for pre-transition economic development patterns in Lithuania. The integrity of regions was neglected and came second to the requirement for inter-ministerial co-operation. Where the regional dimension was important, as in the case of energy, regions much larger than a single Soviet republic were used. Economic development based on such principles resulted in a distortion of natural economic structures and patterns.

The natural resource base and geographic location of Lithuania also influenced the way in which it was developed within the former Soviet system. The principal natural resources in the country are arable land and timber, as well as the raw materials for the production of cement, glass and construction materials. Modest reserves of high-grade oil have also been commercially exploited. However, the focus of Soviet development of Lithuania was agrarian, reinforced by stable climatic conditions suitable for agriculture. The other important locational dimension is the country's position at the junction of Eastern and Western Europe and of key transport corridors with access to the Baltic Sea. Within the confines of Soviet development, the Lithuanian authorities attempted to use Soviet planning practices to develop higher-wage sectors such as electronics, machinery and equipment and military production. Production of final goods in high domestic demand, such as food and light industry goods, was also promoted. Lithuanian planning bodies followed a policy of the uniform development of the entire territory in order to absorb the local rural labour force.

The development of the energy sector is worth noting, focused particularly on oil refining and the production of electricity. Oil production of 12 million tons per year supplied an area much larger than the country itself, where the demand was not even a third of this total. Similarly in the electricity field, a nuclear power station was constructed at Ignalina to compensate for the shortfall in power in the north-western electricity system of the USSR. All primary energy sources – crude oil, gas and nuclear fuel – had to be (and still have to be) imported from Russia. Energy-intensive industries were also developed to exploit the surplus of energy produced. This sector has been significantly affected by the process of economic transition which led to a marked drop in production following price rises for primary resources and the inability of energy users to pay for supplies. Exports were cut almost entirely and, in 1998, the oil refinery and electricity generation facilities were operating at only half capacity. A modernisation of the refinery and the construction of electricity lines into the Western European grid could help to re-achieve full capacity over the next 4-5 years.

The economic impact of transition has been marked in Lithuania. Changing statistical methodologies make comparisons between the early and late 1990s problematic and thus data from 1993 has been used in this analysis. However, the most dramatic economic decline occurred between 1991-92, introducing significant structural change. In 1990, industry accounted for 32.8 percent of GDP, agriculture for 27.6 percent, construction for 10.5 percent and trade for 8.4 percent. The changes in this structure by 1997 are presented in Table 10.1 – the principal trends include a considerable decrease in manufacturing and financial intermediation, which flourished briefly in 1993, and relative gains in construction, trade, real estate, public administration and education.

An important qualitative characteristic of the economic structure is the ability of individual sectors to export their production. The industrial diversity of Lithuania is a positive contributor in this regard, although exports in food, textiles and mineral (oil) products show the largest and fastest growth rates. Other important exported products include fertilisers, pharmaceuticals and enzymes. Export levels are one indicator of the competitiveness of products, although in many areas, this has been negatively affected by the Russian economic crisis.

Table 10.1 Structure of economy by GDP and employment in 1993 and 1997

	Share of GDP %		Employment, %	
	1993	1997	1993	1997
Agriculture and forestry	14.2	12.6	22.5	21.8
Industry	34.2	24.1	25.7	20.0
Mining and manufacturing	30.1	20.8	23.8	17.5
Electricity, gas and water supply	4.1	3.3	1.9	2.5
Construction	5.1	7.3	7.1	7.1
Trade	14.0	16.9	9.7	15.1
Hotels and restaurants	1.3	1.7	1.1	1.3
Transport and communications	9.8	9.2	5.6	5.6
Financial services	7.3	2.4	1.2	1.0
Real estate, renting and business activity	4.2	8.3	2.2	2.4
Public administration and defence	2.9	6.3	3.2	4.1
Education	2.8	5.7	7.7	8.9
Health and social work	1.8	3.2	5.4	6.4
Other service activities	2.4	2.4	8.6	6.2

Source: Statistical Yearbook of Lithuania, 1998.

Lithuania has a relatively well-educated population and, now that the immediate economic crisis is over, is moving towards the objective of developing higher-technology products and increased R&D capacity. A range of high-technology goods is already produced, although R&D-intensive production remains limited. The most promising fields for future development include opto-electronics, bio-technology and precision instruments.

Economic transition reforms

A wide range of legislative changes relating to the liberalisation of economic activity was adopted in the first 2-3 years of transition. Many of these have subsequently been amended or revised, taking the experience of market economic structures or the new demands of EU directives into account. Since 1997, the latter area has had increasing influence on the design and amendment of legislation. The move from the provision of widespread to only limited economic subsidies took approximately six years and now only communal services for the poorest section of the population and some agricultural prices are still subsidised. Recently, State aid rules similar to those of the European Community have been adopted. Restrictions on economic activity only exist in relation to 27 economic activities, for which licences have to be obtained. Customs duties, except for timber, were fully abolished by 1998, and import duties are among the lowest in the transition countries.

The creation of market institutions has been slower than the development of new economic activity due to the requirement for additional organisational and financial investment. Banking and monetary policy was a particular failure in the early transition years. The principal responsible organisation, the Bank of Lithuania, was inefficient in stabilising the financial situation and developing commercial banking. A currency board model was introduced in 1994, and the litas was pegged to the US dollar from April of that year. Plans to move gradually away from the currency board model have been approved, and the currency will be pegged to a basket of the dollar and the euro from 1999. A National Stock Exchange of Lithuania also started trading in late 1993. The banking and monetary system is now stabilising, following the bankruptcy of more than ten commercial banks and serious crisis at the end of 1995, and even the recent Russian crisis did not have a serious destabilising effect.

One of the most successful components of economic reform in Lithuania has been the privatisation process. Mass voucher-based privatisation started in September 1991 and, by 1993, more than half of the economy (in terms of production and employment) and virtually all residential housing and agricultural properties had moved into private ownership. The voucher privatisation, which excluded large infrastructure enterprises, was completed by mid-1995. Commercial privatisation was initiated in 1996 and the privatisation of infrastructure was emphasised the following year. Overall, the privatisation process was due to be completed during 1999 with the exception of Lithuanian Railways and the electricity supply system, both of which require essential restructuring and management reform in advance.

Regional disparities in economic contraction and growth

Stable economic growth, which started in 1995, is anticipated to continue for at least a decade at an annual rate of 5-7 percent of GDP - although the Russian crisis has made this projection less certain. In addition to growth factors identified in previous sections, foreign investment and the development of physical infrastructure are expected to play a key role in both national and regional economic growth. However, it is also exactly these factors which may exacerbate the regional disparities which have been emerging in the economic development of Lithuania.

In *demographic* terms, Lithuania is a relatively small country with only 3.7 million inhabitants, 68 percent of whom live in urban areas. The introduction of political and economic reform has reversed demographic trends in the Soviet era, and the country is now experiencing negative natural growth as well as negative net migration (although a positive balance was recorded in 1997). This migration pattern is influenced by the two-way repatriation process following the country's independence and the collapse of the Soviet Union. The ethnic composition of the population is over 80 percent Lithuanian, with eight percent being Russian and a further seven percent Polish. Regional demographic data are presented in Table 10.2. Positive natural growth rates are evident only in the western part of the country, and the highest rate of depopulation is in the north-eastern county of Utena.

Economic contraction during the transition period has affected regions differently. The regions worst hit tended to be those dominated by a single small number of large enterprises which either went bankrupt or significantly reduced their production. Simultaneously, economic renewal in these regions is more difficult because of their disadvantaged situation in relation to the attraction of investment as well as unfavourable longer-term growth factors. Unfortunately, the regional share of GDP is not available as a statistical indicator in Lithuania although it would best show the relative economic development at regional level.

The overall trends affecting total *employment* comprise a reduction of jobs in agriculture and the creation of new jobs in the services sector.

Employment in industry and construction combined changed relatively little over the period 1995-97 (see Table 10.3).

Table 10.2 Population and unemployment by counties

Region	Pop'n '000	Density per sq. km.	Natural increase		Net migration		Unemployment	
			'94	'97	'94	'97	'94	'98
Alytus	202.3	37.3	-0.5	-1.2	126	79	4.6	8.7
Kaunas	754.2	92.4	-1.3	-0.4	-675	-556	2.4	4.7
Klaipeda	415.5	72.3	0.8	0.5	-276	-82	4.4	5.4
Marijampole	198.6	44.5	-1.3	0.2	127	2	2.4	8.1
Panevezys	322.5	41.0	-2.0	-1.4	-53	-386	4.7	8.0
Siauliai	401.9	45.9	-0.6	-0.5	-162	315	4.6	9.5
Taurage	130.2	33.6	0.2	-1.2	-398	27	9.7	8.5
Telsiai	182.6	44.1	2.3	0.8	-205	-203	2.9	6.8
Utena	202.4	28.1	-4.9	-4.9	736	207	4.4	6.4
Vilnius	895.4	92.8	-1.3	-1.6	-2,600	612	3.2	5.4
Lithuania	3,705.6	56.8	-1.0	-0.9	-2,582	-7	3.8	6.5

Sources: Districts of Lithuania, 1997, 1998.

Clearly, the actual number of jobs is not the only important feature affecting the regional labour force. The value-added of jobs also differs around the country, partly reflected in monthly earnings. In 1997, average monthly earnings per job were highest in more urban counties such as Vilnius (928 litas[1]) and Klaipeda (843 litas) and fell to 656 litas in Taurage and 653 litas in Marijampole.[1] Utena had the second highest rate (866 litas) principally because of the high wages paid at the Ignalina nuclear power station. The Mazeikiai oil refinery had the same skewing effect on wage levels in the county of Telsiai. These averages also hide the most depressed former *rajonas* along the state border including Skuodas, Akmene, Zarasai, Ignalina, Svencionys and Lazdijai. These municipalities have poor conditions both for agriculture and for the development of industry and services. Special support is required, with financial assistance from development funds and the input of expertise, to develop non-traditional small business activity in these areas.

The counties most affected by unemployment include Siauliai, Alytus and Taurage where large electronics and machinery enterprises have gone bankrupt and new businesses are slow to appear. The unemployment rate in

Utena has also increased over the last four years from 3.8 to 6.5 percent. The official unemployment data, based on the statistics of the Labour Exchange, do not take unregistered unemployment into account. According to a survey carried out by the Statistics Department, the real national unemployment rate is much higher - 17.4 percent instead of the officially quoted 3.5 percent in September 1994 and 14.3 percent instead of 6.2 percent in May 1998.

Table 10.3 Employed population by economic activity (annual average, '000)

Region	Agric., hunting & forestry		Industry		Construction		Services	
	'95	'97	'95	'97	'95	'97	'95	'97
Alytus	25.8	17.9	19.3	21.6	5.6	5.5	29.1	39.1
Kaunas	65.9	62.9	76.0	72.3	25.4	26.9	155.6	172.0
Klaipeda	29.6	26.6	36.9	31.1	14.0	13.8	107.1	116.0
Marijam-pole	34.1	30.2	12.0	13.3	5.0	4.7	28.8	32.4
Panevezys	48.5	43.5	31.9	32.6	9.5	9.1	59.8	60.8
Siauliai	54.8	53.6	28.4	25.6	11.6	9.9	83.9	89.7
Taurage	19.3	19.3	5.4	4.7	2.4	2.0	24.9	26.3
Telsiai	18.3	16.7	18.6	18.7	6.5	7.2	32.7	33.9
Utena	31.1	25.9	17.1	17.8	9.1	8.5	31.5	36.7
Vilnius	62.6	66.4	102.9	96.3	25.6	31.1	237.0	246.6
Lithuania	390.0	363.0	348.5	334.0	115.0	119.0	790.4	854.0

Source: Districts of Lithuania. Economic and social development, 1998.

The inflow of foreign direct investment (FDI) is gradually increasing and is likely to grow further as continued economic reform is carried out. Lithuanian statistics on FDI do not include State or State-guaranteed loans and portfolio investment which is less than one-tenth of a company's shares. Per capita FDI in 1991 was only US$ 2.25 and remained relatively low until 1995 (US$ 94.7). By 1996, per capita FDI had increased considerably to US$ 189 and US$ 281 in 1997. Preliminary data suggest that, in 1998, total FDI of US$ 2 billion, or a per capita figure of US$ 540, came into Lithuania in 1998 from EU countries. The regional disparities in FDI receipts are very stark, with Vilnius accounting for over 50 percent of the total and a further 13 percent each flowing into Kaunas and Klaipeda. The remaining 22 percent is spread over the other seven counties.

It is clear that political and economic transition has introduced regional disparities into what was formerly a uniformly developed territory. The comparative advantages of regions differ considerably and some are much more able to attract investment than others. Vilnius, as the capital, together with the seaport of Klaipeda, for example, are the clear leaders in terms of investment attractiveness.

Regional policy response

The emerging regional disparities are currently not very severe but the government has introduced some measures in awareness of them. State sectoral programmes, as well as programmes supporting areas such as SMEs and tourism, offer regionally differentiated awards for investors to support more disadvantaged regions. Further, in 1998, the government passed a decree on the principles of regional policy which will form the basis for a future law in this area. According to the decree, a National Council for Regional Development will be created, as well as corresponding councils and agencies at county level. These institutions will implement regional development plans and programmes using appropriate legal, economic and financial measures.

Note

1   £1 = 6.4 litas (December 1999).

References

Department of Statistics (1998a), *Foreign direct investment in Lithuania*, no. 01, Vilnius.
Department of Statistics (1998b), *Survey of Lithuanian economy*, no. 2, Vilnius.
OECD (1998), *Investment Guide for Lithuania*, Centre for Co-operation with Non-Members, Paris.
Vilkas, E. (1997), 'Computations of General Equilibrium: Lithuanian Energy', *Monetary Studies*, vol. 1, no. 1, pp. 51-60.

11 Poland

GRZEGORZ GORZELAK

Introduction

Poland covers a relatively large territorial area (312,000 km^2) and is highly regionally differentiated, manifested in geography and landscape, demography, economy, culture and politics. Two major factors are centrally responsible for this differentiation - structural issues, often of a historical nature, and the urban-rural dimension – and their interaction shapes the structure of the Polish territory. This chapter presents a brief review of the historical dimension of the Polish regional structure before looking in more detail at the regional impact of the process of economic transformation which has taken place during the 1990s. It highlights some of the most important aspects of regional transformation before concluding with a brief overview of the regional policy response and the related process of administrative decentralisation.

Territorial administrative structure

The territorial organisation of the state was fundamentally changed after 1989 in two steps. First, self-government was introduced at local level in 1989 and, second, since 1999, it has been introduced at the intermediate and regional levels. The current structure of the Polish territorial administrative structure is illustrated in Figure 11.1 and includes the following.
- There are 16 regional units (*voivodships*) with a strong, directly elected, self-government and presided over by a marshall. Parallel to the self-governmental authorities, there is a government administration, headed by the *voivod* and nominated by the prime minister which is responsible for the implementation of State policies (which should be limited to policing duties, i.e. the maintenance of national standards etc.) Big *voivodships* assume many of the current responsibilities of the

national government, a situation which would make the central government smaller but stronger. They will also be able to undertake new tasks which are currently not carried out at all including the creation of regional systems of innovation, technology transfer centres, international promotion etc.
- Over 300 fully self-government districts are taking on some of the responsibilities previously performed by the 49 old *voivodships* (such as post-graduate education, roads, employment services etc.).
- Over 2,500 local self-government units (*gminas*) continue to be responsible for basic service delivery to the population, as well for basic technical local infrastructure. None of the competencies of the *gminas* has been transferred up to the districts.

Figure 11.1 Administrative division of Poland from 1 January 1999

Poland is the only post-socialist country which has introduced a full decentralisation reform of its territorial organisation. Despite the shortcomings of the new system, which should gradually be eliminated as the decentralisation deepens, the self-government system has proved its virtues and has been a good framework for democracy and the efficient management of public funds. However, as in economic processes, the performance of local governments is strongly differentiated and follows the general east-west divide of Poland. This differentiation is likely to deepen further the regional and local disparities in the country.

Recent processes of economic transformation

Poland has undergone rapid and deep post-socialist transformation since 1990 which, to date, has generally been successful and has embraced all walks of socio-economic life (see Table 11.1). The Polish economy shifted from the so-called planned system to a market economy, and expanded its external linkages from the closed framework of the former COMECON to the open global market.

The post-socialist transformation should be regarded as a 'normal' process of technological and organisational change, undertaken later than would have been the case if Central Europe (and other socialist countries) had been incorporated earlier into the global economy. The decline in economic output, which occurred in the post-socialist countries after 1990, was the price of restructuring similar to that which the West paid during its change of socio-economic structures after 1973. To a great extent, the Polish success is based on the radical nature of early reforms, among the harshest of the post-socialist block, which set the Polish transformation on a firm footing. Poland has gone through one of the steepest J-curves with a corresponding potential for the future. The accelerated process of transformation to a market economy has reaped positive benefits, and Poland is gaining international confidence with the majority of Poles finding their place within the new political and economic framework. The economic decline in Poland was part of the necessary adaptation to new internal and external conditions. It was the result of superimposing a post-Fordist organisation of economic, social and political life onto a structure shaped by a Fordist paradigm of development. However, along with other post-socialist countries, Poland is now catching up with the rest of the developing world as the process of restructuring continues.

Table 11.1 Economic development trends in Poland, 1989-1997 (previous year=100)

Categories	1989	1990	1991	1992	1993	1994	1995	1996	1997
Gross Domestic Product	100.2	88.4	93.0	102.6	103.8	105.2	106.5	106.1	106.9
Industrial production	99.5	75.5	92.0	102.8	106.4	112.1	109.4	108.3	110.8
Agricultural production	111.0	99.7	106.8	87.7	108.0	89.2	117.8	99.1	101.7
Fixed capital formation	97.9	89.4	95.6	102.3	102.9	109.2	126.0	120.3	120.2
Consumption	104.9	84.3	107.5	103.5	104.8	103.9	104.1	107.5	106.2
Exports	100.2	113.7	97.6	97.4	98.9	118.3	116.7	109.7	113.7
Imports	101.5	82.1	137.8	113.9	118.5	113.4	120.3	128.0	122.0
Foreign investment	.	.	185.0	233.0	253.0	109.3	195.0	142.0	.
Working pop. (total)	99.0	97.3	94.1	95.8	90.9	101.1	100.3	101.9	101.9
Working pop. (public)[a]	.	93.1	85.4	89.1	103.4	95.1	95.7	96.2	93.7
Working pop. (private)[a]	.	102.1	104.8	102.4	103.6	105.5	103.3	107.1	105.3
Unemployment rate	.	6.3	11.8	13.6	13.7	16.0	14.9	13.2	10.5
Inflation*	351.0	686.0	171.1	142.4	134.6	130.7	126.8	119.8	113.3
Households' real income	.	.	100.6	98.7	99.2	100.6	101.9	106.4	.
Households' real outlays	.	.	104.2	97.2	102.5	96.9	97.8	105.9	.

Source: Roczniki Statystyczne (Statistical Yearbooks), 1990-1998.
Notes: * December-to-December basis.

The regional patterns of the Polish transformation

The spatial development of Poland has been shaped by historical factors as far back as the pattern of urbanisation in the 13th and 15th centuries. Other factors, including the nature of the industrialisation process of Polish cities last century and the administration of Polish territory between 1795 and 1918 by three separate powers (Russia, Prussia and Austria), have also had a significant influence. The different developmental conditions of the three territories, which in 1918 joined to form the independent Polish state, left behind deep traces in the level of economic development, the infrastructure (roads, railways), the level of urbanisation, the legal system, the education and attitudes of the population and the cultural landscape. After World War II, Poland's borders were shifted westward at the expense of the eastern (and less developed) territories.

The historical processes created the following divisions within the Polish spatial structure:
- the territories situated west of Vistula, long under the influence of the West, which undoubtedly constitute a part of Western Europe;
- the territories situated east of the line dividing Slavic Christendom into two parts: western (Roman-Catholic) and eastern (Orthodox), under the influence of the East, and which belong to Eastern Europe;
- the territories between these two historical borders, constituting a 'transitional area' in which the influences of Western and Eastern Europe are intertwined and have jointly shaped their social, economic and spatial structures.

The East-West division is nothing strange in this part of Europe. In the Czech and Slovak Republics this has been a traditional spatial pattern, shaped by the long history of these territories. In Hungary it emerged after 1990, and replaced a historical division of the country across the line which separated better developed regions in the north-western part of the country from the less-developed ones in the south-eastern part. Nowadays, the Danube river is the main line of division of Hungary.

The post-socialist transformation has also had a clear regional pattern, with certain regions appearing better prepared for the new economic conditions and others less able to adjust. Not surprisingly, the historically more developed regions display better adaptability to the competitive, open economy. Their richer and more modern economic structure, higher qualified labour force, and better institutional and physical infrastructure make them more attractive to both domestic and foreign investors (see Figure 11.2). As a result, structural changes have been deeper in these regions and the dynamics of transformation greater.

In general, the level of development of the *urban* areas is higher than that of the *rural* ones. This is particularly true of the big cities which are evenly distributed over the country's territory, although relatively less densely in the East. These cities comprise the nodal system of the economic, scientific and cultural life of the country. Virtually all the positive elements of the process of transformation, including institution-building, the rapid growth of university education, foreign linkages[1] etc, were concentrated in the largest urban centres of Poland. In the education field, for example, nine academic centres account for over 70 percent of students and 80 percent of faculties. The qualitative dimension of transformation is even more concentrated spatially than the quantitative one. Warsaw, for example, is the location for less than a third of national R&D staff, but 38 percent of all professors working in the country (in Kraków these figures are 11 and 13 percent, and in Wrocław 7.5 and 10 percent, respectively). Warsaw, Kraków, Poznań and Wrocław may currently be considered European cities and, assuming the continued success of the Polish transformation, these cities may improve their position in the ranking of Europoles. Szczecin, Gdańsk and Lublin belong to the Polish 'second division', although these cities play an important role as supra-regional centres of national importance. In the case of Lublin, this is more future potential and will depend to a great degree on developments of Poland's easterly neighbours. Katowice and Łódź, as old industrial regions, are currently in the process of transition.

The traditional rural-urban split has become even more evident than was the case within the industry-driven planned economy of the socialist system - related to the fact that Polish *agriculture* in general comprises one of the weakest sectors of the national economy. It is also the sector which has the greatest regional differentiation. Polish agriculture is characterised by three different types of production structure:

- Large farms of several hundred (or even a few thousand) hectares, based on hired labour and functioning according to the principles of a capitalist enterprise. This type prevails in north-western Poland, where the huge State farms, after a few years of decline, transferred into private hands and, in general have good future prospects for improved efficiency and development.
- Big, dynamic family farms (up to few hundred hectares), functioning in accordance with the principles of the free market and aspiring to the family enterprise model. This type of agriculture is concentrated in the mid-western region of Wielkopolska which has the greatest tradition of high agricultural culture in Poland.
- Numerous small farms (1-5 hectares), with primarily social (self-provision, reproduction of a certain lifestyle) and psychological functions (sense of security in uncertain times). This type prevails in south-eastern Poland, where the farms are smallest and hidden rural unemployment is highest - while in the central and north-eastern parts of the country the farms are larger (though far less effective than in Wielkopolska). In north-eastern regions, the rural areas are subject to rapid de-population as a result of out-migration.

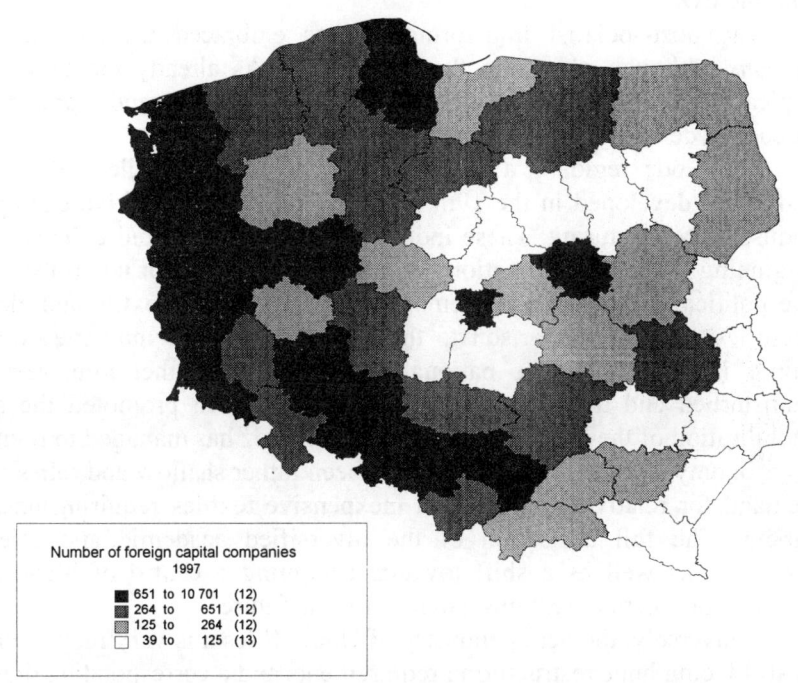

Figure 11.2 Companies with foreign capital in Poland, 1997

The regional structure of agriculture is an important aspect of the Polish transformation as this sector will present particularly sensitive problems in relation to Poland's accession to the European Union. Paradoxically, it is unlikely to be the regions with the weakest agricultural structure which will be most endangered by accession – although this is the perception of current EU Member States. The agricultural products of the small subsistence farms are not sold on the domestic, and certainly not the international, market and therefore their impact on an enlarged EU would be negligible. However, the global-market conditions will immediately influence the largest Polish food-producers, and, at the same time, these producers will create a competitive threat for their counterparts in the EU. It is, therefore, not the weakness but the strength of Polish agriculture which is likely to cause the difficulties in the future integration of Poland into the EU.[2]

The post-socialist transformation has embraced the *old industrial regions*, although not all in the same way. As already mentioned, two typical examples include Łódź (a case of rapid change) and Upper Silesia (a case of delayed industrial change).

The Łódź region - a traditional centre of the textile and clothing industries developed in the 19th century - provides a positive example of industrial restructuring. These industries underwent a rapid collapse at the beginning of the transformation period. There was little or no protection for the politically weak, mostly female, workforce in the textile and clothing factories and, in comparison to the coal mines, these industries were of minor importance to the national economy. Łódź, therefore, remained undisturbed and this was one of the factors which promoted the social mobilisation of the regional and local elites. Łódź has managed to revitalise its economy, although this process has been rather shallow and relies on the demand for relatively simple and inexpensive textiles requiring unskilled labour. The full utilisation of the diversified academic and scientific structure, as well as a shift towards becoming a centre of high-quality garment production, remains a matter for the future.

Conversely, the heavy industry of Upper Silesia is very inefficient and is still facing huge restructuring requirements and a corresponding dramatic decline in employment. Despite the requirement for extensive subsidies and the problem of excessive supply, the extraction of hard coal increases annually. This is partly a result of a lack of political will and determination by consecutive post-socialist Polish governments which have been afraid of the political consequences of bold or radical attempts to change these obsolete regional economic structures. As both European and American experiences prove, however, the more postponed the adjustment of employment in a region, the more dramatic and far-reaching the future employment reductions and the higher the social costs will be. A costly, but perhaps finally effective, regional restructuring programme has only very recently been introduced. It proposes the provision of major payments (up to 40 times average monthly wages) to those miners who take voluntary redundancy, as well as covering the cost of mine closures, industrial site recovery and the re-development of the regional infrastructure. Even under this programme, regional restructuring will take several years and the later the process is initiated, the more difficult and expensive it is likely to become.

Regional polarisation has been an obvious result of the transformation process. This polarisation is apparent even when the lagging regions demonstrate a positive rate of growth given that this is generally lower than the corresponding progress in more dynamic areas. In economic-statistical terms, Poland is a country with relatively mild regional disparities. The ratio of GDP per inhabitant of the poorest and the richest regions (see Figure 11.3), for example, based on the division of the country into the former 49 *voivodships*, was approximately 1:2.5 - much less than in countries such as Italy or Spain assuming their division into a similar number of regions. The statistical inter-regional disparities are slightly smaller under the new regional division of the country into 16 units, although intra-regional differences have become higher (as much as 4:1 in one of the new regions - see Table 11.2).

Assuming the truth of the thesis that organisational and technological imports from the West will remain a key factor in the modernisation of Central Europe (as has been the case in recent years), the *East-West split* will shape the future regional structure of Poland (and its Central European neighbours), reinforcing the trends towards spatial polarisation. There are also no signs that the peripheral, backward regions will achieve a faster rate of growth than the Polish metropoles - on the contrary, it seems that, within the new quality and innovation-driven development paradigm, less-developed regions have an even smaller chance of catching-up than would have been the case within an industrial development paradigm. As a result, the urban-rural split is likely to become increasingly strong within the Polish space.

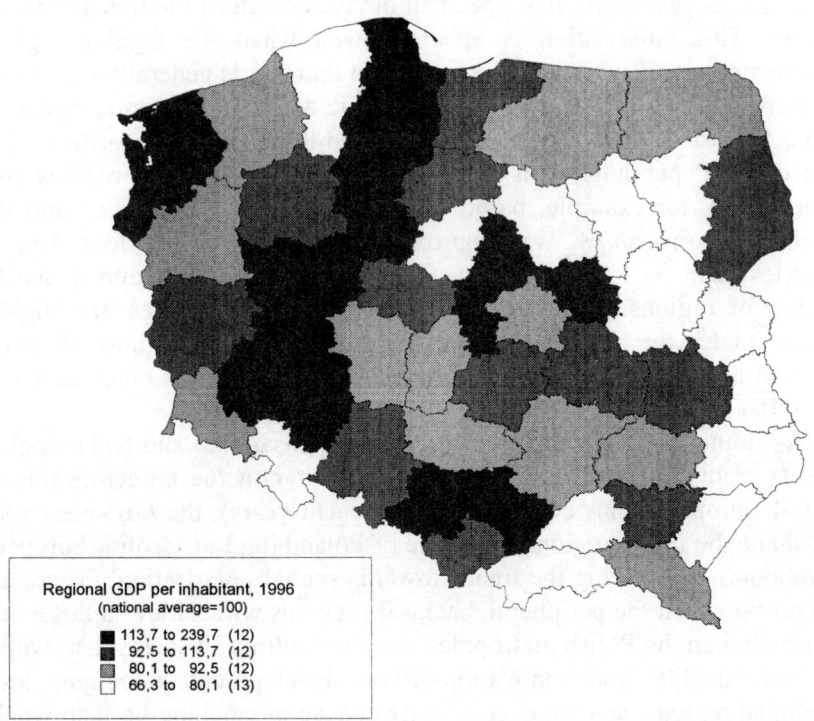

Figure 11.3 Regional GDP per inhabitant, 1996 (national average=100)

Regional policy

Over the last few decades, the regional policy of the Polish state has been more formal than real. Programmes of regional development, often of very different quality, were formulated by appropriate government agencies and the principles of regional policy were drafted, although few were put into practice. In the 1970s, when capital formation was considerably greater, central authority decisions overruled any spatial considerations of the planning bodies. In the 1980s, little was done in the Polish socio-economic space as the socialist system, in the throes of collapse, attempted to prove its ability to create economic development. The liberal approach of the

1990s has also left little room for regional policy, and the weak measures undertaken under this heading have taken a reactive and passive approach, intervening where the process of transformation has created serious problems, generally based on the criterion of unemployment.

To date, no institution responsible for the formulation and implementation of national regional policy has been created in Poland. Certain central government departments do distribute considerable amounts of public resources among particular regions but with a wholly unco-ordinated approach. As a result, there is a wide redistribution of resources through the central budget - public revenue comprises almost 50 percent of GDP, of which over 60 percent (30 percent of total GDP) goes through the central budget. In general, richer regions lose and poorer regions gain from this redistribution, but this is the result of sectoral (vertical) policies with little territorial (horizontal) co-ordination.

The discussion about an appropriate regional policy model for Poland, adequate for the future accession of the country to the European Union, is taking on an increasingly high profile. Although not openly admitted by government officials, the old equity-efficiency dilemma has to be resolved, albeit within new economic and political conditions. As elsewhere, politicians prefer to avoid the issue of efficiency, preferring to talk about regional equalisation. This is problematic for a number of reasons. First, it appears that, within the new knowledge-driven development paradigm, the equity goal is increasingly difficult to achieve, and efficiency is becoming more widespread as better responses are made to contemporary challenges. Second, the intervention of European Union regional policy, itself currently under reform, will increasingly influence the Polish policies in a way which is currently difficult to foresee.

Third, the decentralisation reform has a significant bearing on regional development and policy in Poland. Since 1999, the regions themselves, now politically and economically stronger, undertake several responsibilities previously restricted to national government. However, as the abilities of the regional and local political élite vary, the activities of different bodies of the territorial self-government will result in differentiated development trajectories among individual territorial units. The wiser will become richer, and the less able will not be in a position to cope with the challenges of the global, competitive economy. The development chances of new big Polish regions are summarised in Table 11.2.

Finally, in the new decentralised system, it will be the principal responsibility of the regions themselves to decide how regional potential can best be utilised. The central government should intervene in the regions only when such intervention would be beneficial for the whole country. The construction and modernisation of major transportation corridors, enhancing trans-border co-operation, assisting the regions in developing their educational and R&D potential, for example, are among the activities which could increase the international competitiveness of the Polish regions - and, as result, the competitiveness of the country as a whole.

Table 11.2 Strengths and weaknesses of the new Polish regions

Regional capitals (new region)	Strengths	Weaknesses
Białystok (podlaskie) a=72 b=2.1*	Clean environment. Higher education. Border location. Tourist potential.	Peripheral location. High share of agriculture. Low educational level.
Bydgoszcz–Toruń (kujawskopomorskie) a=84 b=2.4	Favourable location on North-South axis. Higher education.	Internal periphery. Deteriorated urban structures. Inefficient transport infrastructure. Conflicts within the regional elite.
Gdańsk (pomorskie) a=100 b=2.6	Maritime location. Big harbour. Cultural heritage. Tourist potential. International airport.	Deteriorated urban structures. Inefficient transport infrastructure.
Katowice (śląskie) a=115 b=2.6	Good transport connections. Higher education and R&D potential. Big urban agglomeration. Industrial traditions.	Derelict industrial and urban structures. Heavy pollution. Low educational level.
Kielce (świętokrzyskie) a=69 b=2.2	Central location.	Low endogenous potential. Poor infrastructure. Deteriorated rural space. Low educational level. Internal periphery.
Kraków (małopolskie) a=90 b=2.9	Cultural heritage. Positive image. Tourist potential. Higher education and R&D potential. International airport.	Deteriorated urban structure. High pollution in the city.
Lublin (lubelskie) a=73 b=2.7	Higher education. Border location.	Peripheral location. High share of agriculture. Low educational level.
Łódź (łódzkie) a=94 b=2.8	Higher education, R&D potential. Central location. Proximity of Warsaw.	Deteriorated urban structure. Shallow restructuring. "Shadow" of Warsaw.
Opole (opolskie) a=86 b=1.8	Location between two major metropoles. Rich infrastructure. Industrial traditions. Contacts with Germany.	Low endogenous potential. Pollution.
Olsztyn (warmińsko-mazurskie) a=77 b=2.2	Clean environment. Tourist potential.	Peripheral location. High share of agriculture. Low educational level.

Regional capitals (new region)	Strengths	Weaknesses
Poznań (wielkopolskie) a=108 b=2.1	Western location. Higher education. R&D potential. Organisational skills and traditions. Diversified economic structure. International airport. Good image.	Inefficient transport infrastructure. Deteriorated urban structure.
Rzeszów (podkarpackie) a=75 b=3.0	Higher education. Clean environment. Tourist potential.	Peripheral location. Poor infrastructure. Low educational level. Difficult restructuring of agriculture.
Szczecin (zachodniopomorskie) a=97 b=2.4	Proximity to Berlin. Maritime location. Big harbour.	Inefficient transport infrastructure. Deteriorated urban structure.
Warsaw (mazowieckie) a=151 b=4.2	National capital. Higher education. R&D potential. Cultural heritage. Diversified economic structure. International airport.	Deteriorated urban structure. Chaotic urban development. Inefficient transport infrastructure.
Wrocław (dolnośląskie) a=94 b=2.0	Higher education. R&D potential. Diversified economic structure. Cultural heritage. Tourist potential. Western location.	Deteriorated urban structure.
Zielona Góra (lubuskie) a=86 b=1.7	Border location. Tourist potential.	External periphery. Inefficient transport infrastructure.

Notes: *a=GDP per inhabitant, Poland=100, 1997 and b=highest/lowest value of GDP per inhabitant in districts within a given region, 1997.

Notes

1 Over 30 billion dollars came to Poland as direct foreign investment. In 1998 this inflow equalled to US$10 billion, over 50 percent more than in 1997.
2 Restructuring of Polish agriculture will remain the internal task of Poland, and EU funds should not be regarded as compulsory aid for Poland from the common budget.

12 Romania

IOAN IANOS

Introduction

Romania can be classified as one of Europe's medium-sized countries with a surface area of over 235,000 km^2 and a population of 22.5 million and is the second largest Central and East European country after Poland. The country is characterised by considerable territorial diversity due to its socio-economic disparities, the wide range of natural conditions and its location at the crossroads both of different climatic and cultural systems. Romania has achieved a limited degree of success in the implementation of political and economic reforms and, although this has fallen short of original expectations, the relatively low starting point in comparison to other CEE countries should not be forgotten. Particular barriers to the transition to a market economy have included the absence of an adequate political, economic and social legislative base, resistance to change both among the population and certain socio-economic actors, and ambiguity in the setting of priorities.

One goal of economic policies and the creation of a new institutional and legal framework in Romania is to facilitate the integration of the country into wider European political and economic structures. Ensuring the role of regional development within this process is viewed as an increasingly important political objective – both to bridge existing economic gaps and to help prevent the emergence of future problems. It is clear that regional disparities do exist in Romania and the process of transition and restructuring is, if anything, encouraging their deepening. This chapter reviews the process of economic transition to date, before focusing in more detail on the regional disparity situation and the evolving regional policy response.

The current state of transition

In common with other CEE countries, Romania faced considerable political, economic and social challenges following the fall of the totalitarian regime at the end of 1989. This challenge was exacerbated by the particular severity of the former dictatorship. At a political level, a series of key events showed progress in this area including the adoption by referendum of a new constitution at the end of 1991 and free presidential and governmental elections in 1992 and again in 1996. These events have helped to secure popular belief in the growth of democracy in the country.

In the economic field, an initial analysis shows sharp GDP decline in the first 2-3 years of the transition period followed by economic growth from 1993 onwards. This is, however, misleading as it hides continued policies of industrial and energy subsidies, price and currency exchange control and debt protection. In fact, the economic trends had more similarities to experience in other CEE countries, with sharp production decline in the initial years and the emergence of mass unemployment, exacerbated by a sharp rise in the number of people entering retirement. Rural commuters and the workforces of large manufacturing plants located in rural areas under the socialist planning system were initially the worst affected by unemployment. Machine-building and textiles were sectors particularly hit following the collapse of foreign and especially CMEA markets.

Economic policy measures and the privatisation and restructuring drives of 1993 and 1994 did have some effect, with unemployment falling from 11 percent in 1994 to 6.6 percent in 1996. The private sector has also increased, contributing 52.5 percent of GDP in 1996. The implementation of reforms at enterprise level was hampered by the philosophy that a lack of resources and the changing economic conditions made it necessary for economic restructuring to precede privatisation. This contributed in part to the fact that the structure of economic activities did not change significantly, apart from a slight rise in service sector activities. Small and medium-sized enterprises, however, grew in number, particularly in trade and service industries, although the adverse economic conditions meant that the death rates were also very high. The emergence of medium-sized firms in particular was also related to the restructuring of large firms and their sub-division into a higher number of smaller units.

A new approach to economic development was undertaken from 1997, focusing on privatisation and economic reform. Important subsidies for mining, inefficient industries and State farms were withdrawn, resulting in falls in production and GDP as well as high inflation. This move was very important and marked an important step away from continued heavy State intervention in the economy. The State remains an important owner, however, in the mining and energy sectors and the privatisation of transport systems has only just begun. New privatisation legislation introduced in 1998 is a further attempt to speed up the process and change the underlying ownership structures in the country.

Foreign direct investment into Romania totalled ca. US$3 billion between 1990 and March 1998. Joint venture capital is concentrated in productive activities, trade, services and construction. The main investor countries include Germany, the Netherlands, Italy, South Korea, France and the USA. In common with all the CEE countries, foreign investment activity is focused on the capital city (accounting for 56 percent of total capital investment) and better developed regions such as Dolj, Timis and Constanta – although these regions have significantly lower shares of generally less than five percent. Continued economic reform and legislative changes are anticipated to improve conditions for foreign investment.

Territorial administrative structure

Romania is currently divided into 41 counties and the capital city of Bucharest, and, below the county level, 2,685 communes which include over 14,000 villages and 263 towns. A series of changes to the territorial structure of Romania have occurred over the past few decades. Following the end of the Second World War and the introduction of a Soviet model of territorial structure, Romania was initially divided into 20 and, from 1960, 16 administrative districts and 177 *raions*. A new structure was introduced in 1968 with the re-introduction of the former *judet*, or departments, although their number was reduced from the former 60 to only 39 and the Bucharest municipality. The only subsequent amendments were the creation of two *judets*, Calarasi and Giurgiu, in the surrounding area of Bucharest and the transformation of the Ilfov *judet* (reduced in size) into the seventh sector of the capital ('Sectorul Agricol Ilfov'). In 1995, this sector was made into the Ilfov *judet*.

The County Councils were granted decision-making powers over the administration of *judet* resources following local elections in 1992. There were, however, a number of important restrictions associated with the use of local income. The Public Finances Act (No. 189) of 1998 regulates the make-up of local financial resources. Fifty percent of the total salary tax is given to the State budget, 40 percent to the local commune and ten percent to the *judet* budget.

Effective regional development and policy is difficult within the current territorial administrative structure in Romania as the sub-national level is too small and corresponds only to NUTS III of the European Union categorisation. If Romania as a whole were considered a NUTS I region, it is necessary to create the NUTS II level. This was addressed by the 1998 Green Paper on Regional Development Policy which proposed the creation of eight new, voluntary macro-regions (see Regional Policy section below). This regional division has, in part, been based on a historical territorial unit, the province, and comprises the regions of Moldavia, Transylvania, Muntenia, Banat, Oltenia, Bucovina, Crisana-Maramures and Dobrogea.

Regional disparities

Regional disparities in Romania are caused by a wide range of factors and, while apparently diminishing during the former socialist regime, have become very apparent with the introduction of economic reforms. Regional statistics in Romania are relatively poor with certain indicators being unavailable and others, such as per capita GDP, unreliable. In the analysis of regional disparities, therefore, meaningful indicators for demography, living standards, economic activity and infrastructure have been chosen.

Demographic indicators

Four key demographic indicators can be used to highlight the regional disparity situation. First, the human pressure on a given area can be most accurately measured by the number of inhabitants in the total area of inhabitable space. This qualifies the more general population density indicator which does not take the existence of particular environmental or natural features such as forestry cover, water bodies etc. into account. This human pressure indicator ranges from 67.1 inhabitants per km^2 in Tulcea county to 282.3 in Prahova. The highest values are found in hilly areas with a large number of settlements. Two large areas have more than 150 inhabitants per km^2 – the central-south (Valcea, Arges, Dambovita and Prahova counties, together with Brasov) and the north-east, encompassing

Moldavia's counties (except Vaslui and Botosani) and Maramures. The lowest human pressure levels are in the plains and in some of the less-populated central areas. The highest values are clearly registered in Bucharest (8,935 inhabitants per km^2) and in the most urbanised areas including the Brasov Depression, Jiu Valley, Central Mures Valley, and the Constanta area.

Second, the net migration index is a useful indirect tool for appraising the attractiveness of a region. Significant disparities are apparent between the north-eastern and south-western counties, the former having negative values. Three distinct areas have net migration of less than two percent: the northern counties of Maramures, Salaj and Bistrita-Nasaud; all the counties surrounding Bucharest (except Ialomita); and, the eastern counties of Botosani and Vaslui, both of which have a negative net migration index. In 1996, the areas with the highest net migration included Timis and Arad, both in Banat province (5.5 and 3.8 percent respectively), Constanta in Dobrogea (2.6 percent), Sibiu (2.7 percent), Brasov (2 percent) and Hunedoara (1.5 percent). Economic restructuring policies can directly affect migration levels with recent redundancies in the mining sector, for example, leading to the out-migration of over 5,000 people from Hunedoara.

Third, the demographic structure index (ratio of the population aged 15 or under to that aged 60 or over) ranges from 0.72 to 1.79, with the lowest values registered in the counties around Bucharest (Teleorman, 0.72 and Giurgui, 0.8) and parts of the Banat province. There is a number of reasons for this including the pull factors of Bucharest on younger age groups which have the greatest reproductive capacity and the traditional one-child family patterns. Moldovian counties have much higher values (Iasi, 1.7; Bacau, 1.5; Suceava, 1.5) as well as Constanta (1.8) and Brasov (1.7).

Fourth, the urbanisation index is given by a standard urban/total population ratio. Once again, the counties surrounding Bucharest have the lowest levels (Ilfov, 7 percent; Giurgiu, 31 percent; Dambovita, 31 percent and Calarasi 40 percent) with the highest values being registered in the south of Transylvania (Brasov, 76 percent; Hunedoara, 76 percent) and Dobrogea (Constanta, 74 percent). The urbanisation level as calculated by this index is often distorted by the pull effect of a large urban centre on its rural surrounding area.

Two different trends characterise population distribution in rural and urban areas. On the one hand, the repeal of former laws banning migration into urban areas resulted in a sharp increase of people moving into the cities and towns, with urban areas growing by as much as 15-20 percent. On the other hand, the passing of the 1991 Land Law encouraged reverse urban-rural migration and, to some degree, lessened the positive pull effect of more developed regions such as Banat, Brasov, Constanta and Bucharest. The privatisation of land through the Land Law also led to a process of extreme fragmentation with an average farm size of only ca. 2.6 ha. New legislative endeavours are now underway to change the Law and increase the minimum property size.

Taking the four demographic indices together, three areas emerge with a high overall demographic index: the city of Bucharest and the counties of Constanta, Brasov and Sibiu. At the other end of the scale, the counties of Teleorman, Giurgiu, Olt and Calarasi have important demographic problems. The main problem for these counties is the decrease of demographic potential. The ageing of the population has been exacerbated through the arrival of a large number of retired people (the result of the agricultural re-privatisation). One ramification of demographic homogenisation is that the Moldovian *judets* will remain an important labour force reservoir while the Banat area will lose in this regard. Changes within the agricultural sphere and rising poverty, particularly in over-populated areas, are likely to result in a large-scale movement of people towards the cities.

Economic activity

Regional disparities in terms of economic activity can most accurately be shown using two main indicators. The first presents the proportion of the working population involved in services in comparison to agriculture in a given region. The industrial sector is much more unstable during the transition and restructuring period and thus a ratio based on the primary and tertiary sectors is more reliable. Regions where this ratio is high are those where there has been a strong service sector development, often based on tourism and commercial activities, and where agriculture is a less attractive or available option for the workforce. The Romanian counties where this is the case include Brasov (209 percent, ie. where the working population employed in services is at least twice as high as in agriculture), Sibiu (189 percent), Hunedoara (184 percent) and Constanta (163 percent). At the other end of the scale are counties including Teleorman (39 percent), Calarasi (41 percent) and Vaslui and Botosani (49 percent). There is a strong inverse correlation between this index and rurality with the highest county levels generally found in south Transylvania and south Dobrogea and the lowest in the south Romanian plain and eastern Moldovia.

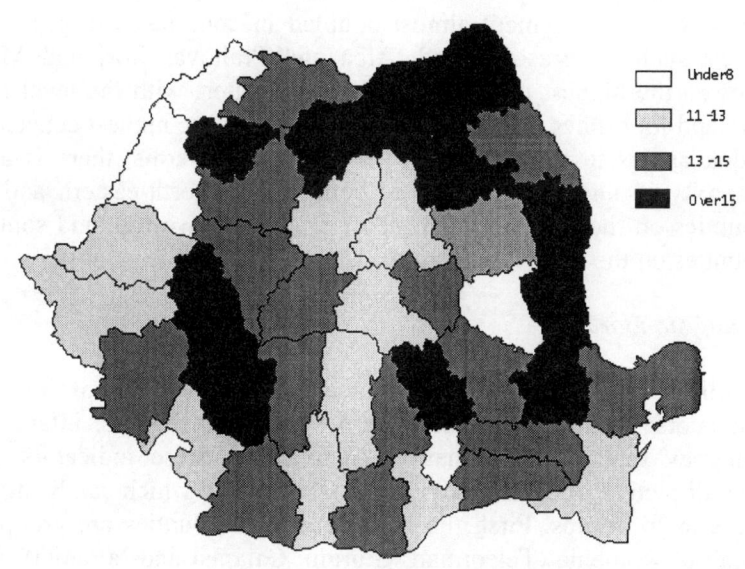

Figure 12.1   Unemployment by county in Romania, July 1999

The trends in industrial activity and restructuring are better reflected in the second index of economic activity which is the unemployment rate. This indicator broadly mirrors the above pattern of regional disparities. In 1996, the counties with low unemployment were located in the Banat region (Timis, 2.9 percent and Arad, 2.7 percent) and within the Transylvania, Crisana and Maramures regions. Areas with low unemployment were and are not always the best developed areas – Gorj (2.3 percent), for example, retained a low unemployment rate because the mining sector continued to receive considerable state subsidies and therefore maintained an artificially high level of employment. Unemployment is particularly high in Neamt (13.1 percent), Valcea (12.5 percent), Vaslui (11.1 percent) and Botosani (10.5 percent), which were all part of a forced industrialisation under the former socialist regime.

The economic reform measures of the current government during 1998 have resulted in significant changes to the unemployment rate, particularly in those counties heavily dependent on mining activity (Hunedoara 14.2 percent; Gorj, 11.6 percent; Maramures, 11.1 percent). Over the period 1996-98, unemployment almost doubled in counties with previously low levels such as Brasov, Arad, Alba and Prahova. Gorj and Maramures showed the highest unemployment growth rates, with the level increasing five and four times respectively – the impact of the highest concentration of redundancies in the autumn of 1997. In broad terms, there is an overall disparity in unemployment rates between the north-eastern and southern counties on the one hand and the central, south-western and south-eastern counties on the other (see Figure 12.1).

Living standards

Family living standards can be assessed on the basis of four principal indicators: number of private cars per 1,000 inhabitants; infant mortality; illiteracy rate; and criminality. Aggregating these indicators shows an overall picture of considerable regional disparity which can be divided into three main groups. First, the least developed counties are grouped in the south of Romania (Teleorman, Giurgiu, Calarasi and Ialomita), forming a ring around the capital city which stands out as an island of development, in the province of Moldovia (Botosani, Vaslui, Neamt Suceava, Bacau and Iasi) and in the north-western part of the country (Bistrita-Nasaud, Salaj and Maramures). Tulcea county, encompassing the Danube delta, is an isolated county also belonging to this group.

Second, moderately developed regions include the counties of the Oltenia province and Caras-Severin, as well as a number of individual counties spread across Romania. Finally, the highly-developed areas in terms of living standards, include a group of counties in north-west, south-west and south-east of the country. These areas are characterised as ones with a concentration of the most viable industries and a good infrastructure provision. The Constanta county also belongs to this group because of its port activities and the location of certain profitable industries. Development trends to date suggest that the current group of moderately developed areas are likely to decline and become less well developed.

Overall, the counties undergoing the greatest economic difficulties in Romania are situated in Moldovia and south Muntenia. In the case of south Muntenia, this is related to the effect of development in Bucharest which has resulted in under development of this area. Moldovia's problems conversely are linked more to historical, cultural and economic reasons, and the demographic pattern is characterised by large families. New industrial activities introduced under the socialist regime were based on imported raw materials and demand from the former Soviet Union. This made the industrialisation process artificial and unable to compete within the changed post-transition economic framework conditions. Unless there is a real change to the local and regional development policies, the Moldovian counties are likely to continue a trend towards greater economic poverty.

Regional policy development

The considerable economic and political challenges facing Romania in its transition from a very severe socialist regime to a functioning democracy and market economy mean that priorities for development must be set. The role of regional development and regional policy within these priorities needs to be approached realistically, bearing in mind the availability of resources and institutional capacity. External assistance, for example, through EU-sponsored programmes is available and may help the process and the requirement to reduce deepening regional disparities is recognised. However, the continued need to ensure national economic growth and combat the deep-seated social impact of the restructuring process mean that there is likely to be a staged response to the need for regional development policy.

In this context, the choice between focusing resources on less-favoured regions or actively supporting the better regions despite the risk of further exacerbating the disparity levels is a pertinent one. There is an argument that the latter is better suited for the current Romanian reality in an attempt to bring the better regions up to a position where they match Western European development levels and can act as a driving force for the economy as a whole. This growth and the related attractiveness for investment (domestic and foreign) could result in the diffusion of positive benefits to less developed areas. It could be argued that only once this has occurred can resources realistically be directed towards less-developed areas which, in any case, could experience trickle-down development.

Against these considerations, a regional development policy has progressively been formulated in Romania over the last 3-4 years, initiated in part by the external impetus of the EU Phare programme and the worsening social problems resulting from economic and industrial restructuring. A Green Paper has been drafted which outlines the regional policy approach and lays down the basic principles for the creation of an institutional framework. On the basis of this Paper, a Regional Development Act was passed in 1998. The institutional framework is emerging slowly and includes a National Regional Development Council, the creation in early 1999 of Regional Development Agencies in the eight new macro-regions and a National Regional Development Agency. So-called 'unfavourable zones' have also been designated, currently focused on mining areas, and a range of financial incentives, as well as support from a National Fund for Regional Development, is available.

Considerable challenges face the further development of regional policy in Romania. Above all, the issues of administrative structure and institutional framework, as well as the wider questions of regional development priorities under the current economic conditions in the country, will be critical to the future development, effectiveness and credibility of this policy area.

13 Slovak Republic

JURAJ SILVAN

Introduction

The Slovak Republic became a sovereign democratic and legal state from 1 January 1993 following the division of the former Czecho-Slovak Federal Republic. The Slovak Republic is a relatively small country in Europe, encompassing a total area of 49,036 km^2 and with a population of 5.4 million. The capital, Bratislava, has 451,000 inhabitants. The country borders other Central and Eastern European nations (Czech Republic, Poland and Hungary) as well as the EU (Austria) and the NIS (Ukraine). The national territory is heavily forested, covering over 40 percent of the total area, the remainder comprising principally arable and pasture land. Mountainous areas also account for 40 percent of the country's territory, rising to a height of over 2,500 metres.

The process of socio-economic transformation was initiated in the Slovak Republic in late 1989 when it still comprised part of the former Czechoslovakia. Economic transformation resulted in dramatic national economic change, such as an increase in unemployment during 1991 alone from 1.5 percent to 11.8 percent. The reform process, particularly in the economic sphere, has also had a significant spatial impact, and the theory of centrally planned, equal socio-economic development of all territorial units, in place for the last 40 years, was reversed. Socio-economic disparities in the spatial structure of the Slovak Republic have increased significantly. This chapter reviews the current situation as well as the regional policy response which as been developed during the 1990s.

Basis for regionalisation

Territorial administrative structure

The most recent territorial and administrative reform in the Slovak Republic took place in July 1996 (see Figure 13.1). It established the first steps towards the creation of a decentralised territorial-administrative system which could support the future introduction of more decentralised management systems. The 1996 reform did not affect the whole public administration and encompassed only the creation of new State administrative units at regional level. Eight regions (*kraj*, provinces) and 79 districts were established in place of the former 38 districts (see Table 13.1). Below the district level are 2,875 municipalities, 136 of which have the status of towns. The primary purpose of these regions is to act as channels for the decentralisation of State management tasks as self-government powers at this level have not yet been put in place. Self-governmental regions in this context would be defined as lower or higher level territorial units with governments which are independent from the State administration and are equipped with local or supra-local/regional competencies (Ivaničková, 1998).

The designation of these new State administrative regions and their centres, or capitals, was to be based on a range of criteria. These included their size, relative socio-economic stability, historical, cultural and ethnic identity, the functional nodality and the accessibility both of the individual units and their centres and the degree of urbanisation. In addition, issues such as their perceived ability to absorb new decentralised tasks were taken into account. The average number of inhabitants in 1996 was ca. 671,000 for the regions and ca. 68,000 in the districts.

In reality, not all of these criteria were fulfilled as originally intended. Some of them, such as the size of districts and their relative stability were not entirely respected. One of the smallest districts, Kysucké Nové Mesto in North Slovakia, for example, was created from the immediate hinterland of the regional centre Žilina, and encompasses only 174 km^2, or 0.35 percent of the total national area. The district of Medzilaborce in North-East Slovakia, has only 12,850 inhabitants, or 0.24 percent of the total national population. The small size of these districts means that their development ability in terms of human and economic resources, as well as the options open to them for combating structural problems, are inevitably weaker than larger and much stronger districts. The districts of South

Slovakia remained unchanged by the reform. Overall, the districts broadly comprise the catchment areas of economic and commuting centres. The new pattern of districts was also guided by the results of the long-term application of central place theory by urban and regional planners in the Slovak Republic.

Figure 13.1   Territorial administrative structure of the Slovak Republic

One of the objectives of regional development policy is to strengthen these new regional units economically, socially and culturally for internal purposes and also to enable them to integrate within the relevant EU structures (Silvan and Zemko, 1996). In the EU's NUTS terminology, the regions equate to NUTS III regions and NUTS II when aggregated into four groups.[1] The Slovak Republic as a whole is considered a NUTS I region and, at lower levels, the 79 districts are NUTS IV and the 2,875 settlements or administrative communes are NUTS V.

The second key step in the creation of a functioning territorial administrative structure in the Slovak Republic – that is, the establishment of regional self-government – was not initiated until the end of 1998. This development, necessary for the full implementation of the public administrative reform, is likely to be carried through by the new government of the Slovak Republic, elected in the parliamentary elections of October 1998. Directly elected governments are only currently in operation at central government level and at local settlement level where municipal bodies and mayors (lord mayors in 136 towns) are elected. This system is one of the most stable elements of the newly established democracy and is comparable with Western European systems.

The current structure, however, leaves a considerable gap between the local and national government levels. The introduction of a genuine region-level self-government would require a change in thinking within the central government *vis-à-vis* the regions and communes, which would receive greater powers including regional and local budgets. Such a system would grant greater autonomy to all regions, including more peripheral areas, in the management of their resources.

Table 13.1 Selected geographical and demographic characteristics in 1997[a]

Region	Number of inhabitants	Total increase/ Decrease ('000)	Number of districts	Number of settle-ments[b] /Towns	Area in km^2	Pop. density per km^2
Bratislava	618,673	-0,37	8	72/7	2 053	301,5
Trnava	549,621	1,32	7	249/15	4 148	132,5
Trenčín	610,349	0,35	9	275/18	4 501	135,6
Nitra	717,241	-0,48	7	347/15	6 343	113,1
Žilina	689,504	2,52	11	314/17	6 788	101,6
Banská Bystrica	663,845	-0,27	13	515/24	9 455	70,2
Prešov	777,301	5,39	13	665/23	8 993	86,4
Košice	761,116	3,45	11	438/17	6 753	112,7
Slovak Republic	5,387,650	1,62	79	2875/136	49 034	109,9

Source: Selected Data on Regions in the SR. Statistical Office of the SR 2/1998.
Notes: [a] Preliminary data as of December 31, 1997. [b] Number of municipalities as of December 31, 1997. Without cities' sections in Bratislava and Košice, including four military sub-districts.

A final component of the emerging decentralised system comprises the various citizens' groups e.g. NGOs, grass-root support organisations, interest associations and so on. However, it can be difficult to integrate the opinions of such groups and associations into the decision-making channels. The full and rational use of the indigenous potential and resources of cities, towns and communes, and their effective utilisation within the emerging public-private partnership system, will also require integration into regional institutions. There are already examples of successful co-operation between local bodies and units in the cultural, social, infrastructural and environmental fields. Further, the voluntary creation of nearly 50 informal regional associations of towns and communes, encompassing virtually the entire territory of the Slovak Republic, provide a positive indication of the existence as well as the natural requirement for the institutionalisation of regional self-government in everyday life (Silvan and Zemko et al., 1995).

Regional disparities

In the identification and analysis of regional disparities in the Slovak Republic, socio-economic criteria at NUTS IV level (ie. the districts) have been used and evaluation has been carried out on this basis. Per capita GDP data are not available at this level. The Statistical Office of the Slovak Republic provides only three components of GDP creation at the level of the eight regions (NUTS III): gross output, intermediate consumption and value added (see Table 13.2). These data are based on the ESA methodology (European System of Integrated Economic Accounts). It is unlikely that the statistical methodology to provide GDP data at NUTS IV level will be available in the near future.

Table 13.2 Components of creation of the gross domestic product[*] - first half year 1998

Region	Gross Output per person	Gross Output % of SR total	Intermediate Consumption per person	Intermediate Consumption % of SR total	Value added per person	Value added % of SR total
Bratislava	451,715	35.2	273,143	32.1	178,572	33.3
Trnava	135,328	8.7	78,791	8.2	56,537	9.4
Trenčín	121,766	8.7	74,946	8.7	46,821	8.6
Nitra	106,521	8.9	68,433	9.3	38,088	8.2
Žilina	118,231	9.5	74,517	9.8	43,714	9.1
Banská Bystrica	127,738	9.9	69,748	8.8	57,989	11.6
Prešov	80,876	7.3	49,089	7.3	31,787	7.4
Košice	163,286	14.5	109,304	15.8	53,983	12.4
SR (average SKK)	159,258	-	97,658	-	61,600	-
SR (average US$)	13 496	-	8 276	-	5 220	-

Source: Statistical Office of the SR, 1998 (own calculations).
Notes: * The estimates are on the basis of preliminary quarterly accounts SKK (Slovak koruna) to US$ in PPS.

Calculations of GDP in 1997 for the four NUTS II regions, and comparisons to the EU average are presented in Table 13.3 (Buček, 1998). On the basis of this GDP calculation, the disparities between the eight NUTS III level regions are even more pronounced. In 1997, there was a six-fold difference between the strongest (Bratislava) and the weakest (Prešov) regions.

The most frequently used data for the analysis and evaluation of socio-economic regional disparities at district level are provided below, together, for the first half of 1998, with the districts at the two extremes for each indicator (Statistical Office of the Slovak Republic, 1998):

- *Production of industrial goods and construction output*: Bratislava II (397,331 SKK per person^2) and Sobrance (2,863 SKK).
- *Average monthly wage*: Košice II (13,930 SKK) and Snina (7,102 SKK) and Svidník (7,150 SKK). The national average was 9,677 SKK.
- *Total acquisition investments per inhabitant.*: Bratislava I-V (178,199 SKK) and Svidník (960 SKK). At regional level, Bratislava had the highest rate (131,648 SKK) and Prešov (5,498 SKK) the lowest.

- *Unemployment rate (registered)* (30 June, 1998): Bratislava IV (3.1 percent) and Rimavská Sobota (27.9 percent), Revúca (27.6 percent), Trebišov (25.5 percent). An unemployment rate of over 20 percent was recorded in 18 districts. At regional level, sharp disparities were evident between the capital region of Bratislava (4.4 percent) and the other three regions of Prešov (19.4 percent), Košice (19.2 percent) and Banská Bystrica (16.3 percent) (see Figure 13.2).

Table 13.3 Comparison of GDP levels for Slovakian regions and EU

NUTS II Regions	GDP per person				Slovak Republic (% of total)	
	in SKK	euro	% of EU average	% of GDP	Inhabit.	Investment
Bratislava	292,900	21,536	122.5	35.0	11.5	52.1
West Slovakia	70,070	5,152	29.3	25.4	34.9	20.9
Central Slovakia	73,975	5,438	30.9	19.3	25.1	13.8
East Slovakia	68,880	5,065	28.8	20.3	28.5	13.2
SR (average)	96,500	7,096	40.4	25.0	12.5	25.0
EU (average)		17,580	100.0			

- *Entrepreneurial activity measured as number of profit-oriented organisations per 1,000 inhabitants*: Bratislava I (91.5) and Poltár (3.5). At regional level, the disparities are still sharp although not as marked as at district level, with Bratislava still having the highest number (27.9) and Prešov the lowest (7.1). In terms of *number of entrepreneurs (persons) per 1,000 inhabitants*, Bratislava I was again the top district (113.7) with Sobrance having the lowest figure (30.6). The regional pattern was the same as for the other indicator: Bratislava (82.8) and Prešov (42.7). The national average was 53.1.
- *Index of economic burden* (ie. the proportion of post- and pre-working age population to working age population x 100): Košice III (39,7), Bratislava V - Petržalka (44.8) and Sobrance (83.5), Medzilaborce (80.3), Stará Ľubovňa (79.4). At regional level, Bratislava had the lower index (60.1) and Prešov the highest (71.5) using data of the first half of 1997.

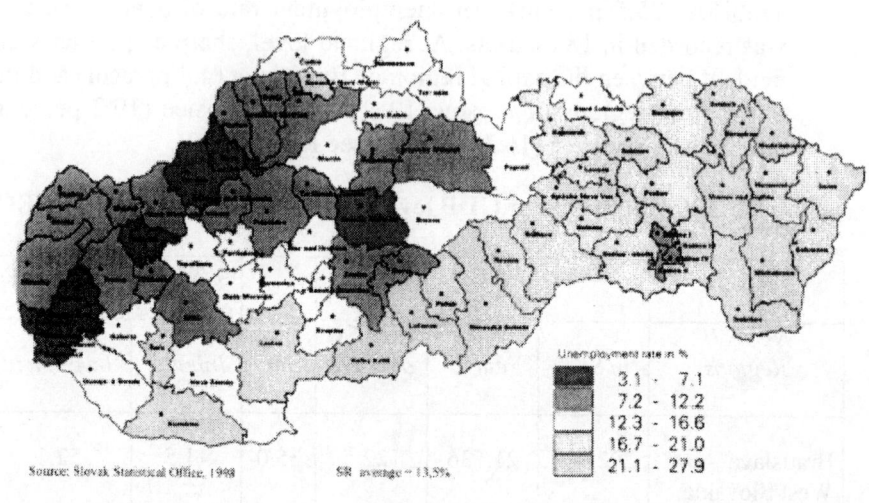

Figure 13.2 Unemployment at district level in the Slovak Republic, June 1998

- *Total population increase per 1,000 inhabitants*: Košice I (18.0), Kežmarok (10.9), Námestovo (10.2) and, at regional level, Prešov (5.4). The highest total population decrease was recorded in Bratislava I (-10.4), Turčianske Teplice (-4.7), Sobrance (-4.3) and at regional level in Nitra (-0.5) and Bratislava (0.4) using preliminary 1997 data. In terms of *population density*, the national average is 109.9 inhabitants per km^2, with district levels ranging from 30.1 in Medzilaborce district in north-east Slovakia to 4716.5 in Bratislava I.
- *Number of hospital beds per 1,000 inhabitants*: Levoča (13.8) and Banská Bystrica (11) with the region of Bratislava one of the lowest levels (7.7). There is no hospital in eight districts of the Slovak Republic.
- *Number of completed dwellings* (in the first half of 1998): Žilina (221), Michalovce (176), Dunajská Streda (137) and Bratislava V (6). The Bratislava V district is a new high rise residential housing

area. There are a further six districts in the Slovak Republic with under ten completed dwellings in 1997. At regional level, the figures were Žilina (600), Košice (544) and Nitra (216), Trenčín (345). There were 6,536 dwellings under construction at the end of June 1998 in Prešov, 6,078 in Bratislava and 4,180 in Nitra.

From this detailed data it is possible to identify considerable regional disparities between the strongest and weakest districts in the country. The negative socio-economic indicators and trends are most significant in the East Slovakian districts and in the border districts of South and partially North Slovakia. There are some exceptions including the position of the metropolitan areas of Košice and Banská Bystrica, Zvolen, and districts containing significantly developed and urbanised centres within the Trnava, Nitra, Trenčín, Žilina and Prešov regions. Settlements located in the hinterland of central cities (not just the above-mentioned centres) also adopt certain urban functions including industry, recreation, storage and recreation/second homes which indirectly improve the environment of the central cities (Silvan, 1992). The richness of the historic and cultural heritage and the integrity of many urban historic sites and monuments is one basis on which future improvements can be built. The region of Bratislava has the best infrastructure, R&D potential, FDI concentration (62 percent of the Slovak total) and is situated on the border with the European Union.

Three main categories of territorial unit (at district level) can be identified on the basis of development levels, socio-economic and demographic structures, the degree of infrastructural provision and underlying conditions for adaptation to market economic systems.

Territorial units/districts with developed economic basis

This group of districts are the leaders of the transformation process in the Slovak Republic. The process of adaptation to new economic conditions and their share of production services are positive, principally as a result of underlying diversified economic structures. These districts contain a substantial share of the highly qualified inhabitants of the Slovak Republic and the maintenance of a qualified labour force is likely because of the university and vocational training base.

The urban agglomerations of the eight regional capitals and their hinterlands are the principal location for this group of districts. The two metropolitan areas of Bratislava and Košice have the largest hinterlands, as well as the third virtually metropolitan area in central Slovakia of Banská Bystrica–Zvolen. The other five urban agglomerations which play an important role in the settlement system are the capitals of the Trnava, Nitra, Trenčín, Žilina and Prešov regions. All these agglomerations have relatively good road accessibility from the main centres. The more remote eastern and central Slovakian centres compensate for their geographic position through the presence of local airports with regular flight connections to neighbouring European capitals and centres (eg. from Košice and Žilina to Vienna). A European communication corridor (IIA) from Bratislava to Žilina-Poprad-Košice and Ukraine is under construction and is planned to be of motorway standard by the first decade of the next century.

Territorial units with lagging economic development

This group of territorial units is characterised by lagging economic development with a relatively low capacity for adaptation within the transition to market economic conditions. The stimulation of development in these regions will require regional policy tools similar to those used in the European Union, and it is recognised that it is likely to be a long-term process. These districts are located principally in the two east Slovakian regions of Prešov and Košice, the southern part of the Banská Bystrica region and three northern districts of the Žilina region. The list of territorial units facing lagging economic development levels in the longer-term includes around 20 districts: Bardejov, Kežmarok, Medzilaborce, Sabinov, Snina, Stropkov, Svidník and Vranov nad Topľou (in the Prešov region); Gelnica, Košice-countryside, Sobrance and Trebišov (in the Košice region); Detva, Poltár, Revúca, Rimavská Sobota, Veľký Krtíš (in the Banská Bystrica region); and Bytča, Čadca and Námestovo (in the Žilina region). Most of these districts are located on the border areas with Hungary, Ukraine and Poland.

The reasons for their lagging economic position include poor technical, transport and telecommunication infrastructures and accessibility. The traditional agricultural areas, farmed through north-eastern Slovakian systems of sub-mountain forest and extensive agricultural management, have only gradually undergone a process of industrialisation. The more positive features of these districts include a healthy environment with a large proportion of these territories under State nature protection within the institutional framework of national parks, protected landscape areas, natural reserves and special protected areas with rich and high-quality sources of drinking water. It is also true that this environmental and nature protection places limits on the economic development options open to these areas.

Many of these districts have a high tourism potential although the tourism infrastructure has often not been developed in line with modern-day requirements for recreation and leisure. This could be used to future advantage if focus is placed on the development of areas of peaceful, unspoilt nature with good hospitality and culture. The principal Slovakian tourism centres in the High and Low Tatra mountains could potentially compete in this environment given their rich agro- and eco-tourism potential.

Certain patterns of rural development should also be highlighted, particularly the role of agro-industrial complexes. These were established partly because of the very different soil and climatic conditions in the mountain and sub-mountain areas of the country as compared to the more optimal conditions typical around the Danube and in the east Slovakian lowlands as well as in the basins of south Slovakia where intensive agricultural production is possible. A characteristic feature of these areas now is the rapid fall in the number of agricultural jobs and the ecological aspect of more extensive agricultural production provides insufficient direct income possibilities. The problem of the lack of economic support for extensive agriculture in mountain and sub-mountain areas is not specific to the Slovak Republic and can also be identified in EU countries. Despite the knowledge that such systems are in accordance with nature protection principles and contribute to the maintenance of valuable landscapes and biodiversity, this approach is insufficiently supported through agricultural policy.

The development of these areas requires a number of key elements including:
- pro-active, regionally differentiated development funds, taxation and support policies;
- improved transport and telecommunication infrastructure; and
- a regionally based educational infrastructure (including regional universities and vocational training schools) to support the educational level.

The creation of equal development conditions in these areas, in comparison to more advanced territories within the country, will be necessary to prevent further economic and demographic decline and environmental damage. This task is further complicated by the location in some of these territories of Romany populations where adaptation is sometimes socially more difficult.

Another factor which could contribute to future development potential is enhanced cross-border co-operation with neighbouring countries at both regional and local level. The extent of such co-operation differs between country and region. The best co-operation basis is in areas bordering Austria including co-operation between the capital cities of Vienna and Bratislava, as well as where considerable potential exists to create a genuine agglomeration based on positive human, economic, infrastructural and physical (the Danube river) potential. The level of cross-border co-operation in other areas reveals different levels of intensity with better results between so-called twinned cities such as Komárno-Komárom and Štúrovo-Estzergom on the Hungarian-Slovak border and in areas of shared common interest such as the two sides of the High Tatras mountain range where initial steps have been taken create a Slovak-Polish Euro-region 'Tatry'. The triangle of the Beskydy mountain area involving the Czech Republic, Poland and the Slovak Republic has also been proposed as a future Euroregion. Close co-operation also exists between the two regional Commerce and Industrial Chambers in Zilina (Slovak Republic) and Bialsko-Biala (Poland).

The division of the former Czechoslovakia has created a new state border between the two now independent nations which has specific characteristics. In addition to traditional economic links between the two countries, strong cultural and human relationships also exist. The absence of a language barrier and the fact that both countries had a similar starting point for the transition process (although the Slovak Republic had to create a wholly new State administration following the division) contribute to the above-average potential for cross-border co-operation and mutual relationships. The future development of cross-border co-operation in the Czech-Slovak border zones will require the identification of new areas of development factors and areas of effective economic activity (Halas, 1998).

Territorial units with on-going structural difficulties

These districts can be categorised as those experiencing on-going structural difficulties principally as a result of their economic structures which are dominated by coal or ore-mining industries and traditional, mono-sectoral engineering industry. The areas involved include the districts of Spišská Nová Ves, Rožňava, Prievidza and Martin and Považská Bystrica which incorporate both mining and engineering industries within their territories. The last two districts had huge engineering complexes which, until the Velvet Revolution, comprised the most developed industrial areas in the Slovak Republic able to compete with similar districts in the Czech Bohemia. However, the collapse of their principally armaments-based production in the early 1990s has left them with considerable difficulties in establishing a stable production programme.

An important consideration *vis-à-vis* these regions is that they have a good supply of technical, transport and social infrastructure as well as a large and well-qualified labour force. These factors, together with a re-orientation of the structure of their economic base, could be exploited to accelerate the adaptation process. A considerable invested resource is represented in their infrastructural provision in particular.

Instruments of regional development policy

Prior to 1990 regional policy principally had a regulatory character through administrative plans relating to prices, currency and the financial sphere. This policy had little significance in practice given the framework of central planning, subjective decision-making and price distortion. It was not possible to identify a coherent strategy or theoretical concept in the field of regional policy. Problems of regional disparity were addressed through the central allocation of principally industrialisation-related resources in given regions and districts (Buček, 1998a).

The regional policy focus changed following the initiation of the process of socio-economic transformation in the Slovak Republic in late 1989. New directions included an initial focus on the monitoring of growing disparities and the identification of problem regions, the implementation of regional policy instruments within a market environment and the activation of regional and local institutions as well as private and public-private organisations (Buček, 1998a). It became clear, however, that the process of transformation could not be managed on the basis of previously developed patterns and methods, and the problem facing the Slovak Republic, together with other CEE countries, was a lack of a model relating to such an economic and political transition. This is equally true within the sphere of regional development co-ordination to help guide the creation of a new legislative and institutional framework for regional development, taking account of the specific historical, socio-economic, territorial and environmental aspects.

The challenge in the Slovak Republic is the development of a more comprehensive and integrated regional development policy, taking the above factors into account. Further requirements include the strengthening of regional development institutions, the allocation of regionally based budgetary resources and financial control mechanisms and the deepening of co-operation between bodies responsible for different types of regional development, including cross-border co-operation. This process was initiated as early as 1990-91 with the creation of a network of information, advisory and consultant activities oriented to regional development. A number of entrepreneur funds were established by the Foundation for Development of Regions and the Phare Pilot Project Programme and a National Agency for Regional Development was created. The National Labour Office, through Regional and District Offices, contributes both to the solving of the unemployment problems and stimulating employment policy within certain sub-national units.

There has been a limited use of direct financial instruments, with current government support accounting for around 0.02 percent of GDP. Several other forms of regional development support have been emerging, and regional policy in the Slovak Republic is gradually creating the broad framework for the development of diversified policy instruments (Buček, 1998a) – although a number of difficulties require remedies for future regional policy to be truly effective.

The implementation of regional policy priorities is important both for the successful application of EU principles and procedures and for the preparation and management of regional development projects. A number of strategic developments, such as the Strategy and Concept of Regional Development of the Slovak Republic, drafted in 1998, have been applied to the short- and medium-term programme for regional development at national level and within individual regions and districts. Both of these regional policy-related concepts must be further developed and applied within the framework of the new, central government programme of

November 1998. The principles and procedures of the European Union will also have to be taken more into account in line with accession negotiations, and EU supported regional development programmes have already been implemented within the country eg. Phare, CBC, Credo, Ecos, Ouverture and Partnership 2000.

The above-mentioned conceptual documents have shaped the strategic aims, objectives, priorities and measures of Slovak regional policy - although the 1998 Strategy of Regional Development has never been formally adopted and remains a working document only. The first proposed strategic aim is to support the Slovak regions and increase national prosperity. It has four objectives:
- the reduction of disparities between regions/districts and the increase of their competitive capability;
- the re-conversion of regions/districts particularly affected by industrial decline and structural crisis;
- the increase of the employment rate and the tackling of labour market problems at regional/district level; and
- the development of rural areas (eg. through the Programme of Village Renewal which already incorporates almost 800 villages).

The second proposed strategic aim is to improve the institutional and administrative capacity for the implementation of a comprehensive regional policy integrated with structural tools. In this case, two objectives are defined:
- the development of a comprehensive integrated regional development policy and a corresponding legal framework; and
- the creation and enforcement of budgetary and financial control institutions as a mechanism for regional development and other structural tools which would be compatible with EU standards as well as the available manpower.

The intention was to update the Strategy every four years but to re-examine the measures and priorities more frequently on the basis of the socio-economic situation at regional and district level. This would allow on-going consideration of changing circumstances in line with the progress of the reform as well as the shifting development gap between the Slovak Republic and the European Union.

Conclusion

The Slovak Republic, as well as other transition CEE countries, requires new and positive development impulses. An effectively managed regional development policy, involving a combination of both bottom-up and top-down approaches, could be considered such an impulse. The Slovak Republic has achieved a sound initial basis within its regional and district system for the support of regional economic development, although further progress is clearly still required. In particular, the creation of stable institutions for regional policy, including a structure of regional self-government, is necessary to ensure more efficient future implementation of the EU Structural Funds and better co-ordination is required between central governments, regions and other players including the private sector.

Notes

1   Bratislava (Bratislava); West-Slovakia (Trnava, Nitra and Trenčin); Central-Slovakia (Banská Bystrica and Žilina); East-Slovakia (Košice and Prešov).
2   £1= 67 koruna (SKK) (December 1999).

References

Buček, M. (1998a), 'Regional Policy and its Instruments in Transformation Period in the Slovak Republic', *Region and Public Administration* no. 3, Economic University, Bratislava.
Buček, M. (1998b), 'Regional Policy of the Slovak Republic', in Majer, G. F. and Tödling, F. (eds) *Regional and Urban Economics*, Elita, Bratislava.
Halas, M. (1998), *Changes in Cross-Border Activities of Population in the Slovak-Czech Border Area*, Proceedings of the 12th Congress of the Slovak Geographical Society, September 9-13, Prešov.
Ivaničková, A. (1998), 'Regionalisation and Spatial Organisation of Regional Development', *Ekonóm*, Bratislava.
Office for Strategy of the Development of the Society, Science and Technology of the Slovak Republic (1998), *Strategy of Regional Development of the Slovak Republic*, Bratislava.
Rajčák, M. (1998), *The Strategic Intentions and Objectives of the Slovak Regional Policy*, Session of EAG (ARL Hannover), Sušice, Czech Republic.
Silvan, J. (1992), 'Eastern Europe', in Stren, R., White, R. and Withney, J. (eds) *Sustainable Cities, Urbanisation and the Environment in International Perspective*, Westview Press.

Silvan, J. and Zemko, I. (1996), 'Slovak Republic: 8 Regions and 79 Districts', *European Journal of Regional Development,* no. 4.

Silvan, J. and Zemko, I. et. al. (1995), *Process of Forming of Regional Level of Space Arrangement and Management with Special Regard to the Conditions in the Slovak Republic,* RSS-0SI Project Nr. 261/94, Bratislava.

14 Slovenia

PAVLE SICHERL AND STANKA KUKAR

Introduction

Slovenia has survived the simultaneous and superimposed shocks of socio-economic and political transition and the disintegration of the former Yugoslavia relatively well. Slovenia is a small country in terms both of size (about 20,000 km^2 in area) and population (just under two million inhabitants) and is located at the crossroads of Central Europe. The richness of its cultural and historic heritage is an important asset in Slovenia's potential for further economic and social development. Diverse climatic and landscape conditions provide the pre-conditions for a wide range of economic development and lifestyle options – despite the overall size of the country.

Slovenia can be viewed as a region state, such as Ireland or Denmark, considering the impact of its accession on EU cohesion, but a more detailed and differentiated approach is required for internal development purposes. This chapter provides an overview of the territorial administrative structure of the country, the spatial impact of reform in the country and the emerging regional policy response.

Territorial administrative reform

The basic administrative unit below central government in Slovenia is the municipality. The law on local self-government in 1994 increased the number of municipalities from 62 to 147. The total increased further to 193 in 1998 following the division of some of the larger municipalities into two or more smaller ones, and there is still further pressure for the creation of new ones. The result of this trend is that the municipalities are very small in size; excluding Ljubljana and Maribor, they average fewer than 9,000 inhabitants.

The tasks which should be undertaken by the municipalities include a number formerly carried out by the central government including active employment policy, land-use and environment tasks as well as social services and basic education. The execution of these tasks requires both financial and personnel resources, and the municipalities are generally not well-endowed with either. They are often unable to carry out the tasks they are expected to do and it would be advantageous for them to combine forces on a more regional basis.

Figure 14.1 Territorial administrative structure of Slovenia

There is currently no intermediate level between the central government and the municipalities. Currently, individual ministries and national organisations use different regional breakdowns, usually between 8 and 12 regions in the administration of their activities. Twelve statistical planning regions are used by Eurostat as the basis for NUTS III designation but have no administrative powers. Some debate has occurred in Slovenia about the use of these 12 regions as economic development regions. Overall, a special law on the regions is now under preparation, but no agreement has yet been achieved on the competencies, definition or number of regions.

The current state of transition

The first phase of transition was hampered by the disintegration of the former Yugoslavia. Slovenia, however, enjoyed the advantage both of earlier experience with a self-management system based on a quasi-market economy and of exposure to democratic and market economic influences through trade and the free mobility of people since the mid-1960s. The political situation prioritised the issues of a peaceful division of the former Yugoslavia, the creation of an independent state and its international recognition. There was a high degree of agreement among the Slovenian population with regard to the question of independence but the new political parties were less agreed on other issues. The political structure in Slovenia has not yet stabilised and there are increasing difficulties in reaching consensus on important development and social issues even within the present coalition.

In the economic field, the emphasis was initially placed on achieving macro-economic stability as well as on measures to halt the fall in production and employment. The recovery started during 1993 and the pre-transition level of GDP had been reached by the start of 1999. The balance of payments situation has stabilised with a remarkable structural change in market orientation – in 1997, around 65 percent of all foreign trade was undertaken with EU countries. The budget surpluses of the early years became small budget deficits, although the internal and external debt situation is not yet problematic and is still low in comparison with some EU countries. Inflation remains a problem and stood at around eight percent at the end of 1998.

Slovenia has the highest per capita GDP levels of all the CEE countries. In 1997, per capita GDP indices in purchasing power parity (EU-15=100) were 68 for Slovenia, 63 for Czech Republic, 47 for Hungary, 47 for Slovak Republic and 40 for Poland (Eurostat, 1998). If the disparity between CEE countries and the EU average is expressed in terms of time, the retrospective time distance for GDP per capita is 19 years for Slovenia, 21 years for Czech Republic, 29 years for Hungary and Slovakia, and 33 years for Poland.[1] Slovenia had a similar level of GDP per capita (PPP) as Greece and Portugal in 1997.

The privatisation process has been virtually completed although the privatisation of banks, insurance companies and public utilities is still on-going with a greater role of the private sector in decision-making and management, co-operation challenges between the public and private sector increase. Unemployment remains the most important overall long-term problem in the country and includes a significant spatial dimension.

A number of social indicators continued to improve in sharp contrast to the fall in GDP per capita in the initial years of transition. In general, the degree of disparity between EU countries and Slovenia is much smaller if other indicators are taken into account - a more comprehensive review of a wider range of socio-economic indicators provides a more optimistic picture than is the case with a pure focus on per capita GDP (Sicherl, 1997b). Most of the education in Slovenia is still free and there has been an important increase in the number of students. Social cohesion has not been seriously undermined by the uncertainty and negative impact of transition. However, this should not be taken for granted in the light of worsening regional disparities and income distribution patterns, high unemployment, the lack of agreement on pension reform and the fact that the political situation is not favourable for the efficient implementation of required structural reform.

Slovenia has already achieved, to a great extent, the stabilisation of the economy, the initial phase of recovery, and the creation of a new institutional and legal framework necessary for the market economy – its effective co-ordination and co-operation remain major challenges,. A further important task is the effort to ensure that the formal framework complies with the EU accession requirements and the screening of the country's legislation is now under way. In terms of economic indicators, Slovenia currently fulfils the two fiscal criteria, and may in the next few years be able to satisfy all five EMU convergence criteria.

Demography

The demographic situation is worsening throughout Slovenia because of low birth rates and negative net migration. The total fertility rate is far below the level which would maintain the reproduction level of the population. The Slovenian population is ageing and has no demographic reserves to meet the gap in the active population in the future. It is not expected that the population will exceed two million over the next ten years. The age structure is changing considerably with the ageing index increasing from 76 in 1997 to over 110 by the year 2020.

The Slovenian population has been spatially unequally distributed for a relatively long period. Around a third of the Slovenian territory comprises areas where the concentration of population is increasing and these areas account for 75 percent of the total population. The depopulating areas are agricultural and peripheral regions (Pomurska, Posavska, Goriska, Kraska) and Zasavska region, an old industrial and coal-mining region.

The settlement structure is dispersed, with only two towns having a population in excess of 100,000 inhabitants, and substantial daily commuting takes place. There is also a clear process of sub-urbanisation which is most strongly seen in the Ljubljana and Maribor urban agglomerations, but also in Kranj and Trzic, the coastal cities, Celje, Nova Gorica and Novo mesto. An accompanying trend is the dispersed construction of individual houses, made possible by the lack of restrictions over land-use change and an open urban policy. The rural hinterlands of congested areas have experienced an intense economic and social dynamic and have a relatively progressive market agriculture. The less accessible, peripheral and mountainous rural areas have a weak economic structure and are exposed to further depopulation. Overall, the spatial distribution of population, together with the process of sub-urbanisation, means that only half the total population live in towns although 92 percent of the population is non-agricultural.

Employment and unemployment

The most important long-term economic problem in Slovenia is unemployment. The unemployment rate (ILO standardised rate) increased from 2.6 percent in 1989 to 7.1 percent in 1997 – still below the EU average. The registered unemployment is twice this level. The rate of economic activity of the working age population has fallen by ten percent, and the number of persons in paid employment was about 35 percent lower in 1997 than in 1988. There are also increasing disparities in the distribution of income and opportunity in the labour market. The optimistic expectations that the new private enterprises would compensate for the loss of jobs in large privatised firms have proved unrealistic. The job losses are largest in manufacturing, agriculture and forestry, construction and, in some regions, in trade and catering. The number of jobs in non-market services, and in administration in particular, has increased.

There is a marked regional difference in the structure of the economically active population. Agriculture remains important in three regions (Pomurska, Dolenjska, Posavska) while another two regions could be labelled service regions (Central Slovenia, with the capital Ljubljana, and Obalno-kraska, the most attractive tourist region). Industry remains the prevailing activity in the other regions, with the highest share in Zasavska. The different economic structure of the regions has influenced the intensity of their adjustment problems, and their unemployment rates in particular. The regional disparities in terms of unemployment rates for the 12 statistical regions are presented in Table 14.1. Podravska, Pomurska, Zasavska, Posavska and Savinjska regions show the highest rates of unemployment as well as below average economic indicators.

Related to the employment problem are the health care and the pension systems, which currently still offer good coverage but face serious problems. Within the health sector, the own contributions of users are increasing and the large losses of the pension system have been covered by the budget. A reform of the pension system is inevitable in the light of mounting problems, not least the considerable fall in the ratio of contributors to pensioners. There is, however, considerable debate among the social partners about the basic elements of the pension reform, and considerable difficulties have been encountered in reaching a consensus.

Economy

Regional per capita GDP data for the 12 statistical regions is not available. If per capita gross material product is used as an approximation, Central Slovenia was the leading region in 1990 with an index of 120, and Goriska and the Coastal region were the only other regions with above average indices of 109. The regions with the lowest indices were Koroska (84) and Pomurska (71). A greater range of indices became available in the late 1990s and these are presented for the statistical regions in Table 14.1.

Per capita income tax is the most illustrative indicator of the degree of regional economic disparities, given the difficulties with the per capita gross value added indicators highlighted in the above note. This indicator, as well as the ageing index, show a ratio of 1.5:1 between the highest and lowest values between the twelve statistical regions. The corresponding ratio for unemployment is more than 2:1, and for per capita gross value added rises to 2.6:1. The latter indicator, however, is less reliable both for the coverage reason mentioned above, and on account of the high daily mobility of the workforce between the Slovenian regions. For this reason, per capita GDP figures, even if they were available, would be likely to overestimate the regional differences in the standard of living and access to employment and education.

Studies in the early 1990s identified four groups of Slovenian regions on the basis of the level of economic development in 1990, the economic structure and an evaluation of natural, human, financial and infrastructure potential (Kukar, 1996):
- *most developed regions*, with a good underlying economic structure and positive future development potential (Central region, Coastal region, Gorenjska);
- *medium developed regions* with positive development potential and a relatively good economic structure (Savinjska, Dolenjska, Goriska);
- *medium developed regions,* with a more problematic economic structure but some development possibilities (Podravska, Koroska, Posavska, Zasavska); and
- *less-developed regions* with some development potential (Pomurska, Karst).

The process of economic restructuring and the transition from a socialist to a market economy has influenced the economic position of the Slovenian regions in different ways. Over the period 1991-1997, a process of polarisation emerged with an improvement in the relative position of five regions and a deterioration in the other seven, less-developed regions (Kukar, 1998). The following conclusions can be drawn from a comparison of the regional groupings at the start of the transition process and after seven years of reform:
- the three most developed regions have remained developed and their relative position has improved - the relative position of the fourth region (Goriska) has remained similar;

- Dolenjska, a medium developed region in 1990, has exploited its development potential and has joined the group of economically more developed regions;

Table 14.1 Basic socio-economic indicators for statistical regions (Slovenia = 100)

Region	Ageing index		Gross value added per inhabitant*		Income tax basis per inhabitant		Unemploy. rate	
	1991	1997	1991	1996	1992	1996	1991	1997
Central region	94.3	96.1	140.1	145.4	116.9	120.9	97.4	75.5
Coastal region	115.1	122.4	100.4	101.8	105.0	110.1	121.7	73.7
Gorenjska	88.7	89.5	91.0	95.9	106.3	100.9	106.8	82.2
Goriška	128.3	122.4	108.0	105.5	112.5	106.4	62.3	64.6
Savinjska	90.6	89.5	90.5	87.9	92.1	92.4	84.8	114.0
Dolenjska	84.9	80.3	101.9	107.6	93.8	93.9	64.4	88.8
Pomurska	124.5	113.2	65.0	55.6	74.4	77.5	125.4	126.2
Karst	124.5	115.8	67.4	61.0	103.0	96.8	86.2	83.2
Podravska	107.5	105.3	78.7	71.4	86.3	84.2	127.1	153.5
Koroška	79.2	81.6	56.9	72.8	92.4	87.1	74.1	85.6
Posavska	117.0	106.6	95.5	70.3	82.6	85.2	89.9	115.4
Zasavska	109.4	113.2	84.2	91.9	105.6	96.9	126.7	120.5
Slovenia	100.0	100.0	100.0	100.0	100.0	100.0	100.0	100.0

Sources: Statistical Office of the Republic of Slovenia; Agency for Payments; National Employment Office; Institute for Macroeconomic Analysis and Development.

Note: * Regional estimates of GDP per capita are not available. As an approximation, data is used here for gross value added in enterprises and companies that have submitted their balance sheets to the Agency for Payments. It is estimated that about 40 percent of GDP is not included in this source (eg. farmers, certain SMEs, financial institutions, public administration).

- Savinjska, earlier classed together with Goriska and Dolenjska as a medium developed region with a positive economic structure and good development potential, has fared badly during the transition period. The steel works and heavy equipment production, as well as some other manufacturing branches (eg. textiles and furniture), have gone bankrupt and the rate of unemployment has nearly tripled in only six years. This

region, together with Podravska, Zasavska and Posavska and the three less developed regions (Koroska, Karst and Pomurska), comprises the group of regions whose relative position has worsened over the period 1991–1997;
- the two least developed regions (Pomurska, Karst) have been affected by the restructuring problems a few years later than the more developed regions and have recently shown considerable structural problems. These trends have worsened their relative position.

Regions with a higher percentage of tertiary activity (trade, tourism, and business services) have experienced fewer difficulties in adapting to the new economic and political circumstances – notably Central region (with the capital Ljubljana), Coastal and Gorenjska regions. The two more agricultural regions with a few modern industrial enterprises (Goriska, Dolenjska) and a larger share of tourism have also witnessed fewer problems than regions burdened with old heavy industry (Podravska with Maribor, Savinjska, Posavska, Koroska, Karst). Pomurska remains the least developed region with a high share of agriculture.

Regional policy and regional development institutions

Slovenia has undertaken some form of domestic regional policy since 1971. At that time, the target assisted area covered ca. 16 percent of the population. A new law, which is still in force, was passed in 1990 and focused regional policy on the support of demographically endangered areas. The eligibility criteria for the receipt of regional support were made purely demographic in nature including an ageing index and the rate of population growth, and coverage is currently 24.6 percent of the population (and 55 percent of the territory of the country). The resources available for regional development support are limited and declining - in 1997 they amounted to only about 0.08 percent of GDP. The Ministry of Economic Relations and Development is responsible for co-financing local infrastructure and the Fund for Regional Development and the Preservation of Rural Areas, created in 1996, provides soft loans for investment in agriculture, supporting activities and SMEs in designated areas.

A range of other government policies has an impact on regional development. These include: government support for local authority budgets; the promotion of an economic base for the ethnic minorities (the

Italian minority in the south-west and the Hungarian minority in the north-east); integrated rural development and the village renewal programme; financial support for certain spatially concentrated economic sectors (iron, mining, heavy equipment, hop growing, tourism, fishing); active employment policy and other policies. From a regional development perspective, there is a lack of co-operation and co-ordination of these policy areas between the individual government offices and ministries, as well as between different levels of decision-making. It is difficult to assess to what extent these measures contribute to more balanced regional development.

The limited, under-resourced nature of current regional policy in Slovenia, focused on small, peripheral and de-populating areas, is unable to combat the emerging regional disparities and is insufficient to stimulate endogenous regional development. A new comprehensive regional policy, therefore, is required in the country. The first draft of a new law on regional development was discussed in parliament in 1995 and the second draft entered the government procedures only in late 1998 - highlighting the relatively low priority given to regional development issues. The main objectives of the law are to create the preconditions for sustainable and balanced development of all regions, to reduce regional disparities and promote inter-regional and cross-border co-operation. The second draft defines three types of assisted area or priority objective: economically weak, de-populating areas; industrial areas with structural problems and high unemployment; and border areas and other areas with limited development potential. The reform of the territorial administrative structure has not yet been agreed and this has delayed the passing of the law. The key strategy documents which currently influence the design and implementation of regional development policy include the Strategy of Regional Development of Slovenia, national sectoral programmes containing an explicit regional impact assessment and the regional development programmes for individual regions. The regional development Strategy is designed to help clarify and agree key conceptual issues in this area.

In organisational terms, the creation of a National Council for Development has been proposed, chaired by the Minister for Economic Relations and Development and incorporating the key ministers responsible for relevant development issues. The aim of this organisation would be to promote a higher level of co-ordination between government policies and programmes which indirectly address regional issues and ensure that they are complementary and not in competition. Further, a National Development Agency (NDA) is to be established by the Ministry for Economic Relations and Development. The NDA would become the driving force for the promotion of regional development across the national territory. One current proposal is for the integration of the Fund for Regional Development and the Preservation of Rural Areas within this organisation. In individual regions, regional development agencies will be established which will be responsible for the preparation, implementation, monitoring and evaluation of regional development programmes.

Note

1   For discussion of time distance as a measure of disparities in social and economic development see Sicherl (1997a). Since EU15 in 1997=100, 68 percent of this level was achieved in EU15 in 1978: the time lag of Slovenia behind EU15 thus amounts to 19 years.

References

Eurostat (1998), 'Statistics in Focus', *Economy and Finance*, 28/1998.
Kukar, S. (1996), 'Regional Policy in Slovenia: Results, Problems and Alternatives', *Eastern European Economics*, vol. 34, no. 4, Arizona State University, New York, pp. 41-103.
Kukar, S. (1998), *Regional Disparities in the Transition Period*, Internal paper for the White Book on the Regional Strategy of Slovenia, Ljubljana.
Sicherl, P. (1997a), *A Novel Methodology for Comparisons in Time and Space*, East European Series, no. 45, Institute for Advanced Studies, Vienna.
Sicherl, P. (1997b), *Cohesion in the EU and Accession of Slovenia: Comparisons with Selected Smaller EU Countries*, East European Series, no. 50, Institute for Advanced Studies, Vienna.
Statistical Office of the Republic of Slovenia (various years), *Statistical Yearbook*, Ljubljana.

PART III:
THEMATIC PERSPECTIVES

The national reviews of the ten CEE countries in the previous section show an emerging awareness of the significance of regional development, as spatial disparities widen, but (as yet) weak capacities for regional policies to respond. It is clear, however, that regional policy is assuming a higher profile, especially with the prospect of EU structural assistance. In developing regional policy responses, the CEE countries face weeks to address several key issues. These include: the weight accorded to equalisation of regional differences versus national efficiency; the importance of regional strategies based on enlargement development such as upgrading of production structures through SME development and technological change versus policies promoting the attraction of foreign investment; the significance of environmental improvement as part of regional development; and the potential of cross-border co-operation. The following section considers these issues in a series of five 'thematic perspectives' on regional development in CEE.

15 Regional Disparity, Industrial Development and Technology Change in Hungary

ANNE LORENTZEN

Introduction

The process of transition from a centrally planned to a market economy in Central and Eastern Europe (CEE) was, among other things, assumed to have a positive impact on industrial innovation and competitiveness. This is the point of departure for this chapter on post-1989 technological change in Hungarian industry. Its aim is to detect the impact of liberalisation and privatisation on the industrial technological capacity of a formerly centrally planned economy, with Hungary as a case-study, and focusing on three regions, namely Győr-Moson-Sopron in the West, Borsod-Abaúj-Zemplen in the East and Budapest, the capital, in the centre of the country. Empirical research includes an enterprise study made in 1994 and 1995 of 20 enterprises located in the three regions, revealing the existence of regional disparities in Hungary at the company level as well as at the aggregate level of the regional societies, and the differing impact of transition on company behaviour in terms of innovation.

In this chapter the main conclusions concerning regional differences in enterprise development are summarised. The empirical results need to be put into a wider perspective, and therefore the first part of the chapter contains a brief overview of the process of transition and of the regional economic development of Hungary, rehearsing some of the issues raised earlier in the volume by Gyula Horvath. The remainder of the chapter looks in more detail at various components of company development in the three Hungarian case-study regions.[1]

The process of transition

The process of transition initiated in Hungary in 1989 included economic, social and institutional aspects. In economic terms, the first years after 1989 represented a veritable economic roller coaster. The introduction of a market economy in 1989 threw Hungary into a severe crisis characterised by negative growth rates for three consecutive years. Production shrank, investment ceased. This had severe social implications, including a jump in unemployment rates from 2 percent to more than 13 percent in 1992, and job loss and a diminution of real wages were the immediate impacts of the transition (WIIW, 1996).

However, already in 1993 economic trends turned in an upward direction, and unemployment decreased again. Industrial production had suffered negative growth until 1993, when growth rates again became not only positive, but high. The economic recovery seems to have been based on various factors: internal demand grew again; the private sector expanded; foreign investment flows into Hungary were considerable, and industry managed to expand exports to the West.

Institutional changes have been the nexus of the process of transition. The institutions regulating the Hungarian economy were based on central planning since the 1940s. In relation to industry, central planning implied a strong concentration of industry in a limited number of state-owned trusts, which incorporated a large number of vertically integrated production plants. The system of central planning was reformed somewhat in 1968 under the now famous New Economic Mechanism (NEM), which introduced a simulated market mechanism (Ernst, Alexev and Marer, 1996). In the 1980s reforms were continued: in 1980 the number of monopolised trusts was reduced, in 1985 the managers of state-owned enterprises obtained increased autonomy, and in 1988-1989 the establishment of private companies became legal, foreign ownership was allowed, and the transformation of state-owned companies into semi-private corporations became a possibility.

Then, in the spring of 1989, Hungary opened its borders to the West, thereby initiating an acceleration of institutional, economic and social change. The liberalisation of foreign trade was phased in gradually from 1989. Spontaneous privatisation of State-owned companies had already begun in 1989, and later that year the State Property Agency (since 1995, the Hungarian Privatisation and State Holding Company) was founded to lead the process of privatisation, which took place through tendering of shares. The turbulence of the initial years after 1989 was partly due to the lack of an appropriate institutional infrastructure required to make a modern market economy work including, for example, commercial banks and labour market institutions. Legislation has developed continuously, however, and the initial phase of marked laissez faire is being substituted gradually by a redefinition of the role of the State in the new market economy.

Three structural changes in the economy have characterised Hungary since 1989: first the expansion of the private sector which, in 1997, was estimated to account for two thirds of GDP (OECD, 1997). Second, the inflow of foreign capital, which was the highest in CEE and amounted to $14,583 million in June 1997 (Economic Bulletin for Europe, 1997). Third, the complete change of the structure of foreign trade whereby Western Europe accounted for more than 75 percent of both imports and exports in 1995 (Central Statistical Office).

The regional economic development of Hungary

The background to the present regional disparities can be found in the economic history of Hungary and principally through its industrialisation policies. Before the First World War the industrial development of Hungary was mainly concentrated around Budapest, the capital. The status of the capital as an industrial centre was supported by a centralised railway network (Bernat, 1989) and by the centralising efforts of the government (Enyedi, 1997). The rest of Hungary supplied raw materials from the mines, the forests and from agriculture to the industrial activities of Budapest. Apart from the post-war loss of nearly half of its territory, no major changes occurred in the spatial development of industrial activities in Hungary. The economy grew only slowly, and the industrial concentration around Budapest was further favoured by taxation, subsidies and by a close enterprise co-operation. As a result, in 1949, 54 percent of the industrial labour force was employed in Budapest and, in addition, industries developed in a belt around the capital. Simultaneously, however, mines and energy sources served as a basis for industrialisation in some of the provinces.

The Communists, who came to power in 1949, challenged this centralised model of industrialisation, with the intention of reducing the dominance of Budapest and eliminating regional disparities. At that time, development of backward areas was synonymous with industrial growth, and the efforts of the government actually resulted in considerable industrial development in Hungary.

The industrial policy of the Communists can be divided into five phases of so-called 'socialist industrialisation'. The first phases were based on an extensive development of industry and the absorption of manpower, while a focus on a more intensive industrial development, including technological development, characterised the industrial policy after 1969. Finally, in the 1980s, economic efficiency became a major concern (Bernat, 1989). As a result, between 1950 and 1980, industrial output grew by more than 800 percent, employment grew by almost 500 percent, and the sectoral pattern of industry changed in favour of heavy industry, of which the machine-building and chemical industries were the most outstanding (Bernat, 1989).

In this way, Hungary became industrialised very rapidly and developed new branches to an extent which widely surpassed the requirements of the country itself, for instance in engineering and chemicals. An important component of this strategy was the trade and social division of labour within CMEA (Council for Mutual Economic Assistance). In 1981, 58.1 percent of Hungarian exports and 51.5 percent of imports into the country were sourced in other socialist countries (Bernat, 1989).

Part of the industrial policy was to transform the spatial structure of industry, a process which was also phased (Bernat, 1989). During the first phase, lasting from 1950 to 1959, a large number of new plants, mainly in heavy industry, were located in already developed regions with abundant energy sources and raw materials, and Hungary witnessed the establishment of large investment projects in coal, steel, chemicals and aluminium production.

During the second phase, from 1960 to 1968, the focus was on the development of former economically backward regions, (eg. the Great Plain), and five spatial growth poles were formed, located in Miskolc, Debrecen, Szeged, Pécs and Györ. Outside these growth poles, the location of industry into regions with surplus labour also took place, but the technical levels of such firms were very poor (Farkas, 1995) probably because job creation was the policy focus.

Until 1969, industry was centrally planned in Hungary but, shortly before the third phase of spatial policy from 1969 to 1975, authority over investment decisions was transferred to the individual companies. The enterprises used their newly gained authority to go to the countryside in search of labour. The resulting spatial decentralisation of industry was also favoured by preferential treatment arrangements outside the capital (Bernat, 1989). In rural areas, industrialisation was favoured by the rapid development of agriculture. Agricultural products were, to an increasing degree, used as inputs in the manufacturing industry. Thus, slaughterhouses, meat-processing plants, cold storage plants, vegetable oil factories, maize processing factories, breweries and sugar refineries emerged (Bernat, 1989), and the production of components for the food processing industries also developed.

From 1976, changes in the spatial structure of industry were minimal, as the number of new investments were reduced and the focus changed to the upgrading of existing plants. Towards the end of the 1970s, industry was located more evenly than in 1950, with only 24.2 percent of the people employed in industry working in Budapest. The industrially developed counties were Borsod-Abaúj-Zemplen, Heves and Nógrád in the north, Komaron, Fejer and Veszprém west of Budapest, Györ Sopron in the west and Baranya in the south. These counties counted for 35.1 percent of industrial employment in 1981 (Bernat, 1989).

However, other regional disparities persisted, which became important for the nature of regional development in a longer-term perspective. In particular, Budapest was comparatively much better equipped with infrastructure and a higher educated population, 40 percent of whom lived in Budapest in 1980 (Szalo, 1994).

Eastern and western Hungary, two extremes

The general economic changes after 1989 in terms of competition from Western European goods, the break down of CMEA trade in 1990, stagnation of internal demand and general lack of capital were problems shared by all regions. However, not all regions were similarly equipped to deal with these changes resulting in the post-1989 re-emergence of old regional disparities as well as the appearance of certain new ones. Budapest again became a magnet of investment, western Hungary prospered, and the formerly flourishing Borsod-Abaúj-Zemplen seemed to be caught in a vicious circle of underdevelopment. The regional disparities were partly rooted in different development paths during Communism. Before analysing the recent developments, the industrial past of the three case-study regions will be characterised briefly.

Györ-Sopron borders Austria, and contacts with the West have been a natural part of economic life for many years. Györ was one of the growth poles of the 1960s, but was not so heavily industrialised as other counties with less than five percent of industrial employment in 1981 (Bernat, 1989). Györ is a traditional centre of light industries such as cotton, wool, silk, knitwear, footwear and furniture (Bernat, 1989). The relative diversification of industry around Györ is also seen in the existence of the food industry and engineering, particularly motor-vehicle production and railway carriages and machines (Bernat, 1989).

Borsod-Abaúj-Zemplen (BAZ) is situated in the north-east of Hungary and borders Ukraine and Slovakia. Large investments were made in mining, metallurgy and chemicals in this county, where engineering and light industries also came to play a certain role (Bernat, 1989). In 1981, ten percent of all industrial workers were employed in this county (Bernat, 1989). The global crisis of metallurgy, which has hit the old industrial countries, was also felt in BAZ where employment started to decrease from the mid-1980s, falling from 50,000 to around 20,000 at the beginning of the 1990s (OECD, 1994).

Budapest, the capital, is situated in the central-north of Hungary, and it has been characterised by an extreme concentration of activities for more than one hundred years (Bencze and Tajti, 1972). Over time, Budapest has developed a diversified industrial structure, but the capital lost some of its dominance during the Communist era, and only 24.2 percent of industrial employment was based there in 1981 (Bernat, 1989). Budapest has traditionally been a centre for the engineering industry, accounting for 40 percent of the national total in 1981 (Bernat, 1989). Chemical and pharmaceutical industries are located there, as well as a third of the light industries in 1981 (Bernat, 1989). Also the food industry, although it is represented more evenly than most industries in the regions, has a large concentration in Budapest.

The question is: what happened to these three regions after 1989? Recent data allow a sketchy analysis of the way they have been affected by the transition from a planned to a market economic system during the 1990s.

- *Unemployment*: at the peak of the crisis in 1992, Budapest, with almost 19 percent of the population, had only nine percent of the unemployed; BAZ, where 7.3 percent of the population lived, accounted for 11 percent of the unemployed; while Györ-Moson-Sopron had an unemployment share corresponding to its share of the population (2.5

percent). Following the start of economic recovery in Hungary in 1993-94, unemployment fell across the country by 25 percent. Regionally, the total fell most in Győr (26 percent), implying an economic boom, but sharp decline was also evident in BAZ (21 percent), suggesting renewed economic rigour. Unemployment fell least in Budapest (10 percent) although the starting point was already relatively low.

- *Economic development:* in 1994, Budapest was by far the leading county with a per capita GDP of 180 percent of the national average; Győr was in second place (106 percent); and BAZ in 18th position (second to last in the rank order of counties) with a GDP per capita level equivalent to only 69 percent of the national average.
- *Living standards:* as an indicator of living standards, car ownership in 1995 was almost 300 per 1,000 inhabitants in Budapest, 233 in Győr and 159 in BAZ. Conversely, in the rank order of need, BAZ had a high concentration of needy people in 1995, with 14.4 percent of people receiving unemployment benefits, compared to 8.6 percent in Budapest and 1.8 percent in Győr.

The inflow of renewed investment played a key role in the economic recovery process. In spatial terms, there was a clear preference for Budapest and Győr. Foreign capital concentrated in Budapest, which accounted for 62 percent of the foreign capital in 1994. BAZ, conversely, attracted very little, only 2.1 percent of the foreign capital in 1994, while Győr accounted for four percent of FDI in 1994, growing to 5.5 percent of total FDI in 1995.

The direction of the capital flows can be explained by the relative attractiveness of the three regions. Budapest is a business and administrative centre with diversified industry and many services, for example in connection with tourism. The majority of the R&D staff and the leading business managers are also centred in Budapest (Enyedi, 1997). Győr is close to Western markets, has a diverse industrial structure, and the lifestyle and attitude similarities with Austria make it easy for foreigners to do business. BAZ, on the other hand, is far away from Western Europe, both in distance and in attitudes and tradition. The old industrial plants are not attractive since they are run down and belong to generally troubled sectors. Greenfield investment in new sectors is also easier in more developed regions.

However, in terms of investment in manufacturing, the role of Budapest is less pronounced, the situation of BAZ less depressing and that of Győr quite impressive. Budapest received a quarter of the investment in manufacturing, BAZ 8.2 percent and Győr 9.7 percent in 1994. As a result of the different capital flows, the spatial distribution of industry changed after 1989, but not as much as one might have expected. Measured as persons employed in industry, the major change seems to be the decrease in Budapest's share to 16.6 percent in 1995. BAZ's share of Hungary's industrial employment dropped to 8.7 percent, and Győr's share increased a little to 5.6 percent (Central Statistical Office). In terms of dependence on industry, Budapest has achieved a greater shift towards the services sector, reducing its share of industrial employees to 17.7 percent of the country total. Dependence is considerably higher in BAZ and Győr, where the respective figures are 40 and 38 percent (Central Statistical Office, 1995).

Given the role of industry in Hungary's economic profile (more than 30 percent of the active labour force), the country's future depends very much on the development in this area. This, in turn, is linked to the way that individual companies cope with the challenges facing them. The following section presents empirical results documenting how regional location influences the extent and direction of innovation at company level.

Product change and innovation in the three regions

Product innovation[2] is crucial to competitiveness, and competitiveness is what Hungarian companies have had to accomplish since 1989 in order to survive. Product innovation incorporates a range of changes in a company, including qualifications, organisation and production technique. In this analysis, product changes are considered rather broadly, namely as changes in the volume and composition of production on the one hand, and different degrees of product innovation (the introduction of new products) on the other hand.

Two questions are central to the investigation of product change. First, has the transition process called forward a process of product specialisation, and thus a movement away from the highly integrated and Fordist inspired production system? The answer to this is negative. Indeed, investigation showed that the companies in general were characterised by a very diversified product range. This is a continuation of the structure before 1989 in which Hungarian companies were highly integrated, both horizontally and vertically. Since 1989 the companies have increased their product range, which is the same as a further diversification. The rationale for this is that the market is not considered big enough for product specialisation, that many customers want to get everything from one producer, and that some companies experienced such trouble with supplies that they wanted to control the production of raw materials or semi-manufactured products themselves. Judging from the research, the focus on diversification will continue in the future. In addition to this general picture the data suggest a regional variation, with some signs of a certain product specialisation among companies in Györ, but less in Budapest and none in Miskolc.

The second central question is whether the process of transition, particularly in the light of the many new impulses from the market, has given rise to product innovation at the company level? In this case, the answer was positive. Practically all companies (90 percent) had introduced new products. Most reported that they had adapted existing products, some had introduced alternative products (new to the firm but not to the market) as a supplement to use the existing capacity, and a few had developed new products themselves, ie. products that were new both to the firms and to the market. Interviews revealed that, in future, adaptation in terms of quality development will be a concern in many companies.

The regional analysis shows that companies in all regions have introduced new products and that adaptation was the most widespread strategy. However, there is a difference in that the Györ companies seem to prefer product development to the introduction of alternative products, while the reverse was true in the Budapest companies. Miskolc resembles Györ in that adaptation and product development were main product strategies.

In summary, there are great similarities among the product changes since 1989, but it is possible to distinguish between strategies used in the three different regions. The companies in Györ have been expanding their production, have been able to specialise production a little, and have introduced new products, based on their own adaptation and development efforts. In Miskolc, the companies have reduced their production, and they have compensated for the loss of markets by using a diversification strategy mainly based on adaptation but also on product development. Budapest companies have mostly decreased production volumes and have diversified production. It is striking, however, that product development has not taken place in the Budapest companies.

Production technique

Machinery and equipment make a difference to product quality and price, and a key issue is the change of production technique since 1989. The general picture of the sample is that machinery is very old, with almost half of the companies stating that their machinery is more than 20 years old. Regionally the age of equipment increases with the eastern location of the companies. In Győr, a third of the interviewed companies had relatively new equipment, while the figure fell to 12 percent in Budapest and zero in Miskolc.

A large percentage, namely 40 percent of the companies, have not undertaken any renewal at all since 1989. Most of the companies that have failed to modernise are found in Budapest, while, in comparison, only a small share of the companies in Győr and Miskolc have not modernised their machinery at all.

Changes in qualification profile

Qualification and organisation are among the 'soft' aspects of technology and are closely related to changes in products and production techniques. The share of skilled workers in Hungarian companies is very high, quite unlike the Fordist tradition. There is a notable share of white-collar workers, (27 percent), but with the share in some companies rising to 50 percent. The high share of white-collar workers indicates that planning, co-ordinating and controlling tasks are still widely separated from the shop floor.

All enterprises have highly educated managers with university or college degrees, while the skilled workers have technical school or equivalent backgrounds. Few skilled workers participate in middle management and none in top management. This indicates a qualification gap between top and bottom in the companies and can be interpreted as Fordist type opposition between management on the one hand and the labour force on the other hand. Further, the qualifications of the different groups of employees are mainly technical, while (formal) managerial qualifications are scarcely represented. This indicates that the companies are poorly equipped in terms of qualifications to cope with management tasks in a market economy. Since 1989, however, some upgrading of management qualifications is evident while the number of unskilled workers on the shop floor has generally been cut back in reaction to cost considerations.

Changes in organisation

The process of transition has challenged the way production was organised in the planned economy in several ways. First, companies that were previously very big, or part of a trust, have been split up and privatised. The new individual companies have had to cope with tasks that were earlier resolved at the level of the trust, at ministerial level or at the level of the sector research institutes. Second, cost efficiency has become more important with implications for the way activities are organised. Finally, traditional Fordist-inspired organisational forms have been challenged by new management forms used among competitors in the West.

The Fordist principles that inspired the organisation of industrial production in the planned economies from the 1940s can be summarised as follows: a hierarchical organisational structure; centralised decision-making with vertical, top-down oriented lines of decision and communication; and an extended division of labour and specialisation of different tasks (Boyer, 1989). In the West these organisational principles have been challenged by the emergence of new technology, and by varied and changeable consumer demands which led to the need for more flexible organisational forms better able to utilise human abilities on the floor. Have these new conditions affected the organisation of Hungarian industrial companies?

Research on the present organisational structures of the Hungarian companies and the on-going changes in their structures, suggests that almost all the enterprises are characterised by a functional division of labour, most with a hierarchical, top-down management in which the director has a strong role in decision-making. Delegation of responsibility and horizontal co-ordination are seldom seen. The companies are characterised by a relatively high number of specialised departments, and the companies integrate many different activities, from the preparation of raw materials to quality control, ie. they are highly vertically integrated. New activities like marketing, design and construction were not frequently represented in the department structure.

The most frequent organisational changes made by companies under the new economic conditions include a reduction in the number of departments and the emergence of new departments in areas such as quality control and marketing. In Győr, changes were generally constructive and future oriented while in Miskolc, they tended to be made more in reaction to personnel dismissal and were more defensive in nature.

Changes in trade structure and inter-firm relations

The internal changes of the companies cannot be understood without reference to the external relations of the enterprises. In Hungary, the change of regulation systems from planned and indirect supply and demand managed, for example, through trade companies, to market-based and direct supply is an institutional change of great importance for companies. Market-based supply and demand are more unstable and more direct than within the former planned system, and the ability to manage these relations is necessary for a company operating in a market environment.

Analysis of the overall changes in the market structure affecting companies shows that trade relations today are privatised, decentralised and diversified. Companies have felt the changes since 1989 in two areas: the radical change in the export markets from East to West, and the multiplication of the number of customers. The meso-institutions regulating the relations with customers have undergone considerable change since 1989. Today, all companies communicate directly with their customers, receiving specific demands as well as feed back, and most of them co-operate with customers about product development. The role of the customer has changed from a secondary one to a crucial partner in the life of the company, and companies acknowledge the importance of this relationship.

Concerning supplies, the most important changes have been the emergence of many small suppliers, due to privatisation and the splitting up of companies, and an increase in imports, due to better import possibilities. Unreliable supplies, often the result of the weak financial position of the suppliers, are also a new experience for the Hungarian companies. However, companies continue to undertake all phases of production themselves, based on the purchase of raw materials, although subcontracting and the purchase of components also took place to some extent.

In regional terms, the Győr companies interviewed tend to compete more on the basis of quality, have closer links with customers and be more export oriented than in BAZ or Budapest. Conversely in Miskolc, price is more the competitive strength and little co-operation with customers and suppliers has emerged. Exports to the West have also been forced by the loss of traditional markets. Export was the least important for the Budapest-based companies.

Summary and conclusions

The above analysis shows that similarities exist in the company-level development, structure and change in the three case-study Hungarian regions. This is due to a shared heritage of Fordist-inspired socialist production organisation and to common conditions at the macro-level that have confronted the companies since 1989. However, considerable differentiation can also be identified in the industrial development paths of the two regions.

The companies in Győr have expanded and specialised their production, and have introduced new products based on their own adaptation and development efforts. This has been done on the basis of relatively new production equipment, modernised since 1989. The qualification profile of the companies in Győr represents a steep pyramid with a slim share of administrative staff and a tiny top administration, and a large share of skilled, manual workers. The organisational changes in Győr since 1989 have been constructive and made the companies better able to cope with the challenges arising from the process of transition. They have expanded and upgraded management and a few have reorganised work processes. The Győr companies were more export-oriented, and stress co-operation with customers and suppliers more than other companies. They focus on quality rather than on price. As a whole the companies in Győr are more dynamic, efficient and innovative than the companies of the two other regions studied.

The companies in Miskolc have drastically reduced their production volume, and in the midst of this crisis, have introduced new products based on their own adaptation and development effort and have diversified the range of products to survive. They are bound to a very old assembly of machinery, which the companies have tried to modernise in some aspects. The qualification profile, with a very large share of white-collar workers and large management groups, reflects the continuation of Fordist inspired and plan-based economic tradition. Changes consist mainly of a reduction in the number of departments due to the dismissal of people necessitated by the crisis. In their external relations, the Miskolc companies experienced a serious shock as exports to the East ceased, but westward export has been achieved principally through sales at low prices. The Miskolc companies have not changed the highly integrated structure of production, and they do not co-operate much with customers and suppliers. The socialist Fordist heritage is strongly represented and the crisis makes new investment virtually impossible, although it is noteworthy that the companies show considerable dynamism in product development and changing trade structure.

The companies in Budapest have also had to reduce production and have diversified their production to survive. In Budapest, examples of expanding and specialising production can also be found. The companies produce on the basis of rather old machinery and the few changes made are small, resulting in no general upgrading. The qualification profile shows an extreme weight of white-collar workers, reflecting a complex organisation and low cost-consciousness. The Budapest companies have been more reluctant to change their organisation, and there has been no pattern in the changes reported. In their external relations, the Budapest companies regret the loss of foreign markets, and, although the Budapest companies have differentiated their market scope, their export share is today the lowest among the regions analysed. They have developed contacts with customers and suppliers, and have developed products in co-operation with them. A development of inter-firm relations is maybe the most important change for future innovation and competitiveness of the Budapest companies.

It is too early to explain the marked regional differences noted above. As the companies share the same heritage and macro-economic and institutional conditions, explanatory factors must be sought in regional differences, not only in terms of different industrial heritages, but also in different locations, attitudes and traditions. The regional differences do, however, argue for a regional focus of industrial policy. This has been developed in the BAZ case, for example, with the help of the EU Phare programme (Lorentzen,1998), and represents an important first step. However, the Hungarian experience also shows that industrial policy is required at both national and regional level, and that not only troubled regions, but all regions should take an active part in the identification of their problems, needs and objectives for future development. In line with this reasoning, the Hungarian law on regional development and physical planning from 1996 provides a formal institutional basis for the active involvement of counties, regions and communities - a topic expanded in more detail in Chapter 22 of this volume.

Very tentatively the following industrial development paths could be emerging in the three regions analysed in this chapter: Györ has scope for international specialisation based on high quality products and modern production techniques, in co-operation with foreign partners; Budapest could develop company specialisation and co-operation among local industries as a platform for regional innovation and competitiveness, using foreign partners as a lever for quality development and export; and Miskolc might stress the export of standardised products, make cost-reducing investment and reorganisation at company level, and upgrade product quality. Most of all, the Hungarian government should create a climate in which new investment in machinery and equipment becomes attainable, and in which the home market regains sufficient movement to stimulate industrial growth and innovation.

Notes

1   An earlier version of this article was published in *European Planning Studies*, vol. 7 no. 4 August 1999.
2   The research on innovation in Hungarian industry is based on qualitative interviews in 20 production companies involved in machine building and food processing. The sample consisted of 1 State-owned, 2 foreign-owned, 12 private Hungarian-owned companies and 5 companies under privatisation. The interviews were carried out in 1994 and 1995. The interviews regarded changes at different levels within the companies as well as changes in the relations between the companies and their surroundings, that is in the trade and inter-enterprise relations. A basic idea was to consider innovation at company level as a result of an interplay between different factors, the priority of which could not be decided on beforehand. Both concepts of the technological capacity of society (Lorentzen, 1988), Porter's diamond (Porter, 1990) and of different production systems (Boyer, 1989) inspired the approach (Lorentzen and Rostgaard, 1997).

References

Borsod-Abaúj-Zémplen County Development Council (1995), *Integrated Reconversion and Crisis Management Programme for Borsod-Abaúj-Zemplen County*, Miskolc.
Bencze, I. and Tajti, E.V. (1972), *Budapest. An industrial geographical approach*, Akadémiai Kiadó, Budapest.

Bernát, T. (1989), *An economic geography of Hungary*, Adadémiai Kiadó, Budapest.

Boyer, R. (1989), *New directions in management practices and work organisation. General principles and national trajectories*, OECD conference 'Technology change as a social process - society, enterprises and the individual', Helsinki, 11-13 December.

Central Statistical Office (1995), *Statistical Yearbook of Hungary 1995*, Budapest.

Downes, R. and Horváth, G. (1996), *The Challenge of Regional Policy Development in Hungary*, Regional and Industrial Policy Research Series no. 15, European Policies Research Centre, University of Strathclyde, Glasgow.

Economic Bulletin for Europe (1997), Vol. 49:93.

Ernst, M., Alexeev, M. and Marer, P. (1996), *Transforming the core. Restructuring Industrial Enterprises in Russia and Central Europe*, Westview Press, Oxford.

European Bank for Reconstruction and Development (1997), *Transition report 1997*, London, p. 225.

Enyedi, G. (1997), 'Budapest: return to European competition', in Jensen-Butler, C., Shachar, A. and von Weesep, J. (eds) (1997), *European cities in competition*, Avebury, Aldershot.

Farkas, B. (1995), *Regional Policy in Hungary: Tendencies in the transition period*, Paper presented at the 'Regional Futures' conference, Regional Studies Association, Gothenburg, Sweden, 6-9 May.

Horváth, G. (1996), 'The Regional Policy of the transition in Hungary', *European Spatial Research and Policy*, vol. 3, no. 2.

Lorentzen, A. (1996), 'Regional Development and Institutions in Hungary: Past, Present and Future Development', *European Planning Studies*, vol. 4, no. 3, pp. 259-77.

Lorentzen, A. (1988), *Technological capacity. A contribution to a comprehensive understanding of technology and development in an international perspective*, Technology and Society Series, no. 5, Aalborg University Press, Aalborg.

Lorentzen, A. (1998), 'Transition institutions and regional development in Hungary, BAZ county', in Halkier H. and Danson, M. (eds) (1998), *Regional Development Agencies in Europe*, Jessica Kingsley, London and Bristol, pp. 141-62.

Lorentzen, A. and Rostgaard, M. (1997), *Technological change in Hungarian industry after 1989 - results from empirical research in 20 Hungarian enterprises*, Department of Development and Planning, Aalborg University.

The OECD Observer (1997), no. 207, August 1997.

OECD (1994), *Synthesis report on the seminar: The steel industry in transition. Financial and privatisation issues*, OECD Working Papers 77, Paris.

Porter, M. E. (1990), *The Competitive Advantage of Nations*. MacMillan, London and Basingstoke.

Szaló, P. (1994), 'Influences of structural changes on regional economics in Hungary', in Hajdú, Z. and Horváth, G. (eds) (1994), *European Challenges and Hungarian responses in Regional Policy*, Centre for Regional Studies, Pècs, pp. 79-93.

WIIW (Vienna Institute for Comparative Economic Studies) (1996), *WIIW Handbook of Statistics 1996 - Countries in transition*, Vienna.

16 Inward Investment, Cohesion and the 'Wealth of Regions' in East-Central Europe

ADRIAN SMITH AND PETR PAVLÍNEK

Cohesion and enlargement: inward investment as panacea for enhancing the 'wealth of regions'?

The future enlargement of the European Union to include potential new Member States from East-Central Europe (ECE) will profoundly redraw the map of regional inequality within the Union (Dunford and Smith, 2000). Economic disparities between east and west are substantial, with the wealthiest applicant state (Slovenia) recording a per capita GDP in purchasing power standards in 1995 some 59 percent of the EU average. The poorest applicant (Romania) recorded a per capita income some 23 percent of the average, which places it in a similar position to Russia (not an applicant). At the regional level, data for two of the applicant states (Hungary and Slovakia) indicate that the majority of regions fall below the 75 percent of EU per capita GDP threshold currently used as a basis for identifying Objective 1 regions (Dunford and Smith, 2000). As Iain Begg (1996) has argued, then, the addition of approximately 105 million people in the ECE applicant countries would increase the EU population by 28 percent, while simultaneously adding only between 3.4 percent and 8.5 percent to EU GDP (depending upon whether one uses nominal exchange rates or PPS estimates). Consequently, average EU per capita GDP would be likely to drop by 15 percent. In other words, at current levels and under current criteria applied to EU Member States, all applicant countries would be eligible for Cohesion Fund support in addition to support through the Structural programmes, costing something in the range of 42 billion euro. Such transfers would account for between seven percent of Slovenia's GDP and 51 percent of Lithuania's (Grabbe and Hughes, quoted in Begg, 1996).

It is partly within this context of large-scale disparities in levels of economic development between applicant states and their regions and current EU Member States that claims have developed concerning the role that exogenous forces, such as foreign direct investment (FDI), can play in enhancing regional and national competitiveness in East-Central Europe. Foreign direct investment, for example, has been seen as a mechanism by which peripheral regions in ECE can position themselves within flows of global capital in order to restructure what is claimed to be an out-moded, inefficient industrial structure that represents the legacy of state socialism (Dunning, 1993). As such, within this analysis, inward investment can provide a catalyst for significant levels of restructuring both within enterprises – through new investment programmes, access to new markets and intra-corporate networks, new managerial technologies, etc – and in regional economies – through the creation of local supply linkages, enhanced labour market opportunities, and so on.

Closely related to these claims concerning the role of inward investment in ECE is a set of arguments, largely derived from non-ECE experiences which suggest that inward investment can create conditions for a progressive upgrading of regional economies through enhanced learning, innovation and strengthening the density and 'thickness' of economic institutions. Dicken et al. (1994) have argued that 'probably the most important single indicator of local embeddedness [of foreign investors] relates to supplier relationships'. They argue that embeddedness in networks of local supply contracts assists in the development of spread effects into the local economy dominated by a multinational corporation (MNC). Similarly, Malmberg et al. (1996) have argued that MNCs, 'rather than being in opposition to the notion of local knowledge accumulation, to a large degree follow a similar "learning logic" [which is localised]. They too are dependent upon strong local milieux — or home bases — in the knowledge accumulation necessary for their long-term competitiveness'.

This second set of arguments, then, speaks to an increased role for inward investors in the upgrading of local supply chains and in the creation of regionalised 'learning' to enhance regional performance. In the words of Amin and Thrift (1994), 'the global' can be 'held down' in local economies and the competitiveness of less favoured regions can be enhanced through an engagement with global capital. Inward investment can become a mechanism for 'offensive restructuring' in which local skills and supply networks are developed further, productivity increases, and institutional actors at the regional level enter into co-operative relations enhancing the upgrading of skills and component supply relations. Drawing upon institutionalist and evolutionary theory, Amin and Thrift argue that an alternative to regional peripherality in an enlarged and more integrated Europe can result from the creation of dynamic institutional and endogenous relations (see also Storper (1997) for a parallel argument). For Amin and Thrift, there is a need to create high levels of 'institutional thickness' to guarantee regional economic competitiveness. Such 'thickness' will result in collaborative and collective interactions between a host of regional institutions working for mutual benefit (however, see Smith (1998) for a critique of these arguments in an East European context). In this view, foreign manufacturing plants can be seen as one type of actor potentially guaranteeing a progressive upgrading of local development in collaboration with other firms, regional development agencies, financial institutions, and so on. However, while evidence from Eastern Europe is often piecemeal and based upon case study evidence, it does appear that, while inward investment *has* transformed the productive and technological basis of enterprises, it is having very uneven impacts on regional economic buoyancy (Grabher, 1992, 1993, 1997; Sadler and Swain, 1994; Sharp and Marz, 1997; Havas, 1997; Pavlínek, 1998; Pavlínek and Smith, 1998; Smith and Ferenčíková, 1998). Indeed, as Morgan (1997) has recognised in the context of Wales, innovation policies which stress the development of supply linkages and technological transfer between inward investors and endogenous firms should *not* be regarded as mechanisms to solve many of the key problems of 'less-favoured regions', such as mass unemployment and social exclusion. What such policies can hope to do, however, according to Morgan (1997), is to help "safeguard existing jobs, embed existing foreign plants, promote more robust linkages between these plants and indigenous firms, and [help] ... to disseminate 'best practice' throughout the regional economy" (however, see Hudson (1999) for an important critique of the claims for developing regionalised innovation and learning).

Such claims fail to consider two important aspects of restructuring led by inward investment. First, there is inadequate treatment of the role of corporate power and labour process transformations in the process of restructuring led by inward investment. There is a general failure to consider the way in which labour process control becomes increasingly dominated by multinational firms, concomitant with an exclusion of more democratic ways of potentially organising the work-place. This is of particular importance in ECE where new labour practices and management techniques brought by inward investment have transformed the wage relation and employment contract, but in the direction of labour flexibility rather than work place democratisation.

Second, these claims neglect to consider different forms of industrial and regional restructuring resulting from inward investment. Lipietz (1992), for example, has argued that regions can be differentiated on the basis of whether local and international actors within regional economies adopt strategies for 'defensive restructuring' through a focus on low wage, cost advantages and large-scale worker flexibility, or strategies involving a more progressive upgrading through 'offensive restructuring' in which there is a conservation and enrichment of skills, connected to high wages, increasing productivity and important levels of co-operation and partnership between economic and institutional actors. Indeed, the marginalisation of local economic strengths resulting from inward investment is, in part, the result of cost-cutting, 'defensive' strategies used by foreign investors who have continuously been the dominant actors in inward investment.

This chapter develops these two arguments by drawing upon a number of intensive, in-depth case studies of inward investment in the manufacturing sector in the Czech Republic and Slovakia (see Pavlínek and Smith, 1998, for further details). The chapter develops two main arguments. First, that the experiences of inward investment suggest that reliance upon globalised corporate networks may not be the godsend that many of the proponents of FDI in 'transition' suggest it to be. Second, the paper argues that the role of inward investment in enterprise restructuring varies significantly within a single state, and this alone requires us to question the type of investor strategies and their impacts on regional development and enterprise restructuring.

Inward investment, industrial restructuring and cohesion in the Czech Republic and Slovakia

Recent research on the role of inward investment in regional change suggests that there is a need to examine the locally and nationally specific impacts of FDI along a number of trajectories. Generally, five main conclusions from our research on Slovakia can be arrived at. First, with the exception of the VW auto investment in the capital city region of Bratislava, inward investment has had only a limited effect on local employment levels. In the case of the US company, Whirlpool, investment in Poprad in north-eastern Slovakia, for example, has resulted in employment loss, contributing to the relatively high level of local unemployment in the region. In Bratislava, where employment levels have increased, this has worked to exacerbate labour shortages in the region, and VW has been introducing various employment and training programmes to secure a work force. In part, labour retention is worsened by low wages and high work-intensity in such plants.

Second, skills upgrading is limited across all regions with significant levels of foreign investment. All firms show high levels of labour intensity, rather than technology intensity, and investors have used labour-intensive, 'bottom-end' production to cut costs. In many ways, most of our case studies indicate few research and development functions, and the companies look like typical, low-cost branch plants rather than dynamic 'performance plants' said to be at the forefront of enhanced, FDI-led restructuring in some parts of Europe.

Third, the introduction of new management practices has been one of the most important changes in firms, but nowhere has this enhanced the democratisation of the work place. In Whirlpool Poprad, for example, increased shop floor and contractual flexibility have been used to downsize employment and increase insecurity.

Fourth, inward investment has resulted in the emergence of significant differences in intra-regional wage levels between employees in firms with FDI and in the local economy. In the majority of firms wage levels are higher in foreign-owned plants; up to 80 percent higher in one of the regional economies in central Slovakia, Liptovský Mikuláš. Some would argue that increasing local wage levels through inward investment will boost local demand for goods. But employment increases tend to be marginal and the benefits of such wage increases are limited. In the Bratislava case where employment levels *have* increased, wages are low and less differentiated from those in the local economy which tend already to be relatively high.

Finally, what have been the impacts on local supply networks? Only in one case examined has there been any significant growth in local suppliers (Poprad), which are part of a just-in-time (JIT) supply system increasing work-place flexibility in Whirlpool Poprad. In the automobile sector, where one would perhaps expect to see such networks emerging, virtually all sourcing occurs through VW's European corporate networks and none occurs locally. The low level of supplier embeddedness therefore remains a major constraint on creating more integrated inward investment in Slovakia.

To what extent have the experiences of inward investment in Slovakia been mirrored in the Czech Republic, which has been a much larger recipient of FDI and where the bulk of foreign investment has gone into several, large, formerly state-owned companies privatised in the early 1990s? The four largest investments, for example, accounted for 59 percent of all directly invested capital between 1990 and 1995 (Pavlínek, 1998).

First, it is important to distinguish between two main types of investment – cross border export-oriented investment based on low labour and production costs (in comparison to Germany, Austria and the rest of the European Union) and market capture FDI. The first type of investment has had almost no positive impact on regional development because of virtually non-existent local and national supplier linkages. Such investments are characterised by small branch plants that are vertically integrated into the networks of multinational companies. These branch plants are in a vulnerable position because they are usually first to be closed if cross-border production cost differentials change or if a multinational company tries to cut its losses at times of economic difficulties.

Market-capture investments, however, are typically large investments in existing state-owned companies that often involve the purchase of the entire network of production units across the Czech Republic. After their privatisation, these companies usually underwent rapid restructuring based on the inflow of foreign capital, technology and managerial skills to improve their competitiveness and consolidate their position on the Czech and foreign markets. This type of inward investment has usually attempted to develop linkages with local firms and integrate its operations in local economic networks. Some sectors, such as food processing, depend on local suppliers by virtue of their operations. Others attempt to reap the benefits of relatively cheap and skilled local labour by subcontracting locally instead of importing more expensive components from abroad. Market-capture investments are thus, unlike in the Slovak example, likely to contribute to increased regional economic activity and are more likely to be long-term investments compared to cross-border, export-oriented investments elsewhere in the Czech Republic. Such investments are rare, however, and the potential for this type of investment has been largely exhausted during the privatisation process that took place in the first half of the 1990s. In the Czech Republic, the typical examples include the Volkswagen investment in the Škoda car maker and, to a much lesser degree, the purchase of Vitana, the food processing firm specialising in pre-prepared food, by the Norwegian company Rieber & Son.

However, the associated potential risks include the strong dependence of the regional economy on a single foreign multinational corporation making its decisions in the context of its global and multiple operations. The introduction of new production concepts unacceptable to labour unions in Western Europe, such as has occurred at Škoda, indicates the readiness of multinational companies to exploit relatively weak and inexperienced unions.

Skills upgrading has been very limited in both types of investment. Cross-border, export-oriented investments seek low-wage, low-skilled labour. Typically, young female workers assemble imported components which usually represents de-skilling rather than skills upgrading, a situation similar to the *maquiladoras* on the U.S.-Mexican border and other export processing zones in the less developed countries. Market-capture investment has also had limited impact on skills upgrading because the skill level of Czech labour is relatively high. For example, according to one manager at the Škoda car maker, the skill level of Škoda's workers based on one hundred years of experience of making cars is higher than that of the workers in Western Europe and was (according to him) the most important reason why Volkswagen bought Škoda.

As in Slovakia, one of the most important changes in the foreign-owned firms has been the introduction of new management practices. As a union leader at Škoda argued in 1996, Volkswagen did not bring any new skills to Škoda but it brought "new work organisation and order". Similar changes have been experienced in other foreign-owned companies and joint ventures. What this new 'organisation and order' means in practical terms is the replacement of state socialist work organisation and shop-floor practices with capitalist ones. The anarchy of the production associated with state socialism and typified by continual reorganisation of the labour process (Burawoy 1985) has been replaced with the planned organisation of production.[1] The considerable autonomy workers enjoyed on the shop floor and the control of production they exercised under the previous state socialist system (see Clarke et al., 1994; Burawoy and Pavel, 1993, 1992) has been removed and replaced by increased authority of the foreman and effective managerial control as more efficient horizontal and vertical organisation of the work-place has been introduced. New management practices also include the introduction of western concepts such as JIT production.

Between 1993 and 1996, two-thirds of foreign-owned companies and joint ventures in manufacturing created new jobs while about one-third shed workers (Pomery, 1997; Marek, 1998).[2] Overall, however, the impact of foreign investment on local employment levels has been limited as the total number of people employed in foreign manufacturing plants remains low – approximately six percent of the total workforce of the Czech Republic. Companies with foreign participation are affected by the low level of flexibility of Czech labour in terms of its ability to move because of the non-existent housing market. Based on a survey of manufacturing plants with foreign presence, 63 percent of surveyed companies said that they were having problems finding properly skilled labour in their present location. Almost one-third (27 percent) of foreign-owned manufacturing plants or joint ventures used foreign workers from Slovakia, Ukraine and Poland in 1997 (Pomery, 1997), who are cheaper and much more flexible than Czech workers.

These experiences suggest that inward investment in Slovakia and the Czech Republic is having (at best) a very uneven impact on the upgrading of regional performance. Few 'spread effects' are identifiable and many inward investment projects remain relatively isolated 'cathedrals in the desert' of an increasingly de-industrialised space economy. However, as we suggested earlier, there has been a shift in academic writing about inward investment in 'less favoured regions', such as those of East-Central Europe, to consider the potential role that external investment *could* have if the right kind of policy and institutional frameworks are developed. This recent concern mirrors the rise of interest in the *regional capacity* for learning and innovation in an increasingly globalised economy (Storper, 1997; Amin, 1998; Amin and Thrift, 1994, 1995). The following section outlines some potentials for and constraints on developing a set of regional capacities enhancing the impacts of inward investment in East and Central Europe's 'less favoured regions'.

Regional policy and upgrading the 'wealth of regions'

The recent turn in regional development studies to consider the role of specifically regional capacities in enhancing firm and regional competitiveness and performance (Storper, 1997) has led Amin (1998) to argue that, in European less-favoured regions with high levels of externally owned or controlled firms, four potentials exist for upgrading the status of inward investment and for promoting strategies of 'offensive' rather than 'defensive' restructuring. The focus for Amin is "on building the wealth of regions (rather than the individual firms), with upgrading of the economic, institutional, and social base as the prerequisite for entrepreneurial success" (Amin, 1998). The four aspects stressed by Amin are as follows:

- *building clusters of inter-related industries* with long roots in a local skill or capabilities base to enhance international competitive advantage and *building economies of association* by encouraging "social dialogue and learning based on shared knowledge and information exchange", inter-firm exchange and reciprocity (Amin, 1998);
- *learning to learn and adapt* to changing external firm and sectoral environments and to predict and shape future trajectories of growth, and being able to evolve in order to adapt;
- *broadening and mobilising the local institutional base* to enhance locally democratic and interactive associations between state and non-state actors to unlock local potentials; and,
- *creating socially inclusive entrepreneurship and employment* to nurture skills, expertise and capabilities rather than solely to increase the overall volume of jobs.

Hudson (1998, 1999), however, has warned against uncritically embracing a perspective based around localised learning and supply-side improvements as the basis for enhanced regional performance and for transferring models developed around a small set of largely West-European examples to the environments of East-Central Europe (see also Hudson 1997). As Hudson (1999) argues, learning is by no means "a universal panacea to the problems of socio-spatial inequality and in some respects is used as a cloak behind which some of the harsher realities of capitalism can be hidden. Addressing the problems of uneven development and inequality ... poses very hard policy and political choices for those who seek to devise progressive development trajectories". In particular, Hudson argues that, first, the production of knowledge and learning may be less important facets of corporate success than aspects of corporate practice such as rationalising and increasing the production efficiency of existing commodities or devising new commodities for profitable production. Second, new forms of 'inclusive' work practices and management techniques based around re-skilling and team-work may be less significant than an intensification of the labour process under contemporary capitalism: "Workers are enmeshed within disempowering regimes of subordination, characterised by control, exploitation, and surveillance, accepting arrangements through which they discipline themselves and their fellow workers, while bound together through the rhetoric of team working" (Hudson, 1999). This has clearly been the case in the context of the new work practices discussed above implemented in Czech and Slovak foreign investments. Third, new work practices are increasingly concerned with no-union and one-union agreements and so the basis for inclusion and negotiation of democratic work places is eroded further. Fourth, the proposed role for increased network relations between firms may be less based upon equal exchange and reciprocity than upon "sharp asymmetries in power between companies, and ... subtle coercion if companies wish to keep their customers or suppliers" (Hudson, 1999). Finally, 'institutional thickness' and dense mosaics of state and non-state interaction may be no guarantee for *long-term* innovation, learning and competitiveness as institutional lock-in can constrain change (see also Smith and Swain, 1998).

To what extent then is there a potential for the implementation and development of such 'wealth of regions' policies in the East-Central European context? We would suggest that the scope is limited for four main reasons. First, the corporate strategies of multinational companies investing in East-Central Europe are not conducive to enhancing regional economic performance. Strategies tend to capitalise on the low-wage, low-cost locational advantages of the region and upon gaining access to new markets. It therefore seems unlikely that the significant development divide between east and west in Europe (Dunford and Smith, 2000) will be overcome by enhancing the role of western corporations in the region.

Second, regional capacities *within* East-Central Europe have been starkly eroded as a result of two main processes: the de-industrialisation of large parts of the region in the early 1990s (Smith, 1998; Dunford, 1998) and the continued adherence to neo-liberal policies and macro-economic prudence under a regime of global governance (Gowan, 1995; Smith, 1997, 1998) which constrains the options that are open to policy-makers in the region.

Third, the regional institutional structures of East-Central Europe under state socialism could be characterised as 'thin', and this legacy remains an important impediment to enhancing regional performance. This was true in both the state and non-state sectors. In the state sector there are few actors to build on, aside from those attached to the former hegemony of the Communist Party. In the non-state sector there were few firms with limited sub-contracting linkages between them, a stress upon local autarky (although see the case of VW-Škoda in the Czech Republic (Pavlínek, 1998, Pavlínek and Smith, 1998)) and, outside of the enterprise sphere, little basis for enhancing civic involvement and 'local voice' as has been seen to be important in areas of growth such as those in parts of Italy.

Finally, there is little epistemological basis for arguing that the kinds of models put forward in the 'new regionalist' literature provide the basis for change in East-Central Europe. Such models tend towards voluntarism rather than an understanding of power and control, and the latter is of double significance in considering the inability of, and constraints placed upon, regional and national actors in transition contexts where disempowerment is the norm.

What is to be done? Some concluding comments

Given the above stated limitations to enhancing the 'wealth of regions' using strategies identified in the evolutionary work of Amin, what alternatives are there for progressive local and regional development in ECE? In concluding this chapter we want to identify three main areas for consideration.

First, little can be done to enhance regional performance and to integrate external investors more fully in relation to supply networks and democratisation if the neo-liberal framework of fiscal and monetary austerity continues in ECE. Clear progress has been made in many contexts for reducing inflation, and there is now some scope for major investment in productive upgrading and an enhanced interventionist industrial policy to guarantee effective industrial restructuring. Clearly, the inflationary impacts of such expenditures have to be closely monitored, but macro-economic flexibility must go beyond the hegemony of 'Washington consensus' style policies (see Chapter 3) of limited state intervention and austerity. Indeed, Amin (1998) and Amin and Tomaney (1995) have argued that such forms of expenditure in Western Europe are now essential if the problem of unemployment and exclusion are to be dealt with. In ECE, where mass unemployment and structural unemployment are fundamental issues, and where unemployment levels are invariably high (Smith, 2000), significant action needs to be taken over and above any supply-side solutions. If cohesive and more democratic transitions are to be developed in ECE, then demand-side mechanisms need to be introduced in order to increase consumption and demand among those who are most marginalised and excluded.

Second, such arguments presuppose that action is required not just at the regional level, but that 'the national' is of fundamental importance in securing more equitable and cohesive development trajectories. As Hudson (1998) has argued, "The strong regional economies of western Europe are clustered in the strong national economies, within national regulatory regimes that have made fewest concessions to the worst excesses of Anglo-American neoliberalism". To a large degree, a similar argument can be made in the context of ECE where 'strong' regional economies tend to be those in the 'stronger' national economies (see Dunford and Smith, 2000). The crucial question, however, is what type of national state. In ECE it seems essential that national states are required to implement programmes that will enhance social justice and equity, and facilitate and enable a more egalitarian and inclusive society. If constraining and negotiating the roles of inward investors is part of such a strategy, then the national state is required to make such interventions.

Finally, the above two comments need to be seen within the context of a strategy of economic democratisation. The 'great revolutions' of ECE have largely been about political democratisation. Economic democratisation has been essentially marginalised (see the discussion in Smith, 1998). While focusing on the former Soviet Union, Weisskopf (1993) has argued that democratic worker self-management of enterprises represents the best way of ensuring a 'third way' between the centralised plan and the ravages of the market in post-state socialist societies. Indeed, democratic self-management, it is claimed, is particularly appropriate for the post-state socialist economy because there is only a weak environment for the development of market capitalism, workers were accorded a significant degree of control under state socialism over the day-to-day labour process, which can be built upon in self-management and that there is increasingly a desire in ECE to construct a new system on the basis of 'fairness, stability, and security' (Weisskopf 1993). Furthermore, Schweickart (1993) has also argued the case for work-place democratisation, increased worker motivation by tying wages to productivity, and the combination of self-management with market forms of co-ordination — '[t]he key feature of a market economy is a firm's right to produce what it wishes to produce, to sell to whomever will buy, to purchase its inputs from whatever sources it can find. ... These are the freedoms most essential to making a worker-managed enterprise a responsible economic agent'. However, socialising property relations among inward investors is politically difficult. A start could be made among domestically owned firms, within the context of a rejuvenated industrial policy enhancing technological and labour process upgrading. Yet any form of socialisation must be central to the construction of new wage relations, new forms of control and new development trajectories. As Sayer and Walker (1992) have argued, 'abolishing the capital–labour relation simultaneously abolishes the enormous disparity in mobility — and consequently power — between capital and labour, which contributes so much to uneven development'. While there are inherent dangers in self-management[3] the shift to greater democratic control over the production process should be seen as equally important as the democratisation of the political sphere, and as a way of shifting towards more socially progressive, cohesive and 'offensive' strategies for regional reconstruction in an enlarging and reconstructing Europe.

Notes

1   While the planned organisation of the appropriation and distribution of goods and services (what Burawoy (1985) calls relations of production) typical of state socialism was replaced by the anarchy associated with capitalism.

2   The figure is based on a survey of manufacturing firms with foreign capital participation in the Czech Republic. The rate of survey return was 26 percent (163 out of 621 firms contacted) (Pomery 1997).

3   Weisskopf (1993, pp. 131–4), for example, highlights a potential loss of economic efficiency as the interests of workers may be more short term than those of a capitalist firm, incentives for quality managerial performance may be lost, there may be an inadequate supply of capital, and insufficient innovation, and the development of problematic social forms such as income inequalities between workers in more and less successful self-managed firms and the concentration of worker assets in undiversified portfolios.

References

Amin, A. (1998), *An institutionalist perspective on regional economic development*, Paper presented at the OECD conference on regional development, Boras, Sweden, 29 January.

Amin, A. and Thrift, N. (1994), 'Living in the global', in Amin, A. and Thrift, N. (eds), *Globalisation, Institutions and Regional Development in Europe*, Oxford University Press, Oxford, pp. 1–22.

Amin, A. and Thrift, N. (1995), 'Institutional issues for the European regions: from markets and plans to socio-economics and powers of association', *Economy and Society*, vol. 24, no. 1, pp. 41–66.

Amin, A. and Tomaney, J. (1995), 'The regional development potential of inward investment in the less favoured regions of the European Community', in Amin, A. and Tomaney, J. (eds), *Behind the Myth of European Union*, pp. 201–20.

Begg, I. (1996), *Inter-regional transfers in a widened Europe*, South Bank European Papers, No. 5, European Institute, South Bank University.

Burawoy, M. (1985), *The Politics of Production*, Verso, London and New York.

Burawoy, M. and Pavel K. (1992), 'The Soviet Transition from Socialism to Capitalism: Worker Control and Economic Bargaining in the Wood Industry.' *American Sociological Review*, vol. 57, no. 19, pp. 16–38.

Burawoy, M. and Pavel K. (1993), 'The Economic Basis of Russia's Political Crisis.' *New Left Review*, vol. 198/1993, pp. 49–69.

Clarke, S., Fairbrother P., Borisov V. and Bizyukov P. (1994), 'The Privatisation of Industrial Enterprises in Russia: Four Case-studies.' *Europe-Asia Studies*, vol. 46, no. 2, pp. 179–214.

Dicken, P., Forsgren, M. and Malmberg, A. (1994), 'The local embeddedness of trans-national corporations', in Amin, A. and Thrift, N. (eds), *Globalisation, Institutions and Regional Development in Europe*, Oxford University Press, Oxford.

Dunford, M. (1998), "Differential development, institutions, modes of regulation and comparative transitions to capitalism: Russia, the Commonwealth of Independent States and the former German Democratic Republic", in Pickles, J. and Smith, A. (eds), *Theorising Transition: The Political Economy of Post-Communist Transformations*, Routledge, London.

Dunford, M. and Smith, A. (2000 forthcoming), 'Catching up or falling behind? Economic performance and regional trajectories in a wider Europe', *Economic Geography*.

Dunning, J. (1993), 'The prospects for foreign direct investment in Eastern Europe', in Artisen, P., Rojec, M. and Svetlicic, M. (eds), *Foreign Investment in Central and Eastern Europe*, Macmillan, London, pp. 16–33.

Gowan, P. (1995), 'Neo-liberal theory and practice for Eastern Europe', *New Left Review*, vol. 213, pp. 3–60.

Grabher, G. (1992), 'Eastern conquista: the truncated industrialisation of East European regions by large West European corporations', in Ernste, H. and Meier, V. (eds), *Regional Development and Contemporary Industrial Response*, Belhaven, London.

Grabher, G. (1993), *Instant capitalism: the regional impacts of western investment in Eastern Germany*, Paper presented to the conference on 'Conflict and Cohesion in the Single Market', Newcastle upon Tyne, November 1993.

Grabher, G. (1997), 'Adaptation at the cost of adaptability? Restructuring the Eastern German Regional Economy', in Grabher, G. and Stark, D. (eds),

Restructuring Networks in Post-Socialism: Legacies, Linkages, and Localities, Oxford University Press, Oxford.

Havas, A. (1997), 'Foreign direct investment and intra-industry trade: the case of the automotive industry in Central Europe', in Dyker, D. (ed), *The Technology of Transition*, Central European University Press, Budapest, pp. 211-40.

Hudson, R. (1998), *What makes economically successful regions in Europe successful? Implications for transferring success from west to east*, Working Papers in Contemporary European Studies no. 27, Sussex European Institute, University of Sussex.

Hudson, R. (1999), 'The learning economy, the learning firm and the learning region: a sympathetic critique of the limits to learning', *European Urban and Regional Studies*, vol. 6, no. 1, pp. 59-72.

Hudson, R., Dunford, M., Hamilton, D. and Kotter, R. (1997), 'Developing regional strategies for economic success: lessons from Europe's economically successful regions?', *European Urban and Regional Studies*, vol. 4, no. 4, pp. 365-73.

Lipietz, A. (1992), The regulation approach and capitalist crisis: an alternative compromise for the 1990s, in Dunford, M. and Kafkalas, G. (eds), *Cities and Regions in the New Europe*, Belhaven, London, pp. 309-34.

Malmberg, A., Sölvell, Ö. and Zander, I. (1996), Spatial clustering, local accumulation of knowledge and firm competitiveness, *Geografiska Annaler*, vol. 78 B, pp. 85-97.

Marek, T. (1998), 'Zpracovatelský průmysl vylepšil své pozice' (Processing industry improved its positions), *Mladá Fronta Dnes*, 9, 22:15.

Morgan, K. (1997), The learning region: institutions, innovation and regional renewal, *Regional Studies*, vol. 31, pp. 491-503.

Pavlínek, P. (1998), 'Foreign direct investment in the Czech Republic', *Professional Geographer*, vol. 50, pp. 71-85.

Pavlínek, P. and Smith, A. (1998), 'Internationalisation and embeddedness in East European transition: the contrasting geographies of inward investment in the Czech and Slovak Republics', *Regional Studies*, vol. 32, pp. 619-38.

Pomery, Chris (1997), *The First CzechInvest Annual Survey on FDI in the Czech Republic 1997*, CzechInvest, Prague.

Sadler, D. and Swain, A. (1994), 'State and market in eastern Europe: regional development and workplace implications of direct foreign investment in the automobile industry in Hungary', *Transactions of the Institute of British Geographers*, vol. 19, pp. 387-403.

Sayer, A. and Walker, R. (1992), *The New Social Economy: Reworking the Division of Labour*, Blackwell, Oxford.

Schweickart, D. (1993), *Against Capitalism*, Cambridge University Press, Cambridge.

Sharp, M. and Marz, M. (1997), 'Multinational companies and the transfer and diffusion of new technological capabilities in Central and Eastern Europe and the former Soviet Union', in Dyker, D. (ed), *The Technology of Transition*, Central European University Press, Budapest, pp. 95–125.

Smith, A. (1997), 'Breaking the old and constructing the new: geographies of uneven development in central and eastern Europe', in Lee, R. and Wills, J. (eds), *Geographies of Economies*, Edward Arnold, London, pp. 331–44.

Smith, A. (1998), *Reconstructing the Regional Economy: Industrial Transformation and Regional Development in Slovakia*, Edward Elgar, Cheltenham.

Smith, A. (2000 forthcoming), 'Employment restructuring and household survival in 'post-communist transition': rethinking economic practices on the eastern periphery of Europe', *Environment and Planning A*.

Smith, A. and Ferenčíková, S. (1998), Inward investment, regional transformations and uneven development in East-Central Europe: enterprise case studies from Slovakia, *European Urban and Regional Studies*, vol. 5, pp. 155–73.

Smith, A. and Swain, A. (1998) 'Regulating and institutionalising capitalisms: the micro-foundations of transformation in Eastern and Central Europe', in Pickles, J. and Smith, A. (eds), *Theorising Transition: the Political Economy of Post-Communist Transformations*, London, Routledge, pp. 25–53.

Storper, M. (1997), *The Regional World: Territorial Development in a Global Economy*, Guildford, New York.

Weisskopf, T. (1993), 'Democratic self-management: an alternative approach to economic transformation in the former Soviet Union', in Silverman, B., Vogt, R. and Yanowitch, M. (eds), *Double Shift: Transforming Work in Postsocialist and Postindustrial Societies – A U.S.–Post-Soviet Dialogue*, New York: Sharpe, pp. 127–43.

17 The Spatial Dimension to Environmental Problems

HELMUT KARL, OMAR RANNÉ AND JOHN MACQUARRIE

Introduction

Heavy industrialisation, the inefficient use of energy, obsolete technology and a lack of environmental regulatory controls have all contributed to a serious deterioration in environmental quality in many regions of Central and Eastern Europe (CEE). Furthermore, the true extent of environmental degradation preceding the transition process was largely concealed as a result of unreliable monitoring and governmental censorship.

Although the environmental situation has improved over the last 10 years, mainly due to the decline in industrial output and increased concern by post-communist governments, pollution nonetheless remains serious and threatens sustainable regional development. Water and air pollution present human health risks and pose a threat to natural resources such as forests or ground water, while environmental risks and past contamination discourage foreign investors. Moreover, notwithstanding economic hardship and considerably lower income levels, the countries seeking EU membership must devote substantial financial resources to comply with the more stringent EU legislation. For all these reasons environmental aspects are an important factor for regional development in the transition countries.

This chapter provides an overview over the current environmental conditions in CEE countries and attempts to identify regional development strategies that strike a balance between ecological, economic and social goals without losing sight of political feasibility.

Background and trends

Major environmental problems

In general, the CEE countries face the same environmental challenges as other industrialised European countries, ie. they must adopt appropriate policies that:
- reduce air polluting emissions causing acidification and adverse health effects, particularly heavy metals (eg. arsenic, cadmium and lead), particulates, nitrogen oxides (NO_x) and sulphur dioxide (SO_2);
- reduce greenhouse gas emissions that contribute to climate change, particularly carbon dioxide (CO_2) and methane (CH_4) according to the commitments of the Kyoto Protocol;
- improve the management of water resources and reduce water pollution;
- preserve bio-diversity and stop the depletion of natural resources;
- improve the management of environmental risks, especially those connected with contaminated sites and nuclear safety;
- improve the urban environment; and
- reduce waste generation and improve waste management.

However, despite substantial improvements in the last decade, environmental problems are often more accentuated in CEE countries than in the EU. This section illustrates some general trends concerning all CEE countries as well as regional differences; it mainly focuses on emissions, because data on ambient conditions are less reliable and do not show clear trends.[1]

Overall trends in CEE countries

Air pollution is arguably the most important area of environmental concern in CEE countries. On the one hand, industry in the previous centrally-planned economies continues to be highly polluting, and on the other hand, in some countries the structure of energy supply is problematic. In particular Poland and the Czech Republic and, albeit to a lesser extent, Bulgaria and Slovakia rely heavily on domestic brown coal and lignite with high sulphur contents. In contrast, both Hungary and Romania have greater shares of oil and gas. Furthermore, energy efficiency remains relatively poor in CEE; in 1995 only Slovenia approached the OECD European average, while the other countries used twice as much or even more energy per unit of Gross Domestic Product (GDP).

Over the last 10 years, all CEE countries have realised substantial reductions of various pollutants; this is reflected most impressively in the decreasing emissions of heavy metals, particulates and SO_2. For example, all CEE countries show a marked decline in total SO_2 emissions. Emissions in the Czech Republic decreased from 2.3 million tons in 1985 to 950,000 tons in 1996, or in Poland from 4.3 million tons to 2.6 million tons (1994). Several factors such as fuel substitution and investments in pollution control technologies contributed to this development, but arguably most important was the sharp decline in industrial production in the early 1990s. However, in comparison to the OECD countries, the pollution intensities both per capita and per unit of GDP are still high. In 1994, the OECD average was 41.5 kg SO_2 per capita (2.2 kg SO_2 per 1000 US-$ GDP), while the respective numbers for CEE countries were: Czech Republic 123.4 (13.9), Poland 67.6 (13.7), Hungary 72.6 (11.3), Bulgaria 163.1 (37.2), Slovakia 44.6 (6.5). The decrease in SO_2 emissions is also reflected in decreasing SO_2 concentrations over the region, although emission also depends upon other factors, such as meteorological conditions.

CO_2 emissions show a significant decline in CEE - around 30-40 percent in the decade 1985-94 - which is mainly caused by decreasing energy supply and fuel substitution. The national emissions reduction targets for the greenhouse gases CO_2 and CH_4 according to the Kyoto Protocol are -6 percent for Poland and Hungary respectively and -8 percent for the Czech Republic by the period 2008-12 (taking 1990 as the base year). CO_2 emissions per capita are below OECD average in all the CEE countries except the Czech Republic, while emissions per unit of GDP are higher in all countries. The consumption of ozone-depleting chlorofluorocarbons for general purposes was prohibited at the beginning of 1996 in accordance with the Montreal Protocol.

While NO_x emissions from stationary sources are decreasing in all the CEE countries, the emissions from mobile sources has become a more important source of pollution. From 1990-94, the number of vehicles - often in poor condition and violating emission standards despite modernisation efforts (use of catalytic converters) - increased by 34 percent in Poland and by 25 percent in Bulgaria and the Czech Republic. However, the number of vehicles per inhabitant is still below the OECD average - between 31 for the Czech Republic and 21 for Bulgaria compared to 42 for

OECD Europe. The opening up of CEE countries and the new trading links with Western Europe will lead to further increases in both passenger and freight traffic. Without any regulatory policy measures in place, growth will continue to concentrate on automobile transport and result in increasing NO_x and CO_2 emissions that may well offset the progress regarding stationary sources.

The quality of *water resources* is the second major concern in CEE. Both the standards of sewage systems and waste water treatment facilities, especially in rural areas, are below the European average and require substantial investments. Discharges of nitrogen, phosphorus and organic matter by point sources and agricultural activities are the main contributors to water contamination. However, emissions have been significantly reduced since 1990, and a distinct improvement of surface water quality can be identified in most areas. For example, between 1990 and 1996, the Czech Republic reported a decrease in discharges of organic pollution and petroleum substances by around 70 percent; in Poland the length of excessively polluted rivers fell by 50 percent.

In the early 1990s, the main reason for the decrease in air and water pollution was the dramatic slump in industrial production; in all CEE countries industrial production declined by 30-50 percent between 1989 and 1993. However, the decrease in pollution continued in the period following 1993/94, although in most countries industrial production had returned to growth. This indicates the growing influence of other factors, such as the implementation of environmental policies, the elimination of subsidies, structural changes in energy supply, high environmental investments in both the public and private sector, and a gradual decrease in energy intensity.

While the impact of *agriculture* upon the environment is not as critical as industrial and energy production, it still remains a significant source of environmental deterioration. Soil degradation, pollution and loss of productive land is caused through erosion, salinisation, drainage of wetlands, intensive livestock farming and by excessive use of chemical fertilisers, pesticides and other chemical inputs. The consequences of these processes, such as ground water pollution and soil contamination, can be regarded as a common problem in CEE countries. For example, in Hungary, agriculture uses around 13 percent of all water consumed and is the second largest source of water pollution, while in Lithuania nearly 80 percent of the wetlands were drained under Soviet rule. In some areas, agriculture contributes up to 80 percent of the nitrogen loading and 40 percent of the phosphorus loading in surface waters. However, due to declines in agricultural activity and subsidies for fertilisers, the environmental pressure from intensive agricultural production has decreased during the 1990s. For example, the use of nitrate fertilisers that was relatively high in the 1970s and 1980s fell below the OECD average.

Protected areas are an indicator for the level of *nature and biodiversity protection*. Using the classification of the International Union for the Conservation of Nature (IUCN), land under protection amounts to around ten percent of the territory in OECD Europe. The number is higher in the Czech Republic and Slovakia, lower in Hungary and Bulgaria, and about the same in Poland (under the Polish classification, protected areas cover about 30 percent of the country). However, this indicator does not provide information on the achievement of protection objectives in these territories. According to the report on the state of environment in the Czech Republic, information on endangered species indicate bad conditions in spite of the greater area of protected territories. Slovakia and Romania are among the European countries with the highest percentage of threatened species (36 percent and 30 percent respectively).

Forest degradation, at least partly caused by air pollution, is a widespread problem in CEE with 35-50 percent of the forests damaged or dying. Some regions such as the 'Black Triangle' - the border region of Poland, Germany and the Czech Republic - or Upper Silesia are even more seriously affected. However, mainly as a result of the reduction of SO_2 emissions, the overall state of forests has begun to show the first signs of improvement over the last few years; in the Czech Republic in 1996, the area of forests damaged by emissions decreased to 59.7 percent.

The *nuclear power* industry within CEE poses a potentially major hazard (accidents, disposal of high-level radioactive wastes and leakage of radioactivity). The two reactors at Ignalina, Lithuania, are the largest 'Chernobyl-style' reactors ever built, producing around 80 percent of the electricity generated in Lithuania. Many questions regarding its position on a geological fault line and its effects on the nearby Lake Druksiai remain unresolved. The former military factory in Sillamae, Estonia, has not only caused the extensive dispersal of pollutants into the Gulf of Finland, but has also left behind approximately five million tons of radioactive and toxic substances. Problems regarding soil and ground water pollution as a result of nuclear facilities are also a problem in both Bulgaria and Slovakia, where nuclear power makes up approximately 20 percent of energy supply. Poland is the only CEE country without nuclear power plants. With increased pressure applied since the transition period, governments in CEE have found it necessary to improve safety standards. This has led to an increase in western companies securing business, largely as a consequence of the financial constraints CEE governments had when attempting to incorporate safeguards.

A particular problem in CEE countries is the contamination of soil and ground water with petroleum products and chemicals at former Soviet military bases. For example, in the Czech Republic, 60 out of 73 sites that were used by the Soviet Army are considered highly contaminated, and the projected clean-up costs are considerable.

Another major and developing source of environmental degradation stems from *urban agglomerations*, in particular those areas associated with heavy industry. Urban air quality, measured through annual average concentrations, is significantly worse in CEE for suspended particulates - 'good' examples are cities such as Chorzow (Poland) and Plovdiv (Bulgaria) - and comparable to cities in Western Europe for NO_x and SO_2. Moreover, noise pollution, over-exploitation of ground water resources and water pollution due to inadequate sewage treatment, present serious problems of the urban environment in CEE countries.

One issue that is closely associated with urbanisation is *waste management*. Although many problems within CEE countries are inherited from the socialist era, new problems are emerging as a direct consequence of the opening-up to western markets and changing consumption patterns. The pattern of increasing municipal waste is particularly prevalent in the large urban agglomerations, such as Prague, Warsaw and Bratislava. In Prague, for example, according to estimates, waste levels have increased by 50 percent since 1990.

The increasing volume of industrial and often hazardous waste adds a further problem, in particular because of the inadequate waste management infrastructure. The existing waste management systems are already overburdened and rely mainly on landfilling. For example, the Visegrad countries dispose of nearly 80 percent of their waste in landfill sites - the highest figure in Western Europe is 60 percent (Bisschop, 1996). National and local recycling programmes were curtailed in the early 1990s, while other methods of waste disposal or waste treatment, such as incineration, also result in environmental problems.

Costs and benefits of environmental regulation

Although the necessity of improving environmental conditions is widely recognised in the CEE countries, the financial challenge is considerable and may well forestall rapid progress. Even now, according to a study by the OECD, the GDP shares of pollution abatement and control investment in most CEE countries are comparable to those of EU members (and significantly higher in Poland). However, environmental expenditures are likely to rise. In its Communication on Accession Strategies for Environment, the European Commission projected the total investment costs of meeting the EU environmental standards at around 100 to 120 billion Euro for all the candidate countries. In this context, a key issue for the CEE countries is the strong opposition in many EU member states - both net payers and net recipients - against additional funding or significant redistribution in this round of enlargements. Therefore, domestic financing of environmental expenditures will continue to play the dominant role in the CEE countries. With this in mind, it is clear that environmental measures must be very cost-effective and should focus on priority actions.

Of course, environmental regulation also involves important economic benefits. On the one hand, a region may become more attractive for residents as well as foreign investors (environmental quality is an increasingly important 'soft' factor for locational decisions); moreover, the development of some sectors (eg. tourism) depends upon a clean environment. This in turn creates employment opportunities and income and may help to diversify the economic structure. Further, higher environmental standards may even enhance the competitiveness of indigenous firms, thus increasing employment and income; in this context we can identify two mechanisms:
- *product offsets*: taking account of environmental considerations may lead to the creation of better-performing or higher-quality products which either reduce production costs, eg. by using other materials or less packaging, or which can be sold at a higher price, eg. because of their better image or lower disposal costs;
- *process offsets*: reducing pollution may result in improved resource productivity which in turn reduces production costs, eg. reuse of inputs, higher energy efficiency, reduced waste disposal.

Other positive effects are more difficult to identify, eg. better environmental conditions also contribute to higher productivity of workers.

Furthermore, if environmental considerations are neglected, environmental resources may become an important bottleneck in the near future and will seriously undermine economic growth prospects of CEE countries in the long run.

Regional differences

While the CEE countries face similar environmental problems, there are important regional variations; the main spatial differences in pollution levels occur between urbanised areas and more remote rural regions. This is particularly apparent in most of the CEE countries largely as a consequence of concentrated environmentally damaging production, close to the centres of raw materials and energy resources. The outcome is a strong regional dimension to the pattern of environmental damage. The following sections briefly illustrate this dimension, focusing in particular on six CEE countries - Poland, the Czech Republic, Romania, Hungary, Slovakia and Bulgaria.

In *Poland*, the area with perhaps the worst pollution is Upper Silesia. This region contains a total of more than 700 pollutants registered as causing a major hazard to both public health and the environment. The region produces around 25 percent of all industrial dusts, almost 30 percent of all gases, 25 percent of all non-cleaned sewage and around 60 percent of all industrial solid waste. Depending on the scale of analysis, some areas can exceed average pollution emissions by up to 200 times. The effects clearly endanger public health and exceed averages by: 10 percent more deaths from cancer; 20 percent more due to heart disease; 45 percent more complications during pregnancy and 10 percent more premature births. Other heavily polluted areas are located in the south and south-west border regions - Legnica-Katowice copper basin and the Glogow-Ryback coal basin. Two other major areas of pollution are located in the Baltic coastal region; the first to the north, Gdansk, and the other, Szczecin, on the border with Germany in the north-west.

Waste disposal and generation are also spatially concentrated. During 1992, 85 percent was disposed in six *voivodships* (administrative divisions), 70 percent of which was produced in the two border *voivodships* of Katowice and Legnica.

Environmental problems in the *Czech Republic* are also highly regionally concentrated, with the principal urban areas - especially the capital Prague, Plzen and Brno, as well as the more important industrial centres, such as Northern Bohemia and the Ostrava-Karvina region in Moravia - particularly badly affected. The most severely affected region is Northern Bohemia - especially the area of the Ore mountains together with the adjacent border districts in Germany (Saxony), and Poland (Silesia), referred to as the 'Black Triangle'. Eight out of the largest emitters of SO_2, NO_x and particulates are situated in Northern Bohemia, and lack adequate pollution abatement equipment. In terms of the emission of SO_2, Northern Bohemia, and in particular the district of Chomutov, ranks as the highest, where almost half of the national total is produced. The most obvious sources of pollution mainly evolve from coal extraction, energy production and the chemical industry. Northern Bohemia also produces almost 30 percent of NO_x and 25 percent of particulates, again largely the consequence of coal-mining activities and coal-fired power stations in this region.

Furthermore, serious emissions are also present within towns with a high density of population and growing traffic problems, Prague being the most obvious example. Even though the highest emissions of hydrocarbons are found in South and North Moravia, concentrated sources can often create more severe, localised pollution concerns, highlighting the need for a considered and concise examination of average pollution figures and geographical variations. The general picture regarding pollution is, however, not always a reflection of pollution deposition. As already mentioned, transfers of pollution can be a considerable problem.

In *Slovakia*, there is a substantial spatial pattern in terms of general trends of pollution. Around 40 percent of the population lives in an extremely polluted environment, mainly found throughout nine regions including: Bratislava, Trnava-Galanta; Upper-Nitra River-Basin; Upper-Vah River Basin; Middle-Hron River Basin; Central Spis; Central Gemer; Kosice; and the Central Zemplin region. The districts of Prievidza, Trebisov and Kosice account for the highest figures of particulates, NO_x and SO_2 emissions and all these areas are indicative of heavy industry and high urban density. Although Slovakia has experienced a reduction in emissions, care must be taken when assessing the extent of the problem. The significant problem of trans-boundary pollution complicates any firm conclusions regarding environmental deterioration and illustrates the necessity of trans-national co-operation within environmental policy. Due to its geographical location and resultant climatic patterns, Slovakia suffers from high trans-boundary transfers in the form of atmospheric pollution.

The deterioration of the environment in *Hungary* is perhaps less severe and widespread than in both Poland and the Czech Republic, although the country faces similar problems in certain regions and sectors. The outcome of Hungary's rapid industrial development was a relatively concentrated 'industrial crescent', stretching from Ajka, Gyor and Tatabanya in the west to Miskolc and Ozd in the east. While some industry appeared in provincial cities, it was this 'crescent' where concentrations of industrial activities and domestically produced pollution evolved. As early as 1974, the National Ground Level Concentrations Monitoring Network was established to provide continuous data on the country's atmospheric pollution levels. Results during the 1980s have illustrated a common trend: the three main pollutants - particulates, NO_x and SO_2 - are most prevalent around the Greater Budapest area and the Borsod County Industrial Region. The total polluted area of the country amounted to 11.2 percent of total territory, affecting 44 percent of the total population. With the exception of Budapest, all areas were indicative of heavy industrialised zones.

Water pollution within Hungary is again mainly a problem in the 'industrial crescent'. In particular, the large urban centres such as Budapest and Miskolc are badly affected by discharges of heavy metals and bacteriological contamination from domestic sewage. A number of important rivers, including the Danube, have illustrated significant increases in nitrate and phosphate pollution, as well as increased lead and mercury concentrations. This problem is not confined to the 'industrial crescent', but is indicative of the situation throughout Hungary.

Bulgaria suffers from relatively high levels of transboundary pollution, with the main problem areas in the northern boundary, especially in the areas covered by Ruse-Giugiu, Nikopol-Turnu, Magurele and Silistra-Kalarush. Similar to other CEE countries, sources of air pollution are particularly problematic within urban areas and major industrial centres. The principal sources include thermal power plants, chemical plants, metal works, fertiliser and cement factories and oil refineries; the Maritza-Iztok thermal power generation complex, near Plodiv, accounts for around 50 percent of national SO_2 emissions. Again the use of poor quality lignite compounds the problem.

Water pollution is also a significant problem, with industry, particularly chemical plants, metal works and mining activities as the main source, although domestic sewage and agricultural chemicals also contribute significantly to ground water pollution. The areas of Bourgas, Stara Zagora and Turgoviste all suffer from high levels of nitrates, sulphates and some heavy metals. Another important source of pollution stems from the Kozluduy nuclear power station near Vratsa. This power station has provided around 30-40 percent of the country's electricity in recent years. However, safety problems, a series of accidents and a highly critical report by the International Atomic Energy Agency led to the closure of two of its reactors. Furthermore, much concern has been voiced over the extraction and processing domestic and processing of uranium.

Air pollution in *Romania* is a severe problem predominantly in urban and industrialised areas. The main source of atmosphere pollution evolves from power stations and industrial plants, in particular the metallurgical and petrochemical industries. Furthermore, the dangers to public health are compounded by the close proximity of industrial plants to urban areas: the metallurgical industries at Copsa Mica, Bara Mare and Zlatua, are responsible for high levels of pollution of heavy metals such as arsenic, cadmium and selenium. High concentrations of pollutants are also found in Bucharest where emissions from industrial plants (notably ceramics, glass, chemicals and engineering), power plants, as well as domestic heating and traffic add to the pollution problem. Other major sources of pollution stem from petrochemical plants (Brazi-Ploiesti, Onesti, Craiova, Fagaras), cement-processing plants (Bicaz, Baresti-Targu Jiu, Valea Mare Pravat) and non-ferrous metals (Baia Mara, Zlatna, Copsa Mica).

Both ground water and surface water pollution is an extensive problem in Romania. Large urban areas, such as Bucharest, suffer from pollution as a result of untreated municipal wastewater (as late as 1991, Bucharest had no waste water treatment plant). Other large settlements, such as Iasi, Timisoara, Cluj and Brasov also suffered from either a lack of treatment plants and/or inefficient technology. Discharges from agriculture pose problems in rural areas. During the early 1990s, surveys showed that as many as 90 percent of wells contained bacteria in excess of permissible standards, with some agricultural areas recording even higher levels. The predominantly agricultural areas in the south also suffer from high nitrate pollution. Moreover, by the beginning of the 1990s, around 85 percent of Romania's main rivers provided water unfit for human consumption.

Implications for regional policymakers

The 'greening' of regional development strategies cannot replace environmental policies by national governments, or the integration of environmental aspects into sectoral policies, such as agricultural or energy policy. But the integration of environmental factors into regional policy can nevertheless play an important role, because it may help to change the perception of the environment in the regional development context and among the relevant interest groups by indicating opportunities to realise environmental gain (see Goodstadt and Clement 1997).[2] This involves the identification of measures that exploit the potential for simultaneous improvement of environmental conditions and economic development (ie. 'win-win strategies'), thus illustrating that economic growth and environmental improvement need not be mutually exclusive concepts. This type of more positive perception is also desirable, because the environment is - to a certain extent - forced up the political agenda in the candidate countries by the EU; however, to ensure implementation on the regional level it is important to respect the environmental and economic priorities of the inhabitants in the regions affected.

As a broad generalisation, there are two strategies for achieving environmental gain through regional development policies:

- *Vertical Integration*: environmental gain can be realised through specific environmental projects, ie. measures directly aimed at improving environmental conditions that have a positive impact on the economic potential of the region.
- *Horizontal integration*: environment-oriented provisions could be introduced in areas with primarily economic objectives, such as job creation; the aim is to modify measures that otherwise would have no significant or even adverse impacts on the environment.

Typical measures falling under the first category are improvements of the environmental infrastructure, eg. sewage treatment or waste treatment facilities and reclamation of derelict land. To a certain extent, such measures are prerequisites for economic growth because they also improve the business environment for domestic firms and foreign investors. However, these projects often involve significant costs, and, in view of scarce financial resources, it is necessary to concentrate on projects with broad environmental benefits as well as on the regions which are most seriously affected.

In the long run, horizontal integration perhaps offers a higher potential for improvements and innovative solutions that would more effectively change patterns of resource use and pollution in production and consumption.[3] In this context, regional incentives may support environment-oriented research activities in firms and academic institutions as well as the technology transfer between them. They could also provide technical and financial assistance for developing marketing strategies for environment-friendly products and services, such as ecologically produced agricultural goods, energy-efficient consumer goods or sustainable tourism. These activities may be essential for small and medium-sized enterprises or local companies.

Furthermore, the Structural Funds can help regional authorities to develop sustainability strategies in different sectors, such as tourism, fishery, forestry and agriculture, which are important for regional development, but, in the absence of such future-oriented strategies, would rather create additional environmental problems.[4] Another useful area is the development of energy-efficiency programmes (for both firms and private households) that will help to save costs and reduce consumption of resources as well as pollution. Such programmes can make substantial contributions, because energy intensive industries are often highly polluting.

Human resources measures also offer scope for improvements, whether they are directed towards the workforce, engineering staff or management in industry, employees and self-employed in sectors like tourism or agriculture, or other target groups. Either specialised environmental training or the inclusion of environmental aspects in general training programmes can help to disseminate information and raise awareness. Since employees are often most directly involved in the production processes, they are generally better informed about inefficiencies than outsiders: by raising their awareness on environmental issues the employees might focus more on environment-related inefficiencies, thus finding ways to save costs for their firm while simultaneously reducing environmental burdens. Moreover, the participation of the employees is obviously essential in effectively implementing new technologies or procedural changes.

With regard to the institutional design, methods proposed to advance environmental gain in regional development plans include the incorporation of environmental targets (eg. for pollution reduction, improved waste management, energy-efficiency or reclamation of derelict land), the inclusion of environmental criteria in project selection procedures (eg. by adding environmental factors to other criteria, such as job creation), the consideration of environmental indicators in measuring the performance of programmes (eg. the number of patents for environment-oriented product or process improvements) and the establishment of monitoring procedures in order to assess the on-going and long-term environmental impacts (Clement and Bachtler, 1997).

Summary

Although gradual improvements in the industrial sector will help to reduce the degradation of some environmental resources, the environmental burden in CEE countries remains relatively great. Additionally, the growing individual consumption of energy, fuels and short-term usage goods, as well as the increasing number of motor vehicles, are posing new threats to the environment. Therefore, environmental protection will continue to play an important role in CEE countries.

While regional policy cannot substitute for comprehensive environmental policies, it can nevertheless promote environmental gain through regional development by integrating environmental factors into its programmes. In this context, perhaps the single most important task for regional policymakers is to change the perception of environmental protection as a threat to economic development.

Notes

1   In spite of improvements over recent years, the reliability and comparability of statistical data for environmental monitoring and assessment often remains poor.
2   Within the debate about the integration of environmental aspects into the EU Structural Funds the notion of environmental gain is proposed as an analytical tool for the evolution of a new perspective on the role of the environment in the economic regional development process (Clement and Bachtler, 1997).
3   For example, while improved sewage treatment can help to improve water quality, new production processes may reduce the sewage at the source - often the preferable solution.
4   One such example is tourism. Demands for leisure infrastructure can add strains on nature and landscape: mountains and coasts are affected by urbanisation, sporting activities in unspoilt areas destroy habitats and have negative impacts on animal species sensitive to disturbance and so on.

References

Bachtler, J. and Clement, K. (1997), 'Regional Development and Environmental Gain: Strategic Assessment in the EU Structural Funds', *European Environment*, vol. 7, pp. 7-15.

Bisschop, G (1996), 'Optimism Wanes for a Prompt Clean-Up', *Transition*, May 1996.

Bluffstone, R. and Larson, B.A. (1997), 'Implementing Pollution Permit and Charge Systems in Transition Economies: A Possible Blueprint', in Bluffstone, R. and Larson, B.A. (eds), *Controlling Pollution in Transition Economies*, Edward Elgar, Cheltenham, pp. 253-69.

European Commission (1998), *Communication on Accession Strategies for Environment: Meeting the Challenge of Enlargement with the Candidate Countries in Central and Eastern Europe*, Brussels.

European Environmental Agency (1995), *Europe's Environment - The Dobris Assessment*, Office for the Official Publications of the European Communities, Brussels.

European Environmental Agency (1998), *Europe's Environment - The Second Assessment*, Office for the Official Publications of the European Communities, Brussels.

Fodor, I (1994), 'Characteristics of environmental problems in Eastern-Central Europe', in Fodor, I. and Walker, G. (eds), *Environmental Policy and Practice in Eastern and Western Europe*, Centre for Regional Studies, Hungarian Academy of Sciences, Pécs.

Gooch, G.D. (1994), 'Environmental Policy in the Baltic States of Estonia and Latvia', *Journal of Environmental Planning and Management*, vol. 37, no. 3.

Goodstadt, V. and Clement, K. (1997), 'Environmental Improvement within Regional Economic Development: Lessons from Clydeside', in Bachtler, J. and Turok, I. (eds), *The Coherence of EU Regional Policy: Contrasting Perspectives on the Structural Funds*, Jessica Kingsley Publishers, London, pp. 160-76.

Gorzelak, G. (1995), 'Eastern and Central Europe in the Year 2005', in Kuklinski, A. (ed), *Baltic Europe in the Perspective of Global Change*, Oficyna Naukowa, Warsaw.

Kramer, J.M. (1995), 'Energy and the Environment in Eastern Europe', in DeBardeleben, J. and Hannigan, J. (eds), *Environmental Security and Quality After Communism*, Westview Press, Oxford.

OECD (1996), *Environmental Indicators: A Review of Selected Central and Eastern European Countries*, Paris.

OECD (1998), *Public Exposure to Priority Pollutants Identified in the Environmental Action Programmes: Five Years On*, Paris.

OECD (1999), *Pollution Abatement and Control Expenditure in Central and Eastern Europe*, Paris.

Slocock, B. (1995), 'Environmental Regulation and the Enterprise Sector in Eastern Europe', *ACE Quarterly* (Phare), Issue 4, Winter.
Slocock, B. (1996), 'Regional Management of Industrial Pollution in Eastern Europe: Air Quality in Katowice Province, Poland', *European Environment*, vol. 6.
Toman, M. A. (1997), 'Environmental and Economic Reforms in the Central and Eastern European Transitional Economies', in Kaderjak, P. and Powell, J. (eds), *Economics for Environmental Policy in Transition Economies*, Edward Elgar, Cheltenham, pp. 1-14.
Welfens, M. J. (1993), *Umweltprobleme und Umweltpolitik in Mittel- und Osteuropa*, Physica-Verlag, Heidelberg.

National State of the Environment Reports

Czech Environmental Institute (1998), *State of the Environment in the Czech Republic - 1998*
(Internet: http://nfp-cz.eionet.eu.int/YearBook/Cr97-htm/index.htm).

Ministry for Environment (1998), *State of the environment in Hungary*
(Internet: http://www.gridbp.meh.hu/GRID3VER/AINDEX.HTM).

Ministry of Waters, Forests and Environmental Protection (1998), *State of the Environment in Romania 1998*
(Internet: http://nfp-ro.eionet.eu.int/soe/html/index.htm).

State Inspectorate for Environmental Protection (1998), *The State of the Environment in Poland*
(Internet: http://nfp-pl.eionet.eu.int/SoE/wwwang/index.html).

Ministry for Environment/ Slovak Environmental Agency (1998), *State of the Environment Report*
(Internet: http://www.sazp.sk/english/news/indexfrm.html).

18 SMEs in the Visegrad Countries: On their Way to Europe?

FRIEDERIKE WELTER

Introduction

One of the important issues facing Central and Eastern European countries in the transformation from centrally planned into market economies is the need to develop small and medium sized enterprises (SMEs). The potential role of SMEs includes generating employment, and thereby potentially absorbing labour surpluses which result from economic restructuring, contributing to the development of a competitive economy with diversified structures, and being a source of innovation. Data for the European Union (EU) illustrate the important contribution of SMEs (European Network for SME Research, 1996): they account for 99 percent of all enterprises, 66 percent of employment and turnover. In Central and Eastern Europe a rapid progress with transformation was, in most countries, accompanied by a fast evolving private sector including SMEs due to privatisation and new firm formation.

In view of the possible EU membership of several transformation countries, the progress in developing a viable SME sector is of special interest as are the specific structures of SMEs. The pertinent question is how far advanced the SME sector in the transforming economies is in comparison to the EU. In this context, this chapter investigates SMEs in the Czech Republic, Hungary, Poland and Slovakia, concentrating on the development of SMEs and their structures. Using the still deficient national statistics, the first part looks at the number and development of SMEs while the second part tries to give a more realistic picture of the SME sector taking dormant and part-time entrepreneurship into account. Part three deals with the size distribution, part four with sectoral and regional patterns and part five considers the contribution of SMEs to their respective national economies. The final section summarises the findings and offers conclusions about the 'fitness' of SME sectors in the Visegrad countries regarding their possible EU membership.

Number and development of SMEs: A first approach

The actual development of SMEs, which comprise the main part of the private sector, is difficult to analyse because of the lack of adequate and precise statistics. The national enterprise registers can be used as an approximate indicator for the size and development of the total private sector in Central and Eastern Europe. According to these statistics, the number of newly registered enterprises (excluding agriculture) in the eleven Eastern European countries[1] amounted to 3.4 million in 1995 (Eurostat/Phare, 1996). In the same year, the number of enterprises of all sizes amounted to more than 18 million in the 15 Member States of the European Union (BMWi, 1997).

Corresponding enterprise figures for the four Visegrad countries show an overall enormous increase since 1991 (Table 18.1). In Hungary, the number of all enterprises doubled within five years (1991-1996), while in Poland it rose from 1.5 million in 1991 to more than 2 million in 1995. Enterprise figures are especially high in the Czech Republic due to specific registration procedures, and here they increased more than ten times to 1.5 million in 1997. The Slovak Republic shows the lowest enterprise figures in 1991 as well as in 1995. Growth rates amounted to 5 percent in the period 1991-1992 and a mere 0.1 percent in 1994-1995.

Overall, these developments are due to the upsurge in private and small-scale entrepreneurial activities which immediately followed the introduction of market reforms. Using the number of sole proprietorships as an indicator for newly created SMEs,[2] nearly 750,000 SMEs existed in Hungary in 1996, almost twice the figure for 1990. In Poland, the number of SMEs amounted to nearly 2 million in 1995, but in Slovakia to only around 280,000. In the Czech Republic, around 1.1 million SMEs were counted in 1997, compared to a mere 125,000 in 1991. Poland and Hungary had an already considerable level of private entrepreneurship resulting from previous reforms during the centrally planned period. In the former Czechoslovakia, on the other hand, no private activity was allowed during the past 40 years.

Table 18.1 Development of private enterprises and self-employment in the Visegrad countries

Hungary	Sole proprietorships		Registered companies		Total enterprises
	% of total	Number	% of total	Number	Number
1990	96.8	387,340	3.0	12,678	400,018
1991	92.4	510,459	7.7	42,278	552,737
1992	91.1	606,207	8.9	58,974	665,181
1993	82.6	688,843	9.0	75,272	833,908
1994	80.9	778,036	9.5	90,853	961,177
1995	78.9	791,496	10.5	105,883	1,003,624
1996	74.3	745,247	12.6	125,580	1,002,946
Czech Republic	Private entrepreneurs		Private companies		Total enterprises
	% of total	Number	% of total	Number	Number
1992	93.3	891,872	n.a.[a]	n.a.[a]	955,647
1993	87.8	982,075	n.a.[a]	n.a.[a]	1,118,637
1994	83.6	1,044,635	n.a.[a]	n.a.[a]	1,250,216
1995	76.6	856,509	7.9	88,424	1,118,534
1996	75.7	1,000,375	8.5	1,112,514	1,321,096
1997	75.1	1,103,732	8.9	130,626	1,468,940
Slovak Republic	Natural Persons		Legal Persons		Total enterprises
	% of total	Number	% of total	Number	Number
1992	89.7	300,657	4.2	13,939	335,191
1993	88.1	288,677	6.1	19,838	327,652
1994	83.8	287,002	10.6	55,565	342,567
1995	80.2	275,110	12.7	67,892	343,002
Poland	Natural Persons[b]		Private companies		Total enterprises
	% of total	Number	% of total	Number	Number
1991	94.4	1,420,002	3.5	52,486	1,504,802
1992	94.2	1,630,629	4.0	67,105	1,731,661
1993	94.0	1,783,900	4.4	80,181	1,896,898
1994	93.7	1,950,000	4.5	93,000	2,080,000
1995	95.0	1,995,151	n.a.[a]	n.a.[a]	2,099,577

Source: Own calculations. *Notes:* [a]not available; [b]excluding agriculture.

However, compared to the beginning of the transition process, when small-scale privatisation and new market opportunities contributed to an enormous rise in SMEs all over Central and Eastern Europe (Welter, 1995), the initially rapid growth rate of SMEs has slowed down (see Table 18.1).

In Hungary, the number of SMEs reached its peak in 1995 and has been declining since then, although the corresponding growth rates have been decreasing since 1993. The number of SMEs and growth rates followed similar trends in the Czech Republic and Poland. In the Slovak Republic, sole proprietorship as an indicator for self-employment reached its highest point in 1991 and 1992 and has been shrinking since then.

National enterprise registers only paint a very rough picture of the temporal development of the number of SMEs because of changing regulations over time regarding registration. In addition, due to country-specific regulations, the figures and developments are hardly comparable among countries. To illustrate the development of SMEs, therefore, the share of private entrepreneurs and enterprises in all (registered) businesses might be a more appropriate indicator. Table 18.1 shows, for the four Visegrad countries, a declining trend with regard to natural persons and self-employed respectively while the share of private companies (legal persons) is rising. The same applies to growth rates: those for natural persons is decelerating, while those for legal companies is accelerating.

This general trend is partly due to changing registration procedures which certainly reduced the number of persons registered 'just in case'. Another reason could be 'normal' high market turbulence characteristic for the SME sector, resulting in high rates of market entry and market exit.

In Hungary, this overall development goes hand-in-hand with an overall decreasing share of private legal and natural persons resulting from a shift to limited partnerships as the legal form. However, the predominant legal form for SMEs in all four CEE countries still remains the sole proprietorship - which is the common legal form also for EU SMEs.

Registered, dormant and active enterprises and part-time entrepreneurship: a more realistic picture

Figures and indicators relating to SMEs should be interpreted with great care. National registers normally cover all enterprises regardless of their operating status. Hence, they tend to exaggerate the size of the private sector. They include active firms, sometimes even partially State-owned firms (so-called commercialised companies in the process of privatisation), part-time enterprises and 'dormant' firms (Welter, 1997).

Research by the Rhine-Westfalian Institute for Economic Research (RWI) has estimated the share of dormant firms and part-time activities for

1994 to be around 65 percent in the Czech and Slovak Republics, around 40 percent in Hungary and 30 percent in Poland (Lageman et al., 1994). Dormant firms are defined as those enterprises that are registered but never started their activities or which no longer operate but have not closed down legally. Naturally, the share of registered 'dormant' firms will decline during the transition process due to newly introduced strict regulations and a possibly falling optimism regarding entrepreneurial activities. Nevertheless, there remains a considerable share of registered enterprises that never will become active.

The calculation of active firms, at least for Hungary, proved the initial estimations of the RWI only partly correct. The data on registered and active firms published by the Hungarian Statistical Office showed that, out of one million registered firms in 1996, two thirds were operational (Table 18.2). Interestingly, legal forms and the actual status of entrepreneurial activities correlate. While less than two thirds of sole proprietors are active, the figure rises to around 85 percent when looking at limited liability companies. This is principally related to the requirements (for example, minimum capital) connected with setting up a limited liability company. In Slovakia, the Statistical Office estimates the share of active enterprises at 70 percent for 1996 – that, however, still includes entrepreneurs with more than one business/trade and part-time activities.

Table 18.2 Registered and operational entrepreneurial activities in Hungary, 1996

	Registered number	*Active number*	*as % of registered*
Sole proprietorship	745,247	460,163	61.7
Unlimited partnership	4,394	3,558	81.0
Limited partnerships	122,044	107,782	84.4
Limited liability companies	122,044	104,166	85.4
Company limited by shares	3,536	3,232	91.4
Co-operative	8,362	4,858	58.1
All legal forms	1,002,946	678,901	66.5

Source: Own calculations.

Data on the status of entrepreneurial activities that would allow one to determine the amount of part-time or second-job activities is scarce. Where available, it shows that a considerable, if slightly declining, part of the entrepreneurs must be classified as part-time entrepreneurs. In Hungary, for example, less than half of those self-employed (that is, the registered sole proprietorships) carry out their entrepreneurial activity full time (Table 18.3).

Table 18.3 Self-employment by status in Hungary

Sole Proprietorship	Full time	Part time	Pensioners
		as % of sole proprietorship	
1992	45.5	42.1	12.4
1993	44.4	43.0	12.6
1994	44.6	42.3	13.1
1995	45.9	40.9	13.2
1996	47.0	39.1	13.8

Source: Own calculations based on Institute for Small Business Development, 1997.

Furthermore, taking into account the relation of active to dormant self-employment, only 216,234 businesses (or a mere 29 percent out of a registered 745,247) could be classified as operational full-time activities. The respective share will naturally be notably higher for legal persons where entrepreneurship and minimum capital requirements are connected. Nevertheless, a new correction factor to the calculation of dormant and part-time activities in Hungary would amount to 70 percent for self-employment.

Data for the Czech Republic shows that, in 1996, around 15 percent of all entrepreneurial activities (with or without employees) can be classified as second-job activity (Table 18.4).

The share of part-time entrepreneurship decreased slightly from 16 percent in 1994 to 15.6 percent in 1995. As can be expected, part-time entrepreneurship plays a more important role for those entrepreneurs without employees. Here, only around three quarters of all enterprises state their business as main job while enterprises with employees have only a minor share of part-time businesses, amounting to around four percent. Considering the Slovakian estimates for dormant companies, valid also for the Czech Republic and taking into account the specific Czech regulations for registering plus the share of Czech part-time entrepreneurship, the former RWI correction factor for dormant and part-time businesses of 65 percent appears to hold even for today. That factor, however, neglects any of the above-mentioned differences concerning legal forms. Calculated on

Table 18.4 Main and second-job entrepreneurial activities in the Czech Republic

	Entrepreneurs without employees		Entrepreneurs with employees	
	Number	% vertical	number	% vertical
	12.1994 - 2.1995			
Main job	357,400	78.5	181,300	95.8
Second job	97,900	21.5	8,000	4.2
	12.1995 - 2.1996			
Main job	380,500	79.4	197,700	95.7
Second job	98,600	20.6	8,900	4.3
	12.1996 – 2.1997			
Main job	377,700	79.9	204,700	95.7
Second job	95,300	20.1	9,300	4.3

Source: Own calculations.

this basis, the actual number of enterprises (in terms of registered private entrepreneurs) would amount to only 386,300 in the Czech Republic.

In view of these correction factors,[3] we can calculate self-employment rates that will give a more realistic picture of the extent of new firm formation as an approximate indicator for SME development in the Visegrad countries. Sole proprietorship, or the number of natural persons excluding agriculture, can be an approximate measure of self-employment. Comparisons among all four countries will be more revealing if the self-employed persons outside agriculture are related to the economically active population, because small firms dominate the Polish agricultural sector. Table 18.5 shows the various rates for two selected years within the transformation process.

Compared to the EU average of nearly 13 percent, the 1995 self-employment rates in the Central European countries (and consequently SME development) seem, at first glance, to be extremely low. They range from five percent in Slovakia to slightly below seven percent in the Czech Republic and slightly above in Poland and Hungary (Table 18.5). In this case, however, the average figure for the EU conceals enormous differences between EU members themselves. Self-employment is highest in the less-industrialised southern European countries like Greece (27.7 percent), Italy (22.8 percent), Portugal (19.1 percent) or Spain (18.6

percent). More industrialised states normally show a considerably lower self-employment rate. For example, in 1995, self-employment rates amounted to 8.6 percent in Germany, 9.8 percent in the Netherlands and 9.3 percent in France. These figures, then, allow for the conclusion that, in 1995, self-employment in at least three out of the four Visegrad countries is quite advanced. The low rate in Slovakia is evidence for the overall slow progress in transformation which results principally from the difficult political situation over the past years. Regarding this ever-growing gap in private sector and SME development, and neglecting any statistical explanation, the decreasing rate of self-employment in Slovakia hints at a 'black future'.

Table 18.5 Self-employment in the Visegrad countries and the EU

	Self-employed		Self-employment rate	
	1993	1995	1993	1995
	in '000 (rounded)		in % of labour force	
Czech Republic	344	300	7.3	6.8
Hungary	413	237	10.5	7.2
Poland	1,249	798	8.4	7.3
Slovak Republic	101	96	5.3	5.0
European Union (EU-15)	n.a	18,163	n.a.	12.9

Source: Own calculations and Lageman et al., 1994, for EU BMWi, 1997.

The overall declining rates in Hungary and Poland are merely a statistical phenomenon, mainly based on the new correction factors for calculating active and full time self-employment which are higher than those used in 1993. The situation in the Czech Republic is different; here, the decreasing rate might hint at a 'normalisation' of the start-up process resulting in lower numbers for new self-employed persons and, consequently, a lower rate.

Finally, many SME activities - at least in countries with high administrative barriers - are likely to be carried out in the hidden or informal economy. These activities are either not registered at all or legally registered firms do not declare parts of their turnover. Estimates by the statistical offices of Central and Eastern European countries and published by the European Bank for Reconstruction and Development (EBRD) indicate that the shadow economy accounts, for example, for around 30 percent of official GDP in Hungary (EBRD, 1996).

Size distribution: dominance of micro-enterprises

Compared to the EU countries, Central and East European countries have moved towards the 'normal' structures of mature market economies but nevertheless still show distorted patterns (Table 18.6). Medium and large firms generally account for a similar slice of all enterprises (around one percent) and employment (around 50 percent) in Central and Eastern Europe, as in the EU. Distorted size structures are obvious when looking at smaller enterprises. Regarding the number of enterprises, small and micro-firms are evenly distributed in EU countries, with a share of 49 percent, while in Central and Eastern Europe micro-firms without any salaried employees account for two-thirds of all enterprises. Similar, but slightly less pronounced, distortions in favour of micro-enterprises can be observed concerning employment structures. When looking at single Central European countries, the size structures of enterprises differ even more markedly.

One of the difficulties in comparing size patterns is related to the range of definitions which can differ even further between sectors. For example, micro-enterprises, according to the EU definition, are those without any salaried employees, in Hungary with up to nine employees, and in Poland with fewer than six employees. Small enterprises comprise in Slovakia only those with more than 10 and fewer than 25 employees, but in the Czech Republic, Hungary and Poland all enterprises with up to 49 and 50 enterprises respectively.

Table 18.6 Size structures in Central and Eastern Europe and the European Union, 1996

	CEEC	EU	CEEC	EU
	as % of number of enterprises		as % of employment	
No salaried employees	66.2	49.7	14.9	9.7
1-49 salaried employees	32.4	49.2	34.0	40.1
50 or more salaried employees	1.4	1.1	51.0	50.2

Source: Eurostat/Phare, 1996.

Remembering these differences, the majority of enterprises in Central and Eastern European countries are still very small. Micro-enterprises dominate, while the small and medium enterprise sector is notably underrepresented. In Hungary, for example, micro-enterprises with fewer than 10 employees account for 97 percent of all operating enterprises, while only three percent are small firms and less than one percent medium enterprises (Table 18.7). Slovakian enterprises in 1996 showed a less distorted size structure (but still in favour of very small enterprises) because of the overall slow development of private enterprises. Micro-firms and small enterprises account for 77 percent and around 15 percent respectively (Table 18.7). Micro-enterprises also dominate in Poland: in 1995, out of 2 million private businesses, medium and large enterprises comprise less than one percent, while micro-firms with 1 to 5 employees account for more than 90 percent (Polish Foundation for Small and Medium Enterprise Promotion and Development, 1997).

Looking at the size patterns in various sectors, the overall general tendency towards small and micro-enterprises can be observed across all sectors. This does not change even when differing definitions for size classes are taken into account (Tables 18.7 and 18.8), although it is particularly pronounced in the tertiary sectors. In Slovakia, for example, micro-enterprises employing up to nine persons account for more than half of all enterprises in manufacturing and construction. This share rises to nearly 90 percent in trade. In Hungary, more than 97 percent enterprises in manufacturing and 99 percent construction and trade are classified as micro and small ones (0-50 employees).

Table 18.7 Size distribution of Hungarian and Slovakian enterprises in 1996

Hungary	Micro	Small	Medium	Large
	as % of legal form			
Sole proprietorship	99.7	0.3	0	0
General partnership	97.1	2.7	0.2	0
Limited partnership	98.6	1.3	0.1	0
Limited liability company	85.5	11.6	2.6	0.3
Company by shares	36.6	20.7	24.4	18.3
Co-operative	42.9	30.4	25.6	1.2
All legal forms	96.6	2.5	0.7	0.1

Slovakia	Micro	Small	Medium	Large
	as % of sector			
Manufacturing	58.1	24.6	11.9	5.4
Construction	59.1	28.7	10.6	1.6
Transport and communication	75.9	13.1	7.8	3.2
Trade	89.7	8.5	1.5	0.3
Hotels and restaurants	70.5	24.7	4.2	0.5
All sectors	77.0	14.4	6.9	1.7

Source: Institute for Small Business Development, 1997 and own calculations.

Table 18.8 Sectoral size distribution in Hungary in 1995

Hungary	Manufacturing	Construction	Trade
	as % of sector		
0-20	95.2	97.0	99.1
21-50 employees	2.5	2.0	0.6
51-300	1.8	0.9	0.3
More than 300	0.5	0.1	0.1

Source: Own calculations.

The higher proportion of medium and large enterprises in the Slovakian manufacturing sector is mainly due to the lagging privatisation process in the country plus a generally lower number of start-ups. Even with privatisation completed, a higher share of larger enterprises in industry generally could easily be explained through issues such as higher barriers to entry including, for example, capital investment. In this respect, the rather uniform sectoral size patterns (dominance of micro and small firms) come as a surprise. Even if the fact that, in industry, a large number of these SMEs have emerged from the privatisation process is taken into account, these size structures confirm the ability of SMEs in transformation economies to exploit sales niches also in secondary sectors.

Regarding the general size patterns of the transformation economies with respect to medium-sized enterprises, one obvious reason explaining the overall predominance of micro-enterprises is the considerable share of entrepreneurial activities in transition countries which are carried out as second-job activities. In these cases, only a negligible number of entrepreneurs create additional jobs. For example, in the Czech Republic, 104,600 entrepreneurs classified their business as second-job activity in 1996. Of these, only nine percent had any employees, compared to a considerable 35 percent when looking at the main-job activity.

A second reason results from the difficulties related to the creation of medium-sized enterprises. The currently existing medium-sized firms are mostly split-offs of large privatised companies. As in Western Europe, greenfield investments in medium-sized firms still tend to be an exception, while the vast majority of start-ups are micro and small firms. The observed size patterns point to a rather slow and time-consuming growth process from newly created micro and small firms into medium-sized enterprises. This suggests that the Central European countries still have a long way to go in the creation of a medium-sized enterprise sector.

Sectoral and regional patterns: distorted sectoral structures and regional clusters of SMEs

The sectoral distribution of SMEs in CEE countries is, on the whole, still distorted, especially in industry with its rather low number of SMEs. Low entry barriers, in terms of low capital and skill requirements, and a formerly underdeveloped tertiary sector resulted in high numbers of start-ups in trade and services in the first years of transition. Small-scale privatisation played an additional role in creating SMEs in these fields. More than one third of all enterprises in Central and Eastern Europe were engaged in 1996 in distributive trades, another 29 percent in transport and services, while manufacturing accounted for ca. 17 percent (Table 18.9). In comparison with the EU average, the shares for trade, gastronomy and services are only slightly lower. The still higher share in manufacturing illustrates the former sectoral structure. It indicates the as yet incomplete transformation process.

Table 18.9   Sectoral distribution in Central and Eastern Europe and the EU (percent)

	CEEC	EU
Manufacturing	16.9	13.3
Construction	10.6	12.7
Distribution	37.6	31.8
Hotels, restaurants, cafes	6.1	8.5
Transport and services	28.7	33.6

Source: Eurostat/Phare, 1996.

The sectoral distribution of SMEs in the four Visegrad countries has generally followed this overall transition pattern even after several years of transformation (Table 18.10). In the initial years, start-ups were concentrated in those sectors where barriers of entry were low and niches existed. This resulted in a high proportion of SMEs and new businesses in tertiary sectors. In 1993, the figures for SMEs in trade, for example, ranged from 35 percent in the Czech Republic to 39 percent in Poland, in services from 24 percent in Slovakia up to 29 percent in the Czech Republic (Welter, 1995). Neglecting statistical differences, these structures are broadly still recognisable two years later, although country-specific sectoral patterns are now more pronounced. SMEs, especially self-employed persons, dominate in trade, catering services and transport sectors. In comparison to the EU average in tertiary activities (73.9 percent), however, all four countries are far below average, with Slovakia and Poland ranging around 48 percent, Hungary and the Czech Republic only around 39 percent.

Table 18.10   SME in selected economic sectors of the Visegrad countries

	Czech Republic[a]	Hungary[a]	Poland	Slovakia[a]
	1996	1995	1996[b]	1995
	as % of all enterprises			
Manufacturing	13.4	11.4	18	14.9
Construction	10.7	7.3	7	7.4
Trade	31.8	28.6	40	44.2
Hotels, restaurants	4.1	4.0	2	2.4
Transport	3.5	6.1	5	2.9

Source: Own calculations.
Notes: [a]Czech Republic: registered private entrepreneurs and enterprises; Hungary: up to 300 employees; Slovakia: up to 250 employees. [b]estimates.

These sectoral patterns in transition economies often go hand-in-hand with regional clusters of SMEs. The average density of enterprises in the Central and Eastern European countries (31 enterprises per 1,000 inhabitants) is still lower than in the EU (43) (Table 18.11). Once more, these general figures conceal country-specific regional variations that are also apparent in the EU. In Hungary and the Czech Republic, for example, the country-wide enterprise density (referring to all active private enterprises) is already higher than the average for Central and Eastern Europe and the EU. Only in Slovakia are there still considerably fewer private enterprises.

There are, however, not only regional variations among countries, but also within countries. As a rule, SMEs tend to concentrate in dynamic regions, eg. the capital regions with good infrastructure (OECD, 1996). The density of SMEs in the capitals underlines the pronounced regional concentration, at least for the Czech and Slovak Republics: in 1996, Prague had 57 active self-employed entrepreneurs per 1,000 inhabitants plus 37 private companies. The respective densities for Bratislava were 28 and 21. These figures are considerably above the national average for private enterprises. Hungary, by contrast, shows a more equal regional picture. Here, private enterprises amount to 41 in comparison to a country-wide average of 48 per 1,000 inhabitants. This might indicate slight progress in developing a regionally diffused private sector.

Regional disparities in SME density often follow historical spatial patterns. For example, Slovakia's industrialised regions were formerly concentrated around Bratislava, while the rest of the country was dominated by agriculture. In Poland, the capital, Warsaw, Silesia, the coastal regions around Gdansk and the region of Łódz were the foci of industrial development. In the Czech Republic, the Bohemian regions are the historically most developed ones which applies equally to SME density. In Hungary, the agglomeration of Budapest and the western regions are historically the earliest developed areas in terms of industrialisation and infrastructure. Despite a relatively equitable regional distribution of Hungarian SMEs, one can still observe this pattern, with SME development lagging behind in those north-eastern regions that are predominantly agricultural areas with some highly specialised (former) State industries (Institute for Small Business Development, 1997).

Table 18.11   Regional distribution of enterprises in 1996

Selected Visegrad countries	Self-employed	Private Companies	All private enterprises
	active* enterprise per '000 inhabitants		
Czech Republic	38	11	49
Prague	57	37	94
Hungary	22	26	48
Budapest	32	9	41
Slovakia	17	7	24
Bratislava	28	21	49
Central and Eastern Europe	n.a.	n.a.	31
European Union	n.a.	n.a.	43

Source: Own calculations, Eurostat/Phare, 1996.
Notes: *Active defined as operational and full time. Correction factor for self-employment: 0.35 for the Czech Republic and Slovakia, 0.3 for Hungary; for companies 0.85.

These latter regions, with patterns of specialisation resulting from the era of central planning (cities with heavy industry combines), but also 'old' industrial regions, experience a much slower development of SMEs. This can be observed for the Polish old-industrial regions where SMEs still play a minor economic role (Polish Foundation for Small and Medium Enterprise Promotion and Development, 1997). The Slovakian town of Martin, the location of a former State military enterprise previously employing some 10,000 persons, might serve as another example. SME density here amounts only to 14 enterprises.

Nevertheless, in general, regional and sectoral SME patterns are less distorted today in Hungary, Poland and the Czech Republic than some years ago. This indicates the considerable progress made since the beginning of the transformation process.

Contribution to national economies: SMEs as an important economic factor

SMEs and private enterprises generally play an important role in the development and growth of their national economies. German SMEs, for example, contribute 45 percent to gross value and 68 percent to employment; SMEs in the EU account for nearly two thirds of European turnover and employment (BMWi, 1997; European Network for SME Research, 1996). The situation in the Visegrad countries also shows a rather high contribution of private enterprises and SMEs. Those countries like Hungary or Poland, where private sector activities were already allowed during communism, are still in front position, although countries where rapid progress has been made in mass privatisation (for example the Czech and Slovak Republics) have caught up. In the Czech Republic, for example, the private sector's share of GDP and employment rose from one third in 1993 to roughly 60 percent in 1995 (Borish and Noel, 1996; Lageman et al., 1994). Polish SMEs accounted for approximately one third of the gross national product (GNP) and for more than half of employment in 1995. In Hungary at the end of 1995, SMEs contributed more than half of the GDP (Table 18.12). Hungarian SMEs' contribution to employment was at the corresponding EU level with a share of 66.7 percent.

Contrary to the development of large enterprises, but broadly hand-in-hand with overall economic developments, SMEs have generally improved their economic position rapidly, although with growth rates slowing down in later years. The Hungarian data might serve as an example, bearing in mind that developments in Poland, the Czech Republic and Slovakia might not have been that favourable (Table 18.12). Between 1992 and 1995, the contribution of Hungarian SMEs to employment rose by 28 percent and to GDP by 13 percent. Micro-enterprises, in particular, increased their share in employment (+60 percent), as did medium enterprises to GDP (+32 percent).

These figures, however, cover wide sectoral and size differences that emerge from the sectoral and size-specific developments outlined above. Micro and small firms experience a more dynamic development than medium companies. In Hungary, for example, 44 percent of total GDP and 48 percent of all employment were accounted for by small enterprises, 18 percent and 19 percent respectively by medium-sized firms. In Slovakia, the contribution to output was also higher in micro and small enterprises in the tertiary sectors (trade with 23.8 percent and services with 31.6 percent). In secondary sectors, medium-sized enterprises accounted for a larger part of production, amounting to 37.7 percent in construction and 23.3 percent in industry.

Polish enterprises show similar sectoral patterns. They contributed up to 92 percent to GNP in the trade sector, and 85 percent in the construction sector while industrial SMEs accounted only for slightly more than one quarter. In terms of total GNP and size differences, micro and small enterprises comprised the same share as large companies (both 23 percent) which was more than three times higher than the contribution of medium-sized firms (seven percent).

The SME contribution to employment follows the same patterns in most Visegrad countries. Hungarian micro-enterprises with up to nine employees contribute more than one third, and small and medium-sized firms (10-49 employees) slightly less than one third to total employment (Table 18.12). At first glance, the Polish situation seems to be totally different, with micro-enterprises playing a less important role. Here, the employment share of micro firms in Poland (1-5 employees) amounts to only 19 percent compared with 39 percent in small and medium-sized firms (6-250 employees). The explanation is, however, a simple statistical phenomenon due to the varying size definitions.

In Slovakia, the available data permits a look at sectoral variations. Again, remembering that SMEs in this case are defined as enterprises with up to 500 employees plus tradesmen, SME employment dominates the tertiary sectors (Table 18.14). This is accompanied by employment clusters in micro and small enterprises: service firms with fewer than 24 employees contribute one third of total SME employment in this sector. The figures for trade enterprises amount to 43 percent. The picture changes in industry where medium-sized firms with 100-499 employees account for two thirds of industrial employment in SMEs (NASDME, 1996).

The conclusion is that, looking at sectors alone, tertiary sectors normally account for the highest share in SME employment and SME output. Considering enterprise sizes, it is the smallest enterprises that contribute most, the micro and small firms in tertiary sectors contributing the highest share. Although these patterns are, at first glance, the result of an initially distorted economic structure, they also resemble SME structures in highly industrialised countries in one particular aspect ie. the overall trend towards tertiarisation, and a growing share of services and trade.

Table 18.12   Contribution to employment and GDP in Hungary

	1992		1994		1995	
	Employ.	GDP	Employ.	GDP	Employ.	GDP
	as % of total				
Micro	21.5		30.4		34.6	
Small	9.9	40.9	12.4	43.1	13.1	43.9
Medium	20.5	13.8	19.4	18.1	19.0	18.2
Large	48.2	45.3	37.9	38.8	33.2	37.9

Source: Compiled from Institute for Small Business Development, 1997.

The absorption capacity of SMEs, however, might prove a critical point in relation to the overall employment situation. One of the reasons explaining increasing employment in SMEs is the decreasing employment possibilities in large companies. In Hungary, for example, in the years 1992-1995, increased employment in micro and small enterprises was accompanied by declining figures for medium-sized and large firms (Institute for Small Business Development, 1997). Overall, SMEs were able to absorb 79 percent of the decreasing employment in large enterprises. Taking into account the so far overall positive development of SMEs in Hungary, this share might be considerably lower in, for example, the Czech Republic or Slovakia.

Conclusion: SME sector in the Visegrad countries - fit for the European Union?

The development of SMEs has been progressing remarkably fast since the beginning of transformation, although the rates of start-ups have been slowing in recent years. A considerable proportion of entrepreneurial activities is, however, only carried out part-time.[4] In comparison with the

EU, enterprise sizes are still distorted in favour of micro-companies, with the medium enterprise class more or less lacking. This trend could prove critical in the long run regarding the sustainability of the SME sector. Sectoral distribution generally follows the initial transformation pattern, with SMEs dominating in the tertiary sector and a low number of start-ups in the secondary sector. Compared to the EU, there is still a considerable gap, suggesting further opportunity for SME development. Regional patterns still show a distorted structure, with SME clusters in dynamic regions - a picture also common in EU Member States.

Table 18.13   Contribution to employment in Poland in 1995

	Number of employees million	as % of total employment
Micro	2.0	18.5
Small	2.1	19.5
Medium	2.2	19.8
Large	4.6	42.2

Source: Compiled from Polish Foundation for Small and Medium Enterprise Promotion and Development, 1997.

Table 18.14   SME* contribution to employment in Slovakia

	1993	1994	1995	1996
	as % of sectoral employment			
Industry	36.8	42.9	45.8	48.0
Construction	74.0	78.2	80.7	81.4
Trade	75.7	83.5	89.8	92.8
Selected Market Services	82.4	87.4	91.4	89.9

Source: Own calculations.
Notes: *SMEs: enterprises with up to 500 employees plus tradesmen.

All in all, SMEs made a significant contribution to economic recovery in the Visegrad countries. The drop in national economic production and unemployment would have been much higher without the initial start-up boom. Nowadays, SMEs in the Visegrad countries account for a major part of national production and employment. However, in discussing SMEs' future role in employment, the important question of job quality has to be taken into account including issues such as working conditions, wages and longer-term perspectives. This question has implications for policy-makers and has also been neglected until recently in Western countries.

Furthermore, differences in SME structures and development among these four countries are also becoming more pronounced. Hungary and Poland are still leading, partly due to the initial already high level of private sector activities, and partly because of a generally favourable economic development. The Czech Republic might experience a setback after the rather positive SME development so far due to the slowing of economic growth. Slovakia brings up the rear regarding SME development despite its growing national economy, because of a slow and often reversed reform process. This indicates that SMEs are not only dependent on a smoothly developing national economy but also that they need market-oriented policies and institutions (Welter, 1997).

This is the area where the greatest differences between the Visegrad countries can be observed. Hungary and Poland are far advanced in creating a legal and financial institutional framework, further enhancing SME development. In the Czech Republic, the financial infrastructure is still problematic for SMEs, while Slovakia lags behind concerning workable legal and financial institutions and micro-economic restructuring. The structures of the SME sector in the Visegrad countries might, on the whole, be widely comparable to the EU - the as yet incomplete institutional transformation, however, leaves the future competitiveness of these SMEs in the enlarged single market open to serious question.[5]

Notes

1 The statistical offices of eleven transition economies set up a panel on newly-created enterprises with the help of Eurostat and funding from the Phare programme. The countries comprise Albania, Bulgaria, Czech Republic, Estonia, Hungary, Latvia, Lithuania, Poland, Romania, Slovakia, Slovenia. The first results were published in 1996 (Eurostat/Phare, 1996).

2 The number of sole proprietorships or natural persons is only an approximate indicator for the number of SMEs and start-ups because some SMEs also might be registered as legal persons, eg. limited liability companies. The assumption that sole proprietorships or natural persons alone give a broad, but rather correct picture of the number of SMEs is based on the (empirically proven) observation that this is the predominant legal form for SMEs.

3   The calculated and estimated correction factors for active and full-time entrepreneurship in 1995 (1993) are as follows: 0,3 (0.6) for Hungarian self-employment, 0.35 (0.35) for Czech and Slovakian entrepreneurs and an estimated 0.4 (0.7) for Polish entrepreneurs.

4   That seems to be an (apparently growing) problem also in Western European countries. Recent research for Germany showed that the share of part-time entrepreneurial activities and micro trade might amount to 75 percent of start-ups (Lageman et al, 1999).

5   For a detailed discussion of 'EU-fitness' of all candidates and not limited to SMEs (see Lageman, 1998).

References

BMWi (1997), *Unternehmensgrößenstatistik 1997/98 - Daten und Fakten*, Bonn.

Borish, M. and Noel, M. (1996), 'Ahead - and still gaining? Where the private sector stands in the Visegrad countries', *Moct - Most*, vol. 6, no. 2, pp. 25-57.

European Network for SME Research (1996), *Das europäische Beobachtungsnetz für KMU*, Vierter Jahresbericht, Zoetermeer.

European Bank for Reconstruction and Development (1996), *Transition Report*, EBRD, London.

Eurostat/Phare (1996), *Enterprises in Central and Eastern Europe*, Luxembourg.

Institute for Small Business Development (1997), *State of Small and Medium Sized Business in Hungary 1997*, Annual report, Budapest.

Lageman, B. (1998), *Die Osterweiterung der EU: Testfall für die 'Strukturreife; der Beitrittskandidaten*, Berichte des Bundesinstituts für ostwissenschaftliche und internationale Studien, 38-1998, Köln.

Lageman, B. et al (1999), *Kleine und mittlere Unternehmen im sektoralen Strukturwandel*, Untersuchungen des Rheinisch-Westfälischen Instituts für Wirtschaftsforschung, H. 27, Essen.

Lageman, B. et al (1994), *Aufbau mittelständischer Strukturen in Polen, Ungarn, der Tschechischen Republik und der Slowakischen Republik*, Untersuchungen des Rheinisch-Westfälischen Instituts für Wirtschaftsforschung, H. 11, Essen.

NASDME (1996), *State of Small and Medium Enterprises 1995*, Bratislava.

OECD (1996), *Small Business in Transition Economies*, Paris.

Polish Foundation for Small and Medium Enterprise Promotion and Development (1997), *The Small and Medium Size Enterprise Sector in Poland: A report for the years 1995-1996*, Warsaw.

Welter, F. (1995), 'Development of Small and medium enterprises and entrepreneurship promotion in the Central European Economies in transition.', in Elsässer, J., Brhel, J. and Forst, M. (eds), *The role of intermediary organisations in Entrepreneurship Promotion*, Bratislava, pp. 20-48.

Welter, F. (1997), *Small and medium enterprises in Central and Eastern Europe: Trends, Barriers and Solutions*, RWI-Papier Nr. 51, Essen.

19 Cross-border Co-operation at Germany's Eastern Border: Institutional Limits to Multi-level Governance

EIKO R. THIELEMANN

Potential and institutional limits to multi-level governance

Much of the recent political science and regional policy literature (Hooghe, 1996; Jeffery, 1997; Kohler-Koch, 1997) has viewed European regional policy as the prime example of an evolving system of multi-level governance in Europe. According to the multi-level governance approach, European policy-making and implementation is shared between actors of different levels of government rather than being monopolised by the State. Supra-national and sub-national institutions can have an influence in policy-making, which is independent of their role as agents of state executives (Marks, Hooghe and Blank, 1996). According to the proponents of multi-level governance we can observe "the existence of overlapping competencies among multiple levels of governments and the interaction of political actors across those levels" (Marks et. al., 1996). Through these policy networks, sub-national actors enjoy direct access to the supra-national institutions of the EU.

The essential idea behind the multi-level governance approach is well captured by the concept of 'partnership', which was one of the key principles introduced into European regional policy with the 1988 reform of the Structural Funds. The 'partnership' concept is based on the conviction that in order to deal with the complexities of European policy, a close co-operation between European, national, regional and local authorities is indispensable. 'Partnership' is based on the premise that "regional and local authorities know best the assets and handicaps of their region, and are therefore the ones best capable to define and manage development programmes and actions" (European Parliament, 1996).

After some initial excitement about multi-level governance as a new approach for conceptualising the European policy process, some disillusionment has set in on the part of both practitioners and academics. It has became clear that multi-level participation is not the same as multi-level governance and it has been shown that, notwithstanding the 'partnership' principle, in many countries, central governments have managed to retain their role as a 'gatekeeper' between supra-national and sub-national actors. In that role they have been successful in keeping at bay unwanted policy changes coming from Brussels (Bache, 1998; Kohler-Koch, 1997b).

This chapter pursues two objectives. First, it provides an analysis of one important field of regional policy-making in Europe - cross-border co-operation. Looking at the experience of cross-border co-operation at Germany's eastern border it counters some of the pessimistic conclusions about the potential of multi-level governance drawn by some writers, such as those mentioned above.[1] It is argued that aspects of inter-regional and cross-border co-operation are one of the most significant examples of multi-level governance in Europe. Unlike other areas of EC regional policy, the push for the introduction of multi-level governance into cross-border co-operation was not a top-down Commission driven process but one in which all three levels of government (supra-national, national and sub-national) acted as catalysts. Whereas the influence of national governments has remained strong at the policy design stage, it is shown that in the implementation of cross-border projects, it is the sub-national level which clearly dominates decision-making. This, without doubt, undermines the capacity of national governments to retain their traditional role as 'gatekeepers'. In cross-border co-operation, the role of sub-national authorities (both regional and sub-regional) and non-State actors (eg. trade unions and employer organisations), goes beyond mere participation and is characterised by the exercise of a considerable degree of influence, in particular with regard to the implementation process.

Despite the fact that cross-border co-operation is perhaps the most genuine reflection of the 'partnership' principle, the policy process in this policy area is not without its shortcomings. Instead of looking at the enormous economic, social and political problems that exist at Germany's border to Poland and the Czech Republic, the second objective of this chapter is to draw attention to a number of institutional factors that have limited the effectiveness of cross-border co-operation. Three main factors will be identified: first, differences in administrative structure (unitary vs. federal) of the countries involved; second, incompatibilities in the rule structure of the two main programmes that finance cross-border projects; and finally, it will be shown that Germany's particular co-operative federal structure has enabled the German *Länder* to establish themselves as the new 'gatekeepers' which control the involvement of sub-regional and semi-public actors in the policy process. It is argued that it is not just the obvious, persisting socio-economic problems but, in particular, the less obvious obstacles that result from deeply entrenched institutional traditions that will continue to constitute a principal challenge to effective cross-border co-operation and deeper multi-level governance at Germany's eastern border.

Cross-border co-operation as multi-level governance in practice

Euroregions at Germany's eastern Border: Between symbolism, regional development and pre-accession strategy

Cross-border co-operation is a special form of inter-regional co-operation and refers to regional and local co-operation, which takes place between administrative authorities of adjacent territories. More specifically, it represents co-operation between regional and local public actors (regional and local public authorities), quasi-public actors (universities, regional development agencies, research centres, social partners) and private actors along a common border. In the EU, cross-border co-operation takes place both between authorities of EU member states (internal cross-border co-operation) or between authorities of EU Member States and authorities outside the EU (external cross-border co-operation). There are currently 28 external cross-border programmes that are funded by the EU's Interreg initiative, supplemented by a similar number of Phare CBC and Tacis programmes.[2] These range from the co-operation of Finland and Sweden with Norway and Russia in the Barents Sea area in the north, to Italian-Albanian and Greek-Bulgarian co-operation in the South. The purpose of these cross-border programmes is to facilitate the organisation and financing of local and regional initiatives across national borders.

The focus of this chapter is external cross-border co-operation between three *Länder* at Germany's eastern border (Mecklenburg West Pomerania,

Brandenburg and Saxony) and regional and local authorities in Poland and the Czech Republic.³ Cross-border initiatives at an external border of the EU often require a lot more effort to overcome barriers to co-operation than those at internal borders. This is particularly true for Germany's eastern border, which stretches over 1,275 km from the Baltic Sea in the North, to the Bavarian and Bohemian Forest in the South. Here barriers to co-operation include both physical (eg. lack of cross-border crossings as a result of the ion curtain) and psychological factors (entrenched prejudices). The relationship between the people on either side of the border has been particularly difficult because of the displacements of communities that took place immediately after the World War II. German speaking communities from Western Poland were forced to move eastward over the new German-Polish border and were replaced by Polish speaking communities coming mainly from the Polish-Russian border. Historically speaking, the communities at this border are therefore very recent neighbours with little common heritage.

Between 1991 and 1993, eight so-called 'Euro-regions' were created along this border, the four most active ones being the three German-Polish ones and the one trilateral one which involves German, Polish and Czech local authorities. Euroregions represent the 'institutionalisation' of cross-border co-operation between sub-national authorities on both sides of the border. Most Euroregions are associations with private law status and comprise districts, towns and local authorities. In some cases non-State actors, such as the local Chambers of Industry and Commerce or the regional branches of the trade unions supplement these organisations. The internal decision-making structure of an Euroregion is made up of council, presidium, secretariat and working groups. On each of these bodies, representatives of communities from both sides of the border are represented. In recent years, cross-border activities at Germany's eastern Border have gone beyond purely symbolic forms of co-operation, or what one observer has called "glorified, regional level versions of town-twinning agreements" (Jeffery, 1997b). The emphasis of projects has shifted away from cultural activities (such as orchestra exchanges, joint exhibitions etc.) into areas such as infrastructure projects and joint spatial planning.⁴ Around 60 percent of Interreg money goes into infrastructure, transport and economic co-operation, 25 percent is used for projects in the area of tourism and the environment; and the remaining 15 percent is used in the field of culture, communication, youth and sport. All these activities have led to an increased awareness among the population. A survey conducted in the Euroregion 'Viadrina' showed that 90 percent of those questioned were aware of the existence of Euroregions in the German-Polish border area (Kennard, 1998).

The catalysts for cross-border co-operation at Germany's eastern border

Whereas the introduction of the concept of 'partnership' into the European Structural Policy has widely been regarded as a top-down, Commission driven process of 'institutional formation' (Marks, 1992), the creation of cross-border institutions has resulted from parallel sub-national, national and European initiatives.

Cross-border co-operation at Germany's eastern border predates the availability of EU funds. After the fall of the Berlin wall, the *Länder* and local authorities at the eastern border, aware of their high level of interdependence, were keen to improve relations in the border area. Indeed, it is a goal, which is explicitly enshrined in the constitutions of some of the new *Länder*. Article 2(1) of Brandenburg's Constitution for instance states:

"Brandenburg is a free state, committed to the rule of law, social justice, peace, the protection of the environment and culture. It strives for the co-operation with other peoples, in particular with its Polish neighbours".

Soon after unification, local initiatives sprang up as the populations on both sides of the border exerted pressure on the political and administrative authorities to reduce obstacles to investment and to change nonsensical local and regional arrangements along the border in areas such as the running of emergency services, education and training infrastructures and environmental protection. The changes in the East had cleared the way for substantive co-operation at regional and local levels, and people saw new opportunities for the regeneration of disadvantaged border regions.

At the national level, the normalisation of the situation between Germany and the Czech Republic and Poland was high on the priority list of the German federal government even before re-unification. A number of diplomatic efforts following the fall of the Berlin wall were directed at calming fears on the other side of the border about the *Ostpolitik* of a unified Germany. Chancellor Kohl, after initially dragging his feet because of his fears of alienating Germany's influential associations of exiles (*Vertriebenenverbände*), representing those who fled former German territories now belonging to Poland and the Czech Republic, finally signed treaties guaranteeing the inviolability and permanent status of Germany's eastern border. These were followed by the German-Polish and German-Czech 'Agreements on Friendship and Co-operation'. Interstate spatial planning commissions were set up, which were to encourage transborder initiatives and to promote strategies for the entire border region.

Initiatives at European level have also played a crucial role in developing cross-border co-operation, in particular in the institutionalisation and financing of such regional co-operation. The EU's interest in Germany's eastern borders can be explained by the fact that this frontier constitutes one of the most crucial, external borders of the EU. For the Union, this border region is an important geographic area "linking the EU in the west with the former COMECON countries in the East, and Scandinavia in the north with the Balkans in the south" (Kennard, 1995). As a result, external cross-border co-operation has long been on the agenda of European institutions, in particular the European Parliament. The Community has provided substantial amounts of money for cross-border co-operation at the East German border through Interreg and Phare. Interreg is the largest of the so-called 'Community Initiatives' programmes developed on the basis of guidelines set out by the European Commission itself rather than being based on national initiatives. Community Initiatives account for approximately nine percent of the Structural Funds money. The current Interreg IIA programme receives 2,650 million euro from the Structural Funds for cross-border co-operation in the period 1994-99. About 300 million euro of this sum has been allocated for projects along the East German border. The money is supplemented by a minimum of 25 percent public and private funding as a result of Interreg's co-financing requirements. In 1990, the European Parliament, on the basis of its budgetary powers, took up an initiative of the Assembly of European Border Regions (AEBR) to create a specific budget line within the Phare programme reserved for cross-border projects with third countries (Phare CBC). It is aimed at supplementing Interreg money, which (being part of the Structural Funds), cannot be used outside the Union's territory. Phare CBC was allocated 150 million euro in 1995, 169 million euro in 1996, and 180 million euro per annum for the years 1996-99. It is a crucial part of the Union's pre-accession strategy which started with the European Council in Essen for the countries of Central and Eastern Europe (CEECs). According to the Commission it not only assists "the processes of transition and integration [of the CEECs] with the EU, but can also contribute to the general economic development of the border regions" (CEC, 1996).

Decision-making structures and implementation experiences

The active input of four levels of government was not limited to the setting-up of cross-border programmes and financing instruments. The co-operation across different levels of government also characterises the implementation of cross-border projects. As the EU does not have its own administrative machinery on the ground, implementation of European policies is dependent on the co-operation of national and sub-national administrations. For the implementation of Euroregion projects this involves the co-ordination of four levels of government and non-State actors.

Table 19.1   Participating actors in the implementation of Phare and Interreg

Level of government	Institution
European	European Commission (DG1/DG XVI)
National	National government
Regional	*Länder/Voivodships*
Local	Euroregions
Semi-public/private	Trade unions, employers associations etc.

The involvement of sub-national and non-state actors in Interreg is perhaps the most significant example of multi-level governance in the implementation of European policy. In many areas of mainstream funding through the Structural Funds, the implementation of 'partnership' has been very much limited. In Interreg, the sub-national level of government clearly dominates the implementation process. Even more remarkable than the key role played by the *Länder*, is the significant role played by sub-regional authorities (local authorities/Euroregions) and the economic and social partners (trade unions, employer organisations).

Although there are minor differences, the structure and workings of the Interreg structures in all three *Länder* with an external border to the East are very similar. Looking at the Interreg implementation process in Brandenburg, in particular, the way in which projects are chosen (see Figure 19.1), what is striking is the pivotal role that sub-regional and non-state actors play in implementation. Euroregions are responsible, not only for giving advice to potential project applicants, but also for conducting an initial screening of applications for Interreg money. Euroregions prepare a written comment on the suitability and quality of the project application and then forward applications together with their comments, to the responsible ministry of the *Land*, where applications are examined to establish whether they fulfil the Interreg regulation, and whether *Land* resources for co-financing are available.

After passing this test, the application is discussed and decided upon in the Interreg Steering Committee, which meets four times a year. With regard to implementation on the German side of the border this is where the real power over the choice of projects lies. There are three Interreg Steering Committees, one for each *Land*'s operational programme. In these Steering Committees, decisions are taken on whether or not to fund particular projects and how much assistance an individual project will receive. Four levels of government - the European, the Federal, the *Land*-level and the Euroregions - are represented on this Committee. Crucially, formal decision-making power lies mainly with the *Land* and the Euroregions. The *Land* chairs the meetings of the committee and is represented by the different ministries involved in Interreg. The German representatives of each Euroregion active in the particular *Land* are represented on the Committee with full voting rights. Representatives of the federal government, the European Commission and the Polish representatives of the Euroregions have only non-voting member status.

The final step of the approval process is the notification of the project initiators by the fund managers of the responsible ministries as to whether or not their application was approved in the Committee.

The important role played by sub-national authorities (the *Länder*, the Euroregions, the constituent local authorities and semi-public actors) in the Interreg policy-implementation process thus becomes very clear. Particularly noteworthy is the relatively strong role of sub-regional actors, which is particularly influential because only projects which pass the initial screening by the Euroregions have a realistic chance of success.[5] Also, decision in the Steering Committees and the Monitoring Committees are taken by consensus. Thus, no decision can be taken against the wishes of the Euroregions. By contrast, it is interesting to note the relatively limited role for Germany's federal level of government. Although officially the federal lead ministry (Economics) regards cross-border co-operation as a regional prerogative, behind the scenes the ministry has long been pushing unsuccessfully to gain a vote on the Interreg Steering Committee.[6]

Figure 19.1 Interreg II procedure to approve projects (Brandenburg)

Looking at the Interreg decision-making structures, it can, therefore, be concluded that Interreg implementation process in Germany, is one where the bottom-up approach that is meant to be at the heart of the 'partnership' principle goes beyond mere rhetoric. Not just the role of German *Länder* but also that of the Euroregions in this process is characterised by their exertion of real influence. Although some regard the implementation process as too complex and slow, most officials within the different authorities involved agree that the adherence to the 'bottom-up' principle has improved the quality of assisted projects. Nonetheless, implementation problems have remained. In the following, three institutional factors will be identified, which have limited the effectiveness of cross-border cooperation at Germany's eastern border.[7]

Institutional limits to effective cross-border co-operation

Federal vs. unitary structures

The constitutions, as well as the administrative structures, of the countries engaged in cross-border co-operation along Germany's eastern border, are characterised by substantial differences. In this section, such incompatibilities between different national institutions will be exemplified by comparing Germany's federal structures with the unitary structures that characterise the Polish State. Most of the points apply equally to the relationship between German and Czech institutions.

Germany's federal structures are often incompatible with Polish centralised ones. Intergovernmental relations in Germany are characterised by 'co-operative federalism', as policies are usually made on the basis of joint action between governments. Germany is divided into three levels of local power: regions (*Länder*), districts (*Kreise*) and local authorities (*Kommunen*). Local authorities are responsible for two thirds of public investment undertaken in the Federal Republic.

Polish unitary structures have their basis in the old centralist structures of the communist period and regional and local self-autonomy in Poland is still limited compared to the competencies enjoyed by German sub-national authorities. Decisions, which can be taken independently by regional and local authorities in Germany, cannot be decided upon by their Polish counterparts without having obtained the explicit consent of the central government in Warsaw. This can lead to delays which may obstruct the cross-border co-operation process, especially attempts to co-ordinate Interreg and Phare funding. Moreover, the financial capacity of Polish regional and local authorities is much smaller than that of their German counterparts. In part, this is due to the differences in wealth between the two countries, but more importantly it reflects the limited revenue-raising powers of Polish regional and local authorities.

The creation of Euroregions as a means to facilitate cross-border co-operation was new for participants on both sides of the border. In the beginning, the Polish authorities in particular, felt uneasy about these regional associations, which are located outside traditional administrative structures and therefore potentially challenge control from the centre.

However, over the last decade, Poland has been engulfed in a fundamental reform of its political, legal and administrative system. In particular, it has taken steps towards decentralisation and the devolution of central power. In 1990, in a first step, local self-government was introduced and just under 2,500 local authorities were founded. Local self-government performs many public functions in its own name and under its own responsibility.[8] They are for example responsible for schools, streets and the utilities. Up until 1998, the local level was the only sub-national level exercising such self-governing functions.

It is the regional level where most differences between Germany and Poland can be found. Until recently, the Polish regional level was made up of 49 *voivodships*, which acted as the central government's offices in the regions. The head of the *voivodship*, the *voivod*, is appointed directly by the Polish head of state.[9] In between the local and the regional structures there are 268 counties (*rayons*) which help to fulfil the administrative tasks of the *voivodships*.

In January 1999, the second stage of territorial reforms came into force which has created two new levels of self-government. The former 49 *voivodships* (*wojewódstwa*) were transformed into 16 larger territorial units (regions). These new *voivodships* now consist of 373 new districts (*powiat*). The number of local authorities has remained the same. The reforms also created parallel structures of elected regional assemblies (*sejmik*) but the *voivod* remains the right arm of central government. In crucial aspects, therefore, the reforms followed the French administrative system of parallel structures of regional self-government and government from the centre (Miller, 1998).

These reforms also meant that each *voivodship* has to develop a multi-annual regional development programme on the basis of which a regional 'treaty' between the *voivodship* and central government is drawn up. For it to come into effect, the agreement of the *voivod*, the regional assembly and the national Council of Ministers is necessary. These new structures, it is hoped, will ensure a more co-ordinated regional policy framework and system of regional assistance.

Although, steps towards decentralisation and devolution of powers have been taken with the creation of elected regional assemblies, a strong centralist legacy persists in Poland. It remains to be seen whether the new territorial administrative structures will make it easier to co-ordinate cross-border regional development initiatives. It is clear that the new structures will need some time to work properly and to determine whether they are capable of fulfilling the high expectations placed on them.

From an institutionalist perspective it becomes clear that the differences in territorial administration between Germany and Poland affect the legitimacy of sub-national authorities in the implementation of cross-border projects in the two countries. It also means that German and Polish sub-national actors will differ in their view of 'appropriate' strategies to pursue in trying to achieve their objectives. Whereas German sub-national authorities might instinctively look for equivalent co-operation partners on the other side of the border, Polish regions and local authorities will be expected to pursue their policies through channels that lead though national ministries. However, as will be seen below, Germany's federal institutional structure, which gives a special role to the *Länder*, often does so to the detriment of the sub-regional level of government.

The incompatibility of Interreg and Phare

If the implementation experiences during the first part of the current programming period (1995-1997) are considered, it becomes clear that the effectiveness of implementing cross-border projects can still be improved. The intermediate evaluation report on the use of Interreg II money in Saxony for that period draws a broadly positive picture of the overall implementation process, but stresses that important co-operation potentials have not yet been realised (IfS, 1998).

The most frequently uttered complaint by those involved in cross-border co-operation at Germany's eastern border is over the incompatibility of the two principal European financing instruments in use - Interreg and Phare CBC (Kennard, 1998; Morhard, 1995), each of which represents a very different institutional rule structure. In a position-paper on the reform of the Structural Funds 2000-2006, the Ministry of Economics of Saxony demands that "attempts must be made to increase the compatibility between the Community Initiative Interreg and the Phare/CBC-programme by the use of common institutions for decision-making, parallel administrative processes and necessary financial resources" (Wirtschaftsministerium Dresden, 1998). The intermediate evaluation of the Interreg II programme in Saxony highlighted some of these co-ordination problems. A survey undertaken among project managers reveals that, while over half of those questioned state that their Interreg project is supplemented by a Czech or Polish project on the other side of the border, only 20 percent confirmed that such supplementary projects have applied for/or are funded by Phare-CBC (IfS, 1998). According to the evaluation report, the primary reasons for the lack of supplementary projects, is not a lack of interest or complex co-ordination processes, but lack of national co-funding for such projects on the Czech and Polish side. This is particularly true for projects of a socio-cultural character, eg. tourism and training, as the Phare regulations are not tailored to fund such projects. Of those questioned, only 29 percent felt that the two instruments Phare CBC and Interreg supplement each other well (IfS, 1998).

Reasons for this lack of compatibility of Interreg and Phare CBC rules are manifold, and mostly derive from the fact that Interreg and Phare were created independently from each other and were devised to serve different objectives. Phare was created to help the Eastern European applicant states in their attempts to fulfil the Community *aquis*. Although Phare CBC was created with Interreg in mind, the fact that it remained an integral part of the overall Phare programme has made it impossible to use Phare CBC as a straightforward supplement to Interreg on the eastern side of the border. The territoriality principle of most EU Funds (based on Article 130c of the EC Treaty) prevents Structural Fund money being spent outside the territory of the EU. Whereas under Interreg virtually all economically significant cross-border activities are eligible for funding, only non-profit organisations can apply for Phare money. Also, Phare-CBC often supports basic infrastructure projects which are usually much larger than Interreg projects.

Common projects are also hard to co-ordinate because of differences in programming structure. Under the Interreg regulations, eligible countries are invited to prepare multi-annual operational programmes for the entire multi-annual funding period. Phare-CBC, in contrast, operates on the basis of annual 'indicative programmes', ie. financing proposals have to be submitted every year in accordance with normal Phare rules. The fact that institutional responsibility within the Brussels bureaucracy is divided has also led to co-ordination problems. Interreg, as part of the Community Structural Funds, is under the overall responsibility of the Commission's regional policy directorate (DG XVI). Phare, on the other hand, falls under the responsibility of Commission Directorate for General External Relations (DG IA). The co-ordination of policy between these two directorates has often been characterised by jealous competition over competencies rather than constructive co-operation.

The existing tensions between the institutional structures of Interreg and Phare have led to the fact that, instead of having common or parallel projects on both sides of the border, the majority of projects are autonomous projects which at best have some cross-border effects. When looking at the Commission's proposals for the 1999 reform of the

Structural Funds and the current state of discussion, a single fund that would combine Interreg and Phare cross-border initiatives is very unlikely before the accession of the first CEE countries.

European vs. domestic institutions

A further institutional tension, one which lies in the relationship between European and domestic policy making, can be identified. Taking the Interreg implementation process as an example, one can observe a tension between regional policy-making inside Germany's regional policy structure (based on the principles of co-operative federalism and 'joint decision-making') and European regional policy-making (based on 'partnership governance').[10]

Germany's federal system is based on the special constitutional relationship between the federal level (*Bund*) and the regional level (*Länder*). According to Germany's constitution (Basic Law), sovereign powers are shared between these two levels of government. Regional policy-making is one of the 'joint tasks' which were introduced with the constitutional reforms of 1969.[11] Decision-making in the 'joint tasks' is characterised by complex, multilateral negotiations between the federal government and the *Länder*.

As to the implementation of European regional policy in Germany - in particular with regard to the principle of 'partnership' - the institutional response of the German political-administrative system has been rather mixed. The principal aim of the Commission in introducing 'partnership' was to legitimise and strengthen the participation of regional and non-State actors in the process of European policy implementation. Though one might assume that there would be little opposition in Germany's federal system to the incorporation of this principle, the empirical evidence leads us to a rather different conclusion. 'Partnership' fits the institutional rule structure of joint-decision making only as far as the involvement of the *Länder* is concerned. The *Länder* were indeed quickly incorporated into the 'programming' process of European regional policy-making and today exert substantial influence across all areas of assistance through the Structural Funds. However, as to the involvement of the sub-regional levels, the experience has been rather different.

As seen earlier, in cross-border co-operation the sub-*national* level of government does indeed dominate the implementation process. However, although the sub-*regional* level (Euroregions and semi-public bodies) play an important role its power is limited as the *Länder* have been able to establish themselves as gatekeepers between European institutions and Germany's sub-*regional* level. Although this is less clear when looking at the distribution of *formal* decision making powers, the *Länder* can muster an enormous degree of *informal* power. As shown earlier, the *Länder* chair the most important Interreg committees and are thus in a key position when it comes to questions of membership and decision-making rules. Moreover, the *Länder* can exert power by providing or withholding the necessary co-financing for projects.

Land ministries have used their formal and informal power to limit the participation of economic and social partners. Despite Germany's corporatist reputation, outside the narrow bands of wage bargaining, the tripartite co-operation between the State, trade unions and employer organisations in Germany is limited. In most areas of policy-making, including regional policy, the role of social and economic partners has traditionally been limited to 'negative co-ordination', ie. the responsible government ministry hammers out a particular policy and then co-ordinates it vertically and horizontally with other ministries affected. Typically, only then, are non-governmental actors asked to comment. The purpose of this consultation is not primarily to improve bottom-up information flow, but to minimise potential resistance by these groups in the implementation process. Although, both Euroregions and economic/social partners are directly represented in some of the most important committees and therefore participate in most aspects of policy-implementation, the *Länder* have been able to resist pressures to include these groups in the design of programmes for the next funding period.

It is therefore fair to say that, whereas European regional policy has tried to promote regionalisation and stimulate co-operation between public and private actors at the regional level, these attempts have encountered considerable resistance in the German federal system. The often presumed compatibility of German federal institutions and those of a regionalised European policy therefore does not hold.

Conclusion

Cross-border co-operation is a policy area, which better than others exemplifies the potentials of multi-level governance in European policy-making. It is a policy field in which real flesh has been put on the principle of 'partnership'. The sub-national level of government is not only generally in control of the implementation process, regional and sub-regional actors dominate the crucial decision making bodies and are—unlike in other areas of the Structural Funds—the ones in charge of making decisions on project selection.

This chapter has emphasised the importance of the institutional context in which policy-making and implementation takes place. In the case of cross-border co-operation at Germany's eastern border, institutional tensions have been identified in connection with the interaction between unitary and federal administrative structures, the lacking compatibility of the EU's principal financing instruments and the incompatibility of European and domestic regional policy institutions. While economic and social problems can be expected to continue to decrease, institutional incompatibilities are likely to prove very resilient. An institutional analysis, which looks at the broader institutional context in which cross-border co-operation takes place can help to explain difficulties within the implementation process and point to obstacles that exist for moves towards deeper multi-level governance in European policy making.

Notes

1. Much of the empirical information is based on a set of 30 semi-structured interviews with representatives of the European, the national, regional and sub-regional (Euroregions) levels of government and the economic and social partners, conducted in June and July 1997 and July 1998.
2. Interreg is the EU's principal programme for cross-border co-operation. Phare stands for 'Pologne et Hongrie: Assistance pour la Restructuration Economique'. The Phare programme, which started in 1989 and was originally geared exclusively at Poland and Hungary, has expanded to now include 11 Central and Eastern European Countries. Further East it has been supplemented by the Tacis (Technical Assistance for Commonwealth of Independent States) programme.
3. A wide variety of other inter-regional co-operation agreements exist. Many of these co-operation agreements are facilitated by the EU's Article 10 programmes such as Ecos-Ouverture, Recite, Ernact.
4. Part of the reason for this is a widely shared concern for visible and quantifiable results of cross-border measures. The construction of a border-crossing is something one can point to even years after its construction, whereas the effects of a sponsored cultural event are less tangible. Whereas the Euroregions (sometimes supported by the Commission) have tended to regard cultural projects as a necessary

building block to overcome entrenched prejudices, officials from the economics ministries - at both the national and the *Land* level - have tended to regard such projects as a potential waste of resources.
5 The role of the economic and social partners is worth stressing. They are part of the governing bodies of the Euroregions and have a say on matters of project selection and, indirectly through the Euroregion's seat in the Monitoring and Steering Committees, on financing decisions. In Saxony, the importance of these groups has been further acknowledged by giving them their own seats on the Interreg Monitoring Committee. Represented are members of the four Saxon chambers of commerce and a representative of the trade unions in Saxony.
6 Interview at the Federal Ministry of Economics in Berlin, 29/7/1997.
7 Institutions, as the term is used here, refers to the *context* in which political actors are embedded, ie. legal arrangements, procedures (decision-making rules) and organisational forms that shape and inform human interaction. For a more in-depth treatment of the 'new institutionalist' approach adopted here see Thielemann (1999).
8 Article 16.2 and Article 6/1 of the law on territorial local government.
9 See Chapter VII, Article 152 of the Polish Constitution.
10 This is not to suggest that in the past there have not also been substantive differences between German and European conceptions of regional policy-making, see eg. Thielemann (1998).
11 Germany's main regional policy instrument is the 'joint task for the improvement of regional economic structures' (*Gemeinschaftsaufgabe zur Verbesserung der regionalen Wirtschaftsstruktur*).

References

Bache, I. (1998), *The Politics of European Regional Policy: Multi-level Governance or Flexible Gatekeeping?*, Sheffield, Sheffield University Press.

Commission of the European Communities (CEC) (1996), *On the implementation of Cross-Border Co-operation between the Community and Countries of Central and Eastern Europe in 1994*, COM (95) 661 final.

European Parliament (1996), *Cross-Border and Inter-Regional Co-operation in the European Union*, Regional Policy Series, W-19.

Hooghe, L. (ed) (1996), *Cohesion Policy and European Integration: Building Multi-Level Governance*, Oxford University Press, New York.

Institut für Stadtforschung und Strukturpolitik (1998), *Evaluierungsstudie über den Einsatz der Strukturfondsmittel der EU im Rahmen der Gemeinschaftsinitiative Interreg II in den Freistaaten Sachsen und Bayern*, Endbericht, Berlin.

Jeffery, C. (ed) (1997a), *The Regional Dimension of the European Union: Towards a Third Level in Europe?*, Cass, London.

Jeffery, C. (1997b), *Sub-National Authorities and European Integration: Moving Beyond the Nation-State?*, Paper presented at the 'Fifth Biennial International Conference' of the European Community Studies Association, Seattle, 29 May to 1 June 1997.
Kennard, A. (1995), The German-Polish Border as a Model for East-West Cooperation on the Oder-Neisse Line, *German Politic*, vol. 4, no. 1, pp.141-49.
Kennard, A. (1998), *EU-Funding: a Stimulus to Interregional Co-operation on the Polish-German border, or Symbolic Contribution to the Pre-Accession Strategy*, Paper presented at the Third UACES Research Conference, Lincoln, 9-11 September.
Kohler-Koch, B. et. al. (eds) (1997a), *Interaktive Politik in Europa: Regionen im Netzwerk der Integration*, Leske & Budrich, Opladen.
Kohler-Koch, B. (1997b), 'Leitbilder und Realität der Europäisierung der Regionen', in Kohler-Koch, B. et. al. (eds), *Interaktive Politik in Europa: Regionen im Netzwerk der Integration*, Leske & Budrich, Opladen, pp.229-53.
Marks, G. (1992), 'Structural Policy in the European Community', in Sbragia (ed), *Europolitics*, Brooking Institution, Washington DC.
Marks, G., Hooghe, L. and Blank, K. (1996), European Integration from the 1980s: State-Centric v. Multi-level Governance, *Journal of Common Market Studies*, vol. 34, no. 3, pp.341-78.
Miller, J. (1998), (Secretary of State for the Polish Ministry of Finance), *Regional Reform and Devolution in Poland: the Future Role of the Voivodship in Europe*, Speech at the second AER Summer School, Erfurt, 26 - 31 July 1998.
Morhard, B. (1995), 'Lokale grenzüberschreitende Kooperation in der deutschpolnischen Grenzregion im Spannungsfeld regionaler, nationaler und europäischer Politik', in Jaedtke, E. and Piehl, E. (eds), *Konferenz der Euroregionen zwischen der Europäischen Union und Polen sowie der Tschechischen Republic*, Europäische Kommission/Parlament, Berlin, pp. 35-42.
Thielemann, E. (1998), *Policy Networks and European Governance: The Europeanisation of Regional Policy-Making in Germany*, Regional and Industrial Research Paper Series, No. 27, European Policies Research Centre, University of Strathclyde, Glasgow.
Thielemann, E. (1999), Institutional Limits of a 'Europe with the Regions': EC State-Aid Control Meets German Federalism, *Journal of European Public Policy*, vol. 6, no.3, pp.399-418
Wirtschaftsministerium Dresden (1997), *Positionspapier der Neuen Bundesländer einschließlich Berlin-Ost zur Reform der Strukturfonds nach 1999*, 06.02.1997.

PART IV:
POLICY RESPONSES

Many of the preceding chapters have posed complex questions and challenges for cohesion and regional policy in CEE. In part, they have also discussed the emerging policy responses. This final substantive section considers the evolution of regional development policies in more detail. Focusing on the Czech Republic, Poland and Hungary as case studies, three chapters describe the progress being made to establish institutions and policy for regional development, followed by an overview of the role of the European Union in assisting the design of delivery of regional policies.

PART IV:
POLICY RESPONSES

20 Regional Policy in the Czech Republic and EU Accession

JIŘÍ BLAŽEK AND SJAAK BOECKHOUT

Introduction

In common with several other countries in Central and Eastern Europe, the Czech Republic is preparing itself for accession to the European Union. These preparations started a couple of years ago but have recently intensified considerably in the light of the European Commission's Agenda 2000. Economic and social cohesion is one of the important elements of the pre-accession negotiations with the European Union, given its relation to the EU Structural Funds which could be provided throughout virtually the whole of the Czech Republic to foster regional economic development and growth in lagging regions or those facing particular restructuring challenges. Regional policy is setting the scene for (pre-) Structural Funds interventions in the Czech Republic. Regional policy was virtually non-existent for a long time until the emergence of the spatially uneven rise of unemployment in the 1990s as a result of the restructuring of existing economic activity. The preparations for EU accession gave further impetus to establishing a coherent and systematic policy to foster the (socio)-economic development of all parts of the Czech Republic.

Capacity building is an intrinsic part of regional policy. The former top-down, centrally planned economic system is being shifted into a bottom-up, market-oriented system that provides basic requirements for the economic growth of companies and regions. This will require infrastructure and institutions that can cope with the needs of decentralised units, offering stimuli for further development. Various studies show that this is one of the crucial factors behind why some countries and regions succeed and others fail to develop successfully (Porter, 1992; De Vet et al., 1998).

In this chapter, the Czech approach to regional policy and planning, which has been and will be used to address the structural changes in the economy and the challenge of EU accession, will be presented. In section

2, recent changes in Czech regional policy are addressed, focusing both on factors that have initiated change and steps that have been taken to pursue policies to overcome these changes. Section 3 discusses the main trends of regional development and outlines the present problems and reactions in Czech regional policy. Section 4 examines the main issues relating to the Czech Republic Development Plan, designed to provide a framework for policy action at various geographical levels, before conclusions are drawn in the final section.

Recent changes in Czech regional policy

Several reasons specific to post-communist countries explain why regional development policy issues are an important focus, in addition to the "classical", welfare-state inspired motives often behind the activities of decision-makers in developed countries (Blažek, 1999). These additional reasons include the following.
- The existence of acute crisis in some regions (usually with out-dated industrial structures) which might endanger the transition process.
- The stability of the regional pattern. Experience from developed countries shows that the regional pattern is quite stable. If the emerging regional pattern in post-communist countries can be defined, therefore, it is likely that it will not be altered completely, either in the short-term or over a medium-term period (5-10 years). This clearly has important policy implications.
- The difficulties of measuring economic efficiency under the centrally planned systems with artificially set prices. Under a system of overall redistribution, concepts such as "lagging" or "leading" regions had only limited relevance.
- Empirical observations confirm that a few years of transition changed the regional structure of post-communist countries more than several decades of communism.
- The re-establishment of democracy at local/regional levels and the new opportunities for local/regional initiatives have been important components of the democratisation of society, but also an important source of disparity in the geographical structure of society.

Despite all these reasons, the Czech Republic has hardly had any form of comprehensive regional policy for a considerable time. Up to 1996, this type of policy had a very low priority for the Czech government. There were several reasons for this: historical and geographical (small regional disparities in the former communist Czechoslovakia); economic (until 1996, an unusually low rate of unemployment of only about 3-4 percent); and political (proclaimed one-sided liberalism, unwillingness to intervene and distort market forces since 1990). As a result, regional policy comprised only modest support to SMEs (in the form of soft loans) in assisted areas selected principally on the basis of unemployment rate (eg. more than five percent in 1996).

It is fair to say that, although explicit regional policy was virtually absent, several sectoral Ministries pursued policies and programmes that had very definite (intentional or unintentional) regional effects. Examples of these are: the distribution of resources from the Environment Fund to the most polluted regions (Ministry for Environment); the support to farmers facing less-favourable conditions or in environmentally protected areas (Ministry for Agriculture); the allocation of funds for active employment policy to district job centres on the basis of unemployment rates (Ministry of Labour); the support of public transport in rural areas (Ministry for Transport), the revitalisation of former Soviet military training bases (Ministry of Defence); support of SMEs and foreign investors through CzechInvest (Ministry for Industry and Trade); and, probably the most important, the distribution of funds from the Ministry of Finance to local governments and District Offices. This last area included an equalisation grant to towns and municipalities in districts with below-average tax yields from personal income tax, which exceeded by several times the amount of resources from official regional policy (Blažek, 1999).

Since 1996, the Czech government has changed its attitude towards regional policy due to both internal and external factors. First, the most important of the internal factors is the steadily growing unemployment rate resulting from the economic stagnation in 1997-1998 and also delayed restructuring in dominant sectors of economic activity. Although the present level of unemployment (about eight percent) is still relatively low compared to countries in Western Europe, the rate of unemployment in several districts (notably in old industrial regions) has reached serious levels (almost 17 percent). At the same time, there are considerable labour shortages in other regions (about three percent unemployment rate in Prague and in several other districts).

Second, another important internal factor was the renunciation of the doctrine of economic liberalism by the Czech government following the

1996 parliamentary elections and more forcefully since the election and creation of a Social Democrat minority government in June 1998. This government even declared regional policy as a "outstanding priority" in its programme – although little has actually subsequently been realised.

Third, the external factors relate to the stimuli and pressures from the European Commission which has adopted economic and social cohesion as one of the pillars of European integration. From the start of the 1990s, the European Commission allocated considerable resources to regional development problems through the Phare programme, focusing notably on cross-border co-operation with regions bordering EU Member States (Germany, Austria) and recently also in border regions to adjacent CEE countries (Poland, Slovakia). Pressure from the Commission has come in several forms including the Opinion of the European Commission on the Questionnaires completed by all associate countries (1997) and annual evaluations of the progress achieved. In these documents, the European Commission criticised the Czech government in the field of regional development on a number of issues including the fact that regional policy was almost non-existent, there was poor horizontal co-ordination, the regional level of self-government was lacking, and there was a lack of resources for explicit regional development policy. As a result of this, the Czech government has taken steps to overcome these criticisms.

These changing conditions have resulted in several important steps in the field of regional policy.

- The Ministry for Regional Development was created after the elections of 1996. This new ministry was charged with regional policy, housing and tourism, including an important co-ordinating role regarding other governmental bodies and several regional programmes were transferred to this Ministry. The Centre for Regional Development was also established to facilitate the implementation of regional programmes, to support regional development agencies, and to provide training and information to local and regional actors.
- A special Working Group for Economic and Social Cohesion was created in 1998. This comprises 12 governmental bodies and is chaired by the Ministry for Regional Development. This working group was charged with co-ordinating the preparation of the Czech accession to the EU in the field of economic and social cohesion and dealing with the preparation of programming documents and institutional structures for the implementation of future sectoral and regional programmes. The working group was subsequently transformed into the National

Programming Committee for Economic and Social Cohesion (NPC-ESC).
- A new constitutional law was approved in autumn 1997 on the creation of 14 self-governing regions, to be effective in the year 2000. These regions will play an essential role in promoting the development of their territories and will work closely together with the other tiers of government administration, ie. national government and municipalities.
- The establishment of 14 regional development agencies (RDAs) has been organised to implement regional policy in the respective regions. In the context of the Phare-programme, two RDAs were established in problem regions several years ago. Recently, other RDAs have also been set up as a result of bottom-up initiatives. The existing RDAs differ considerably in terms of the size of their territories, number and qualification of employees, size of budget, ownership structure, and also involvement of regional actors. The intended network of 14 RDAs will work closely together with the Centre for Regional Development at the Ministry for Regional Development.
- The acceptance of several governmental regulations in the field of regional policy, including the new Principles of Regional Policy (April 1998) and the regulations on the Preparation for the EU Policy of Economic and Social Cohesion (January and April 1998, January 1999 - see below). These regulations follow the basic principles of the EU Structural Funds (concentration, partnership, programming, additionality, and subsidiarity) and outline the institutional structures that will be established to implement regional policy, including the responsibilities of the various actors involved.

Current problems facing Czech regional development and policy

Despite various changes in Czech regional policy and the institutional framework, several problems still need to be addressed before the Czech Republic could be said to have a coherent and effective regional policy system. The increasing regional disparities in the Czech Republic accentuate the need for positive action in this area.

Factors of regional development and regional disparities

The general regional development trend in post-communist countries after the collapse of communism can be described as *differentiation* (Blažek, 1997). The relatively modest inter-regional disparities which the Czech Republic inherited from the period of communism (see Fuchs and Demko, 1979) have been swiftly amplified. In general, diversified metropolitan regions have performed better than non-metropolitan, old-industrial and rural regions (Hampl, 1996). According to Blažek (1996), four main factors of regional development can be seen in the Czech Republic:
- the geographic position of the regions (both in a horizontal and vertical sense – see Blažek, 1999);
- the economic structure and degree of diversity (more diversified regions have generally better opportunities than narrowly specialised ones);
- the quality of human resources (especially the quality of education and the entrepreneurial tradition); and
- the quality of the environment (devastation of the environment on a sizeable part of the territory of the country will seriously hinder the future development of these regions not only because of the remedy costs but because the devastated environment also detracts potential inward investors).

After the process of transition had started, an almost textbook pattern of west-east regional disparities emerged in the Czech Republic in line with the macro-regional differentiation of Europe (for similar conclusions for Poland and Hungary, see Lodkovska et al., 1996; Barta et al., 1997; Downes, 1996; and Horváth, 1997). This west-east polarity can be illustrated by the fact that in the first half of the 1990s, the rate of unemployment in Moravia (eastern part of the Czech Republic) was twice as high as in Bohemia (western part of the country) with the worst affected region being North-Moravia. Nevertheless, since the mid-1990s, this pattern has been modified significantly through a rapid worsening of the economic and social situation in the old industrial region in North-Bohemia which became the worst affected Czech region in the second half of the 1990s. Another distinctive feature of recent regional development is a sharpening of inter-regional disparities at a local level caused by the bankruptcies of industrial plants. This is a serious development as it is accompanied by a rapid increase in general unemployment (from 3.5

percent in December 1996 to 8.4 percent in March 1999) caused by the deep economic crisis in 1997-1999.

Empirical analyses of recent regional development trends in the Czech Republic are provided by, among others, Hampl (1996), Blažek (1996), Blažek (1999) and Tomeš (1999). These analyses clearly show an acceleration of the growth of inter-regional disparities since the mid-1990s. This can be most pervasively illustrated by the development of the average rate of unemployment and of its level in the most affected districts.

Table 20.1 Average unemployment rate (district maximum) in the Czech Republic

Year	1991	1992	1993	1994	1995	1996	1997	1998	1999 (April)
Average unemp.* (%)	4.1	2.6	3.5	3.2	2.9	3.5	5.2	7.5	8.2
Highest unemp.* (%)	9.1	6.0	8.7	7.5	7.3	9.4	12.4	15.3	16.7

Source: Czech Ministry of Labour and Social Affairs.
Note: * except for 1999, the data relate to December of respective year.

The data provided in Table 20.1 show that the period of exceptionally low rates of unemployment in the Czech Republic is definitely over. In addition, since 1998, the rate of unemployment in several districts has exceeded 15 percent which is a cause for serious concern. However, the roots of the regional problems are not exclusively regional but relate also to the overall poor economic performance of the Czech Republic and the low level of business confidence and aggregate demand. This situation contributes to an overly high emphasis on sectoral approaches to the solution of regional problems and, to date, have not forced the government to implement integrated regional development support programmes.

Lack of co-ordination and strategy

At present, there is no coherent strategy to tackle regional problems. Regional policy is pursued by several institutions at various geographical levels with only *ad hoc* co-ordination between them. What is still missing is the Czech Regional Development Strategy and Regional Development Plan that will provide a comprehensive framework and integrate the various programmes and interventions at all levels. These programming documents are currently under preparation and are outlined in more detail below. The co-ordination role of the Ministry of Regional Development is hampered by the fact that only limited resources are allocated for official regional policy. This is also the case at the regional level where, in addition, there is no legal and financial framework to support regional strategies prepared through bottom-up initiatives. Without substantial budgets both for the Ministry for Regional Development and at the local and regional levels, sectoral ministries will continue to play a dominant role in solving regional problems.

Weak institutional set up and capacity

The absence of regional self-government (see below), and the limited powers and resources of other actors at the regional and local levels, prevent comprehensive and effective actions and policies being undertaken. Although the institutional framework is due to change in 2001, there is still much uncertainty regarding the competence and financial resources of the self-governing regions. The same is true with respect to the role and capacity of the regional development agencies that will be active in the implementation of regional policies and programmes in the respective regions.

Another aspect that is highly relevant in relation to the role of regional and local actors is the lack of qualified personnel able to develop, prepare and implement projects that comply with demanding EU regulations. The lack of qualified personnel is already a brake factor at national level, never mind the situation at regional and local levels. Recent experience of the Phare Cross Border Co-operation Programme shows that a lack of ability to generate high-quality projects could seriously limit the absorption capacity for additional financial resources to be available through the (pre-) Structural Funds in the Czech Republic.

The issue of regional-level administration

A regional level of public administration is still lacking in the Czech Republic. This creates a major problem given that its creation could facilitate a significant shift of competencies between different levels of government. While the overall idea behind the reform is to decentralise certain competencies to the regions, leaving the responsibilities of municipalities, in principle, unchanged, the specific contours of the competence transfer are still unknown. The lack of regional administration creates many problems in the sphere of regional development and regional policy and is also a cause for serious concern within the European Commission in light of the importance of the subsidiarity principle both for European integration in general and the policy of economic and social cohesion in particular. The remainder of this section looks at the background to this particular problem and the principal dilemmas facing the creation of a new regional level of administration.

According to Perlín (1996) and Illner (1999), the creation and development of regional administration has, since the start of the transition period, been the most cumbersome of all levels of public administration. The main effort towards reforming the public administration has focused on two levels: first, the central level (including new parliamentary elections, the creation of a new government, the election of a president); and, second, the local level. These two levels appeared crucial for the success of the transition. The central level was clearly of priority concern given its significance for the whole of society and, at local level, reform seemed vital because of its closeness to the citizens. Regional level reform, however, was both less straightforward and less rational.

The reform of regional administration in the Czech Republic started in 1990 with the abolition of the eight regions, leaving the district as the only State administrative unit. Consequently, representative bodies were elected only at the central and local (municipal) levels. The most important motives behind the abolition of public administration at regional level were the intention to cut the mutual ties of the former communist *nomenklatura* cadres and the strengthening of the competence of bodies at central and local levels. The lack of any form of self-government bodies between the municipal level and the State caused many practical problems such as the availability of appropriate institutions for the management of services and for dealing with issues at supra-municipality level as well as solving inter-municipality disputes. In addition, the abolition of the eight regions resulted in the consequent partial transfer of competencies to central level, and the ministries were faced with difficulties in carrying out all of the now central-level responsibilities. This resulted in the creation of a network of regional branches or offices ('deconcentrated offices'). This process, however was unco-ordinated, with virtually every ministry designing its own network with a different number of regional offices and a different delineation of serviced territories. This inconsistent approach further multiplied the problems of co-ordination, both horizontally and vertically. It is envisaged that, when new self-governing regions are established, the regional branches of different ministries will be integrated into the administrative bodies of these regions. The significance of these problems was and is, however, often underestimated.

There were several principal arguments against the establishment of new regional self-government. First, there was fear of an increase of bureaucracy within the system of public administration. This was understandable because the former communist state was generally considered hyper-bureaucratic and the abolition of some bureaucracy appeared logical.

Second, there were important political calculations. Contrary to the local government, which was considered primarily a non-political service to citizens, the regional level had a much stronger political dimension. There were concerns that the political leaning of the regional representatives in certain regions could differ from the political direction of the ruling party (or coalition) and thus hinder or even endanger the transition itself. It was often argued that, in the period of transition when radical measures should be implemented, a strong central administration is needed.

Third, at the start of the process of transition in the former Czechoslovakia, there was serious discussion about the new nature of relations between the Czechs and the Slovaks. After three years, this debate resulted in the split of Czechoslovakia into two independent states on 1 January 1993. The problem between the Czechs and the Slovaks was paralleled within the Czech Republic by debate about the relationship between the two historical lands - Bohemia and Moravia (particularly during 1991-1992). There was considerable pressure from Moravia to re-establish the system of historical lands, or create a federal structure within the Czech Republic, but the majority of Czech politicians were reluctant to create a new dualism. Consequently, when the constitution of the independent Czech Republic was prepared in autumn 1992, the description of the territorial public administration incorporated into the Czech constitution was vague in nature and stated that "....The Czech Republic consists of higher self-governing units: regions or lands....". The requirement for a constitutional majority to create a new regional self-government has contributed considerably to the delay in reforming the regional administration given that achieving widespread agreement on such a complicated issue has proved to be very difficult.

Fourth, the issue of regional administration has never been at the top of the agenda either among politicians or the wider public – the rare exception was the consideration by President Václav Havel of the creation of regional self-government as an important pillar of civic society. As a result, this issue has been put on hold for several years during which time only a small number of mayors and professionals has tried to initiate reform in this area. Several different proposals for the design of regional administration have been put forward, although many of the proposals were limited to the delineation of the boundaries of future territorial units. This 'map-drawing race' by professionals and some politicians has contributed to the discrediting of the very idea of regional self-government in the media and among the wider public.

Finally, the situation changed after the 1996 elections when the centre-right coalition lost its parliamentary majority and had to change its policies and make some concessions to keep its power as a minority government. This was the point at which it was considered correct to meet the constitutional proposal to establish a second chamber of the Parliament (Senate) as well as a regional level of self-government. As a result of the changed political situation, in 1997 the Parliament approved a constitutional law stating that, from 2000, the Czech Republic would comprise 14 self-governing regions. Nevertheless, the constitutional law still only established the number and boundaries of the new regions and did not address the issues of their competencies or financial resources. These issues have to be covered by separate Acts. The preparation of these Acts, however, was hindered by an unclear vision of the nature of future public administration as well as by lack of effort. Given the situation by the summer of 1999, it seems unlikely that the original time-schedule will be met given that the whole legal package relating to the operation of the new regions is still not ready.

The delay in establishing the 14 self-governing regions is causing many difficulties. While originally the new regions should have started operating from 2000, the slow preparation process of the whole legislative package means that their introduction even in 2001 is now questionable. The regions should play an important role in the promotion of economic development in their territories – a task which is currently either lacking completely or undertaken by relatively weak regional development agencies. The creation of the regions will clearly allocate responsibility for the coherent development of the respective regions. Even though the new regions will not receive any additional money for regional development projects, as the size of their budget is likely to comprise the sum of the resources allocated for competencies to be transferred to this level, they will at least have the opportunity to determine their own priorities. Moreover, it is anticipated that the creation of self-governing regions will stimulate initiative, co-operation and partnership among various regional subjects. Even when the 14 self-governing regions are established, it will take some time before the regions function properly and all subjects and organisations become accustomed to the new institutional framework. This can be expected to happen in the years 2002-2003.

Definition of the hierarchy of NUTS regions

The negotiations between the Czech government and EUROSTAT on the definition of the regional NUTS hierarchy, to be used for statistical purposes and EU cohesion policy, raised other problems closely related to the regional level of administration. The approved, though still non-existent, 14 regions were considered by EUROSTAT as too small for NUTS II regions and instead were accepted as regions corresponding to the NUTS III level. However, for the Czech Republic, the NUTS II regions are the most important level given their centrality in the eligibility for Objective 1 status under the Structural Funds which the Czech government is keen to obtain. This mismatch has already created problems given that certain provisional structures in the 14 future regions have already been established by the Ministry for Regional Development. These structures, called Regional Co-ordination Groups, comprise representatives in each region selected according to the EU principle of partnership. When the hierarchy of NUTS regions was agreed between the Czech Government and the EU in January 1999, comprising eight NUTS II regions in the Czech Republic, the former 14 Regional Co-ordination Groups had to be transformed into eight Regional Monitoring and Management Committees (RMMC). These Committees are participating in the preparation of regional support programmes and will take part in their subsequent implementation. The definition of NUTS IV and NUTS V units was less problematic and the 77 existing districts were accepted as NUTS IV regions, while the 6,242 municipalities were considered as NUTS V units.

Towards the Czech Regional Development Strategy and Regional Development Plan

An important step in overcoming the current lack of co-ordination and strategy will be the formulation and approval of the basic programming documents in the sphere of regional development and policy. At present, two such strategic documents are under preparation. The first document is the Regional Development Strategy of the Czech Republic, required by the Czech Government, and the second is the Regional Development Plan, as defined by the EU Structural Fund regulations. There are some similarities, but also important differences, between both programming documents. The Regional Development Strategy of the Czech Republic is prepared predominantly as a basic framework for the conception of Czech regional policy and in order to facilitate the co-ordination of diverse sectoral programmes with important regional impacts. The main purpose of the Regional Development Plan is to provide a justification and coherent strategy for the use of the pre-accession aid from several EU financial instruments (Phare II, ISPA and SAPARD), as well as the creation of a proper legal and institutional framework to guarantee the efficient, effective and fair use of the aid. Another difference between the two documents is the basic geographical unit used for programming. In the case of the Regional Development Strategy, the basic unit comprises the 14 future self-governing regions (NUTS III level), while in the case of the Regional Development Plan, the basic unit for regional analysis and programmes is the NUTS II regions.

The preparation of the Regional Development Strategy started earlier than the preparation of the Regional Development Plan and, although the Strategy has not yet been approved by the government, the preliminary version of the Strategy was used as an important input into the Regional Development Plan. Both documents are being prepared by the Ministry for Regional Development which promotes the mutual consistency of both programming documents.

During the preparation of these programming documents several basic problems were identified, including the lessons to be learned from other European countries (see Boeckhout et al, 1999). The main issues, grouped by the principles of EU economic and social cohesion policy, are presented in Table 20.2.

Table 20.2 Principal difficulties in the preparation of the Czech programming documents

Principle	Main problems or dilemmas
Concentration	Focus the strategy on narrowing the gap between the Czech Republic and the EU or on combating increasing domestic regional and social disparities (ie. concentration from a European or Czech perspective)?
Partnership	Missing regional level of self-government; unclear criteria for selection of partners.
Programming	Missing strategy for individual sectors (some sectors are still missing from the overall strategy while others are working on their strategy and on the Plan at the same time), lack of experience with the implementation of support programmes.
Additionality	Lack of multi-annual budgeting of public budgets, unknown absorption capacity.
Evaluation and monitoring	Lack of experience with evaluation and monitoring (esp. setting the targets of measures and interventions, problems with formulation of proper indicators).

In addition to the problems mentioned in Table 20.2, obvious complications emerge both from the unclear time schedule of EU enlargement and from the imprecise indication of the volume of pre-accession aid to be made available to the Czech Republic. However, to date, and despite all these problems, the preparation of the first Czech Regional Development Plan is proceeding in line with the methodological guidance prepared jointly by EU and Czech experts which has clarified many of the problems. The main credit for maintaining a good pace in this preparatory work can be given to the National Programming Committee for Economic and Social Cohesion (NPC-ESC), chaired by the Ministry for Regional Development and comprising representatives of all relevant partners from both central and regional levels of administration and from both the public and private sectors. A key role in the preparation of submissions for the Regional Development Plan is played by the 'drafting committees' subordinated to the NPC-ESC. Drafting committees were set up by each relevant ministry or jointly by several ministries. The membership of the drafting committees also includes the main non-governmental partners relevant in particular areas. It is too soon to draw any conclusions on the process of preparation of the programming documents. The first test will be the opinion of European Commission on the Regional Development Plan while the second, and much more important test, will be the actual results of the implemented measures envisaged by the Plan.

Conclusions

Despite the many particularities of the Czech Republic, the main problems in the sphere of regional development and policy are surprisingly similar to those of Poland, Hungary or Slovakia (see Lodkovska et al., 1996; Czyz, 1998; Ruttkay, 1997; Szaló, 1998; Slavík, 1998; De Vet et al., 1998; Hollanders, 1999). These common problems comprise the domination of sectoral approaches in the solution of regional problems and their poor co-ordination, and a weak legal and institutional framework (all four countries are preparing or have recently carried out a reform of regional administration, and the responsibility for regional policy among the government Ministries is often unclear or uncertain). There are also problems with the design of high-quality projects which would be devised within the framework of a clear development strategy. Other problems are linked to the co-financing of development programmes, particularly in light of the involvement of the private sector and the annual, rather than multi-annual, budgeting approach of the public sector.

The opportunity presented by the availability of EU pre-accession structural aid is challenging and stimulating, and regional development and policy is one area where the influence of the EU practice is clearly visible. After almost a decade of a trial and error approach, or the complete lack of any activity, the package of pre-accession aid offered from 2000 sets a clear direction for work at both central and regional level. Setting a clear perspective has helped to initiate new activity and enhanced mutual co-operation. It is absolutely crucial to achieve at least some positive results from these new activities.

An important goal is to ensure that the clear and strict criteria used in the implementation of programmes within EU economic and social cohesion policy are also applied in the framework of national policies and programmes. The same is true for other principles such as subsidiarity, partnership and concentration. Contrary to the current situation, where two programming or strategic documents exist, one for national and one for EU programmes (although some degree of convergence is evident), it would be highly desirable to prepare a single common strategy for the complementary use of national and EU programmes and resources. Only then will it be possible to pursue a coherent and effective policy to achieve economic and social cohesion in the Czech Republic.

References

Barta, G., Králik, M. and Perger, É. (1997), 'Achievements and conflicts of modernisation in Hungary', *European Spatial Research and Policy*, vol. 4, no. 2, pp. 61-82.

Blažek, J. (1996), 'Regional Patterns of Economic Adaptability to the Transformation and Global Process in the Czech Republic', *Acta universitatis Comenianae – Geographica*, no. 37, pp. 61-70.

Blažek, J. (1997), 'The Czech Republic on its way toward the West European structures', *European Spatial Research and Policy*, vol. 4, no. 1, pp.37- 62.

Blažek, J. (1999), 'Regional development and regional policy in CEECs in the perspective of the EU eastern enlargement', in Hampl, M. (ed), *Geography of Societal Transformation in the Czech Republic*, Faculty of Science, Charles University, Prague, pp. 183-99.

Boeckhout et al (1999), *Preparing the Czech Regional Development Plan: lessons from Europe*, Ministry for Regional Development, Prague.

Czyz, T. (1998), *The territorial organisation reform and the regional structure of Poland*, Paper presented at Regional Conference of IGU, Lisboa, August 1998, p. 12.

De Vet, J.M., Boot, L. and Hollanders, M. (eds) (1998), *EU-Accession and Regional Development*, Proceedings International Conference Tartu, NEI Rotterdam, p. 120.

Downes, R. (1996), 'Regional Policy Development in Central and Eastern Europe', in Alden, J. and Boland, P. (eds) *Regional Development Strategies: A European Perspective*, Regional Studies Association, Regional Policy and Development 15, Jessica Kingsley, London, pp. 256-72.

Fuchs, R. J. and Demko, G. (1979), 'Geographic inequality under socialism', *Annals of the Association of American Geographers*, vol. 69, no. 2, pp. 304-18.

Hampl, M. et al (1996), *Geografická organizace společnosti a transformační procesy v České republice* (Geographical organisation of society and transformation processes in the Czech Republic), Faculty of Science, Prague, p. 395.

Hollanders, M. (1999), *Regional Development and EU-accession in Central and Eastern Europe*, Erasmus University Rotterdam, Rotterdam.
Horváth, G. (1997), 'The regional policy of the transition in Hungary', *European Spatial Research and Policy*, vol. 3, no. 2, pp. 39-55.
Illner, M. (1999), 'Territorial Decentralisation: An Obstacle to Democratic Reform in Central and Eastern Europe?', in Kimball, J.D. (ed), *The Transfer of Power: Decentralisation in Central and Eastern Europe*, The Local Government and Public Service, Budapest, pp. 7- 42.
Lodkowsa-Skoneczna, A., Pyszkowski, A. and Szlachta, J. (1996), *Regional Development in Poland 1990-1995*, Task Force for Regional Development, Warszaw, p. 133.
Perlín, R. (1996), 'Problematika organizace státní správy a samosprávy' (Problems of state administration and self-government), in Hampl, M. (ed), *Geografická organizace spolecnosti a transformační procesy v Oeské republice*, Faculty of Science, Charles University, Prague, pp. 315-32.
Porter M.E. (1992), *The Competitive Advantage of Nations*, The Free Press, New York.
Ruttkay, É. (1997), *Hungary on the way to EU: consequences for regional policy*, Paper presented at the Conference "Integration and Transition in Europe", Ministry for Environment and Regional Policy, Budapest, p. 11.
Slavík, V. (1998), 'Územnosprávné usporiadanie Slovenskej republiky v medzinárodných porovnániach', (Territorial administration of Slovakia in international comparison), *Geografia*, no.1/1998, pp. 4-7.
Szaló, P. (1997), *Hungary's Experiences of the Transition from a Planned Economy to a Market Economy*, Ministry for Environment and Regional Policy, Budapest, p. 18.
Tomeš, J. (1999), 'Specifická nezaměstnanost v České republice v regionálním srovnání' (Regional patterns of specific unemployment in the Czech Republic), *Geografie-SČGS*, vol. 101, no. 4, pp. 278-95.

21 Regional Development Policy in Poland in the 1990s

MAREK KOZAK

Introduction

In 1999, Poland introduced four reforms considered to represent the last elements of institutional transformation, relating to the national health system, education, social security and, last but not least, the decentralisation and reform of the territorial organisation of the State. Each of those reforms is a major undertaking, both costly and politically difficult.

The territorial reform and decentralisation of the State as of 1 January 1999 has to be seen in the overall context of reforms undertaken since 1989. There were at least two general reasons for the decentralisation of the State: a centralised State with only two levels of public administration could not cope effectively with the dynamically developing market economy and problems arising at the regional level; and a high level of centralisation was inconsistent with the model of democracy introduced after 1989 and the aspirations of the regional communities. The principles of the territorial reform can be summarised as follows:
- decentralisation of power - by delegating competence and resources to the territorial self-government bodies;
- deconcentration of State administration - by strengthening the *voivodship* (regional) structure at the expense of the departmental structure; and
- the application of the principle of subsidiarity by the State central authorities towards the local authorities in lieu of centralised distribution of developmental resources.

Against this background, this chapter concentrates on the institutional and policy issues which have emerged in the 1990s. It begins by outlining recent trends in regional policy during the reform period and the process of decentralisation and territorial reform. The chapter then discusses the debate over regional policy, concluding that the foundations of a modern regional development policy are now in place.

Regional policy 1990-1998

A fundamental shift from a centrally planned to a market economy began in Poland in 1989. Economic policy at the beginning of the transformation (during the period called, with some exaggeration, the "shock therapy") focused exclusively on macro-economic stability. In particular, in the period 1990-1992, there was no specific regional policy. The only instrument of intervention was support for the unemployed which offered preferential conditions both for the unemployed and local businesses. This was provided in addition to general support available in around 400 municipalities, or *gminas* (out of a total of 2,489).

It was only after successful economic stabilisation, at the turn of 1992/93, that the idea of introducing regional policy received support. At that time, despite the lack of a developed regional policy and corresponding institutional basis, a growing number of sectoral policy areas had begun to identify a regional dimension (environment, agriculture, industry etc.). In 1992, the Polish government decided to embark on two interconnected courses of action. At the *policy level*, a major effort was made by the Central Office of Planning (CUP) to develop the concept of regional policy. At the *implementation level*, the decision was taken to develop a modern pilot regional development programme with technical and financial support from the EU and to implement it through the newly created (1993), State-owned and controlled Polish Agency for Regional Development (PARR). The Phare-Struder programme has, to date, been the most complex and largest *sensu stricto* regional development programme in Central Europe[1]. Its experience and regulations were extensively used by subsequent, though less complex, programmes.

Both diagnostic studies and practical experience revealed serious institutional constraints. Systemic changes initiated in 1990 were limited to the local (municipality) level. The absence of elected bodies at the regional level limited the capacity of the regions to solve their problems and to implement State regional policy. At central level, until 1996, responsibility for regional policy was shared by the Central Office of Planning and the Ministry of Labour. Other important constraints included a relatively low level of GDP and a hard budget. It is not surprising, therefore, that among key recommendations for the Government (put forward by almost every study) was the strengthening of central co-ordination of regional policy and the decentralisation of the state.

An early outline of regional policy proposals prepared by the Central Office of Planning (1995) was followed by a number of diagnostic studies, development concepts, and spatial analyses. In 1996, the Task Force for Regional Policy in Poland (a joint initiative of the EU and the Polish Government) produced a highly detailed diagnostic report on regional development and an outline of a regional development strategy. One year later, the Task Force for Structural Policies in Poland published its findings and recommendations, also connected with the creation of regional development policy. Among other key documents, the diagnostic and conceptual foundations for regional policy were further developed in *Poland 2000 Plus – the Assumptions of the Concept of the Long-Term Spatial Policy* (Central Office of Planning – 1996, approved by the Government and the Parliament) and its more developed version, *The Concept of Spatial Policy in Poland* (Government Centre for Strategic Studies, 1999).

None of these proposals was translated in practice, thwarted by a lack of political will and successive administrative reorganisations. For example, the reform, or more accurately, reorganisation, of the central government introduced on 1 January 1997 did not change the actual situation regarding regional policy, but simply transferred responsibility both to the newly created Ministry of Economy (short and medium-term regional planning) and to the Government Centre for Strategic Planning (long-term regional planning). Meanwhile, the Government Sub-committee for Regional Policy and Rural Areas Development, an opinion-making body established in 1995, was disbanded.

In the first half of 1999, there was a debate on a draft regional policy Act developed by the Ministry of Labour. Its proponents consider it vital, while critics say that such a regulation could be more effectively enforced by ensuring coherence of the existing laws and state aid law (currently under preparation). They also criticise its centralistic spirit (which may stem from the public finances law) and in particular the lack of any reference to a central government regional policy department. Yet another debate was started in April / May 1999 focusing on the rationale and concept of the strategy for regional policy in Poland, and based on two projects by the Ministry of Economy and Government Centre for Strategic Studies. A final document from this debate is expected by October 1999.

In the absence of progress at national level, practical economic development actions were being undertaken among the regions. A specific Polish feature was the spontaneous establishment of c.70 regional and local development agencies. Most of them were established in 1991-1994 and, for those involved in foreign assistance funded projects and programmes in particular, managed to gain significant know-how in terms of regional instruments and techniques. The option exists for the shares belonging to the Treasury (through the former 49 *voivods*) to be transferred to the appropriate regional (local) self-government. It is not clear yet how many of them will become controlled by the self-government as a main shareholder or what role they will play as the process gets underway. Surprisingly, the agencies (and the national co-ordinating body, PARR) turned out to be the most stable part of the institutional system. Even before the territorial reform, many regions had started work on regional strategies; six of them, supported under the Phare-Struder Programme, successfully produced strategic documents complying with EU standards. Another four were financed under Phare-RAPID. These can be used by new authorities of new regions.

Decentralisation and territorial reform

There are few non-federal countries which are as deeply decentralised as Poland after the recent territorial reform of 1999. From 1 January 1999 the following levels of elected territorial authorities have been instituted:
- Region *(województwo):* There are now 16 regions in Poland (see chapter 11 by Gorzelak) replacing the former 49 provinces. Each region has an elected regional assembly *(sejmik)* and the regional government *(zarząd)* is headed by a *"marszałek"* nominated by the assembly. The regional government has, among other powers, full responsibility for the strategy and economic development of the region. *De facto*, this power at the regional level is shared with the central government representative *(voivod)*, whose responsibility concerns mainly public safety, standards, and ensuring conformity of laws enacted by the regional assembly.
- County *(powiat):* There are 373 counties, each governed by the county council and the county executive body. As a rule, the *powiat* provides public services which cannot be effectively provided by the municipality.

- Municipality *(gmina):* In existence since 1990, the 2,489 municipalities have full responsibility for the provision of typical public services and local development, including the preparation of the local strategy.

An indisputable outcome of this reform has been the creation of 16 economically stronger regions, based mostly on dynamically developing agglomerations (see Table 21.1). It should be noted, however, that this is not true in all cases and the Parliament has the right to dissolve any of the weaker regions not considered to be viable before the end of 2000. The key challenges facing the new structure relate to finances, institutional framework and legal arrangements.

Table 21.1 Basic data for 16 new Polish regions (*voivodships*), 1998

Voivodship (capital)	Pop. (mill)	Pop. density	GDP per cap. 1997: Poland =100	Number of			Unemp.	
				powiat	gmina	powiaty grodzkie*	%	Fem. '000
Dolnoślaskie (Wrocław)	2.9	150	94	26	169	4	12.3	93
Kujawsko-pomorskie (Bydgoszcz)	2.1	117	84	19	144	4	13.6	75
Lubelskie (Lublin)	2.2	89	73	20	213	4	9.6	60
Lubuskie (Gorzow)	1.1	73	86	11	83	2	12.4	30
Łodzkie (Łodz)	2.7	147	94	20	177	3	11.0	74
Małopolskie (Kraków)	3.2	212	90	19	182	3	7.1	67
Mazowieckie (Warsaw)	5.1	142	151	38	325	4	7.3	106
Opolskie (Opole)	1.1	116	86	11	71	1	9.8	28
Podkarpackie (Rzeszów)	2.1	118	75	20	160	4	11.7	75
Podlaskie (Białystok)	1.2	61	72	14	118	3	9.5	32

				Number of			Unemp.	
Voivodship (capital)	Pop. (mill)	Pop. density	GDP per cap. 1997: Poland =100	powiat	gmina	powiaty grodzkie*	%	Fem. '000
Pomorskie (Gdańsk)	2.2	119	100	15	123	4	10.4	56
Śląskie (Katowice)	4.9	398	115	17	166	19	6.2	89
Świętokrzyskie (Kielce)	1.3	114	69	13	102	1	11.9	46
Warminsko-Mazurskie (Olsztyn)	1.5	60	77	17	116	2	18.9	69
Wielkopolskie (Poznań)	3.3	112	108	31	226	4	7.8	75
Zachodniopomorskie (Szczecin)	1.7	75	97	17	114	3	13.1	54
POLAND	3.9	131	100	308	2,489	65	10.8	1 032

Source: Ministry of Internal Affairs and Administration. GDP estimation from Orlowski, Saganowska and Zienkowski. Table prepared by Polish Agency for Regional Development.
Note: * Cities with the status of *powiats* ie. over 100,000 inhabitants or former *voivod*ship capitals.

First of all, there is a financial barrier. Due to technical reasons, no final data are available on the public finance share of the different tiers. Very rough estimations suggest that *voivodship* self-governments' budgets amount to c. 1.13 percent of the State budget, while the *powiats* have 8.53 percent of expenditure. Altogether, general subsidies for the regional and local self-governments amount to 15.6 percent of the State budget (see also Table 21.2). While the data presented here do not offer a comprehensive picture, it is clear that, for the time being, the newly created units have lower than expected own incomes and will have to rely heavily on State subventions. To what extent the finances available are adequate for the required tasks remains to be seen. An ability to improve financial management will also be of obvious importance.

It is even more difficult to discuss expenditure in the field of regional development. *Sensu stricto* regional policy expenditure (spending on regional restructuring programmes and central investment projects) varied from 0.10 percent of the State budget in 1993 to 0.17 percent in 1998

(Gorzelak, 1998). It should be remembered however, that there is a significant transfer of funds within sectoral policies which can often have a strong regional dimension (labour, environment, mining etc). There is no estimation of the impact of those funds on the regions.

Table 21.2 Budget of the new territorial self-government units, 1999 ('000 PLN*)

	Powiats	Voivodships	Total
Total	14,714,447	2,476,359	17,190,806
of which:			
General subsidies	6,972,671	1,125,518	8,098,189
Grants to implement certain tasks of State administration	4,670,556	39,094	4,709,650
Grants to implement own tasks	2,531,362	757,461	3,288,823
Share of personal income tax (PIT)	310,436	465,654	776,090
Share of corporate income tax (CIT)	-	86,286	86,286
Other income (own income)	229,422	2,346	231,768

Source: Ministry of Internal Affairs and Administration, 1999.
Note: * £1 + 6.8 PLN (December 1999); In 1998, the budgets of these units were exceptionally prepared by the central administration in the absence of the new regional units. The budgets for 2000 (prepared by *powiats* and *voivodships* themselves) are not yet known.

Second, there is an organisational barrier. The regional and *powiat* administrations must, at the same time, both fulfil their duties and create their internal structures and procedures and this will require serious investment in human resources. In addition, the reforms require skills and expertise which could not previously be acquired or practised. Despite the official optimism, it is clear that making the new institutions operate smoothly will take years, rather than months.

Third, there is an inadequate regulatory framework. The main legal acts referring directly or indirectly to regional development are: the *Voivodship* Self-Government Act (June 1998); the *Gmina* Self-Government Act (March 1990); the Spatial Economy Act (July 1994) for 'physical planning' or 'territorial management'; and the Public Finances Act (November 1998). In general, according to the *Voivodship* Self-Government Act, the *voivodship* is responsible for preparing the development strategy, multi-annual programmes and the spatial programme. In turn, the municipality is responsible for preparing the local spatial plan and economic programmes. The Spatial Economy Act additionally requires that the municipality has to work out a study of conditions and goals of its physical planning to take account of the *voivodship* development strategy.[2] The regulations on public finances are also important. Among others things, these stipulate that public sector co-financing cannot be higher than 50 percent, well below the grant aid ceilings under the Cohesion Fund or Objective 1 of the Structural Funds. Higher involvement is allowed but only in the case of projects listed in multi-annual programmes approved by the Cabinet or, if the programme value exceeds PLN 100 million, by the Parliament.

The above-mentioned legislation is not very specific (with the exception of the public finances law) and does not define in detail the structure, methodology or content of the required programmes, strategies and studies. This is a source of concern for regional and local authorities as they expect more guidelines. Paradoxically, from the point of view of European integration, it will make it easier to introduce, for instance, Structural Funds regulations in the future. In the short term, however, it does not help and, while a handbook on regional strategies (such as the one published by the Polish Agency for Regional Development) may serve as an aid, it cannot substitute for the regulations.

Debate on regional policy: key issues

Before presenting the most important issues, it is necessary to note that the regional policy debate has been taking place in a changing environment, and at a changing pace. The acceleration of the EU accession preparation process, in particular, has had an extremely significant influence on issues raised at various times. The same can be said for the influence of the devolution of the State and the territorial reform. Clearly, the devolution of the State created suitable conditions for the introduction of regional policy, but despite this achievement, the most difficult problem turned out to be which government institution should be responsible for regional policy. It has been generally clear that the Committee for Regional Policy and Sustainable Growth, (a purely opinion-making body established in 1998), chaired by the sectoral minister, is not in a position to co-ordinate and/or implement this policy area. There are three alternative proposals: a) to create a separate government department; b) to transfer responsibility to an existing sectoral ministry in terms of both competencies and resources; and

c) to strengthen (along the lines of Office of the Committee for European Integration), the Committee for Regional Policy and Sustainable Growth. Those against proposal "a" cite the danger of having an overly small, potentially weak department. Those against "b" stress that sectoral ministries will be pre-occupied with their core (sectoral) tasks and will marginalise horizontal measures. Certainly, mining, steel and other sectors which are not restructured and privatised are, and will be, of key political importance in future years. As for "c", the question is of whose resources and competencies should be transferred to the Regional Policy Committee in order give it the required powers of co-ordination.

A further point of key importance relates to the objectives of regional policy. Initially, the discussion focused on an artificial (particularly in a country where GDP per capita is only c. 42 percent of EU average) debate of "equality vs efficiency" or "competitiveness vs counteracting disparities". Today it is clear to the majority that it is not a problem which can be explained in terms of a dichotomy. This is not only because of the EU notion of cohesion which has to be taken into account by Member States when implementing any structural (economic) policy. Recently it has also been acknowledged that the regions' responsibility is to develop strategies and programmes which make optimal use of available resources in order to assure endogenous growth and improved competitiveness. Thus, government policy would address national structural policy issues, and in particular cohesion – a notion also reflected in the Regional Policy Act, which is currently under preparation. Indeed this general concept is also reflected in the public finances law, which defines the method of subsidy distribution between regions and envisages a relatively steady lowering of the 'levelling' subsidy in *voivodship* budgets. The first year of operation of the new regional authorities created some confusion when it became clear that the own incomes of both *powiats* and *voivodships* were far below expectations, making them dependent on various subsidies to perform their own tasks (not to mention the tasks commissioned by the Government).

The Regional Self-Government Act transfers all the responsibility for socio-economic development of the region to elected regional bodies and their executive representations. The public finances law does not, however, envisage the possibility of direct transfer of development funds (pre-accession or structural or any other) to the regional self-government. Some believe that such a transfer should be possible to the *voivod* which (possibly in the form of a contract) would finance various measures and projects identified by the self-government and selected for implementation by bodies such as Regional Steering Committees. The *voivod* (in consultation with the self-government) would establish principles and criteria for project selection. Thus in some regions, parallel regional policy units (*voivod* and *marszałek*) exist which still have to agree on the practicalities of co-operation. The French example (where such a double administration exists) may help to anticipate and solve potential problems.

Another aspect of discussion on objectives relates to the scope of regional policy. While the Ministry of Economy concentrated its efforts on a speedy preparation of six strategies related to Structural Fund goals (regional, labour, fishery, agriculture and rural development, environment, transport), many experts stress that these strategies cannot be developed in isolation from other policies (industrial restructuring, SME development etc.) and should be defined within the framework of a comprehensive national development plan. The above-mentioned strategies are, in most cases, ready, in their final draft versions. The regional policy strategy is in the form of two parallel documents, prepared by the Ministry of Economy and by the Government Centre for Strategic Studies. These two documents, though not approved yet by the Parliament, are to a large extent compatible. In terms of general differences, the Ministry of Economy is more Structural Fund oriented, while the Government Centre focuses more on a need to have a coherent national development strategy which does not evade global issues.

As Poland has a long tradition of spatial (physical) planning, some experts have raised various spatial-related issues of regional policy, often insisting that neither regional policy nor physical planning can be developed separately. There are also other concerns which have prompted many experts to ask whether Polish spatial (and regional) policy can be reduced to issues defined under EU structural policies.

From the above presentation it is obvious that the recent discussions have concentrated mainly on relatively basic decisions. Other questions also exist, which are often technical in nature, but have serious consequences. The NUTS structure for instance, raises concern. Some experts point out that giving the new *voivodships* NUTS II status may penalise large underdeveloped areas of Mazovia because its capital, Warsaw, as a booming agglomeration, will make the region as a whole appear better in GDP per capita terms. This could result in the area failing to be designated under the future Objective 1, or being quickly de-designated, and these concerns apply to areas other than just the capital region.

Another point of concern is the allocation (or not) of NUTS III status to the *powiats*. In comparison with a typical NUTS III unit in the EU, a *powiat* is small, both in terms of population and territory. This could result, for instance in case of Interreg, in the support of an overall smaller population than in the equivalent partner NUTS III region, thus to some extent continuing the already visible asymmetry in cross-border co-operation with EU regions.

Conclusions

The decentralisation and territorial administrative reform of the State in Poland, despite problems which have arisen in connection with this process, has provided a good regional and local base for the implementation of a modern regional policy. At central level, Poland urgently needs a decision on the central institution to be responsible for regional policy formulation and co-ordination, and the legal system has to be further developed. The adoption of the EU *acquis* and, in particular, of regional policy principles (additionality, programming, concentration, partnership) would be a major step forward.

Despite all the conceptual work carried out in recent years, Poland still has to take the final step to develop and introduce its own regional policy. A coherent national strategy has to be worked out before any specific programme for utilisation of the pre-accession or Structural Funds can be presented to the European Commission; a strategy which clearly defines priorities and roles, develops mechanisms of co-ordination, implementation and monitoring arrangements and which integrates appropriate elements of sectoral policy with regional development objectives and actions. Fortunately, most of the required elements are available, which should make the task easier, potentially even capable of finalisation during 2000.

Notes

1 Phare Struder PLN 9207, 76.7 million euro EU support, implemented in six "problem" regions, using several instruments and approaches practised from Structural Funds. It offered support for regional institution-building, financial support to SME investment (equity, grants, guarantees), training and advisory services, training for bank staff, co-financing for local infrastructure projects. Due to the leverage principle used, it mobilised ca

3 euro of regional and local capital (public and private) per each one euro of aid.

2   By law this Act expired on 31 December 1999. If it is not replaced by a new law, or if it is not prolonged for say, two years, municipalities will lose the right to take any decision on construction projects (commercial, municipal, housing).

References

Central Office of Planning (1995), *Raport o polityce regionalnej (Report on Regional Policy)*, Warsaw.

Central Office of Planning, (1996), *Poland 2000 Plus - The Assumptions of the Concept of the Long-Term Spatial Policy*, Warsaw.

Domański R. (ed), (1998), *Emerging Spatial and Regional Structures of an Economy in Transition, Polish Academy of Sciences*, Committee for Spatial Economy and Regional Planning, Warsaw.

Gorzelak G. (1998), *Regional and Local Potential for Transformation in Poland*, EUROREG, Warsaw University, Warsaw.

Gorzelak G., Kozak M. and Roszkowski W. (1998), 'Regional Development Agencies in Poland', in Danson M. and Halkier H. (eds) *Regional Development Agencies in Europe*, Jessica Kingsley Publishers, London and Bristol, Pennsylvania.

Kozak M. and Pyszkowski A. (eds) (1999), *A Phare-Struder Pilot Regional Development Programme*, Polish Agency for Regional Development, Warsaw.

Kozak M. and Szewczyk R. (1998), *Regional Development in Poland – Basic Facts*, Polish Agency for Regional Development, Warsaw.

Kropiwnicki J. and Szewczyk R. (1998), *Regional Profiles of Poland*, Polish Agency for Regional Development, Warsaw.

Kuklinski A. (ed) (1997), *Polska przestrzeń w perspektywie drugiego trwania, (Polish Space in the Long Term Perspective)*, Polish Academy of Sciences, Committee for Spatial Economy and Regional Planning, Warsaw.

Kuklinski A., Mync A. and Szul R. (1997), *Polish Space at the Turn of the 20th Century*, Polish Agency for Regional Development, Warsaw.

Government Centre for Strategic Studies (1999), *The Concept of the Spatial Policy in Poland*, Warsaw.

Task Force for Regional Development in Poland (1996), *Outline of a Regional Development Strategy for Poland*, Final Report, Warsaw.

Task Force for Regional Development in Poland (1996), *Regional Development in Poland*, Diagnostic Report, Warsaw.

Task Force for Structural Policy in Poland (1997), *Final Report*, Warsaw.

22 Regional Policy Evolution in Hungary

RUTH DOWNES

Introduction

Hungary faces considerable regional development problems, as highlighted in Chapter 8, many of which have emerged or been exacerbated by the process of economic and political transition during the 1990s. These include a marked east-west divide, with the eastern counties generally showing the worst levels of economic development, and the over dominant position of Budapest in the country's socio-economic framework. An increasingly mature policy response to these issues has been gradually emerging throughout the 1990s and is now one of the most advanced in Central and Eastern Europe (CEE). This chapter examines the evolution of Hungarian regional policy, its principal objectives and implementation measures, as well as related difficulties such as the issue of territorial administrative reform.

Evolution of Hungarian regional policy

Hungary has a tradition of regional planning which dates back considerably further than the initiation of political reform at the end of the 1980s. Regional planning was undertaken during the 1970s, although generally dominated more by sectoral than regional concerns. A Parliamentary Decree in 1985 specified the long-term tasks and aims of regional policy which included the idea of creating preconditions for indigenous development through restructuring and modernisation. However, financial and institutional constraints severely limited the overall impact of spatially concentrated regional planning resources.

The political and economic liberalisation of the country gradually introduced a new era for regional policy in Hungary. Tangible signs of this were evident as early as 1990 with the establishment of the Ministry for Environment and Regional Policy and the Regional Development Fund a year later. A resolution on regional development, passed in 1993, was the first clear definition of regional policy aims and instruments. It specified the principal tasks of the policy area which, at that stage, included establishing the basis for internal and international co-operation, regional crisis management, infrastructure projects focused on the most underdeveloped areas and achieving an overall reduction in disparities in the distribution and function of the settlement infrastructure. While the 1993 legislation was important, regional policy activity remained reactive and rather *ad hoc* in nature, lacking an overall concept or strategy. Increasing political awareness and agreement on issues such as the requirement to try and reduce disparities through public expenditure and the need to reinforce the role of the counties, however, paved the way for the next developments.

The landmark piece of legislation came in 1996 with the passing of the Act on Regional Development and Physical Planning (XXI/1996). The Act, which still forms the legal basis for regional policy in Hungary, came into force in July 1996 and was an attempt to introduce a more comprehensive regional development policy, taking European models and principles into account. The Act was the first among the CEE countries to provide a legal framework which was broadly in line with the structural policies of the EU - a pattern which has subsequently been followed in the majority of other countries in the region.

The Act specified the key objectives of regional policy as follows:
- to assist the development of a market economy in every region, to create the required conditions for sustained growth, and to improve economic conditions and quality of life through co-ordination of social, environmental and economic interests;
- to create conditions for self-sustaining development;
- to reduce adverse disparities (in terms of living, economic, cultural and infrastructural conditions) between Budapest and the remainder of the country, as well as between advantaged and disadvantaged regions; and,
- to encourage initiatives by regional and local communities and co-ordinate them with national objectives.

In a pattern common to regional policy evolution in a number of CEE countries, these objectives have a certain dual equity and efficiency element in the policy approach, emphasising both development in every region and the need for the reduction of regional disparities. This is linked, in part, to the continued national economic difficulties and the efforts to promote overall high levels of growth.

The 1996 Act was a significant step in the regional policy field in Hungary for a number of reasons. First, it looked outside the borders of the country and attempted to make its basic principles and directions compatible with European practice. This is necessary at least from the point of view of EU accession negotiations – although ensuring that nationally-based priorities and approaches are sufficiently considered is an important balancing act. Second, the Act attempted to create new organisational clarity by establishing the scope of authority and responsibilities of the parliament and government, as well as sub-national authorities and actors. Third, it incorporated the notions of partnership and decentralisation as well as evaluation of instruments.

A further conceptual step was taken in 1998 with the drafting of the National Regional Development Concept. This was designed to determine the regional development principles, guidelines and aims for the government's regional development activity and act as an orientation point for other actors in the field. It was also seen as a way of outlining regional targets to be met by government sectoral policies and help ensure that the division of tasks specified in the 1996 Act was fulfilled.

The Concept is very wide-ranging and specifies both medium and longer-term objectives. The former comprise more immediately practical initiatives in both crisis and more developed areas such as tackling the crisis caused by acute social and employment related problems and focusing restructuring intervention on the key areas of economic crisis. In more developed areas, the Concept points to the need for the removal of institutional and technical barriers, the use of business promotion measures and the creation of industrial parks and enterprise zones. Wider aspects of regional development are highlighted in the requirement for policy to reduce social, demographic and ethnic segregation.

The longer-term objectives are formulated as more general goals and include the alignment of the spatial structure of economic activities with the needs of sustainable development and the natural/environmental potential of regions and the creation of equal economic, business and income-related opportunities for communities in different regions. A wider European view is incorporated with the objective to ensure that Hungarian regions, cities and large settlements are integrated into the European system and to create conditions for the development of European regional centres. While the Concept is over-ambitious and presents the development objectives as a mix of practical tasks and principles, it does represent a move towards raising the political profile of regional policy and substituting regional development concerns over traditional sectoral ones.

The reform of territorial administrative structures

It is important before looking in more detail at the implementation structures for Hungarian regional policy to address the question of territorial administrative structures and their reform. This has been a central issue for all the CEE countries, the majority of which are missing an intermediate regional tier of planning or government between the central and local administrations. Another common development has been a fragmentation of territorial units following a post-liberalisation attempt by the localities to (re)gain control of local development affairs. Both these trends are evident in Hungary and, although considerable recent progress has been made in creating functional regional units, important issues remain unresolved.

Hungary is a unitary state comprising 19 counties, plus Budapest which has a similar legal status. The lowest tier of the territorial structure is the settlement, or local authority, and fragmentation is most evident at this level. The local government Act of 1990 introduced a 'one settlement, one local government' principle which dramatically increased the number of settlements to over 3,000. Of these, 35 percent have fewer than 500 inhabitants and the average population is 3,400, lower than the European equivalent.

The 1990 Act also changed the power balance between the settlement and the county levels, increasing the power of the former. The principal responsibility of the settlements includes the provision of basic services such as basic education, social and health services, water supply, public roads and sanitation. The 1996 Regional Development Act further allows settlement local governments to co-operate as 'small regions' for economic and infrastructural development of relevance to that spatial unit. This co-operation is voluntary and takes the form of so-called regional development partnerships or associations. The county level, therefore, is only legally responsible for services which affect the county when settlement authorities either do not, or do not wish to, undertake them.

The weakest tier of the territorial administrative structure, however, remains the region - although more recent developments are attempting to address this issue. The 1996 Act, in addition to allowing co-operation between settlement local governments, also permitted counties to co-operate as 'development regions' for economic development initiatives to be governed by Regional Development Councils (RDCs). These regions and bodies were voluntary except for the Budapest agglomeration and the Lake Balaton area whose creation, on account of their economic significance, was required by the Act. By 1997, six development regions were in operation covering most of the Hungarian territory.

The voluntary and flexible nature of these development regions, however, influenced their efficiency and effectiveness. Further, they comprise an insufficiently stable basis for a final designation of EU NUTS II regions, the territorial unit which would administer Structural Fund resources following the accession of Hungary to the EU. The Parliamentary decision in 1998 which accepted the National Regional Development Concept, therefore, also established seven statistical planning regions which would comprise the future NUTS II regions. These are:

- *West Transdanubia* - Gyor-Moson-Sopron, Vas and Zala counties
- *Middle Transdanubia* - Veszprém, Fejér and Komárom-Esztergom counties
- *South Transdanubia* - Baranya, Somogy and Tolna counties
- *Middle Hungary* - Budapest and Pest counties
- *North Hungary* - Heves, Nógrád and Borsod-Abaúj-Zemplén counties
- *North-Alföld* - Jász-Nagykun-Szolnok, Hajdú-Bihar and Szabolcs-Szatmár-Bereg counties
- *South-Alföld* - Bács-Kiskun, Békés and Csongrád counties

The borders of the former development regions and statistical planning regions are broadly similar, although not identical. Zala county, for example, was included in the South Transdanubia development region but is now incorporated with the western border regions into the West Transdanubia statistical region. The former North-East region, comprising six counties, was also divided into two groups of three making up the current North Hungary and Alföld regions. Regional development agencies are now being established and development plans elaborated for the seven statistical regions. Voluntary development regions may still operate, although it is anticipated that, over time, the new seven regions will become the principal regional level structure.

Institutional structures for regional policy

The institutional infrastructure for regional development has developed through the 1990s in line with legislative change, practical experience and some external impulses such as EU requirements under the accession negotiations. In general, the trend has been towards a greater clarification of roles and responsibilities, although there remains a degree of uncertainty in some areas.

National level

At the highest level, the role of Parliament was initially reinforced at the start of the 1990s to include regulation, financial distribution and Government supervision although, in practice, activity was restricted principally to the distribution of financial resources. The 1996 Act defined Parliamentary tasks essentially as comprising the approval of the framework for regional policy. This involved the agreement of national and regional development plans as well as the overall principles and priorities of regional policy, the establishment of guidelines for regional development support, designation criteria, funds and self-government responsibilities and a supervisory function.

In the Hungarian government, the responsibilities for and approach to regional policy has shifted considerably through the decade. The Ministry of Environment and Regional Policy was created in 1990 but initially held a weak position within the government system for a number of reasons. It had relatively few resources to spread over a wide range of competencies and conflicted directly in terms of authority with the Ministry of the Interior, which had retained responsibility for settlement planning. The lack of clear strategic direction, as well as the stronger focus on initial national level economic crisis management, also made it more difficult for the Ministry to find its niche and work effectively.

The 1996 Act, as for Parliamentary competencies, also specified the role of the Ministry more clearly. Four key tasks were identified: administering the implementation of regional and spatial development; preparing government recommendations for national regional development policy; preparing regional development plans and regional planning schemes for the whole country and for problem areas; and administering regional and spatial development tasks.

Further developments came in the wake of the May 1998 elections and the subsequent ministerial reorganisation. This moved regional policy competence to a new Ministry for Agriculture and Regional Development (MoARD) under the jurisdiction of the smaller of the new coalition parties, the Smallholders Party, which has a strong rural backing. The new Ministry brought together most of the regional policy related competencies of the government in the department for regional development.

The former subordination of regional policy to sectoral interests is still evident to some degree and is reflected in the continued role of other ministries in regional development issues. These include, for example, the Ministry of Interior's responsibility for settlement, local government activities and regional programme management, the Ministry of Finance's remit in regional financial regulation and the role of the Ministries of Economic Affairs and Labour in regional programmes for the labour force, tourism, enterprise zones and so on. The Ministry of Economic Affairs also has the primary responsibility for the drafting of the National Development Plan, clearly of relevance to regional development. This Plan will form the basis of the country's future CSF within the EU Structural Fund framework, and the Ministry is also involved in key pre-accession instruments such as the ISPA programme.

Wider ministerial involvement also reflects an understanding that measures in other policy areas have a spatial impact. More explicit attempts at inter-ministerial co-ordination between regional development activities and other initiatives with spatial implications have been made in the latter half of the 1990s, although genuine co-operation remains relatively weak in practice. It is still the case that regional policy related decisions are often vulnerable to political bargaining and individual political motivation.

In addition to ministerial competence for regional policy, other institutional structures have also been established with responsibilities in this field. The 1996 Act created a National Council for Regional Development, a new body designed to assist the government in carrying out regional development. Chairmanship of the Council is held by the Minister for Agriculture and Regional Policy and its membership incorporates both national and sub-national bodies including ministries, chambers, some representatives of the county development councils and national local government partnerships. Other relevant bodies such as the Hungarian Foundation for Enterprise Promotion and the Hungarian Bank for Innovation and Development have an advisory role.

The remit of the Council includes the preparation of decisions for the Hungarian parliament and government and the co-ordination of regional development activities, particularly between different levels of government. The Council had significant input into the drafting of the National Concept for Regional Development and is involved in consensus-building as regards regional development subsidies and the implementation of regional policy related resolutions. Its secretariat is the National Regional Development Centre, responsible for regional co-ordination, promotion and harmonisation of national and regional development initiatives and technical support to responsible sub-national implementing bodies.

Sub-national level

The autonomous operation of a large number of settlements and the fact that a more formal regional division has only emerged very recently has proved an important obstacle to the operation of coherent regional policy in Hungary. However, the higher profile of regional development issues and the legislative progress in this area have involved steps to strengthen the sub-national institutional structures and this process is likely to be reinforced, for example, by considerations of future EU Structural Fund implementation.

The 1996 Act again proved an important milestone in its creation of County Development Councils (CDCs), designed to co-ordinate regional development tasks within the county. Two CDCs were originally established within the framework of the first Phare Regional Development Programme (1993-96) for the eastern counties of Borsod-Abaúj-Zemplén and Szabolcs-Szatmár-Bereg, and a positive experience of their operation formed the background to the creation of CDCs throughout the country. Responsibilities were granted to these organisations in four main fields: the co-ordination of development ideas from central and local governments and other actors; the socio-economic evaluation of the county and proposals for medium- and longer-term development; participation in decision-making on the allocation of local government support and other funds; and the determination of evaluation guidelines for programmes. CDC membership comprises representatives from the county assemblies and county-of-right cities, local government, economic chambers, employee interest groups and the MoARD.

The CDCs have played an important function in the creation of a platform for the distribution of funds at sub-national level and as a planning tier. They have increased the self-organisation capability of the municipalities and provided them with a framework for more active participation in the shaping of development policy for their area. They also have the potential to contribute to a more cohesive approach to regional policy through their co-ordination role between national and local government. Their rather ambiguous legal status, however, has led to some conflict about their role and concern over the lack of mechanisms to ensure operational effectiveness and financial accountability.

With even more limited powers are the Regional Development Councils (RDCs), created originally to govern the voluntary 'development regions'. The RDCs were assigned the tasks of drafting regional development plans and organising and co-ordinating the economic development process in their territories. Their membership included representatives from the CDCs, the MoARD, other national ministries, economic chambers and the local government partnerships. The RDCs to date have not been well integrated within the territorial and regional development system and have had only limited resources and powers at their disposal.

The relative strength and position of the regions is, however, gradually improving. The State Budget Act for 1999 provides HUF 1.1 billion[1] for the creation of regional development agencies within the seven new statistical regions, the preparation of regional development programmes and the financing of pilot projects. This represents a considerable step forward in the active financing and support of regional level institutional structures and activities.

The spatial focus of Hungarian regional policy

Regional policy, by its nature, is a spatially focused policy area. The actual system of designation is linked to a number of factors including the underlying policy philosophy and the range of available regional level statistical indicators. Hungary has one of the most sophisticated systems of area designation among the Central and East European countries, drawing on a historical traditional of spatial targeting which, from the mid 1980s, concentrated regional support on the eastern counties of Borsod-Abaúj-Zemplén and Szabolcs-Szatmár-Bereg. While this geographical focus has broadly been maintained, the system of designation has become increasingly sophisticated over the past decade.

The first principal piece of assisted area legislation after the introduction of political and economic reform came in 1993 and defined four categories of area for regional development purposes. These were: backward settlements defined on the basis of socio-economic criteria; settlements located in backward regions but not backward in themselves; settlements of employment zones where unemployment was at least 1.5 times higher than the national average; and settlements requiring modernisation. The basic unit of designation was the settlement, the lowest level of the territorial administrative structure, and the selection was hampered by restricted data availability at this level.

The key 1996 regional policy legislation shifted the method of area designation from the ranking of settlements to an assessment of counties and statistical areas. It also clearly reflected the influence of the EU Structural Fund framework in its composition – a trend subsequently seen in most CEE countries. Four categories of designated area were identified accordingly (see also Chapter 8):

- *socially and economically less developed areas* – small areas where a complex development-level indicator of demographic, economic and infrastructure factors is less than 75 percent of the national average (akin to EU Objective 1);
- *industrial restructuring areas* – those regions with higher than national average industrial employment, higher unemployment and an unfavourable ratio of people employed in industry compared with the 1990 situation (criteria for EU Objective 2 areas);
- *agricultural areas* – regions complying with EU Objective 5b criteria, adjusted for Hungarian characteristics (using, for example, per capita personal income tax base rather than profitability of agriculture and the incorporation of a migration balance);
- *areas of high unemployment* – small areas where the rate of permanent unemployment (more than 180 days) was 1.25 times the national average.

The common West European indicator of per capita GDP was introduced in subsequent 1997 legislation.

A Parliamentary Decision in 1997 stipulated that over the period 1997-99, only one third of the total Hungarian population could be included within the assisted areas at any given time. An annual adjustment is viewed as necessary given the rapidly changing economic situation during the continued process of socio-economic transition and reform. For this reason, an annual Government Decree adjusts the register of communities and regions designated as eligible for regional development support. The assisted areas map designated in 1998 included 33.5 percent of the Hungarian population.

Regional policy instruments

The first post-liberalisation fund specifically for regional development issues, the Regional Development Fund (RDF), was introduced in 1991. A government Decree of the same year also covered more generally the provision of State grants for regional development (including infrastructure) and job creation. The RDF was initially a highly centralised instrument, partly a consequence of the continued sectoral focus of regional issues and the corresponding disputes between ministries about funding sources and target areas. Legislation in 1992 and 1993 helped to clarify the aims and objectives of the RDF and established it as a separate State fund with ten distinct sources of income including central budget subsidies, international aid and privatisation revenue. The tasks for RDF support moved increasingly in line with Western European regional development foci including job creation, business services (including incubator and innovation parks), regional transport and telecommunications systems, social infrastructure, environmental support and tourism. The Fund operated through the provision of non-repayable and repayable subsidies as well as interest rate subsidies.

The system for the provision of regional policy support changed in 1995 with a public finance reform which transferred the previously separate government RDF subsidies (worth HUF 8 billion in 1995) into the general State budget. In 1997, two government Decrees detailed the conditions and targets of the two main regional development specific budget lines.

- The *Targeted Budgetary Allocation for Regional Development* (TBARD) has a number of objectives including the reduction of regional disparities, the co-ordination of various sectoral grants to facilitate integrated regional programmes and the encouragement of international finance and cross-border co-operation. The range of objectives and types of assistance are similar to those under operation during the later years of the RDF as cited above. Award levels vary by type of assisted area with a number of general criteria such as a maximum ceilings on awards.

- The *Spatial Equalisation Financial Assistance* (SEFA) provides subsidies in priority regional development areas to support investment made by settlement local governments. A key component of this budget line is its decentralised administration, with the County Development Councils responsible for decision-making on allocated subsidies worth, in 1997, HUF 15 billion. Factors taken into account in the distribution of the SEFA support include the characteristics and development needs of the county, the resources available to local governments for investment in their area and the implementation of other relevant development objectives.

These two budget lines are the principal regional development specific financial provisions, although other incentives with a regional dimension are also in operation. Tax relief for longer term investments, for example, are available in regional development areas, areas of high unemployment and enterprise zones.

Some attempt has also been made more recently to achieve better co-ordination with other sectoral budgets which could have an important impact on regional economic development. A government Decree in 1997 included a matrix which identified the relationship between all the principal State funds of the various Ministries. This was designed to raise awareness of the links and require greater co-ordination where an explicit connection between two funds existed – although the extent to which this actually occurs in practice is more questionable.

Current regional policy thinking in Hungary focuses great attention on this issue of co-ordination and ensuring that all national resources which have a spatial impact in their implementation take regional development considerations into account. In light of the size and influence of some of these budgets, this is considered a better medium- to long-term approach than focusing on raising regional development specific resources – although these are currently recognised to be low in European comparison. Other key challenges for future development in this area include the reinforcement of a decentralised system of administration and the creation of a sound monitoring and evaluation structure.

Conclusions

In the context of the emergence of regional policy in virtually all of the CEE countries, Hungary offers one of the most advanced examples in the region. The 1996 legislation established a more robust legal basis and institutional structure, clarifying the principles and objectives of regional policy, strengthening the position of the former Ministry of Environment and Regional Policy and creating a new National Council for Regional Development. The 1998 National Regional Development Concept, while still very wide-ranging, at least lays down the framework and objectives for future development and, at sub-national level, CDCs and RDCs are also developing more localised development plans. The budget for regional development specific purposes increased three-fold between 1994-98, and more attempt is being made to ensure regional awareness in the implementation of other sectoral budgets. The process of area designation for the targeting of these funds has also become much more sophisticated. The 1999 budgetary allocation for the creation of regional development agencies and the elaboration of development programmes and pilot projects is also an indication of the renewed emphasis on regional issues.

Hungary is no stranger to spatial and regional planning and this tradition has clearly been built upon and refined since the introduction of political and economic reform. However, the challenge of re-defining regional policy within the new market economic conditions is still considerable. Many of the positive developments of the 1990s require continued refinement. The emergence of sub-national structures and the move towards decentralised implementation of certain budget lines, for example, requires corresponding efforts in co-ordination and the allocation of sufficient decision-making and financial responsibility to make them meaningful. More experience is required at different administrative levels in longer-term planning as well as the process of drafting, co-ordinating and implementing regional development plans.

Regional policy is likely to remain high on the future political agenda of the country. The serious regional disparities and the continued spatial impact of economic reform will raise its domestic profile. Probably more importantly, however, will be the external impetus from the EU in the context of accession negotiations and the requirement to have suitable structures for the implementation of the Structural Funds. This may present a positive stimulus for reform and progress, putting in place a framework which can facilitate exchange of experience such as the twinning arrangements and the Special Preparatory Programmes. It will also be important, however, to ensure that the continued development of regional policy in Hungary is not forced down a road which is incompatible with the current regional development situation and policy priorities of the country. The process of regional policy evolution, taking useful lessons from Western European and EU practice and balancing them with national traditions and approaches, will be an important, if difficult, challenge for the next decade.

Note

1   £1 = HUF 406 (December 1999).

References

Bachtler, J., Raines, P. and Downes, R. (eds) (1999), *First Report on Economic and Social Cohesion – Study Area 3: The Impact on Cohesion of EU Enlargement*, Regional and Industrial Research Policy Series, No. 34, European Policies Research Centre, Glasgow.

Bachtler, J. and Downes, R. (1999), 'Regional Policy In The Transition Countries: a comparative assessment', *European Planning Studies*, vol. 7, no.6.

Downes, R. and Horvath, G. (1996), *The Challenge of Regional Policy Development in Hungary*, Regional and Industrial Research Policy Series, No. 15, European Policies Research Centre, Glasgow.

European Commission (1997), *Commission Opinion on Hungary's application for Membership of the European Union*, DOC/97/16, European Commission, Brussels.

Government of the Hungarian Republic (1998), *National Regional Development Concept*, Background Document of the Parliament's Resolution No. 35/1998 (III.20) OGY, Budapest.

Horvath, G. (1998), *Regional and Cohesion Policy in Hungary*, Discussion Paper No. 23, Centre for Regional Studies of Hungarian Academy of Sciences, Pécs.

Ministry for Agriculture and Regional Development (1998), *Regional Development in Hungary*, Budapest.

Ministry for Agriculture and Regional Policy (1998), *New Developments and Policies in Hungary*, Budapest.

23 Regional Policy in Central and Eastern Europe: The EU Perspective

JEAN-FRANÇOIS DREVET

During the period of change in Central and Eastern Europe since 1989, regional policy has not so far been at the forefront. However, in the context of accession to the EU, the applicant countries are increasingly realising the need to develop strong regional policies in order to intensify and accelerate the integration process. The prospect of receiving Community structural funding is also a strong incentive for them to get down to designing and organising the management of regional policy structures.

This chapter deals only with the ten countries applying for EU membership,[1] even though there are interesting developments in some of the other Central and Eastern European countries.[2] Although the applicant countries are by no means all in the same situation, their common past as much as their Community future does set them on comparable paths.

A major challenge

For the applicant countries as well as for their partners in the European Union, the tripling of the per capita GDP of a population of more than 100 million represents an unprecedented challenge, which is of the same order of magnitude as German unification (Table 23.1).

Table 23.1 Comparison of German unification and enlargement to 26 Member States

Increase in	Area %	Population %	GDP %
Germany after unification/West Germany	50	25	7
EUR 26/EUR15	33	29	9

Source: EUROSTAT.

But this is not a new challenge. Each enlargement has resulted in a fall in the Community average per capita GDP (see Table 23.2).

Table 23.2 Impact of the successive enlargements of the EU

1995 data	Increase in area %	Increase in pop'n %	Increase in total GDP %	Change in per capita GDP	Average per capita GDP EUR6 = 100
EUR9/EUR6	31	32	29	-3	97
EUR12/EUR9	48	22	15	-6	91
EUR15/EUR12	43	11	8	-3	89
EUR26/EUR15	33	29	9	-16	75

Source: European Commission.
Notes: including German reunification.

The potential fall measured today (-16 percent) is on its own greater than the previous ones added together. The vital issue in the enlargement process is therefore how effectively policies can reduce disparities.

In view of the very limited resources available in the applicant countries, it is in the first instance up to European structural policy and more specifically regional policy to take up the challenge. There are budget appropriations for that purpose (over 30 percent of the budget, 0.46 percent of Community GDP), and instruments were modernised as part of the recent revision of the regulations through Agenda 2000.

For their part, the beneficiary countries need to devise and implement new policies and provide themselves with the capacity to manage efficiently a complex system ranging from the formulation of objectives to the definition of the appropriate procedure for managing complex financial instruments. This approach of establishing new regional policies geared to assistance from the Community Structural Funds is the reverse of that seen in Western Europe, where regional policies were created a long time before Community Funds came into being.

The need for institution building

In the euphoria of the return to the market economy, the new governments often rejected regional policies, fearing that they would stand in the way of economic advance. In Poland and the Czech Republic, the neo-liberal economists persuaded the politicians that it was better to do without what they saw as an antiquated means of managing change. Rising unemployment rates, in particular in the areas affected by the conversion of the primary industries or the armaments industry, forced the governments to take action. They at first targeted the social area, before realising that these problems had a major regional dimension. However, the establishment of a regional policy is facing a large range of obstacles.

- Given its horizontal nature, regional policy, more than other policies, needs a sound inter-ministerial co-ordination structure, a system of arbitration and a procedure for selecting priorities. This will be essential for Objective 1 type programmes, covering a broad range of projects, from infrastructure to human resources, taking in industrial conversion and rural development. In the coalition governments of the post-communist era, as elsewhere, rivalry between ministers, and the unavailability of premiers does not facilitate the emergence of technically well prepared choices.
- The powers relating to regional policy are poorly defined or entrusted to several different government departments, which ignore or compete with one another. Added to this situation, which can also be observed in Western Europe, are difficulties stemming from badly organised ministries lacking the requisite human and financial resources. There are still very few countries which have equipped their government departments to manage future assistance from the Community Structural Funds.

- In almost all the applicant countries, a decentralisation process has been undertaken, bringing to prominence new local authorities which will have elected councils: *powiats* and *voivods* in Poland, counties and regions in Hungary, macro-regions in Romania, regions in the Czech and Slovak Republics. They provide new geographic frameworks for assistance and represent potential partners for implementing Community funding. But the new territorial structures are still fragile, their powers are not clearly defined, and they have very little experience.

The new scope of regional policies

With their entire territory potentially eligible for Objective 1 assistance, the applicant countries are preparing national policies to narrow the development gap with the EU. Therefore, as experienced in Portugal, Greece or Ireland, a number of future structural programmes will be designed at national level. In the smaller countries (the Baltic States and Slovenia), the national geographic framework will logically play the most important role.

However, the new territorial organisation, which is being put in place in the large countries (16 new *voivods* in Poland, eight macro-regions in Romania, the regrouping of counties and regions in Hungary and the Czech Republic), should facilitate the development of a reasonable number of major regional development programmes covering the entire territory.

Initially, pending progress in the decentralisation process, programmes will inevitably have to be launched and managed by the State administrations. The ministries responsible will thus be well placed to apply appropriate weightings between the regions with high growth potential and the others. Action to combat their internal disparities will be a second priority, at least until the large cities or the most developed regions have crossed the fateful threshold of 75 percent[3] of the Community average GDP per capita.

Preparations

Phare's general interventions

Unlike previous enlargements, the European Union is this time in a position to support the process of integrating the applicant countries with substantial aid from the Phare programme, which is currently the main channel for financial and technical co-operation with Central and Eastern Europe. Set up in 1989 to support economic and political transition of Poland and Hungary, Phare had by 1996 been extended to include 14 partner countries.[4] From 3 billion euro for 1990-93, the Phare budget was extended to 4.5 billion euro for the period 1994-97 (1123 million euro/year, see Table 23.3).

Table 23.3 Evolution of Phare allocations by country (1990-97)

	1990-93 million euro	1994-97 million euro	1994-97 million euro per year	Population '000	1994-97 euro per head per year
Bulgaria	308	297	74	8400	9
Czech Republic[5]	60	284	71	10300	7
Estonia	22	113	28	1500	19
Hungary	406	366	92	10200	9
Latvia	33	142	35	2600	14
Lithuania	44	184	46	3700	12
Poland	803	734	183	38600	5
Romania	440	384	96	22700	4
Slovakia[5]	40	134	33	5300	6
Slovenia	19	96	24	2000	12
Albania	192	259	65	3200	20
Bosnia	37	213	53	3500	15
Macedonia	35	108	27	2100	13
Multi-country	383	399	100	114100	1
Other	210	782	196	114100	2
Total	3030	4493	1123	114100	10

Source: Phare annual report, 1997.

Phare's assistance takes the form of grants, and its area of intervention has grown to encompass a wide range of activities. Throughout the 1989-96 period Phare has shown a continuing flexibility, adapting to the changing priorities of the reform process in each of its partner countries. The most recent period, 1994-96, has been characterised by a large increase in support for the legislative framework and administrative structures.

Phare's structural activities

In comparison with the Structural Funds, Phare activity extends beyond economic investment to various actions, for instance projects promoting democracy and civil society. Another difference is the absence of significant matching funding from the beneficiary countries.

Since 1994, Phare is participating in cross-border co-operation, matching the interventions of Interreg on Phare-EU borders. With the exception of Romania[6] the applicant countries have already implemented cross-border co-operation programmes, in addition to the Community Interreg initiative, at their borders with the Member States of the EU. An extension of this experiment includes the borders between the candidate countries and those with their Tacis and MEDA neighbours.[7]

A number of regional development programmes have also been implemented, some of them following the EU regional policy format. Phare has provided assistance for programmes for industrial conversion, initially in the east of Hungary and in Poland (Struder), then in the Czech Republic. More specific operations have been undertaken in the Baltic States, Bulgaria and Romania. In all these cases, the Phare actions have represented relatively large financial commitments compared to the very restricted public budgets of the recipient countries.

The development of these actions has also shown how the authorities in charge of regional development lack experience. It was therefore considered important to contribute, before accession, to the development of the applicants' implementing capability, not only at the level of the central administration (inter-ministerial co-ordination, reinforcement of the ministry responsible for regional policy) but also at regional level (support for decentralisation).

Pre-accession strategies

Since the Essen European council of December 1994, Phare has become the financial instrument of the pre-accession strategies supporting the ten

candidate countries in their preparation. This orientation has been reinforced in 1997, with Agenda 2000. Drawing the lessons from the opinion given on the applications for membership, the Commission decided to refocus Phare on two priorities.
- The first priority will be to help the administrations of the partner countries in acquiring the capacity to implement the *acquis communautaire*. Thus, Phare will support the *institution building* process of the national and regional administrations, as well as their regulatory bodies to familiarise themselves with Community policies and procedures.
- The second priority is to help the candidate countries to bring their industries and major infrastructures up to Community standards by mobilising the investment required. This effort will be largely devoted to the areas where Community norms are becoming increasingly demanding.

Accession partnerships

A step further is being implemented, with the *Accession Partnerships*. Approved by the Council in 1998, they even make the continuation of aid conditional upon the effective implementation of Community legislation. In developing its pre-accession strategies, the Commission decided in March 1997 to make Phare change from a demand-driven system into an accession driven one. Even before accession, the methods of Community assistance are therefore set to develop on the lines of those of the Structural Funds and more specifically the Objective 1 programmes.

Preparing for the future implementation of the Structural Funds

Under the so-called institution building priority, a special preparatory programme for the implementation of the Structural Funds was launched by DG IA and DG XVI[8] at the end of 1997. It includes various measures to support the applicant countries in designing, programming and managing future structural assistance.

These guidelines are all the more important as the ERDF area of assistance will remain the responsibility of Phare until the date of accession. Therefore, Phare will participate in the preparation of Objective 1 type regional programmes as already envisaged in Romania and in the Czech Republic. On the model of the Cohesion Fund,[9] the Instrument for

Structural Policies for Pre-Accession (ISPA) provided for in the Commission's Agenda 2000 proposals will be confined to part-financing transport and environment infrastructures.

The applicant countries therefore face a complex operation: preparing to incorporate the legislation on the Structural Funds (in fact the ERDF) using another financial instrument which subjects them to different management procedures. Phare practises annual management by projects, while the 1988 reform generalised a system of pluri-annual programmes for the ERDF and the other Structural Funds.

The challenge will not be easy. But it will be worth it: under the Phare programme, applicant countries receive approximately 10 euro per head per year. As from 2000, this amount will be increased to just under 30 euro per head per year. Between the date of their accession and 2006, the first acceding members could receive appropriations totalling five times that amount[10] to fund their first Objective 1 programmes.

In increasing its financial contribution, the EU is expecting an acceleration of the integration process, both in legal and practical terms. On the one hand, a strong improvement of administrative and budgetary capacity is necessary to deal with Community policies. This problem was successfully tackled in Spain and Portugal in the 1980s, in particular in the area of the Structural Funds. As the candidate countries are to start this process a number of years before accession, the management of the funds is supposed to be at an efficient level by the time of accession. On the other hand, the funds should contribute to the catching-up process, improving infrastructures, boosting public investment and attracting enough private investment to create economic growth and employment. This has been reasonably successful in Ireland, Portugal and Spain. It is the common responsibility of the candidate countries and the Union to pave the way for the most efficient process.

Notes

1   Estonia, Poland, the Czech Republic, Hungary, Latvia, Lithuania, Slovakia, Romania and Bulgaria. Cyprus and Malta, which have also started accession negotiations, are not dealt with here.
2   Central and Eastern Europe also includes Albania, Macedonia and Bosnia-Herzegovina as well as Croatia and Serbia Montenegro.
3   After enlargement this threshold will be lower than it is today, since it will be calculated for a Europe of 21 or 26 Member States.

4	The ten candidate countries, plus Macedonia, Albania, Bosnia, and Croatia, which is currently suspended.
5	Since the division of the former Czechoslovakia.
6	Romania has no common border with the EU.
7	Tacis: technical assistance to the Community of Independent States; MEDA: programme of financial co-operation with Southern and Eastern Mediterranean non-member countries.
8	Now DG Enlargement and DG Regio.
9	The Cohesion Fund is not one of the Structural Funds.
10	In the financial perspectives, 2000-2006, the Commission reserved 38 billion euro in the budget of the Structural Funds for the new Member States.

24 Transition, Cohesion and Regional Policy in Central and Eastern Europe: Conclusions

JOHN BACHTLER, RUTH DOWNES AND
GRZEGORZ GORZELAK

Introduction

Among the many challenges presented by the process of European integration, the creation of a new architecture for the European Union associated with its eastward enlargement is surely the most difficult. With profound economic, political, institutional and socio-cultural implications, the speed, form and consequences of enlargement are key issues for debate and research. Central issues are naturally the differences between EU and CEE countries, collectively and individually, but also the internal disparities within CEE countries, their nature, magnitude and evolution in the course of transition. Related, there is the question of whether and how the institutional capacities in CEE countries are able to respond to disparities and the potential support that the EU could usefully provide to assist economic and social cohesion within individual countries and across an enlarged European Union.

As a contribution to the debate, the aim of this volume has been to assess the impact of transition on economic and social cohesion in the countries of Central and Eastern Europe and to examine the significance of regional policy. In the first chapters, the book examined the progress of transition in its economic, political and social dimensions. It then undertook a systematic review of regional disparities, territorial structures and regional development policies in each of the ten 'candidate countries' and also discussed selected regional development themes relating to technological change, inward investment, environmental problems, small and medium-sized enterprises and cross-border co-operation. Lastly, the book considered the progress of regional policy, illustrated with case studies from the Czech Republic, Hungary and Poland, and the role of the European Union in supporting the development of regional policy institutions and instruments.

In bringing the volume to a close, this final chapter reviews the issues discussed in the preceding chapters and the main conclusions to emerge, notably the dimensions of transition, the spatial implications and the embryonic policy institutions and measures in the regional development field. The chapter concludes by speculating on the impact of enlargement of the EU to cohesion and the role of the EU in promoting structural change.

The dimensions of transition

On a journey without a route map, the transition towards a market economy and democratic government in Central and Eastern Europe (CEE) has taken various paths under different national political and economic conditions. Notwithstanding the varying contexts and uneven progress, there is general agreement on various common features of systemic change that has led to the embedding of market economic reforms (Yndgaard, 1999; Poeschl, 1999; Carlin and Landesmann, 1997; Frydman et al., 1998 Gomulka, 1998; de Melo et al., 1996; Gros and Steinherr, 1995). Macro-economic stabilisation was the initial priority to address high foreign debt, hyper-inflation and commodity shortages which emerged following the collapse of socialist regimes (Blejer and Skreb, 1998; Fischer et al., 1996; Ickes, 1996). Restrictive monetary policies, the reduction of enterprise subsidies and price liberalisation were also common components of reform in most countries. Such measures exposed the lack of international competitiveness of many State enterprises, accelerating reforms to industrial organisation and shifts in industrial structure through the dismantling of the planned economy via privatisation and changes to banking, tax and capital market systems (Krajnyak and Zettlemeyer, 1998; Amsden et al., 1994).

The impact of reforms was immediate. Sudden falls in output, rising prices and hyper-inflation accompanied the open emergence and growth of unemployment and (partly) a fall in living standards. From 1992, following the so-called 'J-curve', signs of stabilisation were evident in countries such as Poland, Hungary and Slovenia which have now experienced positive rates of growth for several years. Recent economic difficulties in the Czech Republic have cast some doubt on its inclusion in this group. In the Baltic

States, and moreso in Bulgaria and Romania, it took longer to achieve a degree of economic stability, and GDP growth only resumed during the second half of the 1990s. Until 1998, according to the EBRD, Poland was the only country to have achieved the 1989 level of real GDP, with Slovenia and the Slovak Republic projected to reach this level by 1999 (EBRD 1998a) – although other statistical sources (eg. Polish statistical yearbook) indicate that these two countries had also achieved 1989 levels by 1998. Privatisation of the state sector is advanced, having started with the privatisation of small-scale enterprises, followed by a more extensive transfer of larger State-owned industrial assets and enterprises. Combined with the increase in private entrepreneurial enterprise, it has led to a major shift in the ownership structure of CEE economies (Welter, 1997; Zemplinerova, 1997; Bilsen, 1997). The share of the private sector in GDP exceeds 40 percent throughout the CEE region, with figures of 70 percent and above in some of the more advanced countries (Slovenia, Czech Republic and Hungary) (EBRD, 1998). The EU review of Candidate Countries as part of Agenda 2000 noted that substantial progress has been made in establishing 'single market' reforms, particularly in education, R&D, telecoms, SMEs and trade relations, although the rate of progress varies by country and sectors (CEC, 1997).

Foreign trade and investment have been important contributors to the reform process. Measures to liberalise domestic trading conditions, support international trade and encourage foreign investment were taken early on in CEE countries. These included the removal of national trade restrictions and barriers for the benefit of domestic companies, the introduction of currency convertibility at international rates and a range of incentives, such as the sale (in some countries) of key enterprises through the privatisation process to foreign investors (OECD, 1997; Zemplinerova, 1997). Trade and investment patterns have been realigned: as early as 1993, EU countries accounted for around half of Polish, Czech and Hungarian exports and imports. By the late 1990s, the EU market accounted for 50-60 percent of all CEE exports – approximately the importance of the EU market for EU nations themselves (Baldwin et al., 1997; Grabbe and Hughes, 1997).

Foreign direct investment flows were initially slow in light of political and economic uncertainty but increased considerably during the 1990s, with Hungary, Poland and the Czech Republic taking nearly two-thirds of the CEE total (Estrin et al., 1997). Recent figures show the accumulation of FDI over the period 1989-98 to be US$ 16.9 billion in Hungary, US$ 12.4 billion in Poland, and US$ 8.4 billion in the Czech Republic, then falling to

US$ 3.4 billion for the next highest recipient, Romania. At the bottom of the scale, Estonia received US$ 1 billion and Bulgaria US$ 1.2 billion over the period (EBRD, 1998). Arguably, FDI has been a mixed blessing. On the one hand, in order to restructure their legacy of inefficient industries, CEE countries have used FDI as a means to position themselves in global capital markets, often resulting in restructuring based on low-cost competitiveness and an erosion of wage relations and worker flexibility (Grabher, 1997; Smith and Swain, 1998). On the other hand, FDI has the potential to upgrade national and regional economies through, for example, the creation of good local supplier networks (Malmberg et al., 1996; Amin and Thrift, 1994).

Labour markets have been reshaped extensively, with declines in labour force participation and overall employment. In agriculture, dramatic falls in agricultural employment of up to 40 percent were recorded in Hungary and the Czech Republic, though less so in Poland and Romania where agriculture was a more significant sector and, in the Polish case, where private sector ownership was already dominant. Agricultural employment actually increased in Romania, Bulgaria, Lithuania and Latvia during the early 1990s, acting partly as a reservoir for job losses in other sectors; agricultural smallholdings also became a necessary source of additional income and insurance against unemployment. There has been a marked contraction in manufacturing, but industrial production as a share of GDP still exceeds the EU average in a number of transition economies (Martzanis and Petrakos, 1998), and a universal growth in services, especially in finance, retailing, hotels and trade (EBRD, 1998; OECD, 1997).

Democratic political and institutional systems have been established to a greater or lesser extent across the countries of the region, with a separation of powers between the executive, legislature and judiciary and the progressive development of new constitutions (Grey, 1997). Whereas in some more advanced countries (eg. Poland and Hungary), the primary task is to consolidate institutions to ensure their effective operation and maintain the separation of powers, elsewhere (eg. Bulgaria and Romania) there are still important institutional deficits (Elster et al., 1997). The political landscape is characterised by numerous political parties covering the entire spectrum and fluctuating in form and composition (Gábor, 1997; Ágh, 1998). Such factors contribute to the difficulties in forming and maintaining coalitions, and cause political instability and inconsistency in the direction and commitment of policy (Dawisha and Parrott, 1997; White et al., 1998).

New private sector institutions and institutional structures have been created, in some cases accelerated through Western support, but many are still operating imperfectly, lacking expertise or resources. In many cases, institutions such as banks operate in a very centralised manner, concentrated in the capital cities. Financial services remain underdeveloped, burdened by the legacies of central planning and early macro-economic crisis. Key future challenges include the creation and enforcement of legal and regulatory frameworks for the financial sector, the promotion of greater competition between private financial institutions and the privatisation of state banks (Mullineux and Green, 1998; Anderson and Kegels, 1998; EBRD, 1998; van Wijnbergen, 1998).

There are enduring negative effects of transition. Unemployment is the most obvious phenomenon to have emerged. Rates in 1998 ranged from 6.1 percent in the Czech Republic to almost 13 percent in Bulgaria and Slovakia. However, these rates are inadequate as a true indicator of labour market conditions as a result of under-registration of hidden unemployment and ineligibility for benefits among those out of work for prolonged periods. The impact of unemployment is differentiated, with growing levels of youth and female unemployment, as well as long-term unemployment (Commander and Coricelli, 1995; Jackson et al., 1995; Porket, 1995; OECD, 1994; Burda, 1994). In most countries there has also been a decline in average incomes and purchasing power and an increase in poverty and insecurity for large sections of the population – the disparities between social groups have increased considerably. The political instability evident in some countries (eg. Slovakia, Bulgaria and Romania) is partly a result of a certain 'reform fatigue' with respect to popular commitment to reform given that, for the majority of people, their social situation has worsened over the period. The negative effects of transition have led to a certain political backlash against liberal, reform-oriented parties and the rise of anti-reform parties and extremist groups (Higley et al., 1998).

Regional disparities and problems

The regional economic effects of transition are increasingly uneven. Prior to the start of transformation, the regional structure of the CEE countries was relatively equitable compared to Western European countries. Notwithstanding the severe limitations of data availability and reliability, the evidence from the chapters in this volume and elsewhere suggests that

CEE regional disparities in income, investment and employment have grown quickly and significantly since 1989, with a prediction of widening disparities in future and fragmentation of regional economies. Not all indicators are diverging at the same rate. While the distribution of foreign investment and entrepreneurship varies greatly across the CEE countries, and labour market indicators (unemployment, employment change) also show considerable disparities, regional differences in GDP or wage levels appear to be more limited (especially if the capital cities are excluded) and, in some cases, with less variation than in EU countries (Abraham and Eser, 1999; Bachtler, Raines and Downes, 1999; Blažek, 1999; Dunford and Smith, 1998).

Examining the patterns of regional development across CEE, the 'leaders' are those regions most able to progress along a steep J-curve path and prepare themselves for the new paradigm of an information economy. They tend to be regions that started from more favourable positions and have shown greatest potential for rapid restructuring and adaptability to market economic conditions. In general, it is the major agglomerations and urban centres which demonstrate the most advanced features of transition with higher rates of new firm formation, tertiary sector growth and concentrations of foreign investment (Bachtler and Downes, 1999). Unemployment rates in urban areas are usually low, to the extent of causing shortages of workers, requiring immigration from neighbouring countries. There are also difficulties associated with pollution, congestion and housing shortages. Intra-urban social inequality is emerging as the larger urban areas become increasingly stratified by social groups and polarised along Western European lines (Fassman 1998, Duke and Grime, 1997).

The most prominent examples of these trends are the core and capital city regions. Several CEE countries – Hungary, the Czech Republic, Estonia and Latvia – have an urban hierarchy overwhelmingly dominated by the capitals, primarily the legacy of historically reshaped borders. The capitals, and other regional centres particularly in Poland, Romania, Bulgaria and Latvia, benefit from the best communications infrastructure, skilled labour, business environment and tourist facilities. The impact of mono-centric settlement structures is huge: the Tallin area (Estonia) has 80-90 percent of foreign investment and tourism and 40 percent of all registered enterprises; Riga (Latvia) has 30 percent of the national population and almost half of the FDI stock; in Prague (Czech Republic), GDP per capita is approaching a level twice the national average, and wage levels are almost one third higher than the Czech average; Budapest

(Hungary) accounts for 40 percent of the total urban population, 35 percent of service sector employment, and nearly two-thirds of all FDI flowing into Hungary, contributing to a GDP per capita level three times that of the worst-placed county in Hungary (Szabolcs-Szatmár-Bereg). The absence of major secondary centres means that, outside the capital cities, spatial disparities in growth are relatively small. In the countries with multi-polar urban structures, the capitals also have more favourable economic indicators (especially for foreign investment), but other centres act as important centres for economic development eg. Kaunas and Klaipeda in Lithuania; Varna and Plovdiv in Bulgaria; and Poznań, Kraków, Wrocław, Gdańsk, Katowice, Szczecin and Łódź in Poland.

Apart from the major urban areas, there are other 'winners' among the CEE regions which have been able to take advantage of macro-economic change and exploit their position. Notable examples are regions close to borders with CEE countries. By contrast with EU Member States, where proximity to CEE countries is generally viewed as disadvantageous (for instance, the Burgenland region in Austria), the reverse has been true for CEE regions along the borders of Germany and Austria which have benefited from investment, tourism, cross-border co-operation and shopping.

Less favourable has been the situation for certain 'lagging regions' which, having proceeded along a 'shallow' J-curve, face difficulty in adapting and demonstrating positive growth potential. Some have experienced sharp economic and social restructuring costs as well as political constraints to restructuring. The lack of an economic base, barriers to external impulses and weak political will make the prospects for some of these regions very serious. Certain underdeveloped rural areas, for example, offer few alternative employment opportunities and attract little foreign investment, resulting in high rates of unemployment and the out-migration of the young and better qualified population. These areas are particularly evident on the eastern borders of CEE and have generally witnessed little improvement in their socio-economic position since the start of the transformation process (Gorzelak, 1996, 1999; Bachtler, Raines and Downes, 1999; Fassmann, 1998; Hajdú and Horváth, 1994; CEC, 1996).

The principal disadvantaged regions are the old industrial areas, the former drivers of economic development under the socialist central planning regime. Most of these regions have been severely affected by business closure, privatisation, rationalisation and the loss of markets and subsidies and present some of the most serious economic, social, political and environmental challenges to the transformation process – and ultimately to integration and EU enlargement. Few such regions have been politically sheltered from the hardships of restructuring and many of the costs of restructuring still lie before them.

This pattern of regional disparities is likely to continue in the near future, with the mono-structural industrial areas and peripheral rural areas facing serious deficits. In the absence of external investment or endogenous development, these will be difficult to overcome in the short term, constraining the potential of these regions to adapt and transform – and further reinforcing the pattern of regional disparities (Dunford and Smith, 1998). Four main types of deficit can be identified. First, they lack a solid infrastructure base, particularly in transport, where the current stock is overloaded. Second, labour force difficulties are likely to intensify with the increased requirement for technological, management and entrepreneurial skills. Third, environmental problems are severe in the old industrial regions, in particular, and there is a mismatch between the areas with the worst difficulties and the availability of resources for clean-up operations. Finally, the capacity of businesses to maintain competitiveness through innovation is hampered by skills deficits, access to technology as well as socio-cultural, attitudinal problems.

Regional policy responses

To what extent is there a regional policy response to the above disparities and problems? As the preceding discussions of regional policy in the national reviews and policy chapters illustrate, the policy situation varies greatly among CEE countries. For the most part, regional development questions were sidelined for much of the 1990s in most countries. Structural reforms were concentrated in the 'sectoral' policy sphere, and the interplay between 'regional' and 'sectoral' issues has not been fully developed. To some extent this is understandable. The pressure of major problems, like macro-economic equilibrium, the dynamics of growth, external economic relations and balance of payments, industrial restructuring, and social problems like unemployment and poverty have preoccupied the political élites and governments in countries that, in general, have not enjoyed social and economic prosperity. For most countries, problems like growing regional differences or the marginalisation of certain territories are considered to be of secondary importance. The main exceptions are cases where economically and/or politically important regions face problems that may threaten national political stability - in such situations, intervention (usually less successful than planned) is being undertaken (Brada, 1998; Desai, 1998; Drabek and Brada, 1998).

In assessing the characteristics of actions in the regional policy sphere, four issues are worth highlighting: the reform of territorial administrative structures, the institutional infrastructure for regional development, the introduction of regional policy legislation and instruments, and the designation of assisted areas (Bachtler and Downes, 2000; Bachtler and Downes, 1999).

Reform of territorial administration

There has been extensive debate in most CEE countries to establish the appropriate structures for territorial administration and/or self-government, especially with a view to implementing regional development more effectively. Early reforms generally gave more powers to the local level, creating a gap between central and local administrations. Central governments have a high concentration of political power, while regional or provincial levels tend to be weak, having lost power and resources either to central government or to communes and municipalities. Broadly, this has resulted in a fragmentation process, both vertical and horizontal, in the relationships between different levels of government and among actors at regional/local level. The Hungarian reforms, for example, doubled the number of local authorities in 1990, giving each the right to local self-government (Horváth, 1998). In other countries, such as Slovenia, the number of municipalities has risen steadily throughout the 1990s, creating overly small units for government administrative purposes. Several countries face a highly fragmented structure of territorial units, comprising numerous small local government areas (3,000 municipalities in Hungary, more than 6,000 in the Czech Republic) and the lack of a regional or district-level administrative tier capable of exercising a self-government role.

Table 24.1 Territorial administrative structures in CEE countries

Country	Regional tier	Sub-regional tier
Bulgaria	28 regions	262 municipalities
Czech Republic	14 regions	77 districts 6,242 municipalities
Estonia	15 counties	254 local administrative units
Hungary	7 regions[a]	19 counties[b] + Budapest 3,126 settlements
Latvia	26 districts	7 cities 77 towns 486 parishes
Lithuania	10 counties	55 municipalities[c]
Poland	16 regions	373 counties 2,489 municipalities
Romania	41 counties + Bucharest	2,685 communes
Slovakia	8 regions	79 districts 2,875 municipalities
Slovenia		193 municipalities

Note: [a] for statistical and planning purposes only (level of Regional Development Agencies); [b] highest level of sub-national government; [c] planned reform in 2000 will increase the number of municipalities.

The issue of the so-called 'vacuum' between central and local government has been a contested political issue, with different models of territorial organisation proposed as a base for decentralising central government powers and responsibilities. Nevertheless, new self-government structures are progressively emerging (see Table 24.1). In Hungary, the role of the 20 counties has been revived and, in the Czech Republic, the 77 districts have been grouped together into 14 new administrative regions from the start of January 2000. In Poland, wide-ranging territorial administrative reform, which came into force on 1 January 1999, reduced the former 49 *voivodships* to 16 larger regional units, introduced self-government at this level to co-exist with the former government administration, and created 373 self-governmental districts (*powiat*). Elsewhere, regional devolution is seen as either premature, as in Romania and Bulgaria where regional structures are for State administrative purposes, or unnecessary, as in the Baltic countries where the priority has been local government reform.

Institutional infrastructure

Allied to the reform of territorial administration is the adequacy of the institutional infrastructure for regional development. Reflecting the points made above, most of the key institutional developments have been at central government and local government levels.

The low profile of regional policy has led to it being sidelined in the institutional structures of most CEE countries, policy responsibility being exercised by weak ministries or as a secondary function in mainline government departments. Most symptomatic of this situation is the continued lack of any significant central government regional policy responsibility in Poland, where the government reshuffle in late 1999 once again did not consider regional policy important enough to allocate departmental resources to the Ministry of Economics nominally responsible for this policy area. In the Czech Republic, regional policy functions are carried out by a Ministry of Regional Development (encompassing also planning and housing functions), but the ministry is small, poorly resourced and periodically under threat of disbandment. In Hungary, regional policy was one of the departments 'traded' between ministries following the 1998 elections with a ministerial re-shuffle creating a new Ministry for Agriculture and Regional Development.

A distinctive feature of the institutional arrangements for regional development in CEE countries is the emphasis placed on inter-ministerial co-ordination. Virtually every CEE country has set up a national council, board or committee for regional policy, representing not only different central government departments but also sub-national bodies such as regional/county councils, development agencies, local authorities and business interests. In the first instance, these bodies have been tasked mainly with co-ordinating the preparation of national development concepts and plans for accessing EU funding as well as overseeing the implementation structures for delivering these funds. Although some early signs are encouraging (as in the Czech Republic), it is unclear whether the impact of these councils or committees will go beyond compliance with the regulatory and methodological requirements of the EU and actually exercise a strategic influence on the regional allocation of central government resources. It is notable that their remit is often restricted to consultative and advisory functions rather than decision-making powers, and the continued tension between sectoral and regional policy interests will prove difficult to resolve (as in Western European countries).

Another characteristic of the institutional landscape is the creation of specialist support organisations in the regional policy field, in some respects comparable to DATAR in France or the specialist intermediaries (national boards and agencies) in Austria and the Nordic countries. They include a range of organisations established to co-ordinate the delivery of regional policy initiatives, such as: the Estonian Regional Development Agency, which manages the administration of regional development programmes and incentive instruments; the Bohemian-Moravian Guarantee and Development Bank, which administers the main regional assistance schemes in the Czech Republic; the Polish Agency for Regional Development, which manages the administration of regional development programmes funded by the EU and other donor agencies; and the recently established National Agency for Regional Development in Romania, intended to oversee the implementation of funds under the emerging regional policy structure. Several specialist agencies providing technical assistance (eg. policy advice, research, information and training) also exist, notably the Governmental Centre for Strategic Studies (Poland), the Centre for Regional Development (Czech Republic) and the Institute for Macroeconomic Analysis (Slovenia).

Decentralisation is a perceived weak point of the reforms implemented in Central and Eastern Europe, again partly because of the supremacy of sectoral over regional interests. Even in Poland, where the local self-governmental units are strongest, the local budgets depend - to a great extent - on the decisions taken at central level. The Polish case also demonstrates clearly how central governmental administrations only reluctantly concede competencies and financial resources to regional levels of self-government. Arguably, State bureaucracies are keener to decentralise problems than money and decision-making responsibility. This is sometimes supported by the contention that local government is not mature enough to undertake tasks that are (or have been) in the hands of the State – somewhat reminiscent of statements issued by former communist authorities that the Central and Eastern European societies have not 'matured' to democracy. This paradoxical analogy supports the observation that the central-regional-local splits are of a more fundamental and universal character than just a leftover feature of authoritarian communist rule.

This applies in part to regional development. It is true that the design and implementation of regional development policies has hitherto been predominantly 'top down', with the delivery of almost all State government resources through the regional offices of central government ministries, especially in the Baltic States, Bulgaria and Romania. Further, an important constraint has been the weak institutional capacity and shortage of qualified personnel, a bottleneck to institutional development at national level let alone among regional and local bodies. However, there are some signs of decentralisation. In Poland and the Czech Republic, a regional level of self-government has only just been established with important responsibilities for regional development. Further, the negative impact of the absence of national institutional leadership for regional policy in Poland has partially been offset by the activity of c.70 local and regional development agencies which have attempted to fill the vacuum between public administration and the private sectors in economic development tasks. In countries such as Bulgaria and Romania, the newly created regional development agencies and boards are expected to consult widely among local governments in drawing up development plans. Lastly, in Hungary, it has to be acknowledged that a growing proportion of the (albeit limited) regional development budget is being channelled through decentralised decision-making mechanisms, with the county/regional development councils taking on increasingly important responsibilities for the targeting and utilisation of regional policy funds.

Regional policy measures

Before 1997, major regional policy legislation had only been passed in Hungary. In the absence of regional policy institutions or measures, other sectoral government departments undertook policies or programmes that had intended or unintended spatial consequences, especially in the sphere of labour market, transport and environment policies. During the late 1990s, growing regional disparities and pressure from the European Union led to a rapid development of regional policy, involving three main trends (Bachtler and Downes, 1999).

First, regional policy is increasingly being given a legislative basis. In 1998-99, laws on regional development or territorial development were submitted for parliamentary approval or passed in Bulgaria, Latvia,

Romania and Slovenia. Elsewhere, lesser government measures in the form of decrees or regulations have been approved (Czech Republic, Lithuania, Slovakia, Poland) pending the drafting of legislation. What is striking about the laws or principles of regional policy in most CEE countries is their all-encompassing nature, combining a mix of equity and efficiency objectives. On the one hand, regional policy is expected to promote transition by 'embedding market economic reforms in every region' while, on the other hand, compensating for the negative effects of transition by reducing regional disparities or addressing specific regional problems such as industrial restructuring, agricultural decline or peripherality.

Second, as part of the process of complying with the regulations for pre-accession EU structural assistance, each CEE country has been developing a hierarchy of concepts, strategies, plans and programmes for regional development. These have several common characteristics. At the apex tends to be a 'national concept' or 'strategy' for regional development providing a conceptual regional policy framework, including a statement of aims and objectives, an outline of the institutional structures and identification of the different policies with a regional dimension or impact. This concept or strategy is then translated into a multi-annual regional development plan, describing in detail how the EU financial aid (under ISPA, SAPARD, Phare) will be allocated between policy areas, managed and delivered. As with the Structural Funds in EU countries, the regional development plans are intended to be submitted to the European Commission for approval and implemented through a series of operational programmes.

Third, various regional policy instruments have begun to emerge. Regional policy legislation tends to be drafted broadly, allowing a wide range of instruments to be implemented. For example, the regional development law in Bulgaria refers to 'regional policy measures such as investment subsidies, interest subsidies, directed investment, preferential state and local charges, financial guarantees etc' as well as 'certain administrative measures governing, for example, the allocation of municipal building plots for construction activities or the granting of building permits'. In practice, the most common form of regional support is delivered through a 'regional development fund' or 'regional development programmes' (eg. in Hungary, Latvia, Romania, Slovenia, Estonia). Generally, these provide targeted assistance for individual municipalities or groups of local governments to undertake: infrastructure projects in areas such as transport, communications, utility services, environmental improvement; and (re)training of the local labour force. In addition, there is a limited amount of direct support to businesses (especially new start-ups and SMEs), mainly through loans and credits rather than grants. Aid in the form of 'technical assistance' is also provided in some countries to encourage municipalities to undertake joint planning or development projects, often with the aim of establishing 'planning regions' (eg. Latvia, Hungary). In Poland, 17 special economic zones have been created, although only a few have been successful in attracting major investment.

Designating assisted areas

As regional policy legislation or regulations are introduced, a key component is the mechanism for spatially allocating resources from limited budgets. The designation or zoning of areas eligible for regional policy support is constrained by institutional deficits, methodological problems and data inadequacies. For example, even basic, up-to-date (un)employment data is not always available and surrogates are often required in place of regionalised GDP statistics. With the exception of Hungary and Poland, data availability is usually at the level of the municipality rather than more relevant statistical units such as labour market areas. The dynamic characteristics of economies and labour markets also make it difficult to identify areas of relative disadvantage accurately. Nevertheless, almost every CEE country has proposed or introduced some form of area designation method for operationalising its regional policy (Bachtler and Downes, 2000).

The basis for designating 'assisted areas' is generally a mix of labour market, demographic, income and infrastructure data to yield an index of disadvantage. The most sophisticated combination of indicators is in Hungary, where regional policy-makers use: a complex combination of demographic, economic and infrastructure criteria to identify low levels of underdevelopment (less than 75 percent of the national average); various labour market criteria (including unemployment and change in industrial employment) to define areas of industrial restructuring; and indicators of migration trends and per capita incomes to designate agricultural areas. A simplified version of this system is under consideration in Slovenia. In Estonia, regional policy areas are defined using a combination of employment, income and development potential indicators, while in the Czech Republic eligibility is accorded to so-called 'structurally affected areas' (based on indicators of industrial employment, number of entrepreneurs, unemployment) and 'economically weak areas' (primary sector employment, population density, tax receipts). Uniquely, the Bulgarian system of area designation not only uses the above types of criteria for designating underdeveloped rural areas and regions in industrial decline, but also uses a mix of demographic, income and unemployment data to identify growth districts and development districts which may also qualify for regional policy support. In Poland, some measures targeted at the unemployed and local firms are provided for local labour markets particularly endangered by structural unemployment.

The outcome of these area designation systems is not always clear. However, an 'assisted areas map' covering 25-35 percent of the national population applies in Hungary, Slovenia and Bulgaria. Once again, a driving force behind this aspect of regional policy is the European Commission, which is keen to see designation systems that reflect the EU approaches to determining Structural Fund eligibility. In particular, systems are encouraged to be transparent, allowing the criteria, designation procedures and outcomes to be externally assessed.

Cohesion and EU enlargement

Looking beyond regional development issues within individual countries, the major challenge facing Europe over the coming decade – discussed in the penultimate chapter of this volume - is the eastward enlargement of the European Union and the role of the EU in promoting economic and social cohesion in an enlarged Union. Ten CEE countries have applied for membership of the European Union, with negotiations with the initial five 'front-runners' CEE countries (Poland, Hungary, Czech Republic, Estonia and Slovenia) and Cyprus currently the furthest advanced.

What will be the impact of enlargement on cohesion? In sectoral terms, the integration of CEE states into the EU could increase competition for agricultural products, simple mechanical engineering, chemicals and plastics industry products and also parts of the car industry, consumer electronics and shipbuilding (Huber and Pichelmann, 1998; Illés, 1997). The product structure in agriculture in the CEE countries is similar to that of the rural regions of Western Europe, with production in Mediterranean countries seen as complementary to CEE. If the CEE states could increase their currently low rates of productivity in comparison to EU levels, the peripheral rural regions of the western EU Member States could come under adaptation pressure. Within CEE countries, this would require continued privatisation as well as land reform, capital intensification and infrastructure renewal. In the industrial sector, the main areas of manufacturing likely to be affected by enlargement have been declining in the EU countries at an above-average rate for some time. In the event of an eastward enlargement, this relocation process would change more in terms of direction than substance, subject to transport costs and wage cost advantages.

In the EU, the countries most susceptible to being disadvantaged by such developments are the southern European members of the Union which have previously been the key targets for investment in these areas. Overall, enlargement would create competitive pressures particularly for those EU countries (and regions) which depend on: agriculture, with a typical product range for central Europe (grain, vegetables, fruit, cattle and pig farming); industrial operations with labour intensive but not particularly human resource intensive production; primary chemicals plants or shipyards with relatively low level product ranges; and assembly plants.

The development differences between the EU and the CEE countries are particularly marked at regional level. Regional data is less readily available than national level statistics, but, where analysis has been undertaken (Bachtler, Raines and Downes, 1999; Hallett, 1997), it is clear that the vast majority of CEE regions are generally well below the Objective 1 threshold of 75 percent of the EU15 average. Of relevance to the current 'cohesion countries' is the fact that the Czech regions and Slovenia may be higher placed than some of the weaker EU regions (mainly in Portugal), and the capital city regions of Prague, Warsaw and Budapest have income per head levels apparently in excess of the weaker regions in Portugal, Greece, Spain and Germany and somewhere in the range of 75-100 percent of the EU average.

The development challenge remains considerable. Outside of some capitals, most of CEE is estimated to be below 40 percent of the EU average and numerous other regions are below 30 percent. Even on the basis of the most optimistic projections of growth over the next 5-6 years, much of CEE would still have a considerable development gap relative to the EU at the time of enlargement, and the more underdeveloped regions are, in any case, unlikely to share higher rates of growth. This means that a large proportion of the CEE regions will only be able to exploit their potential competitive advantage over regions of the present EU Member

States to a relatively small extent, and the adaptation pressures on current Member States may only intensify after a long time delay.

It is virtually certain that an eastward enlargement of the EU would lengthen the belt of structurally weak regions in the south of the Community towards the east. The location of the CEE countries and regions is relatively peripheral to the economic core areas of the Community, and they exhibit considerable handicaps with regard to their integration in European infrastructures. It would be premature to consider any short-term re-orientation of the current corridors or axes of Western European development to include regions (even the capital cities) of Central and Eastern Europe. It is also clear that the EU will not face any fundamentally new problems in eastward enlargement given that, apart from the overall development gap, the old industrial and peripheral rural regions of CEE constitute the core of the regional problem in a very similar way to the structural difficulties of the EU15. It is also these areas which are likely to experience the greatest problems once integrated within the wider EU framework.

This regional dimension heightens the debate on the future implementation of the Structural and Cohesion Funds (Martin, 1998; Kirby, 1998; Molle, 1998; Hallett, 1997). Under ISPA and SAPARD and Phare, increasing sums of money are being poured into CEE countries in the form of pre-accession funds - even more is expected by the end of the 2000-2006 period, when the new members might be eligible for the Structural Funds. Enhancing the absorption ability at all levels (national, regional and local) has become the highest priority for all levels of government and for most of the institutions that operate in the field of local and regional development – in response to the inflow of both current and future EU finance. It is doubtful if this can be done in a centralised manner, especially in the bigger and spatially differentiated countries (like Poland, obviously, but also in the Czech Republic and Hungary). Preparations for future accession to the EU could be considered as one of the strongest arguments for decentralising territorial structures in those countries where this has not yet occurred.

The negotiations with the European Commission open up another set of problems: how much freedom should the future Member States have during these negotiations? Should they blindly follow the recommendations (if not the diktat) of the European Union, or can they suggest their own solutions? In the field of regional development and regional policy this dilemma becomes clear: should 'cohesion' and eliminating interregional differences be the priority of the national regional policies in the countries aspiring to become EU members - or may they pursue more efficiency- and growth-oriented regional policies, which necessarily would lead (at least in the initial phase) to greater interregional differences? For example, the recently elaborated Polish national strategy of regional development opts for a more growth-oriented regional policy and admits that enhanced regional polarisation is an acceptable result of this orientation. Will - and should - Poland be allowed to adopt its own approach to the regional question - or should it be forced to follow the official doctrine of the regional policy of the EU?

The methodological approach to delivering EU pre-accession aid is also questionable. Preparations for structural assistance involve a colossal bureaucracy of regional development concepts, strategies, plans and programmes, driven by highly detailed regulations and guidelines. While the need for rigorous accountability of expenditure is undeniable, there is evidence of institutional systems for regional development in CEE being overloaded from the need to comply with the ISPA/SAPARD/Phare administrative requirements. CEE regional policymakers are expected to accept the EU principles of 'programming' and 'partnership', regardless of their suitability as mechanisms for responding to prevailing regional development challenges.

There are, however, spheres where the European Union's suggestions should not be disputed. These are the accelerated restructuring of the old industrial regions; the development of infrastructure, with special stress put on motorways and high-speed rail; the improvement of the natural environment and education - the four sectors in which the communist regimes, regardless of their national denomination, have left the greatest deficits. Some Central and Eastern European countries (like the Czech Republic and Hungary) are more advanced in overcoming the infrastructure deficits, while others (like Poland) still seem to underestimate the importance of these goals. For example, the natural environment, though greatly improved, still presents the worst conditions in all of Europe; and while the educational gap is slowly closing up, it will be there for another decade. The role of the European Union is simple: it should support, in its own interest, developments in these spheres, since the better equipped the CEE countries are with infrastructure, a good environment and highly qualified manpower, the stronger the entire Union will be against its global competitors.

References

Abraham, T. and Eser, T.W. (1999) 'Regionalentwicklung in Mittel- und Osteuropa im Spannungsfeld von Transformation und Integration am Beispiel Polens', *Raumplanung und Raumordnung*, vol. 2, No. 3.

Ágh, A. (1998), *The Politics of Central Europe*, SAGE Publishers, London.

Amin, A. and Thrift, N. (1994), 'Living in the global', in Amin, A. and Thrift, N. (eds) *Globalisation, Institutions and Regional Development in Europe*, Oxford University Press, Oxford.

Amsden, A.H., Kochanowicz, J. and Taylor, L. (1994), *The Market Meets its Match: Restructuring the Economies of Eastern Europe*, Harvard University Press, Cambridge.

Anderson, R. W. and Kegels, C. (1998), *Transition Banking - Financial Development of Central and Eastern Europe*, Oxford University Press, Oxford.

Bachtler, J. and Downes, R. (1999), 'Regional Policy in the Transition Countries: A Comparative Assessment', *European Planning Studies*, vol. 7, No. 6.

Bachtler, J. and Downes, R. (2000), 'The Spatial Coverage of Regional Policy in Central and Eastern Europe', *European Urban and Regional Studies*, vol. 7, No. 2.

Bachtler, J., Downes, R., Helinska-Hughes, E., Macquarrie, J. (1998), *Regional Development in the Transition Countries*, European Policies Research Centre, University of Strathclyde, Glasgow.

Bachtler, J., Raines, P. and Downes, R. (eds) (1999) *First Report on Economic and Social Cohesion - Study Area 3: The Impact on Cohesion of EU Enlargement*, Regional and Industrial Policy Research Paper, No. 34, European Policies Research Centre, University of Strathclyde, Glasgow.

Baldwin, R., Francois, J. and Portes, R. (1997), 'EU Enlargement – small costs for the west, big gains for the east', *Economic Policy*, April 1997.

Bilsen, V. (1997), *The Enterprise Survey for Bulgaria, Hungary, Romania and Slovakia, 1996*, LICOS KU Leuven, Belgium.

Blažek, J. (1999), 'Regional Development and Regional Policy in Central East Euorpean Countries in the Perspective of the EU Eastern Enlargement', in Hampl, M (ed) *Geography of Societal Transformation in the Czech Republic*, Department of Social Geography and Regional Development, Charles University of Prague, Prague.

Blejer, M.I., Skreb, M., (1998), 'Macroeconomic stabilisation in transition economies', *Review of World Economics*, vol.134, No.3.

Brada, J.C. (1998), 'Introduction: Exchange rates, capital flows, and commercial policies in transition economies', *Journal of Comparative Economics*, vol.26, No.4.

Burda, M.C. (1994), *Structural Change and Unemployment in Central and Eastern Europe – some key issues*, Centre for Economic Policy Research, London.

Carlin, W. and Landesmann, M. (1997), 'From theory into practice? Restructuring and dynamism in transition economies', *Oxford Review of Economic Policy*, vol.13, No.2.
CEC (1996), *Fifth Periodic Report on the Social and Economic Situation and Development of the Regions*, Commission of the European Communities, Brussels.
CEC (1997), *Agenda 2000 – For a Stronger and Wider Union*, COM DOC/97/6, Commission of the European Communities, Brussels.
Commander, S. and Coricelli, F. (eds) (1995), *Unemployment, Restructuring and the Labour Market in Eastern Europe and Russia*, World Bank, Washington DC, USA.
Dawisha, K. and Parrott, B. (1997), *Politics, Power and the Struggle for Democracy in South-East Europe*, Cambridge University Press, Cambridge.
de Melo, M., Denizer, C., and Gelb, A. (1996), 'Patterns of transition from plan to market', *World Bank Economic Review*, vol.10, No.3.
Desai, P. (1998), 'Macroeconomic Fragility and Exchange Rate Vulnerability: A Cautious Record of Transition Economies', *Journal of Comparative Economics*, vol. 26.
Drabek, Z. and Brada, J.C. (1998), 'Exchange rate regimes and the stability of trade policy in transition economies', *Journal of Comparative Economics*, vol.26, No.4.
Dunford, M. and Smith, A. (1998), *Trajectories of change in Europe's regions – cohesion, divergence and regional performance*, Paper to Workshop "Regional Inequality in an Enlarged Europe: Regional Performance and Policy Responses", Centre on the Changing Political Economy of Europe, Sussex European Institute, 12-13 March 1998.
Duke, V. and Grime, K. (1997), 'Inequality in Post-Communism', *Regional Studies*, vol. 31, No. 9.
EBRD (1998), *Transition Report 1998*, European Bank for Reconstruction and Development, London.
Elster, J., Offe, C. and Preuss, U. (1997), *Institutional Design in Post-Communist Societies – Rebuilding the Ship at Sea*, Cambridge University Press, Cambridge.
Estrin, S., Hughes, K. and Todd, S. (1997), *Foreign Direct Investment in Central and Eastern Europe: Multinationals in Transition*, Royal Institute of International Affairs/Pinter Publishers, London.
Fassmann, H. (1998), *Die Rückkehr der Regionen: Beiträge zur regionalen Tranformation Ostmitteleuropas*, Beiträge zur Stadt- und Regionalforschung, Band 15, Vienna.
Fischer, S., Sahay, R. and Vegh, C. (1996), 'Stabilisation and Growth in Transition in Transition Economies: The Early Experience', *Journal of Economic Perspectives*, vol. 10, No. 2.

Frydman, R., Murphy, K. and Rapaczynski, A. (1998), *Capitalism with a Comrade's Face – Studies in Postcommunist Transition*, Central European University Press, Budapest.

Gábor, T. (1997), *Political Parties and Democratic Consolidation in East Central Europe*, Centre for the Study of Public Policy, University of Strathclyde, Glasgow.

Gomulka, S. (1998), 'The Polish model of transformation and growth', *Economics of Transition*, vol.6. No.1.

Gorzelak, G. (1999), *The Regional and Local Potential for Transformation in Poland*, EUROREG, Warsaw.

Gorzelak, G. (1996), *The Regional Dimension of Transformation in Central Europe*, Jessica Kingsley Publishers, London.

Grabbe, H. and Hughes, K. (1997), *Eastward Enlargement of the European Union*, Royal Institute of International Affairs, London.

Grabher, G. and Stark, D. (eds) (1997), *Restructuring Networks in Post-Socialism: Legacies, Linkages and Localities*, Oxford University Press, Oxford.

Grey, R. D. (ed) (1997), *Democratic Theory and Post-Communist Change*, Prentice Hall Publishers.

Gros, D. and Steinherr, A. (1995), *Winds of Change – Economic transition in Central and Eastern Europe*, Longman Group, London.

Hajdú, Z. and Horvath, G. (1994), *European Challenges and Hungarian Responses in Regional Policy*, Centre for Regional Studies, Hungarian Academy of Sciences, Pécs.

Hallett, M. (1997), 'National and Regional Development in Central and Eastern Europe: Implications for EU Structural Assistance', *Economic Papers*, No. 120, Commission of the European Communities, Brussels.

Higley, J., Pakulski, J. and Wesolowski, W. (eds) (1998), *Postcommunist elites and democracy in Eastern Europe*, St. Martin's Press, New York.

Horvath, G. (1998), *Regional and Cohesion Policy in Hungary*, Discussion Papers No. 23, Centre for Regional Studies, Hungarian Academy of Sciences, Pécs.

Huber, P. and Pichelmann, K. (1998), Osterweiterung, struktureller Wandel und Arbeitsmärkte, *Wirtschaftspolitische Blätter*, vol. 45, No. 5.

Ickes, B. (1996), 'How to Stabilize: Lessons from Post-Communist Countries: Comment', *Brookings Papers Economic Activity*, No. 1.

Illés, I. (1997), 'Der Strukturwandel in den mittel- und osteuropäischen Ländern und die Erwartungen an die Europäische Union', *Südosteuropa Aktuell*, vol. 26.

Jackson, M., Koltay, J. and Biesbrouck, W. (1995), *Unemployment and Evolving Labour Markets in Central and Eastern Europe*, Avebury, Aldershot.

Kirby, S. (1998), *Cohesion and enlargement: perspectives for the European Structural Funds*, Action Centre for Europe, London.

Krajnyak, K., Zettelmeyer, J., (1998), 'Competitiveness in transition economies: What scope for real appreciation?', *International Monetary Fund Staff Papers*, vol.45, No.2.

Malmberg, A., Sölvell, Ö. and Zander, I. (1996), Spatial clustering, local accumulation of knowledge and firm competitiveness, *Geogr. Annaler*, vol. 78B.

Martin, R. (1998), 'Financing EU cohesion policy in Central and Eastern Europe: a budgetary timebomb?' *Intereconomics*, May/June 1998.

Martzanis, H. and Petrakos, G. (1998), 'Changing Landscapes in Europe's Economic Structure', *Transition*, Vol 9:2, World Bank.

Molle, W. (1998), *Economic Integration and Cohesion in Europe: Past and Future*, Keynote speech at 'EU Accession and Regional Development' conference, Tallinn, 15-16 June 1998.

Mullineux, A. W. and Green, C. J. (1998), *Economic Performance and Financial Sector Reform in Central and Eastern Europe – Capital Flows, Bank and Enterprise Restructuring*, Edward Elgar Publishers, Cheltenham.

OECD (1994), *Unemployment in Transition Countries: Transient or Persistent?*, Organisation for Economic Cooperation and Development, Paris.

OECD (1997), *The New Banking Landscape in Central and Eastern Europe – Country Experience and Policies for the Future*, Organisation for Economic Cooperation and Development, Paris.

OECD (1997), *Lessons from Economic Transition: Central and Eastern Europe in the 1990s*, Organisation for Economic Cooperation and Development, Paris.

Pavlínek, P. and Smith, A. (1998), 'Internationalisation and Embeddedness in East-Central European Transition: The Contrasting Geographies of Inward Investment in the Czech and Slovak Republics', *Regional Studies*, vol. 32, No. 7.

Poeschl, J. (1999), *Czech Republic: Medium and Long-term Economic Prospects*, WIIW Analytical Forecast, WIIW, Vienna.

Porket, J. L. (1995), *Unemployment in Capitalist, Communist and Post-Communist Economies*, St. Martin's Press, New York.

Smith, A. and Swain, A. (1998), 'Regulating and institutionalising capitalisms: the micro-foundations of transformation in Central and Eastern Europe', in Pickles, J. and Smith, A. (eds), *Theorising Transition: The Political Economy of Post-Communist Transformations*, Routledge, London.

Van Wijnbergen, S. (1998), *Bank Restructuring and Enterprise Reform*, Working Paper No. 29, European Bank for Reconstruction and Development, London.

Welter, F. (1997), 'Small and Medium Enterprises in Central and Eastern Europe: Trends, Barriers and Solutions', *RWI-Papiere*, No.51, Essen.

White, S., Batt, J. and Lewis, P. (eds) (1998), *Developments in Central and East European Politics*, Macmillan Publishers, Basingstoke.

Yndgaard, E. (1999), Differences of transition patterns in Central and Eastern European countries, *Nationalokonomisk Tidsskrift*, No.SISI.

Zemplinerova, A. (1997), *The Role of Foreign Enterprises in the Privatisation and Restructuring of the Czech Economy*, WIIW Research Reports, No. 238, Vienna.

Zemplinerova, A. (1997), 'Small enterprises and foreign investors - key players in enterprise restructuring and structural change', *Ekonomicky Casopism*, vol.45, No.10.

DATE DUE